A World of Language for Deaf Children
Part I. Basic Principles

Modern approaches to the diagnosis and instruction of multi-handicapped children

4

A World of Language
for Deaf Children
Part 1. Basic Principles

A maternal reflective method

Dr. A. van Uden

With a preface by Professor Emeritus
Sir Alexander Ewing, M.A., Ph.D., L.L.D.

Third revised edition

1977

SWETS & ZEITLINGER, AMSTERDAM and LISSE

First edition 1968 by The Institute of the Deaf, Sint Michielsgestel
Second edition 1970 by Rotterdam University Press

391.912
U d 3w
112708
Feb. 1980

Typesetting by The Pitman Press Ltd, Bath
Printed in The Netherlands by Princo b.v. Culemborg

ISBN 90 265 0253 2

Preface

This book may well prove a basis for new progress in education of the deaf. Dr. van Uden, an international authority, offers us the results of his comprehensive and fully up-to-date review of publications in the fields of linguistics and psycholinguistics. Detail by detail he has related those scientific findings to their functioning in the language development of (a) normally hearing and (b) hearing-impaired children.

As he himself states, he has worked and taught in the residential school for the deaf at Sint Michielsgestel for more than thirty years. In this book he has reported applications of his principles and methods with children varying much in the character of their handicaps and as to whether or not they had been given pre-school or nursery training. The years intervening since the writing of the first edition of this book have made it possible to include in this revised edition data drawn from longitudinal studies.

Evidence of high standards, in time achieved by a number of pupils, includes samples of written compositions as well as results of tests. Also, we read a transcription of an oral lesson given to a difficult class. A very important addition, in this revised version, is an appendix dealing with the teaching of dysphasic, aphasic and cerebral-palsied children. Parts of the original book have been revised and extended.

There are certain additions, which, I believe, are of outstanding importance. One of them is the completely new Chapter One. In the first part of this Dr. van Uden has identified the psycholinguistic steps and innate principles upon which are based the processes by which a hearing child, bit by bit, acquires a mother tongue. He relates these processes to existence of particular factors in the child's experience and mental growth, all the way from Mother's forms of response to his early emotional, non-verbal utterances, via his systematization of his words to "Conversation Again Again, Reading and Writing, Belles Lettres". I find this first part of Chapter One, with its quoted examples of actual incidents, a most clarifying approach, using psycholinguistic and psychological terminology, to the second part of the Chapter. There, applying the same findings and principles, three different methods of teaching language to deaf children are evaluated. Mental difficulties associated with pre-lingual deafness are carefully and practically considered. Methods of developing in deaf children ability for true personal conversation are described, starting from very early childhood with what Dr. van Uden calls the "seizing methods" whereby mothers and teachers, recognising indications of what a young child desires to express, provides him with the needed verbal utterance, in sentence form, thus following the essence of normal patterning.

Presentation of that key principle, with exposition and practical examples of the methodology and related mental processes that are necessarily involved to make it continuously effective for deaf children, is surely the heart of this book. We are prepared for the detailed and research-based studies reported in the following chapters.

There is an addition to Chapter Five which concerns all teachers of the deaf who are or have been attracted to "Total Communication". Dr. van Uden brings considerable first-hand experience of manual forms of communication to this subject as well as his ability to give it objective and scientific analysis. After consideration of all aspects of "sign language" and review of researches that have been claimed as supporting "total communication" he states that "... there are of course a few deaf children who because of multiple handicaps need a sign-education". He points out that none of the researches in question give any information about the results of auditory training nor have any of them included the making and analyses of recordings of real conversations in the different communicative modes. He states a conclusion of vital importance that if their children are taught total communication parents will see them "going away from them into another culture which is not theirs".

Finally, there is far more information in this book than I have found it possible to indicate in this preface — such data as technically planned and controlled management of hearing aids in the classroom, rhythmic training and provision of individual speech lessons, special use of diaries. I am convinced that this will be a valuable text-book for a good many years to come.

A. W. G. Ewing

Contents

13

15

Introduction

The paradoxical combination of 'teaching' and 'mother tongue' is the central and perhaps most difficult problem in the education of deaf children.

The problem has intrigued me for many years. In discussions with the teachers of our school there has been assembled so much material on the subject. It had been said to me that it would be worthwhile to put together modern thinking of psycholinguistics and didactics of the deaf in a book, in order to open a fruitful discussion.

The immediate occasion to write this book was an invitation by Prof. Dr. I. G. Taylor of the University of Manchester, Department of Audiology and the Education of the Deaf, to read a paper in his seminar about educational problems of deaf children in September 1967. Further an invitation of the Irish Association of Teachers of the Deaf to explain our principles of language acquisition by deaf children at its first General Meeting in St. Mary's School for the Deaf, Cabra, Dublin, November 1967. After two editions published in 1968 and 1970 respectively, the author here presents a third, completely revised and extended edition. This book will be a precursor of a longer manual still in preparation.

Deafness

By the term 'deaf' children the following will be meant in this book: *prelingually* deaf children who are so *deaf* that – even with the best hearing-aid and the best possible auditory training – they never will reach a level of understanding speech mainly by hearing (van Uden 1951). In general these are children with prelingual hearing handicaps of more than 95 db. (Fletcher-index, ISO standard, Davis 1965, 'high tone-deafness' or 'low-pass hearing loss' excluded). As Dale (1962) said, these children are 'more vision than hearing dependent', and they will always be so. These are precisely the prelingually deaf children dealt with in this book, Sr. Nicholas (1965) strikingly calls them 'visualizers' (originally German 'Augenmenschen', Schmähl 1931). – Nevertheless all these children can wear hearing aids, even the deafest among them, as a help to lipreading, especially with respect to the rhythm of language (van Uden 1952). We said 'all', because the

19

physiologically totally deaf children still have vibration-sense, which too is a form of sound-perception and supports lipreading significantly (van Uden 1958, 1970, 1972, Eggermont 1964).

Prelinguality

By 'prelinguality' is meant in this book below the age of 1 yrs 6 months; because from 1;6–4;6 years of age the symbolic function develops in a hearing child (Sleigh 1972). At about 3;0 years of age a hearing child has already the main structure of the language of the hearing environment (McCarthy 1954). So we distinguish a period of pre-, inter- and post-linguality. The period of pre-linguality is that period of life in which the child has not yet a symbolic system. It uses some signals and understands symbols of others as signals without building up itself a system of symbols. – During the period of inter-linguality the child builds up a system of signals and symbols, which is in some way different from the symbolic system of the environment and in some way similar to that system. – During the period of postlinguality, continuing until the end of man's life, the child has already acquired the system of its environment: in its spontaneous utterances it uses almost all words correctly as regards their positions in the sentences.

If we symbolize the life of a child by a line, we can indicate these three periods (pr-l., in-l., and po-l.) for a normal hearing child, for a mentally defective hearing child (cf. O'Connor et al. 1962, Lenneberg 1966) and for a well-educated normal prelingually deaf child, in general as follows:

Normal hearing child:

pr-1.	in-1.	po-1.
age: 0;0 ———▶	———1;6———▶	———4;0———————▶

Ment. defect. hearing child:

pr-1.	in-1.	po-1.
age: 0;0 ——▶	——3;0———▶	———8;0————▶

Prel. deaf child:

pr.1.	in-1.	po-1.
age: 0;0 ——▶	——3;0 ———▶	———12;0————▶

Linguistics; – Psycholinguistics

Language can be considered as a system but also as a skill, i.e. as a process of inner and outer behaviour. Linguistics studies the system, psycholinguistics the processes (e.g. Hörmann 1967).

It is not at all certain that the rules of linguistics coincide with the laws of psycholinguistics (Miller 1963), i.e. of the processes of receiving and understanding language, of expressing and producing language, of learning language, of conversing in language, and so on.

An illustration of the difference between linguistics and psycholinguistics may be the finding of Leopold (1956): what linguistics calls a subject-predicate-combination may be a question-answer-structure in psycholinguistics.

Perhaps psycholinguistics will appear to be more fruitful than linguistics for the didactics of language. We will discuss such findings of modern psycholinguistics, which are in our opinion important for our work with the deaf.

A Mother-tongue

By a 'mother-tongue' is meant in this book: a wide system of satisfying cultural communication which is used as a second nature (i.e. usually originating from 'mother').

We said 'used'. 'Using a language' is not only producing sentences but also – and perhaps even more – understanding them. Direct understanding of English (may be by hearing, by lipreading or by reading) presupposes a lot of *automatism* in internal and external behaviour. This in contrast to the indirect understanding, i.e. by translation from another language. This latter behaviour happens, e.g. when an Englishman is just starting to learn Dutch and has his first conversation that way: he has to translate more or less the Dutch sentences into his English before he is able to understand them and vice versa in producing sentences; this process hampers a smooth conversation, because the language-control is only indirect and not yet automatic. He does not use that other language as second *nature*. The same, when a deaf person, mainly conversing in signs, has to translate spoken or read English into his sign-codes, and vice versa in producing English sentences. – Here the term 'mother'-(tongue) has a second meaning as the '*origin*', from which the ability to utilize a foreign language arises ('mother' = 'origin').

The term 'mother-tongue' can be used in a very strict sense as 'native language': only the first language, that has been learned very informally from early childhood, usually taught by the '*mother*' (i.e. by the whole family) (Pei-Gaynor 1958, Hartmann and Stork 1972). – In these modern times, however, more and more people are found who have been taught a second language, which perhaps in the beginning was a foreign language to them (mainly indirectly controlled), but who learned it by daily conversation so fluently and smoothly that it should be called a mother-tongue too, in a broader sense, although not trained as *informally* as the native language: they are either competent in two (very seldom in more) coordinated languages, or they have simply forgotten their native language more or less completely.

21

But there is still a third situation. Summarizing we distinguish:

(a) a first language, learned mainly informally and directly, quite automatized: this is a 'native language', a 'mother-tongue' in its strictest sense.
(b) a second language, learned mainly formally, and in the beginning more indirectly used, but after a time used directly and quite automatically: this is a mother-tongue in a broader sense.
(c) The third situation, a *first* language, always used directly and quite automatically, although learned *more formally* than in the first situation: this too is a mother-tongue in a strict sense. – This third situation happens for instance in children with developmental dysphasia after a successful education.

The central problem which we try to solve in this book is: does psycholinguistics give us sufficient principles which can help us to teach deaf children a cultural language in such an automatized way that it should be called a mother-tongue? We say: yes. This mother-tongue can and should be their first language, although not taught as informally as a native language to a hearing child. This can and should be a mother-tongue in its strict sense, according to the mentioned third situation.

A Cultural Language and the Purely Oral Way

Let us first give a definition of the 'purely oral way for deaf children':

The monolingual education of prelingually deaf children in such a way that rhythmic speech and lipreading with sound-perception become their directly automatized way of conversation.

Some scientists (e.g. Chomsky 1957, Moores 1970, 1972, cf. De Saussure 1916) think, they can distinguish between language and its formal appearances, i.e. its *codes*. Language would abstract from its code, i.e. from its spoken, auditory, or written appearance. I do not agree; certainly not if this principle was to be applied to sign-languages too, which in our opinion are not cultural languages of the same value as oral languages, not even when metamorphosed into so-called 'manual English' (Stokoe 1960, 1972; 'manual Dutch' van Beek 1827).

Prerequisites of the Code

Are there some prerequisites which condition a code to be the 'stuff' of a cultural language? The following:
The code must make *human conversation* as smooth as possible, i.e.:
(1) the code must be usable in a *successively* serial way: giving the partners alter-

22

native turns in order to participate in the 'exchange of thoughts' (i.e. conversation);

(2) the code must be as *unequivocal* as possible;

(3) the code must be usable in a quick *tempo* in order to convey messages in a time as short as possible:

(4) the code must give the opportunity to be organized in sub-units in order to enlarge the extent of the message according to the 'magic number 7 ± 2' (Miller 1962) of *Short Term Memory* (STM)-function;

(5) the code must have sub-units which can be *exchanged* between the partners of the dialogue;

(6) the code must convey the *intentions* of the partners' messages: their assertions, questions, appeals;

(7) the code must be such that as many *partners* as possible can be reached simultaneously;

(8) the code must support abstract thinking, thinking in relations, with easy *transfer* of meaning and figuration, so that the code itself is very 'empty', i.e. arbitrary, not conveying a meaning by itself (cf. Ervin-Tripp 1966);

(9) the code must be capable of an *unlimited* enlargement.

A Rhythmic-melodically Organized Code

It may be clear that only a spoken *rhythmic-melodically* organized language has all these humanizing aspects. So it is understandable that all the human languages of earth are encoded that way.

The *finger-spelled* (=the hand shapes itself to show a letter, e.g. the V for victory) words have insufficient rhythm, no melody, insufficient accentuation: so rhythmic sub-units and intonations are impossible; besides the tempo is much too low; STM-function is hampered, unless re-encoded orally.

The same must be said of *sign-language*. Additionally signs are not arbitrary codes, but iconic and dramatizing ones, keeping thinking much too concrete. Also their number is much too limited. We conclude: the sign-language cannot be acknowledged as a fully humanizing language contra Stokoe 1970, only to be used when no other way of communication is possible.

The *graphic* form has its insufficiencies too: no rhythmic grouping, no melody, too slow a tempo unless trained throughout. Additionally this form is simultaneously presented which implies typical reactions where the serial order is concerned; so a deaf, graphically educated child correctly reproduced the sentence 'Why did you forget to give the bird its food in time?', by arranging the words written on loose cards, as follows=(1) Why (2) forget (3) food in time (4) did you (5) give (6) to (7) the bird (8) its

<pre>   1   4   2   6   5   7   8   3</pre>
"Why did-you forget to give the-bird its food-in-time".

NB. The basic function of STM in language-behaviour is often if not always forgotten in the theory of language and its didactics. This will be emphasized very much in this book.

What Now about the Spoken Language in a Deaf Child?

It is possible and indeed it happens very often that a normally hearing child of say three years old who *loses its hearing* (without contracting an additional handicap, thus a '*postlingually deafened child*'), does not loose its rhythmic speech, although it may forget the auditory effect of that speech in a rather short time. This child can be educated so well that it, notwithstanding a delay in its development, controls its mother-tongue perfectly at an age of about 10–12 years, which may be concluded from its intelligible speech, smooth lipreading, correct reading and writing. I have met many of these children.– In which *form* would the cultural language appear to such a child? This seems to be a mainly non-auditorily oral and visually lipread form, albeit that vibration-sense and hearing-remnants play a relatively important supporting part.

This same thing may be said of such so well educated *prelingually deaf people* who possess a perfect rhythmic control of the oral language and behave in an analogous way as the deafened child just mentioned. The number of these people may still be rather small, there are, however, more and more deaf people who – by better and better methods and educational training, last but not least by their own efforts – approximate this ideal very well, even get a better control of language than many hearing. I have met so many of this type of deaf people, both intelligent ones and not so intelligent ones. Failures, apart from multiple handicaps, are usually due to organizational and didactic factors. -- The *form* in which the cultural language learned appears to such deaf people seems to be again mainly the non-auditorily oral form. The 'stuff of thinking' in language will imply its articulatory coding. All the prerequisities of a cultural language, except its melody, are essentially fulfilled, although of course not to the same extent as in hearing people.

A Cultural Language in a Non-oral way

The three formal appearances of a cultural language, mentioned above, are purely oral. There are, however, other forms possible, not mainly oral, but *verbal* in a non-oral way. Thus the term verbal is not quite identical with oral. All oral appearances are of course verbal, but not all verbal appearances are oral.

Alexander Graham Bell (1884) succeeded in teaching a congenitally deaf boy, George Sanders, the English language, without any speech, in a graphic way: he conversed with him graphically. He composed 'deposits' of his graphic conversations with him as reading-lessons in copy-books, which are preserved in the library of the Volta Bureau in Washington D.C. An example of such a reading-lesson is printed on page 39. Bell treated him from 5 to 7 years of age: it has been acknowledged that his language-control was superior to that of other deaf children when he entered a school for the deaf.

Bell's method has been followed in our country, more or less, by Nanninga-Boon (1929, 1934), with like success, that her prelingually deaf son, who had never been in a school for the deaf, could learn French, English and German and complete his studies at the Technical University of Delft. He himself told me that the main form in which language appeared to him, was its graphic form. Speech has been added afterwards.

Helen Keller (1880–1970), the famous deaf-blind (from 1½ years of age) woman of high cultural standard, learned perfect control of English by the manual alphabet, felt into the palms of her hand (cf. Schmitt 1954). The main form of English was for her a tactile-kinesthetic form, although she added Braille to it and afterwards speech too, by the Tadoma-method.

Hofsteater (1932), a prelingually deaf son of deaf parents, learned finger-spelling of the one-hand manual alphabet of Rosellio (1579) and Bonet (1620), from early childhood, the first years of his life with no, or very little speech. His control of English at adult age is said to be perfect. The main form of that English may appear to him the visual-kinesthetic form of the hand movements, integrated with reading and writing, although he learned speech and lip-reading afterwards.

From all this may be concluded that it is possible to learn verbal languages in different forms.

Have All These Formal Appearances the Same Value?

There are in my opinion two criteria for an evaluation of these forms:

(a) The social interaction with the hearing environment.

> NB. The social interaction within a deaf community is not considered crucial here, albeit an escape in some less desirable cases. – A deaf person who is able to integrate into the hearing environment will be able to integrate into a deaf environment of the same cultural standard. This does not seem to be a special criterion (van Uden 1973).

(b) The psycholinguistic functioning of the subject itself, which may be subdivided into two aspects, as mentioned above:

aa. Transfer of meaning and abstract thinking;

bb. Rhythmic clustering and grouping of words, related to the STM-function, automation of linguistic behaviour and exchange of thoughts.

It may be clear that the spoken auditory form of language of the normal hearing is the most essential and complete form and that all other forms are either participations or derivatives.

The non-auditory rhythmic spoken form seems to approximate this essential form nearest of all, as a real participation (= taking a satisfying part of it). The graphic form is only a derivative. It may limit the interaction with the environment very much, and there are reasons to suspect that the development of speech and lipreading may be hampered, which inhibits the social interaction once more (cf. Yale 1931). The function of abstraction may be preserved, but the STM-function is not developed to its full extent. Brill (1953) found that the memory-function for written words in deaf children, not rhythmically trained, was limited to 5 words. It may be predicted that the graphic method can be successful with respect to perfect language-control in very *gifted* deaf children only, because only these can compensate in memory-difficulties and in the slowed down process of automation. The same must be said of the visual finger-spelled form of the manual alphabet. (As far as I know, no researches have been done on the STM-function of tactile manual language of the deaf-blind.)

It may be concluded that these non-oral forms of verbal languages should be used in exceptional cases only, as a last escape where the purely oral form is not possible for some reason, for instance because of brain dysfunctions.

The purely oral way remains the ideal for the prelingually deaf children: more deaf children can be brought to the full culture of language, and this can be done on the average, better and sooner than by any other means, provided that the right methods are followed by qualified teachers.

I. A Model of Teaching a Mother-tongue to Prelingually Deaf Children, Based on Psycholinguistic Principles

1. SUMMARY

It seems very important to the author of this book that the student has a good survey of the *whole* didactics of language to hearing-impaired children.

Therefore the treatment is concentric: in this chapter we will summarize the whole work, to obviate the student not seeing the wood for the trees. The other chapters fan out from this one and we hope that the reader will put the problems from the beginning in their right settings.

Let us introduce this chapter with a short explanation of our thinking:

The development of language in *hearing* children is described in three steps:
− the external behaviour from early childhood with an emphasis on the flexible understanding and on the conversation of the baby with his mother;
− the 'cognitive' mediating processes with an emphasis on the memory-functions related to intonation and rhythm in language and on the child's reflective ('trial and check') behaviour;
− the role of reading and writing in this normal linguistic development.

We have attempted to show how these steps can be followed in the linguistic development of a *deaf* child, with an emphasis on conversation, flexible understanding of language (including learning to read) and making the child detect language-rules (or -laws) himself.

2. SURVEY OF SOME IMPORTANT FINDINGS OF PSYCHOLINGUISTICS IN HEARING CHILDREN

We can distinguish three essential steps in the process of acquiring a mother-tongue by a hearing child, which steps may be described as a model of teaching and learning a mother-tongue.

(1) The External Behaviour

(a) *Conditioning*. The natural babbling of a hearing child and its natural attention

27

to the 'vocalizations' of the environment are moulded and developed by the operant conditioning, the classic conditioning and the evocative influence of the environment, based on the child's tendency to imitation (e.g. Irwin 1948, McCarthy 1954, Menyuk 1969). This process of profiling attention to words and sentences onto a *passive language*, and of profiling and expanding (Fry 1966) babbling onto an active vocabulary (*active language*), is especially stimulated by the *instrumental* value of some vocalizations, both in understanding and producing them.

For example an 'operant' (=incidental) babbling of *mama* is reinforced by the mother by cuddling, is therefore repeated and produced by the baby in some situations as a signal of some need: the child uses this 'vocable' as an instrument in order to be picked up by the mother. *Milk*, in different contexts, is understood by the baby as a signal of food: the baby receives this word as an instrumental stimulus which predicts that he will be fed. And so on. The example of *mama* is one of operant conditioning, the example of *milk* of classic conditioning.

This process, however, should not be conceived too 'mechanically' or 'behavioristically' or 'reflexologically': there is a *personal* relationship between the baby and his mother and vice versa, from the beginning.

(b) Especially a child's *passive* language (=comprehension of speech of the environment) is far *ahead* of its active language (Stern 1907, McCarthy 1954, Lewis 1951, 1968, McNeill 1970). We must emphasize the following two aspects:

(1) Attention to both the code and the situation (persons included) is perfectly integrated as one whole. Very exceptional is 'formal' training, i.e. training of the form of the code as such, so that the attention is mainly focused on the form detached from its content, – e.g. 'You should say two tables and not two table'. The language-code is quite *transparent*, i.e. quite open to and integrated with its content. Nevertheless, it should be emphasized that as soon as the baby starts with speech, this speech is already in some way formally systematized: so his speech is immediately actual acquisition of the system of language. 'The child's perception and production of speech sound sequences considered apart from his acquisition and development of the grammar of his language, is a serious mistake' (Menyuk 1972). Especially the mime and the intonation (those of questions, statements and appeals), already understood by the child within the spoken words and before these words themselves are distinguished, are a link between the form and the content of the language.

(2) The child recognizes 'vocalizations' of its environment in a very *flexible* way. For instance *milk* may be used towards him in very many combinations of linguistic and extra-linguistic contexts. So words are understood in ever richer *combinabilities*. This is the basis from which *creative behaviour*, within and out-

side language, can be developed (Torrance 1962, Barron 1968, 1969). It may be conceived how this creativity is important for the spontaneous outgrowth of language and by means of that for the development of the whole personality. Too much restriction may be dangerous for a whole lifetime.

(c) Active and passive language meet each other mainly in the *conversations* between mother (and others) and child. In the beginning these conversations are usually connected with *doing* something together: the child is spoken to while being cared for; mother plays with and talks to the child. This doing things and playing together are the basis from which conversations originate. Without that, conversation is hampered and because of it, the whole acquisition of language (cf. Rutter 1972, Greenstein 1975).

A second feature of these first conversations between mother and child is that the mother follows a '*seizing method*' (van Uden 1955, 1968), i.e. she seizes what she supposes the child is wanting to say, and gives it back to him in better words and forms. At the same time she says what she herself is wanting to say, which is more and more generally and intuitively understood by the child. By means of this method she enters, little by little, into conversation with a still speechless child. Many teachers of language think that they first have to build up a *vocabulary* before they can start a conversation. The mother, however, in teaching her native language to the baby, immediately starts with conversation by the 'seizing method' and by the 'playing of a double part' (van Uden 1955, 1968). An example:

Hearing child 1; 2:	*Mother:*
'Mama, want wea wea!'	
(with a sign of pulling over head)	'Yes! You want your sweater?
	The blue one?
'Bue bue'	'Yes, the blue one!'
'Bue bue . . . one'	'Yes, the blue one' . . .
	And so on.

Although content, and the transparency of the codes, remain the strongest incentives to developing both mental processes and speech forms (Cazden 1965, 1968, Tizard et al. 1972), grammar as such seems to play an important part too: the child and its mother systematize, and the *conversation* seems to be the 'proving ground' of the child's learning a language by trial and check, supported, corrected, taught by its mother.

(2) The 'Cognitive' Mediating Processes

NB. We take the term 'cognitive' from the learning theory of Tolman and the

Gestalt-psychologists (cf. Hilgard 1956), although these 'internal' processes of the 'black box' are not only just cognitive: they are also feelings, wants, questions, 'mappings', and also eupraxic (Cobb 1948) programmed motor-processes.

(a) The function of *memory*, Short Term Memory (STM) and Long Term Memory (LTM). Mandler (1967, quot. Furth and Milgram 1973) calls STM 'primary memory' and LTM 'organized memory'.

The child uses for example his STM in echoing its mother:

Mother (Dutch):	*Child* (2;1):
Dat is ome Lewie.	
(=that is uncle Lewis)	Ome.wie!
	Ome.wie!
	Ome.wie! (and so on).

Uncle Lewis went out and came back one and a half hours later. He was welcomed with 'Ome.wie' in the same melody and the same rhythm. The child had clearly stored that name in this LTM.

It is a matter of course that this function is basic in the serial behaviour. The length and structure of sentences, both in understanding and producing them, depend on it. If a child suffers a defective memory-span (STM), it has forgotten at the end of a sentence how it had started: this creates misunderstandings and dysgrammaticisms. To illustrate, a boy at a school for learning disabilities said 'He me my arm bumped, has me bumped, arm bumped'. Such dysgrammaticisms are found in children with so-called developmental dysphasia (van Uden 1969). – The next example may show how understanding is hampered too. An intelligent hearing child of 12 years of age could do errands for her mother, notwithstanding still 'clumsy speech'. Mother said to her: 'Will you go and pay the monthly bill at the grocer's shop? I will give you money'. Child: 'What should I buy?' Mother: 'No, you should pay the monthly bill. This is the bill'. Very often the child could not understand an instruction which was a little bit long. Then mother had to break it up into small pieces, in order to be understood by the child.

It may be clear that the utterances of every child are limited according to the span of its STM and of his LTM too (Miller 1951). This memory-function is always stimulated by the mother. See the example above: 'Mama, wea wea' (two words plus a sign) becomes in mother's seizing behaviour 'Yes, you want your sweater?' (=five words, without a sign). 'Bue bue' becomes 'the blue one'. The attention of the child for the whole is rewarded by its successful understanding from the mother. The inverse: the mother rewards the more and more expanded utterances of the child by approving behaviour: 'bue one' – 'Yes, the blue one'.

Brown and Fraser (1963) made hearing children imitate spoken sentences. Here are some examples:

Model:	Imitations:	
	2;1 old	*2;7 old*
I showed you the book.	I show book	I show you the book.
I do not want an apple.	I do – apple.	I do not want – apple

It should be emphasized again that the memory of speech in the child is aided very strongly by *rhythm* and *melody*. When a mother speaks to her child, she sings rather than speaks. . . .

(b) Braine (1963) found that a child of 2 years of age *systematizes* his words, almost as soon as he starts his 2-word stage. This system – his own – is not a direct imitation of adult speech. This implies that the child uses his memory not only in an echoing way, but also in planning his sequences. This planning first of all concerns the positions of the words; some words call for fixed positions, of course via the memory of these words. E.g. 'Want wea wea' of the example above contains the words 'want' which appeared to have gained a fixed position in the series, as 'want ball', 'want this', and even 'want mama?' (=what does mama want?). – Braine does not mention the rhythm of speech, or its melody, but it seems not too unlikely to assume that rhythm in these storing processes plays an important part. In our opinion we may say that the rhythmic grouping of words (forming '*accent-groups*') is the first and most fundamental systematization used by the child. This seems to be very akin to the phrase-structure of sentences (Chomsky 1957, Johnson 1965). This tendency to systematization with fixed positions of some words could be termed a congenital mediating function, although not linguistic in itself, because more or less the same happens in other types of serial behaviour, e.g. the sequences of phonemes: a child very soon takes over the specific positional laws of the phonemes of his mother-tongue, so that, e.g. mbawa or pwa or ftee etc. soon become impossible for him to pronounce, although these combinations may have occurred in his spontaneous babbling; – the same phenomenon happens in music, e.g. the interval-sequences according to the tonic and dominant; – the same happens in body positions of movements as walking, climbing, sitting, and in interacting serial plays, as playing at fives, bowling, playing tennis and so on.

(c) The child *reflects* on language. To give an example, a boy of 4;7 years of age said: 'Father *drived* his car into the sandy pathy'. He showed he had relatively understood the typical behaviour to change the verb when speaking about the past, but not yet the meaning of the flexion-y of sandy, although the grouping of the words is correct. Nobody had ever said to him *drived*. But he found the law himself and applied it (cf. Stern 1907, Lewis 1951, Bellugi 1973). The first feature, however, of linguistic system found by children is the grouping of words by rhythm and melody.

(3) Conversation Again and Again. Reading and Writing. 'Belles Lettres'

The advantage, born of all this, is a better and more independent conversation and communication. According to my observational findings (van Uden 1955) the mother stops her 'seizing method' when the child becomes 5 or 6 years old. A normal hearing child does not need it further. But I found some mothers of mentally defective hearing children who became more inclined to imitate the clumsy speech of their children instead of helping them, which behaviour may be very dangerous. Then the school years come, in which – by *reading* and *writing* – the power of language usage becomes much more conscious to the child, which again affords better and more independent conversation. 'Independent' means: independent of the 'seizing method'.

Thus the process of language acquisition has the form of a *spiral* from the bottom upwards:
   I. From conversation through the 'seizing method' and 'playing a double part', –
  II. via internal cognitive mastering
 III. to independent conversation;
      I. from this independent conversation,
     II. via stronger internal cognitive mastering, by way of reading and writing too,
    III. to still more independent conversation, towards the joy of poetry and 'belles lettres'. . . .

3. APPLICATION OF THIS MODEL IN THE DIDACTICS OF LANGUAGE TO DEAF CHILDREN

We will follow the model in its three steps.

(1) The External Behaviour

(a) Communication should start as early as possible (Ewing 1947, 1954), at least not later than 1;6 years of age (van Uden 1957, 1959, Greenstein 1975). Such methods should be preferred which follow the principles of classic and operant *conditioning* and of evoking imitation (van Uden 1955), i.e. the most natural methods, being tied to the behaviour of the child itself. The methods of the Ewings (1934, 1943, 1964) and of De Werd (1942, Reichling 1949; cf. Krijnen 1967 and

32

Postma 1936) have shown that it is possible in the pure oral way, i.e. without a mixture with signs of finger-spelling.

How to Prevent Sign Language?

A conventional sign-language can be prevented: this means that the *exchanging* code is not one of signs. The deaf child will make signs, at least dramatizations, even the hearing child does so (Hirsch 1923, Beaver 1932), but if the mother does not answer in self-made signs, i.e. if she orally answers normally with of course the usual gestures, so that the full attention of the child becomes face-directed, no sign-*language* comes up.

Heider (1940) found after two years of preschool training a lot of dramatization in deaf children but almost no conventional signs.

The Instrumental Value of Language

Not only the identifying use of language ('matching-exercises', 'that is that' – method) should be emphasized, but more its *instrumental* value (Ewing 1964). Some examples: Mother Williams tells her deaf child the names of some of the foods on the table: 'That is bread' 'That is marmalade' 'That is butter'. She writes the words on cards, putting them by the food concerned. This is an identifying method both for spoken and written language. – Mother Johnson does it rather differently: she knows that her deaf child likes marmalade so much, so she does not put marmalade on the table, keeping it hidden in the cupboard. As soon as her child at the table looks for the marmalade and tries to express himself to get it, she says 'Oh, you want marmalade? Marmalade?' and when the child nods yes, or, still better, tries to say something like 'marmalade' (for instance 'ml. .'), she goes happily to the cupboard and shows it to her child. In this way the spoken word 'marmalade' receives an instrumental value.

The same goes for written language (for instance for dysphasic deaf children). She then prepares 3 cards, e.g. one card with 'bread', another one with 'marmalade', yet another saying 'butter'. She does not put them to the objects concerned but simply places them on the table. Purposely, again the bread, marmalade and butter are not on the table. The child will ask for it, perhaps 'operantly' taking one of the cards or pointing to it, e.g. butter. Then the mother says: 'You want butter? Butter? I will show you!' She goes to the cupboard and shows the child the butter putting it on the table: 'That is the butter!' And so on.

We call this latter method the 'anticipatory method', because the word is given, in spoken form and even written form, *before* the child sees or gets what he wants. This way is much more effective and evokes the interest of the child, because the word, the language becomes an instrument to gain satisfaction of his wishes.

(b) *Two dangers* in the field of language acquisition threaten the deaf child, even in the early stages from 2;0 till 5;0 years of age:

Lack of Transparency

(1) Too much attention to the *form* of language. This is especially dangerous in the identifying methods mentioned above, i.e. the names may stick to only very concrete situations, without evoking the interest of the child, so that he forgets very soon. If for example a deaf child of 6 years of age accepts a new word, without immediately asking for its meaning, this behaviour shows, there was something wrong in its early development. The training should be as situational as possible, totally connected with the feelings and experiences of the children: the language code should be *transparent*.

Language Production First?

(2) Too much emphasis on making the child produce language initially, instead of giving him a *large* background of *language comprehension*. This impedes general intuitive understanding.

Sometimes teachers choose a set of colloquial utterances of daily life. The children learn to use them in the right situations, by a lot of pretending activities in which they have to produce these sentences by heart. Although this can have a nice impression on visitors, who are not aware of the poor background of intuitive understanding, this way is wrong, because it is far too formal. The same thing can be taught and learned by real conversations, within the variation of real situations. A too formal approach emphasizing the production of sentences, gives a too limited language, in words, forms, spans and situations, which hampers flexibility in adjustment to others (van Uden 1955). E.g. if a deaf child of 6 years of age is asked: 'Did you like that apple? *How* was it?' and it answers: 'The apple is round', this would show that there was something wrong in his mental grasp of the combinability of words, originating from a too constructive, too limited background of language in previous years. The effect of a free conversational approach will be for the child to immediately answer: 'Oh fine!' or 'The apple was delicious' and so on, *without* this having been officially taught.

(c) The '*seizing method*' and the '*playing of a double part*' by the mother can and should be followed as soon as possible with deaf children too (van Uden 1955). It is not necessary to build up a certain amount of vocabulary *before* conversation can start. – The seizing method on the other hand presupposes a large amount of daily experiences (Furth 1961, 1966), and most of all playing and doing something with others together: the basis of language should not only be the building up of a vocabulary but most of all the creating of situations which evoke communication: *this* calls for vocabulary, not the inverse.

For instance a child of 6 years of age was spoken to in this way: 'John, give your brush to Mary. You use the pencil'. This was not understood, although the vocabulary was known to the child. Also John was willing, because after pointing and signing to him, he did what was asked. Mostly these misunderstandings show a lack of doing *and* communicating together, a detachment of vocabulary from conversation. John knew the words 'brush' and 'pencil' and 'Mary' too, mainly by matching exercises, thus by the identifying method, and now when these words were used in the normal conversational setting, he went astray.

How can the 'seizing method' and the 'playing of a double part' be applied to deaf children? An example. A mother (a farmer's wife) told me this (it happened after the birth of a litter of rabbits; the conversation was reconstructed afterwards):

Annette (3 years old):	*Mother:*
Brrr (pointing towards the cage of rabbits) . . . (t)a(t)a (with a sign of going to sleep).	The rabbit is sleeping? (Dutch: sl*a*pen). Do you want me to come?

Mama (with a sign of 'come').
Both went to the cage. One small rabbit had died . . .

Annette:	*Mother*:
Brrr (pointing to it).	The rabbit is not sleeping! It is dead!

They buried the dead rabbit. It was a terrible discovery by the child. Such a conversation can be visualized as follows:

The rabbit is sleeping.

No! It is dead Poor rabbit!

Annette   Mother

35

These sentences are understood from the situation ('ideo-visual reading'). Perhaps a drawing of a dead rabbit can be added. This drawing, however, should not be done in such a way that the picture expresses the whole situation: *experiences* should be the interpreter of language, not pictures!

NB. It is a great pity that Annette's speech was so backward at that time. It is quite possible to develop much better speech even at that age (Reichling 1949).

(2) The 'Cognitive' Mediating Processes

(a) *Memory*

The function of *memory* is one of the greatest difficulties in the teaching of language to deaf children. Therefore we have to train deaf children in the memory of *that* language in which we will educate them, first of all in speaking longer and longer normal sentences, and also in copying by heart written sentences. If this memory-function has not been trained, it cannot be expected of the vast majority of deaf children, even of 18 years of age, to utter correct sentences, if the series of words becomes longer than 5.

(b) *Spontaneous systematization*

Deaf children, too, of their own accord, somewhat *systematize* their utterances.
This can already happen in young deaf children. Like the deaf child of 3 years of age who said 'Oooh' for all that was very big, very far away and very important. After a time this was connected with words and also with some signs, e.g. 'Oooh auwo' signifying: 'Oh what a big car' or 'I want into the big car' or on another oc- casion 'We were in the car for a very long time'. The same with 'Oh ball' (=I want that big ball, a big plastic ball used in the swimming-pool); further 'Oooh' with a sign of swimming (=I want to go for a swim in the sea) etc. etc. – This looks rather similar to the systematization of a normal hearing child. Usually, however, the systematization of a deaf child is different from that of a hearing child.

Visual Order of Symbols

Brannon (1966, 1968) found that young deaf children in their spontaneous spoken language very often follow a *visual* order of the words; for example they will say 'Ballpen give me!' instead of 'Give me (a) ballpen' = one has to pick up a ballpen before one can give it. This reminds us of the order of ideas in so-called 'iconic thinking' or 'picture-thinking' or 'image-thinking' (Krabbe 1951), found in normal- ly hearing children with developmental dysphasia. An example of a hearing adult 'image-thinker', a stutterer in addition: 'Oh yes, certain, flowers I like to paint flowers, one-flower, preferably one flower'. So it seems that the origin of the visual order is both the overemphasized visual behaviour of deaf children ('visualizers'), and their poor short term memory.

Emotional Order of Symbols

The same must be said of the *emotional* position of words, a fact which may be observed by everyone knowing the deaf. For example, a deaf child said: 'Hat forgotten' (=I forgot my hat). Another one: 'Daddy drawing. . . .' (=I will give my drawing to daddy). Still another one: 'In . . In! Bag!', shaking head (=I can't put it in my bag) etc. These are not visually determined orders, but emotional ones. In our rhythmic speech we can give the third or fourth word the accent, but such a rhythmic flow does not yet work in the speech of young deaf children. So practically the only way to give a word emphasis is to put it in the first position of the sequence.

But I found (van Uden 1960) in well-trained deaf children of 8–11 years of age that they very often put the emphasis on the second, third or even the last word of their spontaneously spoken utterances. They had conquered their original inclination with their rhythmic speech. – If *young* deaf children are not using the Key (see later; in our Institute they do not learn this), most corrections to the order of words in their written or spoken utterances concern this visual or emotional order. Summarizing we may say: the spontaneous order of words in young deaf children is systematized by visualization and emotional principles on the basis of a lack of STM-function. This does not seem to be a linguistic systematization, i.e. a phrasing behaviour as in hearing children, but it can and should be replaced by a linguistic one, above all by a rhythmic oral education. (About the order of signs in sign-language, see later.)

(c) *A Reflective Method*

We said above that a mother of hearing children of subnormal intelligence is inclined to adjust herself to their poorly structured speech when they are 5–6 years old, and to stop her 'seizing method'. The same thing happens alas in almost all the mothers of deaf children (when they do not have the right guidance), as soon as they become aware of their child's deafness. The consequence of this spontaneous wrong behaviour is that the child never emerges from his very primitive circle of communication. – Professional teachers alas do not usually follow the 'seizing method' either: it is not so easy to train the young teachers this way. Generally they follow the ways in which foreign languages are taught to hearing children and adults: a constructive way of working (see chapter II), the consequence of which is a lack of conversation and again a primitive circle of communication.

Three Different Methods of Teaching Language

Roughly speaking, we can divide the different methods of teaching language to deaf children into three:

The *constructive* methods, in which the children are given models of sentences, programmed from very simple ones until the more complex ones; the children are asked to verbalize experiences, events and facts according to these models; the emphasis is especially on the production of language. The teaching of grammar is usually detached from the teaching of reading. Grammar is used almost only for the production of sentences, that is in active language, how to express themselves correctly, graphically and/or orally.

The *imitative* methods, in which no programmed language is used, only the normal colloquial mother-tongue, but with little training in the structure of language; the children are expected to imitate spontaneously; the emphasis is more on reading. – This method has its origin in Alexander Graham Bell (1847–1922, his publication of 1884; he followed an idea of Dalgarno 1680; the same way has been followed for Helen Keller, see above). As has been mentioned above, Bell trained a congenitally deaf boy during the course of 2 years by always giving him normal language within the situation (in a written form), hoping that the child would imitate him spontaneously. This happened to some degree. His way of working has been followed and propagated by Querll (1922, 1925; see also Forchhammer 1930, Schumann 1940), in addition, however, to lipreading and speech. – To some extent Bell (and his followers) used the 'seizing method' of the mother, not so much by immediately giving George the right sentence replacing his clumsy writing (as far as can be concluded from his report), but afterwards by setting up good reading-lessons. Here is one of his excellent lessons which we have been allowed to reproduce by the courtesy of the Volta Bureau in Washington D.C.:

The Careless Little Girl

Little Mary has been very careless to come out into the cold air with no hat on. Look at her sitting upon the swing. Lilly is standing behind ready to push the swing as it goes backwards and forwards, backwards and forwards, backwards and forwards.

By and by Mary's mamma will come to the swing and say 'Mary, you naughty girl, where is your hat?' And Mary will say 'Please, mamma, it is upstairs'. But her mamma will be very angry and will say 'Stop swinging and go into the house, you careless careless little girl. I am afraid you will be ill tomorrow with a bad cough. If you are so careless again, papa will whip you. Look at Lilly. She is a good girl. She remembered to put on her hat'.

Nov. 23rd – 1873.

The Careless Little Girl

Little Mary has been very careless to come out into the cold air with no hat on. Look at her sitting upon the swing. Lilly is standing behind ready to push the swing as it goes backwards and forwards, backwards and forwards, backwards and forwards.

By and bye Mary's Mamma will come to the swing and say "Mary, you naughty girl, where is your hat?" And Mary will say — "Please, Mamma, it is upstairs".

But her Mamma will be very angry and will say — "Stop swinging and go into the house you careless careless little girl. I am afraid you will be ill tomorrow with a bad cough. If you are so careless again, Papa will whip you. Look at Lilly. She is a good girl. She remembered to put on her hat."

Nov. 23rd 1873

It may be noticed how Bell tried to indicate the accentuated words with big letters. According to the Belgian method of Décroly (1871–1932; see Hamaïde 1922; applied to the instruction of the deaf by Srs. Astère and Odine, Brussels 1930, and Sr. Theresia van Driel, St. Michielsgestel 1934, Sr. M. Helène, Fougères 1971) these lessons are termed 'Ideo-visual reading-lessons'.

Apart from the difficulty of not immediately seizing the utterances of the children and correcting them, and further from the insufficient emphasis on speech and its rhythm, a third difficulty in my opinion is that in general the deaf children are not given sufficient cues to learn grammar both for better understanding and for better control of their own utterances. Whether there is an innate tendency to grammar (Chomsky 1957, McNeill 1970) or not, deaf children need help.

Our *reflective* method tries to combine the normal colloquial language from early childhood with the teaching of the rules or laws of grammatical behaviour.

Is it possible to make deaf children reflect onto their language understood, in order to make them detect and apply the rules of language mainly themselves? We think so (van Uden 1955–1957, 1968). See the examples of oral lessons in the appendices of this book. This development embraces several steps:

1. Real conversation, by the 'seizing method' and the 'playing of a double part', including *all* normal forms of language with all linguistic intentions, thus not only statements, but questions, demands, feelings, calls etc. etc. (orectic language, Lewis 1968).

2. The most important point is: the utterances of the children should be as *rhythmical* as possible, for reasons of memory and also of phrase-structure (Chomsky 1957, Johnson 1965).

3. Because of this lack of memory we cannot omit *reading* and *writing*. This can already be used during hometraining and especially so in the preschool, from about 3 years of age. What the child cannot yet speak, will be written down for him, immediately in the situation. This is kept in the children's diaries in the form of 'reading-lessons' (see the facsimile above; Dale 1968).

Not only statements are written down, but questions, calls, explanations, etc. too, and – as soon as possible – small conversations with sentences not necessarily in their (chrono)-logical order.

4. Learning to reflect on language presupposes much reading and many conversations.

How children show that they have started some reflection, may be illustrated by this example of some 5 year old children in our residential preschool:

Child one:
'My turn hair'.

Teacher:
'Is it your turn to go to the hair-dresser?' (writes on the blackboard:

'It is my turn to go to the hair-
dresser'). 'Say hairdresser' . . .

'Hairedder'
Child two:
'No! Two there!'

'John is already in the salon'
(says this and writes it down
on the blackboard).

'No!' Goes to the blackboard, says
'Two', writes 'Peter' next to 'John'
and changes *is* into *are*.

Of course this child had learned the change of *is* into *are* and vice versa, but he applied it spontaneously in a quite different situation.

Kinds of Conversation

Concerning conversation, we distinguish (van Uden 1970):
a. 'Conversation from heart to heart'.
These conversational 'lessons' are spontaneous conversations in the classroom, in the free time too, the conversations with the parents, the conversations with the house-parents. The flexibility of content and the development of empathy are central here. Of course incorrect forms are corrected immediately ('seizing method'!), but smoothness of the exchange of thoughts is hardly interrupted. The teacher keeps the anthropological and social attitude of every individual child in the foreground in order to develop it.
There are two kinds of these 'conversations from heart to heart':
aa. Quite free conversations, e.g. when a child comes with special news, or when something happened which impressed all the children; this conversation can last 5 or 10 minutes or sometimes a whole hour. These are the main kinds of conversations in preschool and lower grades.
bb. Conversations in order to transmit some information, e.g. why TBC-control is necessary, what the meaning of 'to cope with' is, who Christ is, etc. etc. The older the children become, the more this type of conversation is introduced. The teacher (the children in the highest grades too) composes a reading-lesson which is the 'deposit' of these conversations. See the Appendices.
b. 'Linguistic conversation'.
In these typical 'conversational lessons' the children are made to reflect on language. The material is usually a letter from home, a reading-lesson, or a reading-book. The children have their notebooks (the teacher too). The results of the linguistic conversations and of subsequent individually written tasks are noted down, so that these

41

notebooks could be called: 'growing grammars'. See an example of programming reflective exercises page 234, a summarized 'conversational language' lesson page 243.

NB. Of course there are other exercises too: 'reconstructive exercises' as well as 'constructive' ones.

(3) A Continuous Growth

The linguistic development of deaf children has the form of a *spiral*, from the bottom upwards:

The conversation using the 'seizing method' grows to a more and more independent conversation in the higher grades. This can be mainly independent in the 6–7th grade, i.e. the children need less and less help to express themselves correctly. This growth is wholly connected with the growth of receptive reading and of reflection on language, which again makes the conversations more and more independent. These again enhance reading and writing.

All this is connected with the degree of automatism of language.

II. The False Assumptions of the
Constructive Methods

Confrontation with the Findings of Psycholinguistics

1. A DEFINITION OF THE 'CONSTRUCTIVE METHODS'

a. Characteristics

The constructive methods can be characterized, briefly, as those which take their model from teaching a *foreign* language. They can be described as the methods which:

1. admittedly offer the children living language but start with grammatically limited forms, to be extended later on, more and more to increasingly complex forms, which
2. relying on the ability of the children to construct and to follow learnt analogies, give these children again and again programmed means to build language forms according to learnt models, and which
3. doing so expect that the children will master, receptively and expressively, the learnt language models, and – through these models – other unlearnt language forms.

b. Didactics

The didactics of *teaching a foreign language* to children who already have a mother-tongue can be reduced to three methods (cf. Lado 1964):

(a) Translation-methods: words and sentences of the mother-tongue are translated for the child into the foreign language, according to a special programme. The child is taught to translate for himself from the mother-tongue to the foreign language and the inverse. This process of translation should be speeded up mentally more and more.
(b) Direct methods: words and sentences of the foreign language are identified directly with their meaning, e.g. by pictures: 'Bonjour monsieur' 'C'est une table' etc. Very useful are films and tape recordings to accustom the student to the

pronunciation, the rhythm and melody of the foreign language. This is a big help to their memory too. Films can show small conversations within the situation. The students are invited to imitate the models shown.

(c) 'Natural methods': by conversation-lessons, integrated with the direct methods and completed by the translation-method.

It may be clear that this last way is the best one, i.e. most approximating the way in which we learned our mother-tongue, and the one most able to offer living language. It is only a pity that many teachers of foreign languages do not understand the techniques of the 'seizing method' and of 'playing a double part'.
The 'constructive methods' for deaf children are akin to the methods (a) and (b). The methods under (c) cannot be called 'constructive' in the strict sense.

Concrete Examples

In order to give some concrete examples of what is meant here by 'constructive methods for the deaf', I refer to Fitzgerald (1937), M. Miller (1966), Kreye (1972, 1975) and many others. These methods can be distinguished into two trends, an analytic and a synthetic one: some methods lean more on a categorization of parts of speech from which sentences are constructed (see, e.g. page 50); others immediately introduce some simple sentences, as 'The box is on the table' (see below), which structures are expanded more and more according to a programme. This last method has been stimulated in the U.S.A. recently, based on the principles of the 'generative grammar' of Chomsky (1957, 1965) applied to deaf children by McNeill (1965, 1970), followed by Monsees (1967, 1973), Blackwell and Hamel both at the 'Rode Island School for the Deaf' since 1967 (1970, 1971), and most of all by Streng (1972). Their reasoning is in short as follows: all human beings, therefore deaf children too (even in sign-language? Tervoort 1968, cf. Gardner and Gardner 1969, 1973, working with primates), possess an innate competence in organizing deep-structure of language (especially the subject-predicate-combination, the so-called 'Language Acquisition Device' LAD). Therefore, they say, deaf children should be presented with the simple sentence forms of that deep-structure – 'Daddy slept', 'Mary washes dishes' etc. –, in order to evoke that innate capacity. These simple structures should be increasingly expanded.

Criticisms

The writers above, however, omit to mention that this is not the natural development in a hearing child: the hearing child is presented with *all* forms of language, simple and complicated ones, and it *detects* the language forms mainly himself, according to innate capacities or not. Another difficulty against these methods, which we will point to immediately, is that the rhythmic basis of the language structure is insufficiently understood. A last and most essential obstacle in their reasoning (and that of Chomsky and his followers) is, that the sentence is assumed to be the smallest meaningful unit in language. We will show below that the smallest unit is not the sentence but the conversation. Conversation is the basic means in all language acquisition and without that, the teaching of a language will result in failure. Consequently, the methods mentioned above are in my opinion a real danger to the humanization of deaf children.

2. A DISCUSSION ON THE STARTING POINT OF THE 'CONSTRUCTIVE METHODS'

In order to introduce the problem I will give a sentence used by a teacher following one of the constructive methods, which I discussed with him. When the small children aged about 6 years were in the classroom and had settled down, he put a box on the table and wrote in clear letters on the blackboard:

> The box is on the table

He asked the children: 'Show me the box ... Show me the table ... Where is the box? ...' So much for this lesson. The teacher told me that such a sentence is completely clear to the children and this was the point of our discussion!

In my opinion, this teacher neglected several points in his lesson:

1. *Language-forms* cannot be completely understood unless several of their oppositions are clear too. *The* is not clear unless the indefinite article *a* and the zero-function of omitting the article (e.g. 'milk is good for you') is understood. – The singular-form *box* is not understood unless the plural form *boxes* is understood too. The same with *is-was – have been, has-have* etc., *table-tables, on-in-under* etc.

2. The teacher was not at all sure of the *viewpoints* of the children, i.e. the global intuitive understanding of the situation, which included the persons involved and their intentions in behaviour. If these deaf children were normal, they could not but think of what the teacher *wanted* to do, what the meaning of his behaviour was. One child may have understood this sentence as:

The teacher is putting the box on the table, to get rid of it.

Another one:

The table is under the box.

And:

The box on the table may be opened. The teacher has a surprise for us.

And again:
The box has been put away in order to make us more attentive to the blackboard.
And so on.

3. It is also possible that a child may not have grasped the *unity* of the sentence as it was expressed by flexions and the grouping of the words, but most of all by its rhythmic fluency. The hearing child would understand that unity through rhythm and melody (Reichling 1940), the deaf child through facial mime. But the written sentence on the blackboard had neither mime nor rhythm. This child may have understood:
That is a box. That is a table.
Here we see that *thinking*, although including language, is more than language (cf. Furth 1966, see, however, page 135). To be precise the 'units of thinking' are never *completely* expressed by language. The language code is always something divisable into parts, something spread out in time and/or in space, e.g. 'You were at least able to open the door for me'. In contrast to this spreading out of the code of language, the thought itself is some momentary intuition, a unit, which is in some way an 'indivisible point'. So this thought cannot be constructed, built up from parts, it can only be evoked: if the child lacks this enlightening *intuition*, it will never grasp the meaning of the sentence.

This seems to be a great difference with mathematical or logistic formulas as

$2 + 3 = 5$
or $(a + b) (a - b) = a^2 - b^2$,
or $a > b$ and $b > c$, thus $a > c$,
or $a = b$ (identified), $b = c$, then $a = c$. Etc.

These are *quantitatively* composed units and can be checked by experiencing the continuous or discontinuous quantities. Not so in most of our sentences in language.

4. What is *meant* by table? What is meant by box? It all seems very clear. This cannot be completely understood, however, unless these concepts have been formed by means of their oppositions: What is not a table, but, e.g. a desk? What is not a box but for instance a pot? And so on. This brings us to the problem of the relativity of concepts, with which we will deal later on.

5. Most important:

(a) A real sentence is always uttered to another person, it is a *part of a conversation*. This is another big difference between sentences and mathematical formulas: these formulas are expressions of facts; they are not part of a conversation, but more a help to our thinking. The most important feature of a sentence, however, is that it is a part of the interaction between person and person, it is a *personal* datum.

(b) A sentence, by being a part of a conversation, usually functions as an element in *figure-background thinking*. Piaget (1930, 1951) seems to be right in saying that intellectual thinking views facts as figures against a *background of possibilities*. This implies flexible thinking by making hypotheses and checking their truths. – The teacher, by putting a box on a table and writing on the blackboard 'The box is on the table', detaches this sentence from all conversation, puts it as a clear-cut doubtless fact. But imagine now this same sentence used as part of a conversation:

First example:

Peter: 'Do you know where I may have put that box?'
John: 'Well you must be blind! *The box is on the table!*'
Both Peter and John express the possibilities of other places where the box might be. These possibilities play the part of a background and the sentence as an actual figure against these possibilities.

Second example:
Charles: 'Hey! What a heavy thing! At last, *the box is on the table!*' ...

Third example:
Trudy: 'Now? Isn't that right?'
William: 'I told you to put the box on the windowsill. I now come in with Aunt Lucy and what do I see? *The box is on the table!*'

Fourth example:
Mother: 'Come on boys, clear away all those things! I must lay the table ... Everything into the box and away all of you!' ...
Some seconds later mother returns: 'John, just come here, you bad boy! *The box is on the table!*'

Fifth example:
Father: 'We are going to construct our Christmas stable ... Mary, will you go up into the loft; the box is in the cupboard.'
Voice from upstairs: 'There is no box in the cupboard!'
Father: 'Oh sorry, I forgot to tell you ... *The box is on the table*, that old table, covered with a cloth' ...

These examples may illustrate how conversation facilitates flexible thinking, from possibilities to facts (deductive thinking) and vice versa from facts on to possibilities (inductive thinking).

3. THE 'OPPOSITIONS' IN LANGUAGE: 'VALENCIES' AND 'COMBINABILITIES'

The idea of oppositions has been brought into the modern linguistic science by its founder De Saussure (1916, who said with some exaggeration: 'Dans la langue il n'y a que des différences, sans termes positives'), and developed further by Trubetzkoy, Hjelmslev a.o. (see Reichling 1935, 1962; Potter 1960, Dinneen 1967). Phonemes, words, morphemes, sentences are 'bound' to each other as are atoms in a molecule and molecules in bigger chemical complexes, in which the whole ultimately determines the elements and not the reverse.

Open and Closed Systems

There are open and closed systems of elements. An oppositional system is a closed system, if it excludes to some extent other elements or features. For example the system of bolts, nails and screws is a closed one in so far as it fills a whole field of possibilities in the fixing together of planks. – The 'system' of trademarks of cigarettes is an open 'system'.

The closed oppositional systematization in language happens as early as in the development of *phonology* in hearing children (see, e.g. Fry 1966): at the beginning of real speech the baby uses a few vowels and a few consonants; all words are reduced to that system, such as *chair* becomes *tah*. After a time this system loosens, it is broken up by introducing other phonemes, but again tends to another closed system, a more complex one. So the phonological development of a child is not a continuum by the addition of more and more phonemes, but a growth from one system to another, from one stage, from one phase to another. A closed system in some degree supports itself, 'defending' itself (Klir and Valach 1967).

The same happens in the *semantic* aspect of language: e.g. in the beginning all 'two-leggers' are daddy, as opposed to the mother, a closed system of the persons recognized. All other encountering personalities are pushed away from the consciousness as background phenomena. See page 134 for the other stages of development. – Such a reduction of the environment helps the child (and later the adult) to survey and master the situations, to avoid perplexities, but on the other side, it may cause rigidity in his thinking and adjustment, witness children with developmental dysphasia (Eisenson 1972).

Rigid Thinking?

Deaf children too tend to build up their own semantic closed systems according to the environment. This will remain rather primitive, if we do not expand both experiences and language codes. We said: 'and language codes', (a) because many experiences, memories and images which are not encoded in language tend to remain background phenomena unless occurring very frequently. So 'traffic' will remain an unknown concept for too long a time, if the word is unknown. (b) Some abstractions and concepts are more bound to language than others. Hence a deaf child may abstract 'food' very soon, the same goes for 'furniture', without knowing these words. This is not so for 'metal', 'element', 'uncle' etc. If we don't expand both experiences and language codes for the child, a kind of rigid conversation and thinking will originate.

The same tendency to systematization happens in the development of the *morphology* of language. At first a verb is, e.g. characterized only by its position in the series of words, then afterwards, more features of the verbs (inflexions) are introduced. And so on.

'Valencies' and 'Combinabilities'

These systematizations include a development which grows from simple entireties towards more complex entireties, but always in entireties. These entireties are patterns, Gestalts, figures, structures, which in principle are grasped by global intuition and from which the elements are conceived by differentiation. These elements have different *'valencies'*, i.e. powers of combining with other elements: which could be called *'combinabilities'* (Paardekoper 1966).

Selectivity

These combinabilities are selective. Some words repel each other, e.g. semantically 'quiet rage', or morphologically 'hoping *to* an ice-cream', 'I *is* happy' etc. But other words or morphemes attract each other, e.g. 'quiet happiness', 'hoping *for* an ice-cream', 'I *am* happy' and so on. A selective combinability for the rest can be related both to an opposition and to an affinity. If I say for instance 'For the car' I have a unit of 3 differently ('oppositively') functioning words: preposition-article-noun. If I say: 'market-place', I am combining words which are affiliated to each other, not only semantically but also grammatically: these are 2 nouns or substantives.

4. CONCEPT OF 'SENTENCE' AND 'WORDCLASS'

One of the biggest mistakes in the train of thoughts in the constructive method is its concept of the sentence and of the word-classes, the origin of which is the teaching of Latin in many schools in a so-called logical way as it was thematized in the 17th and 18th century. It was applied in France especially by the school of Arnaud († 1694) in Port-Royal (see Chomsky 1968), and in Germany by Becker (1841). This system has been taken over, particularly from Becker, in the instruction of the deaf (Schumann 1940; Nelson 1949).

In that logical way of thinking the most perfect *sentence* is the proposition, constituted by subject and predicate, functioning as an assertion. So we see, that for instance reading lessons for the small ones, in this constructive method, are built up almost only by propositions.

Word-classes are defined for example in this way:
— substantives = names of things and persons;
— verbs = names of actions;
— adjectives = names of qualities of verbs and adjectives.

The vocabulary is broken up, for the children, in lists of words under such headings as *Who? What? What does ...? How?* and so on.

Sentences are built up in an *associative* way, using words as bricks, usually from left to right, led by ciphers (Sicard 1814), slates (Barry 1893), keys (Fitzgerald 1926), colours (Freunthaller 1932, Schmid-Giovannini 1976, Topley 1964), and so on (Schumann 1940, Nelson 1949).

Streng (1962) gives this example of the use of the FITZGERALD KEY:

What: Who:	verb	What: Whom:	Whom: What:	Where:	For ... from ... etc	When:
Father	bought	me	a box of candy		for birthday	
I	know		that you have a dog at home			
Jerry	likes		to play with his dog			
We	will go			to Chicago		this summer
The doll	is			in the cupboard		

An example from the so-called '*signal-method*' of Freunthaller (1932):

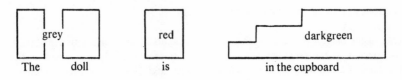

	grey		red		darkgreen
The	doll		is		in the cupboard

Compare this with the 'state diagram' (from Lyons 1972) of so-called modern *Finite State Grammars*, i.e. a sentence grows from state to state until it stops (Hockett 1955, 1958):

START This $\longrightarrow$ man $\longrightarrow$ has $\longrightarrow$ eaten $\longrightarrow$ the bread STOP

We notice immediately how the rhythm of the sentences is broken through this Key. Don't we say:
Father/bought-me/a box of candy . . .
I-know/that . . .
We-will-go/. . .
The teacher has to take care indeed that the children do not say:
Father/bought/me . . .
I/know/that . . .
We/will go . . .
We will not minimize the Key. But there are several dangers.

Criticism of these word classes is obvious. Take '*obedience*'. Is that a quality, or a name of a thing? '*To sleep*'; is this a name of an action? And so on. You will not find such an approach in modern linguistics. In my opinion an approach like that is very misleading to deaf children. The consequences of this method are dreadful: the majority of the children will never attain true reading of normal literature, except perhaps for some very intelligent ones or children who are not truly prelingually deaf (cf. Kreye 1972).

5. DIFFERENT OPPOSITIONAL 'VALENCIES' IN LANGUAGE

It is of course easy to reject a system which in more or less intensity has been so widely used and is still in use in many schools both for the hearing and for the deaf. We will try to bring together several points, discussed in modern linguistics and psycholinguistics. We think we can bridge the gap.

The central idea of modern linguistics is 'opposition'. This word sounds dyadic, i.e. as an opposition between two elements. It is, however, not meant in this way: contrasts between three or more aspects are called oppositions too: 'multilateral oppositions'. Besides, this word sounds analytic. The oppositional aspects of elements of language are seen as valencies precisely: because they are oppositional they have 'combining powers'.
In linguistic behaviour we find the following six oppositional valencies:

51

1. The *phonemes*: e.g. vowels and consonants, plosives and fricatives etc.; some combinations as mbawa are excluded in English: these phonemes repel each other; but mawa and bawa are English combinabilities.

2. The *flexions* (prefixes, infixes, 'Umlauts', suffixes, zerofunctions, e.g. °real – *un*-real, °prove° – *dis*proves, fish°woman – fish*er*man, woman – w*o*men etc.);

3. *Rhythmic oppositions*, different pauses, intonations, i.e. opposed groupings of words such as:

'Turn off the light' – 'Turn the light off'.

How do we know, that in 'the tall boy' *the* has something to do with *boy*? Because very often we say rhythmically: *the boy*. These rhythmic groups *the boy* and *the tall boy* are opposed to each other.

Further the shifting of pauses, e.g. 'John/,who-had-had-an-accident,/has recovered' – 'He had/an accident'.

Shifting of intonations: 'Will you *visit* me?' – 'No! *Tomorrow*'.

4. Intentions of sentences (assertion, question, call, see later);

5. Partners of conversation and referred objects/subjects: 1st, 2nd and 3rd 'person';

6. Polarities of meanings (see Chapter III, 5).

We will pass by the phonematic oppositions (i.e. the structure of phonemes in a special language) and the intonations in this book. We will discuss the following points:

a. The importance of conversation.
b. The intentions of sentences.
c. The phrase structure approach.
d. Lexical meaning and morphological meaning.
e. Rhythm as a language form.
f. Reflecting on the language.
g. When we can say that a language form is really functioning as such in the mind of a child.

6. THE IMPORTANCE OF CONVERSATION

Van Ginneken (1909) was right in saying: 'Conversation is the complete form of language'. This means that, if we want a complete sample of the population 'language', that sample must include conversation. An isolated sentence, even a series of such sentences, is not a complete sample of language.

What is Conversation? Is it a Markovian Process?

Conversation is a two way exchange of thoughts, a continuous anticipatory and reinforcing behaviour of the partners with a continuous feedback. Peter wanting to say something to John already anticipates in his behaviour what he expects John's response to be. John in listening is already preparing what he will say to Peter, and often he will react to sentences uttered by Peter some sentences before the sentence he is uttering now. So: the going on of a conversation is not at all Markovian or a process of serially succeeding probabilities in which the first element is giving information, the probability of the second element is partly explained by this first one, the probability of the third element by the succession of the first and the second, etc. For instance if we see a first letter t we can expect some other letters to come, e.g. a or e, not ch; let it be te; then we can expect again another letter, e.g. a or s etc.; let it be l; then we will expect again another letter; let it be e; so we look for telegram, television etc.; let the next letter be v, we are almost sure, that the whole word will be *television*. (See Shannon and Weaver 1949). We will see later that the Markovian model is applicable (perhaps!) to single words, but not to receptive or expressive language. In contrast to this we will see how the constructive method builds up its lessons rather well in accordance with the Markovian model: each sentence explains the following, e.g.

'The baby saw a big dog.
The dog barked and the baby cried.
The mother ran fast and took the baby home' (M. Miller 1966).

We will see below that actually the 'combinabilities' of the words to each other can be expressed in a stochastic way. 'Stochastic', in contrast with deterministic, means 'guessing' according to given probabilities, which quantitatively can be expressed in percentages. These 'combinabilities', however, do not concern only succeeding words, but preceding words as well. The word 'blue', e.g. has combinabilities both after and before it: for instance 'the blue book'. So the term 'stochastic' comprises a broader field than the Markovian one. In linguistic behaviour the device is not wholly 'deterministic' or 'mechanical' (Bach 1964), as can easily be seen, e.g. in poetry, in free conversation and so on.

The Sentence as an Element of Conversation

We cannot really say that a 'sentence is a construction, which, in the given utterance, is not part of any larger construction' (Bloomfield 1926), because that larger construction is always a conversation. There is no such thing as an isolated sentence in true linguistic behaviour. Every real sentence is 'multipersonal', i.e. presupposes a conversational partner in reality or in imagination. Other sentences before or after, or both before and after the sentence uttered, are said or at least are expected or presupposed in the sentence uttered.
Our criticism of Chomsky's theory and that of his followers is that they put the

sentence much too one-sidedly into the centre of their considerations.

Pike (1967) distinguishes: discourse → sentence → phrase → word. This is a big step into the right direction, but the term 'discourse' is too general, because it comprises a speech, a sermon, an essay, a lecture etc.: these are samples of language which are derivations, derived from the original form of language: conversation.

In conversation specific features of language are almost unconsciously trained, e.g.

a) The 'intentionality' and 'instrumentality' of language (see below).

(b) Such ways of speaking as 'I think' ... 'What do you mean?' ... 'I said' ... etc.

(c) The personal pronouns I, you, your, mine, etc.; the other 'pointer-words' these, that, here, there, etc., the use of which is the basis for understanding and use of the articles.

(d) The shifting of accents, e.g.

A. Did I see *you* in the theatre last night?

B. In the *theatre*? Me? I have *never* been in the theatre.

(e) The use of rhythmical units as phrases, e.g. 'In the theatre?', which units could be called the 'accessories' of linguistic utterances. These are exchanged continuously among the partners. Very often one partner says a phrase, as an incomplete sentence, (according to George Miller about 30% of the sentences in a conversation, 1951), and the other partner supplies the completion, e.g.

Peter: 'Tell me, where the newspaper boy *is*'.

John: 'On the left corner' (= *he is* on the left corner).

In my opinion the dialogic structure of language is closely connected with its phrase-structure.

(f) The flexions, the correct use of which is constantly reinforced by the understanding of the partners and disinforced by misunderstanding and/or correcting reactions (cf. Skinner 1957), e.g.

A. I don't smok*e* any more.

B. Oh, I have never smok*ed*.

A. I wish I had never started smok*ing*.

(g) *Transformations:* the conversations between partners are full of overt transformations in the sense of Chomsky (1965): this means that what has been said by one partner in a positive, active and assertive way, is said differently by the other partner, perhaps negatively, passively, as a question, as a clause, or as an embedded phrase etc., and vice versa, e.g.:

First partner:	*Second partner:*
'How are you?'	'I'm very well, but how is your wife?'
'Oh, not so well really. She has finally been operated on'.	

54

'Who operated on her?'

'The internist' . . .
Etc. etc.

The utterance of the first partner was a question, which was a transformation of the following assertion by the second partner, who transformed it immediately back into a question again. What the first partner had said in a passive voice was said by the second partner in an active voice, and therefore the first partner transformed his passive sentence into an active one . . . See the examples under (d) and (f).

(h) The *question-answer play* and its consequences. Leopold (1954, 1956) found that the first connection of *subject and predicate* appears in a baby between 1;6 and 2;6 years of age. The psycholinguistic behaviour of the child at that time is very striking. The linguistic subject is spoken with the intonation of a question and the linguistic predicate with that of an assertion. To illustrate, his son said: 'Mama? – sleeping' . . . This became: 'Mama sleeping'. Especially, the intonation of the child was very striking and his whole behaviour showed his 'tour de force'. What the child is doing here, is really the presentation of a small conversation. Another example from Bladergroen (1969):

Child: 'What?'
Mother: 'Yes. That is a book!'
Child: 'What?'
Mother: 'Yes. That is a book too!'
Child: 'That?'
Mother: 'Yes. That is a book too!'
Child: 'That? Book . . . That? Book! . . . That? Book! . . . i book . . . i book . . . All book!'
Compare: 'A tobacconist's? Yes, I have seen one'.
Compare this too with this kind of expression by many deaf children: 'I bought. What? Two ice-creams', 'Calling you. Who? Miss Johnson', 'John is glad. Why? Because he has won'. Expressions of this type reflect the way language is learned.

So what the linguistic science calls a subject-predicate combination, may psycholinguistically originate from question and answer play, i.e. from conversation. Here we see again how the neglect of linguistic research on conversation may have led linguistic theory astray. Actually Chomsky's 'deep-structure', i.e. a subject-predicate combination, is an assertion. And every assertion presupposes a question, i.e. a transformation! 'Deep structure' as theorized by Chomsky cannot be the first thing in language growth, let alone its innateness (see page 63). The tendency to *conversation* is innate in men, and that is the origin of the language.

Normal Colloquial English

Concerning deaf children, we should not be afraid to present them with the normal riches of colloquial English, in order to prevent all rigidity of thinking. Constructionalists will shudder at such a 'muddle' as they often call it. But it is the reality of language. And it is indeed possible to make the deaf children master this 'muddle' to a greater extent than constructionism is prepared to believe.

Easy Structures?

Because we do not start from an analytic concept of language but from the global intuitive understanding of the whole, we do not distinguish between 'easy' and 'difficult' structures of sentences, 'easy' and 'difficult' forms. If a form or unit is the correct expression of the child's idea in a normal childlike way, it is the most correct expression, however difficult it may look from an analytic viewpoint. In this respect all forms and sentence structures are equally 'easy'.

Listening to a Conversation and Reflecting on Language Structure

A special advantage of normal hearing chilren must be mentioned here. For example a hearing child is listening to this conversation between its father and mother:
M. 'Daddy, why did you not get shaved?'
F. 'Do you think that my beard is too long?'
M. 'Yes! Look in the mirror!!'
F. 'O yes! you are right. Just a moment! I'll have a quick shave. Could you be getting the car out meanwhile?' ...

Deaf children take in almost only that language which is spoken *to* them, i.e. in conversations where they are personally involved (Vliegenthart 1961). The hearing child also listens to conversations of others, i.e. it is not personally involved, but reflects upon the forms used, upon the melodies, upon the system used by others, e.g. in the given example:
did, you, get, do, you (another!), my, too, long, Yes, look, Yes, you, just, I'll, you, meanwhile; further the flow of rhythms and intonations. The influence of this has not yet been studied, as far as I know, especially not the learning of the grouping of words.
A consequence of this observation for our *didactics* is as follows. The teacher has to ensure that the other children in the class will follow, even when he is conversing with one of them individually; he should call the attention of the other children when two of them are involved in a worthwhile discussion. It is a mistake to think that these happenings are of no importance. – When a deaf child reads the

reading-books read by normal hearing children (in contrast with most of the programmed reading books of the constructionalists), he will meet plenty of conversations in these books and then he will find himself rather in the same situation as the hearing child listening to the conversation of others.

7. THE INTENTIONS OF SENTENCES

Bühler's Theory

Bühler (1934) gives this example: Peter and John are sitting in a room. Peter hears a soft tapping at the panes. He looks up and says to John: 'It is raining'.
Bühler explains that there are three distinguishable intentions of this small sentence:
Reference to the objects ('Darstellung' = representation), in this case the perceived fact of raining (the *symbolic* functioning of language).
Output from the sender ('Ausdruck' = expression) (the *symptomatic* functioning of language).
Call or signal to the receiver ('Appell' = appeal) (the *signalistic* functioning of language).
Bühler elaborated in this way one of Stern's ideas (1907), who saw the spontaneous sentence first of all as a kind of making a stand, i.e. a desire to ask something, to command, to assert. This is already found, Stern says, in the very simple sentences of the baby, which has been confirmed by Menyuk's research (1969, 1972). She found three kinds of intonation in the baby's one-word-sentences (even in his non-verbal vocalizations): the intonation of a statement, of a question and 'emphatic intonations'.

Applications of this Theory

'Intention' means the subjective attitude in a linguistic utterance. Conversation can be seen as a continuous change and exchange of intentions between the partners, i.e. of what they are wanting (consciously or not) to say. 'To intend' literally means to stretch the bow towards a goal. Intention works in an utterance as a catalyst on the words. Of course the partners are not always conscious of that (see below).
In every linguistic utterance the three intentions mentioned above can be distinguished, but not in the same degree:
there is the assertion, in which the representational intention is more prominent, more than in expression and call;
there are the questions, wants, and exclamations, in which the expressive intention

is more prominent;
there is the call, in which the appeal is more prominent.

Intentions and Punctuation-marks

The punctuation-marks we are using are somewhat congruent with these intentions: the full stop, the question mark, and the exclamation mark:
- assertion: The train is late.
- question: Is he coming? Who is coming?
- call (or a sentence 'with emphatic intonation', Menyuk 1969):
a desire: I wish he would come!
an exclamation: What a shame!
an appeal: Don't worry!
a command or imperative: Go home!

 NB. 'Call' or 'appeal' is a broader and to me a better term than 'command' or 'imperative'.

Interaction of Intentions

In free language, i.e. not limited to programmed forms, all these intentions are mixed up in a variegated whole, especially in conversation. Without much conversation it will be almost impossible to teach these ever shifting viewpoints in the minds of the children.
It will then be clear that there is no reason to call the assertion the most perfect and first sentence device. Every assertion presupposes in some way a question, i.e. a need for an answer. We have already seen that the first combinations of subject and predicate in a small child of about 1;6 – 2;6 years (i.e. its assertions) arise from question and answer, i.e. arise from the intentionality of language.

'Baked Sentences'

The conclusion of these findings may be this: a sentence like the one cited earlier, '*The box is on the table*', is strictly speaking, not a sentence at all! It is not a *sentence*, because it does not make *sense* within the normal linguistic setting of a conversation! It looks like an assertion but it is not a true one, because there is no need for such an assertion, neither actually nor virtually, neither in the teacher, nor in the children. It is only a verbalization of a fact, a kind of formula. It is what I call a 'baked sentence'. This is not living language, although constructionalists claim it is. It is not an element of *conversation*; there is no exchange of *intentions*.

58

Constructionism and Signing

The consequences of this way of teaching are dreadful again: because the children do not learn to converse in an oral way, they look for other ways to converse. They have no means other than signs. So the classroom teaching recedes more and more from the real living of the children and will be put more and more into the corner of only teaching a foreign language to these unfortunates. I feel that constructionism is the way to the grave for the oral method.

Intentionalism and Teaching Question-forms

Another conclusion from the important theory of Bühler is the method of teaching question-forms. As I have already said, a question expresses a need for an answer. So a rhetoric question has the linguistic form of a question but psycholinguistically spoken, its behaviour is not a 'true question'; it is just the other way round. The same must be said about most questions asked by the teacher to his pupils: the teacher already knows the answer and – in some aspect – pretends to question his children in order to test them, to make them think and so on.

In my opinion, the best way to teach deaf children to 'express' and to 'receive' questions, is to start from the true questions children utter themselves, as I will explain below.

8. THE PHRASE STRUCTURE APPROACH

Introduction: 'Syntactical Eupraxia'

Neuropathology teaches us that apraxia (Prick and Waals 1958–1965) is a cerebral disorder characterized by loss of ability to execute *planned* movements. If there is a-praxia, there must be in normal subjects 'praxia' or 'eu-praxia' (Cobb 1948), which may be defined as: a cerebral order to execute planned movements. Bühler (1934) spoke of 'intentions' in speech, Külpe (quot. Roels 1934 II) of 'determining tendencies', Hull (quot. Hilgard 1956) of 'anticipatory goal responses', Allesch (quot. Hörmann 1967) of 'impulse figures' and Miller (1960) of 'grammatic plans'.

We go over now to the study of 'syntactical eupraxia', i.e. the planning and 'mapping' functions, according to which we understand and produce correct sentences. From this study we will draw our conclusions for the instruction of the deaf.

Linguistic 'Closed Systems'

We have already spoken of closed and open systems. 'Syntactical eupraxia' has to do

with linguistic *closed systems*. We can imagine such systems according to *two models:*
(a) As an empty programme to be filled by items. The model is the computer. A programme is put into the computer. The elements of this programme are purely symbolic, i.e. without content. Then the items are put in, for instance by means of punch-cards which are 'read' by the machine, resulting in an output.
(b) As a filled programme. The model is taken from chemistry. Every item as such has specific stochastic 'valencies' or 'combinabilities' as mentioned on page 49.

The items for 'syntactical eupraxia' are the words. Chomsky (1957, 1965), followed by many scientists, thinks of an 'empty programme-model', a kind of sentence diagram above the words. A similar diagram is used in the Key by Fitzgerald, – Reichling (1935, 1962, 1970) and van Ginneken (1922, cf. Hjelmslev in Dinneen 1967) think more of a 'filled-programme-model'.

The truth may lay in between. The intentional rhythmic melodies already mentioned, – which in my opinion have to be considered as linguistic, at least psycholinguistic 'programmes' keeping words together –, appear in the vocalizations of the hearing child before the words (Menyuk 1969). They are in some way looking for words, because they express the child's conversational drives and motivations, working as catalysts. The words, as soon as they arise, are integrated into these melodies. These melodies as such are 'empty programmes', but not yet fully syntactical: they can keep words together but seemingly they do not have any influence on the order of the words. They are found in all languages and all kinds of syntactical organizations. But they become virtually syntactical as soon as 'vocables' and 'words' appear: one-word questions, one-word assertions (answers), one-word-calls, i.e. a 'conversational syntax' arises, questions always preceding answers, an alternative behaviour of the partners, and so on. When two words are gripped under one melody, some words appear to gain position-marks ('pivot-words'). Phrases arise. The combination of question-answer grows to subject-predicate-syntax. All words in our western languages receive increasingly some 'position-marks', which are the basis of syntax according to the theory of Reichling, which seems to be the right one.

Reichling's 'Phrasic' and 'Generative' Grammar

Even before the war Reichling (1935, cf. van Ginneken 1922) explained the structure of sentences in this phrasic and generative way (the terms 'phrasic' and 'generative' are not Reichling's, but seem to be appropriate):

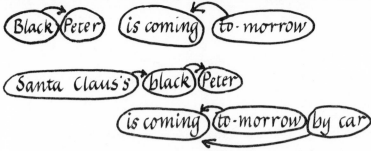

This model has appeared to be very helpful in teaching deaf children. It is a method of not only analysing sentences in word-classes, but of analysing and synthetizing the whole of the sentences, from the undifferentiated whole to the different parts and so back to the differentiated whole. The central question here is – which deaf children of 6 years can already learn to understand –: What *belongs* to what? What does *black* belong to? What does *to-morrow* belong to? And so on. The same model can also be used for exclamations, e.g.

What a shame! What a shame for you !

The principle: 'How words belong to each other', i.e. the rules, or better, the laws of the combinabilities of words generate the phrases and sentences, which are patterns, Gestalts, rather in the same way as the expression H_2O generates the molecule water.

We enlarged the model by using colours in this way: subject blue; predicate (complete, not only the verb) red; e.g.

Santa Claus's Black Peter is coming to-morrow.

To-morrow Black Peter will come.

~~~~~ = red

———— = blue

The children learn these terms: 'What is said about the subject? That is the predicate'. And: 'What is that predicate about? That is the subject'.

Of course the children's exercises should not be done on 'baked sentences' such as 'Santa Claus's . . .', but on normal language taken from the conversations with the children, from their diaries, from their reading books and so on, i.e. in a differentiating way, from the whole to the elements. An example:

A teacher sees that his children are sufficiently mature to follow this approach. He then waits and looks for a suitable sentence in the daily conversations.
Usually he will get one within a few hours:

61

Mary (8 years of age) says: 'To-morrow bus big girls!'

The teacher seizes this and corrects: 'To-morrow the big girls will go out by bus . . . Say it again, Mary!'

Mary repeats it.

Teacher: 'Yes? Is it true?'

All children: 'Yes!' Some of them: 'To-morrow at six o'clock' . . . Others: 'Very early!'

Now the teacher writes this on the blackboard:

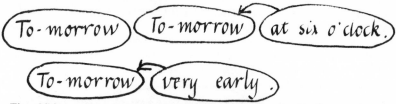

The children will understand these modifying phrases 'at six o'clock' and 'very early' from their own thinking. These phrases *belong* to to-morrow. The teacher makes the children say: '*At six o'clock* belongs to *to-morrow*, and '*Very early* belongs to *to-morrow*'.

Then the teacher says to Mary: 'Say your sentence again, Mary'. Mary repeats it. The teacher writes it on the blackboard: *To-morrow the big girls will go out by bus.* Teacher: 'Who can rearrange this sentence?' (This term is already known to the children from former lessons, from corrections of letters and so on.) It comes out 'The big girls will go out by bus tomorrow.' Then the teacher writes on the blackboard:

Will go out   by bus   to-morrow

Then he draws a circle around the phrases (accent-groups) 'will go out', 'by bus' and 'to-morrow':

Teacher: 'Who can draw some arrows as we did in these accent groups?' (This term too is already known from previous lessons.) He points to the rings around 'at six o'clock' and 'very early'.

After a little trouble it will emerge as, '*By bus* belongs to *will go out*' and '*To-morrow* belongs to *will go out*'.

Later on he will analyse and synthetize also:

In the beginning, however, he should be satisfied with some rather clear structures. This work has to develop over the years. The bases are, the rhythmic feeling of the accent groups (see later) and the feeling of belonging of words to each other, developed from the global intuition.

Chomsky's Phrasic and Generative Diagram

NB. A good introduction to Chomsky's theory within the frame of the whole of linguistics can be found in Dinneen (1967). The linguistics of Chomsky is excellently treated by Lyons (5th 1972), the interaction between Chomsky's theory and psycholinguistics by Greene (2nd 1973), a critical review is given by Derwing (1973), Hammarström (1973) and by Robinson (1975).

The linguistic theory of Chomsky (1957, 1965, 1975) plays an important part in psycholinguistics. It can be summarized as follows:

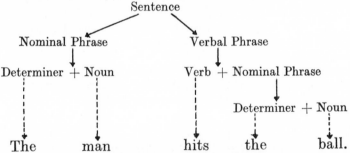

This is his 'phrase-structure' of the sentence; the sentence composed from a 'nominal phrase' and a 'verbal phrase'. Such a simple sentence of a subject, a transitive verb, and a direct object (the subject-predicate structure) is called by him a 'kernel-sentence' or better a 'basic sentence'. In his theory, the passive sentences, negative sentences, question-sentences, imperative sentences, clauses and similar are called 'transformations' of a basic sentence. In this way he comes to a 'generative grammar', because the surface-structure 'The man hits the ball', which can be perceived by other people, is generated by a set of rules, which in this diagram are very simple, called 'rewriting rules' or 'phrase-structure-rules'. When,

63

however, is said, 'The ball is hit by the man' or 'The man does not hit the ball' or 'Does the man hit the ball?' or 'Hit the ball!' or 'I say that the man is hitting the ball' etc., then such sentences are generated by 'transformational rules', because the passive-, negative-, question- and imperative-sentences and clauses are seen as transformations of the basic sentences. They can only be generated (understood and/or produced) from the basic sentences as their source. If I understand 'Does the man hit the ball?', I do this structurally by reducing it to its basic structure. If I say it, I do so by starting from this same basic structure in the 'depth', called 'deep structure' too.

So Chomsky (1962) speaks of 'rule-governed creativity' of men, and supposes that these rules would be poorer in primitive peoples than in peoples of high culture. Some would apply this idea to deaf children and adults (see page 44). So in all languages of the world all sentence-structures would be based on that same 'basic sentence' or 'deep-structure'.

We have already seen that this subject-predicate structure at least psycholinguistically can be explained from the conversational question-answer-structure. The assumption of innateness is at least unproven.

Another assumption of this theory is that the process of producing a sentence is a mirror of the process of understanding it (see the example). Further, that we cannot understand sentences well, if we cannot reduce them to their basic structure. From this it has been concluded that deaf children cannot learn to properly understand, if they have not learned to produce well the sentences of their language previously. All this is pure assumption, and many facts are against it. For example a child already understands a lot before he is able to produce his first sentences. Even in learning a foreign language, the students usually have a much broader 'passive' (= receptive) than 'active' (= expressive) language. See our discussion about the 'conversion-loss' below (Myklebust 1964).

The difference with Reichling's scheme (page 61) is very obvious. Chomsky thinks of an 'empty programme' and Reichling of a 'filled' one. Reichling would schematize Chomsky's example as follows (as a 'chemistry of words'):

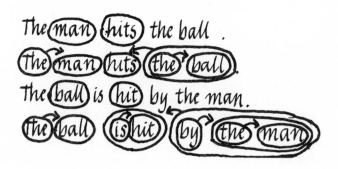

Phrase Structure and Psycholinguistics

The theory of phrase-structure, common to Reichling and Chomsky, in my opinion has appeared to be very fruitful for psycholinguistics, especially how we psycholinguistically produce a sentence. I think we can say: It has been found that the 'phrase structure' is not only a linguistic entity but also a psycholinguistic entity. Thorndike (quot. Hilgard 1956) found that for the memory there is a block between sentences. This series for example:

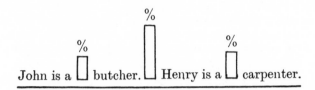

The columns symbolize the amount of mistakes in percentages. The results contradict Guthrie's associative contiguity theory (quot. Hilgard 1956). The combinations *John − butcher* and *Henry − carpenter* are better 'memorised' than *butcher − Henry*. Yet *butcher − Henry* was closer in the training period than the other couples. It may be concluded that sentences in some way are unities in our psycholinguistic inner behaviour.

Johnson (1965, 1966; cf. Levelt 1970 'hierarchic clusters') found the same for phrases within sentences: in a sentence such as *The tall boy saved the dying woman* there were more memory mistakes respectively in the transitions *boy − saved, the − tall* and *saved − the*, than in the transitions *tall − boy, the − dying* and *dying − woman*. In the transition *boy − saved*, there were by far the most mistakes. If we symbolize the percentages of mistakes by means of columns, we get this:

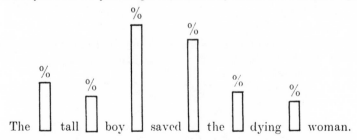

The way of 'living' of such a sentence in the minds of his subjects can be schematized as follows (cf. Yngve 1962): see page 66, top.

65

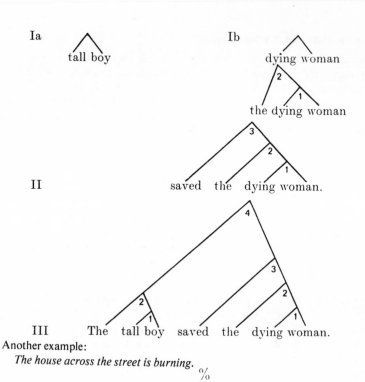

Ia tall boy

Ib dying woman
the dying woman

II saved the dying woman.

III The tall boy saved the dying woman.

Another example:

The house across the street is burning.

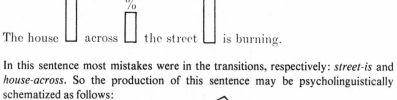

The house across the street is burning.

In this sentence most mistakes were in the transitions, respectively: *street-is* and *house-across*. So the production of this sentence may be psycholinguistically schematized as follows:

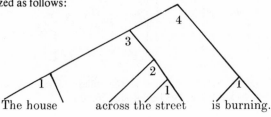

The house across the street is burning.

The numbers in both examples indicate the degree of difficulty in memorizing the respective transitions: low number = easy, high number = difficult.

I notice that the units here – 'the tall boy', 'the dying woman', 'the house,' 'across the street', 'is burning' – coincide almost entirely with the rhythmic phrase, i.e. the 'accent-groups'.

'Phrase Structures' in Analogous Behaviour

Martin (1972) found similar 'phrase structures' in music. He could represent 'musical sentences' and 'musical phrases' by analogous schemes as those of Johnson mentioned above. – Again similar structures are found in dancing (Hartong 1947). – Further rhythm of speech is wholly integrated with rhythmic movements of the body. It is possible to recognize sentences by their rhythm only (Licklider and Miller 1951 quot. Martin 1972; Erber 1974). Speech, music and bodily movements seem to be behaviours affiliated to each other, or better one whole somewhere including each other. 'Phrase-structure' apparently is not something exclusively linguistic. It is more of a general law in rhythmic successive behaviour.

'Feedbacks' and 'Feed-aheads'

Turning back to linguistics, we must conclude that a 'finite state grammar' and more general the 'Markovian concept' is not a right solution of the problems of linguistic behaviour, both in the grammatical and in the semantic respect. If we build up sentences by starting with the first word, going further to the second word etc., we may ask why all the transitions do not have about the same difficulties. According to the grammatical aspect. There must be something of a feedback within groupings, e.g. *woman* feeds back to *die* giving *dying*. There may also be something of a 'feed-ahead', a 'dominating' process (cf. Ashby 1965) in *is* to *burning*, notwithstanding possibly words put between *is* and *burning*, e.g. *is still burning*, where *is* must be stored for a moment, etc. Slips in speech teach us something about these processes, e.g. I heard a person saying: 'I have ... am so afraid'. He first wanted to say: *I have fear* but *afraid* fed back to *have ... am*. The same: '*I am ... have been there*', '*What say ... What do you say?*' and so on.

According to the Semantic Aspect

If in a context words are deleted, it is much easier to locate the deleted word, i.e. to understand the sentences, when there is a context before *and* after it, than when there is only a context before it. The context after it feeds back to the deleted word, in order to understand and find it (Aborn et al., 1959).

Another example: '*Because he was ill, John had to cancel the journey*'. The interpretation of *he* only comes afterwards; the listener or reader should 'feed back' from *John* to *he*.

Still another example: '*The band exploded into a fortissimo*'. *Fortissimo* should feed back to a correct interpretation of *band* (= orchestra) and *exploded* (= figurative meaning). See page 161 on the 'holding-up-function' in interpreting language.

Memory

We make a passing reference to the *memory*, which plays an important part both in producing sentences and in understanding them (cf. Yngve 1962). We will explain this later.

Not Markovian Chains but Structures

It may be clear from all this that the production of sentences is not at all a Markovian process, or let us say a 'sagittal' process such as a trajectory, but one of 'feedbacks' *and* 'feed-aheads', often over some other words, with much reverting and anticipatory activity. Nor can the understanding, the receiving of language be explained in this way, although we hear the words after each other. A sentence, a phrase, is not a Markovian chain, but a structure, a 'Gestalt', a global unit.

Open Positions Before and After Words

An important consequence of this is the following. Each word has its probabilities in respect of both succeeding *and* preceding words, including immediate and mediate pre- and suc-cessions. For instance *woman* has a probability of say 85% of having *the* as a preceding word. In *the woman* we have an immediate precession of *the*. But in *the dying woman* we have a mediate precession of *the* to *woman*. So *the house* has a probability of say 2% of having some form of *burn* as a succeeding word. In *the house burns* we have an immediate succession, but in *the house is burning* or in *the house is still burning* we have a mediate succession. (Mediate pre- and suc-cessions include 'pincer-constructions'.)

So a substantive has some open positions before and after it (van Uden 1960, Wils 1965): e.g.

	flower(s)	
. . . . . .	flower(s)	. . . . .
the	flower	there
John's red	flowers	are withering
with	flowers	behind the wall
		etc.

A substantive has some probability of having a preposition before it. One might think that this probability can be reduced to one of succession: the preposition has some probability of having a substantive after it. But these are two different probabilities. The probability of a substantive having a preposition previous to it, may be e.g. 45%. The probability of a preposition having a substantive after it may be e.g. 95%. So these probabilities cannot be reduced to one alone.

The theory of the so-called 'Finite State Grammars' of Hockett 1955 (see Chomsky 1957) tries to explain the structure of sentences by successive probabilities as a Markovian chain, thus in a linear way, e.g.

the   has a fair amount of probability of having a substantive after it. Let it be
house.   House or the house has a probability of being followed by a verb. Let it be
is.   Is, or the house is, has a probability of having a present participle after it.
          Let it be
burning. And so on.

This theory 'from left to right' or better 'from first to last' as a principle of explanation of grammatical functions (Uhlenbeck, in Reichling et al. 1962; Yngve 1962; Osgood 1963) had better be omitted (as did Chomsky 1957, Miller and Chomsky 1963). These theorists not only forget the rhythmic groupings of the words, the many feedbacks between the words, but also the mediate pre- and suc-cessions, i.e. pincer-constructions.

Stochastic Functions Before and After Words

Because of the importance of this matter, we will further expound a theory of non-linearity of stochastic functions before and after words.

First of all there is a difference in psycholinguistic behaviour between the use of content-words and function-words. For example when we produce a phrase such as *the house, the* will not usually occur first to our minds, but *house*. From many experiments (see Woodworth and Schlosberg 1971), both on free associations (the subject is required to produce all the words after a stimulus word, which occur to his mind) and on fluency (the subject is required to produce words rapidly, as many as occur to his mind, during a time lapse of one or two minutes), we know that the subjects produce, more often than not, so-called content-words (i.e. most meaningful words, see below), and only very exceptionally function-words (such as prepositions, articles, conjunctions and so on, again see below). In so-called 'telegram-style' we omit most of these function-words: the information is concentrated into content-words. Interlingual children use almost only content-words too. Actually in our mental 'plans' for producing sentences (Miller, Galanter and Pribam 1960), we do not always start with the first word we utter. It may be the last word which occurs first to our mind, e.g. 'Umbrella! I forgot my umbrella!'

This is not only true in the production of sentences but also in understanding sentences. From the many experiments on short and long term memory for repeating and recalling given information (see Hall 1971), it is clear that the subjects understand some relevant 'crests' in the 'waves' of the information, which are almost always content-words. They take over those 'crests', and in reproducing the given information they rearrange these crests in their own way, often replacing less relevant words and function-words by others. This means that they have formed for themselves a typical *image* of what the other has said, and that image is not built up analytically from left to right, but is a pattern, a Gestalt, a structure.

The 'Key' and the Stochastic Linguistic Functions

Secondly, we *cannot* arrange our sentences from left to right. Deaf children, those 'visualizers', cannot even do that. Yet this is suggested by the Fitzgerald Key. Tervoort and Verberk (1967, 1974) found that deaf children, trained throughout in the use of this Key, are able to apply it in free conversation in sequences of 4 or at most 5 words (signs). But very often they abandon it, and in sequences of more than 5 words (signs), this is always so (see page 115 concerning the STM-function). So this visual Key cannot be called a real law in their spontaneous thinking.

The Real 'Key' is Rhythm

To me a real law in the arrangement of words into sentences is the grouping of the words by rhythm: thus the phrasic structure, including the opposition of 'pincer'- and 'compound-constructions', with many 'feedbacks' and 'feed-aheads'. This rhythm is something *within* the words; so we do not believe in an 'empty' syntactical diagram, as suggested by Chomsky (1957, 1965) and the Key.

The Visual Empty 'Key' an Artificial Means

Besides in normal language there are so many exceptions in relation to the Key! These exceptions overwhelm the child as soon as it starts reading normal reading-books, which is not programmed language. – Still another, perhaps unexpected effect of the work with the Key is that of deaf children sometimes arranging sentences according to the Key which seem 'perfect English', but are not understood by the children themselves! . . .

An Illustrative Model of Word-grouping Function

Let us give an illustrative model of how the grouping of words in a sample of a language can be a basis from which other groupings can be predicted with some level of confidence. Compare the tape-recordings of 30 children 2;0–2;6 years of age in the study of Brown and Fraser (1963) and of 6 children 1;6–2;6 years of age by Schaerlaekens (1973).

Take this quasi-sample of the language of a child. Let us suppose that it is representative.

1. Ball/be blue.
2. Peter/soon?
3. Ball/be soon.
4. Be blue soon?
5. Peter/blue ball.
6. Peter/be soon.
7. Peter! Be blue
8. Be ball/blue?

It may immediately be clear that this child does not use sentences longer than 3 words, and that its vocabulary comprises only 5 words. We now compose this *matrix* of stochastically functioning combinabilities:

	... Peter ...		... ball ...		... soon ...		... blue ...		... be ...	
	before	after	before	after	before	after	before	after	before	after
Peter	0%	0%	0%	0%	25%	0%	14%	0%	20%	0%
ball	0%	0%	0%	0%	0%	0%	14%	14%	20%	10%
soon	0%	25%	0%	0%	0%	0%	0%	14%	0%	20%
blue	0%	25%	20%	20%	25%	0%	0%	0%	0%	30%
be	0%	50%	20%	40%	50%	0%	44%	0%	0%	0%

We see, that Peter, when used, always has the first position in a sentence. In 25% of the cases Peter has soon after it, in 25% of the cases blue, in 50% of the cases be, and so on with all the words. We see that blue and ball are closely linked, as are ball and be, etc. But ball and soon seem to repel each other. Be appears to be the most frequent word. Etc. etc.

Let us suppose now, that in a given situation these words occur to the mind of this child: quickly after each other:

first soon, then ball, and then Peter. We then have these 'combinabilities':

Peter 25% ← *soon* → 0% ball
Peter 0% ← *ball* → 0% soon
.... *Peter* → 25% soon
.... *Peter* → 0% ball

It can be assumed that the child will use the strongest combinabilities, as it is accustomed to do. So Peter will be the first word in its utterance, although the last in its mind. The strongest 'combinabilities' between Peter soon and ball are: Peter →

25% soon, *ball* being uninvolved.
So we can expect, that this child will say:
Peter soon ball.

Words are put into Categorical 'Cells'

Of course this is only an example, given as a model. The reality of language is much more complicated. We left for instance the *mediate* sequences, the structure of *phrases* within the sentences, the *meanings* of words, phrases and sentences; the *accentuations* and intonations; and last but not least the clustering of words into classes and *categories* ('cells') according to analogic 'combinabilities'. So proper names have their own combinabilities: very soon a baby uses them in an analogic way, i.e. they are stored in one 'cell' of the matrix, by means of which these words call up others themselves, and are easily called up by other ones, according to a special sequence before and after them: e.g. 'for John' never 'John for', or 'John school', never 'school John' and so on, i.e. these words acquire specific combinabilities before and after them. The same happens more and more with other kinds of words, within about a year moving toward substantives, to verbs, to prepositions, to 'pointer-words' etc. A number of researches concerning verbal fluency and verbal memory have shown that we store the words in our mind according to analogic combinabilities (Hall 1971).
It may be clear that language learning and the production of sentences are closely related to 'combinability', and that 'combinability' is closely related to memory (which memory in turn is closely related to rhythm).
These 'combinabilities' further cannot be thought of as detached from the stochastic probabilities of transitions between the words with their 'feed-backs' and 'feed-aheads'. Therefore these systems of combinabilities should not be thought of as deterministic or static structures, but as dynamic ones, with varying degrees of flexibility.

Language Behaviour as Learned Behaviour

All this shows much similarity with the bio-physiology of our brains. It has been found in several physiological researches that our nervous system is able to react to stochastic probabilities in a selective way within the synapses and other connections (see, e.g. Lashley 1951, Miller, Galanter and Pribam 1960, Barbizet 1970). Some stimuli pass easily into special directions and are inhibited into others; they evoke some patterns or Gestalts, sensory or motor or sensory-motor ones, with images and feelings; they build up new ones too through general inventiveness or creativity.
It is very interesting to see how soon a hearing child is able to catch these probabilities, to weigh them, to organize them in classes and 'cells', to fix and free

them, and to imitate more and the more the enormous matrix of combinations offered continuously to him.

This is *learnt* behaviour. We do not need to postulate innate *cognitive* structures in the sense of Chomsky (1957, 1968), or McNeill (1966) in order to explain this. They speak of a 'language-acquisition device' (LAD) as an innate structure, a kind of viewfinder of filtering-structure, namely: the universal features of language as the subject-predicate distinction, the verb-object distinction, the head-modifier distinction. – There is in my opinion an essential difference between innate bio-physiologic-stochastic combinabilities in our brains and innate *knowledge*. Chomsky's theory seems to be a kind of neo-Cartesian or neo-Kantian rationalistic philosophic theory (see page 63), seemingly contradictory in itself: a knowledge which is not a knowledge proper (cf. Lonergan 1958).

It suggests real danger in building up a whole system of training deaf children upon such a weak basis. On the contrary the most general human feature of language is not just subject and predicate and so on, but conversation. This straight away has to do with the structure of language as such: exchange of phrases, questions and answers, many 'transformations' in the overt field of behaviour, imperatives and calls, assertions etc. It is a great pity that Chomsky and his followers tell almost nothing of this basic phenomenon. (For our criticism to Chomsky's theory, see also for example Herriot 1970, Lamendella 1970, Goyvaerts 1972, McElroy 1972, Greene 1973, Derwing 1973). – It seems to be possible to explain the acquisition of language by learnt combinabilities of words and of sensory-motor Gestalts. This is not specifically linguistic, the same happens in non-linguistic serial behaviour, as in learning music (Jett 1968). Compare also this typical process in Jacqueline, the daughter of Piaget (1963), 1;8 years of age. She is entering the house, coming from the garden with bunches of grass in both hands. She tries to open the door by turning the knob, but seeing that she cannot succeed in this way, she puts the bunches onto the ground, turns the knob, pushes the door, picks up the grass and enters. She closes the door without turning the knob. But she goes back, wants to open the door in the same way, and now she sees that the door, turning in her direction, will shove the grass into the corridor. So she puts the bunches aside, distant enough to clear the door ... Etc. Is there a need to postulate innate cognitive deep structures in order to explain the quick development of such serial behaviours? The most clear and parsimonious explanation seems to be the creative flexible use of the learnt combinabilities of elements and of sensory-motor Gestalts. There are a lot of serial behaviours in which learnt operational schemes in the sense of Piaget are creatively used. The schemes are not empty, but have content, i.e. are attached to the elements and Gestalts.

We should not, however, introduce *conscious* thinking too soon either. Very many of those behaviours are built up automatically according to the 'lay-out' of nature, internally and externally. Cybernetics has taught us how these automatisms can grow bio-physiologically. This should be thought of hierarchically, since it has been found that the automatic language functions use stores in the brain, different from conscious creative language functions (Greene 1972, cf. page 119).

The Words as the Kernels of Language

The Key (and other visualized diagrams in use in many methods of instructing the deaf) suggest that there is something of a 'Plan' above the words. Would this be true? It is in agreement with the theory of Miller, Galanter and Pribam (1960). These writers propose to interpret Chomsky's approach psycholinguistically in this way: 'The Plan of the sentence, it seems, must be determined in a general way even before it is differentiated into the particular words that we are going to utter'. I don't think so. This hypothesis looks too mysterious and needs a proof (see the remarks on 'empty diagrams'). In my opinion the immediate daily experience teaches us that the 'mechanism' of the syntax starts to work as soon as one or more words occur to the mind. The Plan of the sentence is a pattern, not above or before the words, but within the words, not least by their rhythmic properties to build up phrases and 'accent-groups'. In producing sentences we are organizing and reorganizing again and again according to the learnt combinabilities of the words, by a kind of 'net-work-grammar' (Woods 1970, Schank 1973, Kempen 1974, 1976).

Criticism of Chomsky's Starting-point

Chomsky and his followers seemingly use two arguments for a sentence-diagram above or before the words: the unlimited number of sentences and their length, and the mechanisms of interpreting homonymous sentences.

a. *An unlimited number of sentences?*

The *number* of sentences, possible in a specific language, is enormous: perhaps billions and billions, but it is not *un*limited as Chomsky (1957) asserts, because it is dependent upon the limited 'combinabilities' of a limited number of *words* of that language (see 'conversion-loss'). An unlimited *length* of sentence presupposes an unlimited memory, which can perhaps only be found in an electronic computer. Is this not a rationalistic presupposition rather than a realistic one?

b. *Do we really reduce homonymous sentences to an empty special simple diagram?*

Chomsky treats two kinds of homonymous sentences, those whose homonymy originates from different groupings of words, and those including different meanings of words. The latter ones will be treated here, the first ones on page 90. A few examples of concerned homonymous sentences:

'*Flying planes can be dangerous*' = '*Flying (in) planes*' or '*(The) flying planes*'. The phrase-structure (= the immediate constituent analysis) is the same in both cases: '*Flying planes/can be dangerous*'. Then Chomsky (1965) proceeds: 'It is

74

... clear that the manner of combination provided by the surface (immediate constituent) structure is in general almost totally irrelevant to semantic interpretation, whereas the grammatical relations expressed in the abstract deep structure are in many cases just those that determine the meaning of the sentence' ... This 'abstract deep structure', relevant to the interpretation, should be either 'planes can be dangerous' or 'flying can be dangerous'. – Is this true? Do we really reduce the sentence to an empty special simple diagram, before we can interpret it? Or could it be that the *words* are homonymous, i.e. 'flying' with a transitive meaning and 'flying' with an intransitive meaning, and that we are able to compose a sentence structure *afterwards*? The interpretation of the whole sentence is already given immediately by the interpretation of the *words*, *before* the sentence structure has been set up. We stress again that this immediate interpretation is given in the full setting of the *conversation* (see there).

Another example: '*Did you see that picture of John?*' = '*Picture made by John*' or '*Picture of (= about) John*'. Do we need 'deep structures' such as: 'John made that picture' or 'Someone painted John?' Can't we reduce the whole homonymy to the multiple meaning of 'of'?

Still another example: '*Mary is easy to please*' = '*Mary easily pleases*' or '*Other persons can please Mary easily*' or '*Mary can be pleased very easily by other persons*'. Chomsky (1965) reasons concerning the verb 'please'. But seemingly that is not the difficulty: the difficulty is the *word* 'easy' which has again a double meaning: a passive and an active one. Chomsky compares this sentence with: 'Mary is eager to please'. The comparison is not to the point, because 'eager' has only an active meaning. The principle of parsimony in explaining behaviour seemingly obliges us to stick simply to the multi-dimensional meaning and combinability of the *word* 'easy'.

NB. *Words and pincer-constructions.* Levelt (1970) did an investigation on complicated sentences to find out how his subjects appreciated the interrelations of the words. E.g. 'Carla takes the book and goes to school'. He found his subjects relating 'Carla' as easily to 'takes' as to 'goes', notwithstanding the distance and the separation of the immediate constituents ('phrase-structures'). He supposes that this behaviour can only be explained when his subjects maintained a deep-structure, bringing subject and predicate together. But this too can be explained more parsimoniously by the combinability of these *words*, semantically, but especially indicated here by the congruent flexions of the verbs. There is a kind of 'pincer construction' (based on rhythmic grouping) working here.

Vocabulary is Basic

An important *conclusion* from all this is that the flexibility of *vocabulary* is basic in our didactics, and that we should not loose too much time by teaching sentence-structures. A further conclusion is that it is necessary to make deaf children aware, as soon as possible, of the homonymy of words.

Flexible Vocabulary, 'Competence' and 'Performance'

Chomsky introduced the terminology of 'competence' and 'performance' in linguistic behaviour. This difference too, in my opinion, originates from the combinabilities of *words*: by 'competence' is meant then the whole of these combinabilities in a particular mind (thus the 'virtual' combinabilities), from which specific ones are chosen when this person is formulating linguistically, i.e. when the virtual combinabilities are actualised onto a specific 'performance'. – We conclude again: a flexible vocabulary, as large as possible, is basic in our whole linguistic training of deaf children.

Syntactic Planning Behaviour, or 'Syntactical Eupraxia'

W can dinstinguish three theories concerning the syntactical 'eupraxia' (see later) according to which we produce correct sentences:

a. We produce correct sentences according to a diagram, which is formed above and before all individual words (Chomsky 1959, Miller et al. 1962).
b. There are first only individual words (in our mind), which are arranged afterwards to correct sentences (Skinner 1957).
c. There is one (or more) beginning individual word(s), which calls forth other words, which in turn are not yet immediately individual but first foreseen according to 'empty places', i.e. foreseen according to their word-class. So the beginning individual word calls forth a sort of diagram according to which we find the correct words, which fit into the 'empty places'.

It may be clear that this last theory is the most correct one. A word calls forth a phrase ('accent-group', e.g. Peter-soon-ball), and this phrase, by means of 'compound'- and/or 'pincer-constructions', calls forth an incomplete and/or complete sentence.

'Phrase Structure' and the Graphic Form of Language

The graphic form of language is a big help even for normally hearing children. It is indispensable for deaf children, most of all because of their memory for language, which is endangered by both lack of 'auditory echoic memory' (Murray 1967) and lagging behind in rhythmic speech. These two functions are the big advantages possessed by hearing children.
Nevertheless the use of this graphic form can be overemphasized, so that the

memory for rhythmic speech is neglected. When a teacher overemphasizes the written, i.e. the simultaneous visual forms of language, he will 'undertrain' the serial successive memory-function of the children, i.e. the short term memory function which they need in producing and receiving spoken phrasic language. This also means that they cannot study language in its essential structure, when they study it one-sidedly in its written forms, because, when a sentence appears in its written form, all stochastics are gone! A written sentence is a simultaneous series of codes: you see the codes almost all together. There is no phrasic structure either. In producing and receiving spoken sentences, however, we must use our short term memory in a specific way, because they are successive sequences: these codes are 'comers and goers'. A teacher who always immediately writes everything down for the children does not train, or insufficiently trains, that typical successive rhythmic short term memory. No wonder, the children have more and more grammatical difficulty in conversing, because their function of spoken short term memory has been 'underfed'.

The Key-approach actually tends to overemphasize the written forms of language. One would expect that a teacher, doing this, *trains* the memory for the written form of language. This is very often neglected, however; it is in some way by many teachers simply presupposed. Then we see in the classroom, if the children are requested to copy words or a reading lesson from the blackboard, a kind of 'chicken-writing', i.e. the children show their bad memory by looking again and again at the black-board, sometimes even for every letter. Another aspect that often is forgotten is the correct integration of the spoken and written forms: the phonetic and graphic analysis of words.

Therefore the teacher should do both: he must continuously train the spoken *and* the graphic STM, both integrated to each other.

The only natural way to teach the structure of language, however, is the phrasic approach, which cannot be used unless in a mainly oral, rhythmic way. This will be explained in the paragraphs 9, 10 and 11.

Transformationalism and Psycholinguistics

Johnson's results are a psycholinguistic confirmation of the phrasic approach of Chomsky et al.

What about Chomsky's theory of transformationalism?

G. Miller (1962) found that the transformation of an active, positive sentence into a passive, negative sentence took more time than the transformation of such a sentence into only a negative or only a passive one. So it looks as if at least a passive-negative sentence is not as directly produced as the other sentences, i.e. that there is something of a 'kernel-sentence' in psycholinguistic behaviour.

Braine (1965), confirmed by Schaerlaekens (1973), found that in children of about 3 years of age, only 4 of 462 sentences could be called kernel-sentences in the terms of Chomsky (i.e. less than 1%). The same applies to the more recent terms 'deep', 'basic' and 'surface' structures.

We have already seen and we will see further that there are a lot of transformations from early childhood in the *conversations* between mother and baby.

So it seems that it cannot be concluded from the linguistic theory of Chomsky that the child psycholinguistically masters first the 'basic-sentence-structure' or the 'kernel-sentences' and then the transformations. Both of them seem to be mastered right from the start. The independent variables apparently are not the 'basic' or 'not-basic' (transformational differences), but both the *memory* of the child (concerning the combinabilities of words, the length and complexity of the structures, namely 'compound' or 'pincer'-constructions) and the *meaning* of the situation.

It has been forgotten in many researches on memory for language, making comparisons between kernel-sentences and transformed sentences (e.g. Savin et al. 1965), that the latter are usually longer than the first ones.

Much depends on the situation. It can happen that the situation is so understood that its 'passivity' comes first to mind, i.e. that the passive sentence is most direct, and that in another situation activity or negativity is signified first. So Slobin (1966, 1968) found that hearing children understood a passive sentence as quickly as an active one, if the situation was clear enough:

easy to understand: 'The patient has been guarished by the doctor';
difficult: 'The patient guarished the doctor'.

Johnson-Laird (1968) found the same in adults, also that the passive voice was more directly understood than the active one in specific situations.

Wason (1965, 1968) found about the same for negative sentences:

easy: 'Johnny has no elephant';
difficult: 'Johnny has no nose!'

Other researches have shown that not so much the number of transformations is crucial in difficulty of recalling, understanding or producing sentences, but much more the combinabilities of *words* (see Martin, Roberts and Collins 1968, Perfetti 1969, Cromer 1970). Cromer found that a homonymous sentence as 'John is easy to see' is understood by children under 6 years of age as active (John is actor, 'easy' as an active word), and that only children over 6 years of age were able to understand it passively. This is not a lagging behind in the comprehending of structures but in the riches of vocabulary, according to the situation.

Actually Miller used only 'baked' sentences in his research and consequently this *situational* setting of sentences did not come to the fore. His subjects had to manipulate sentences very formally and consciously. – Again we see that it seems to be necessary to start psycholinguistic research from real *conversational* behaviour.

We *conclude*: the theory of transformationalism has not been confirmed by psycholinguistic research.

78

It is of course not a must for psycholinguistic kernels or bases to coincide with linguistic ones. 'Mental grammar' should not a priori be identified with 'linguistic grammar' (Greene 1972). Her finding that idiomatic, automatic language of the daily conversations is not stored in the same areas of the brain as creative language points in the same direction.

Both so-called 'basic structures' and 'transformations' seem to be *learned* by the child equally directly by the *combinabilities of words*.

9. LEXICAL MEANING AND MORPHOLOGICAL MEANING

Words as Bricks?

The advocates of the constructive method categorize words according to assumed contents, i.e. to very abstract meanings such as things and persons, actions, qualities etc. So they separate these meanings, as 'lexemes', almost totally from the morphological forms of the words. They conceive words as bricks and morphological forms as cement (cf. Dik and Kooy 1970). Is this right? Are these morphological forms, as such, meaningless? Or must we see the meanings of words as one whole with a contentive and a functional aspect, both meaningful?

Grammaticality Independent of Meanings?

This question can be understood in two ways:
Does 'grammaticality' exist without any meaning? And:
Is it possible that two grammatically different sentences can have an identical meaning?
In 1957 Chomsky taught that the grammar of sentences is independent of meanings; later (1965, under the influence of Katz and Fodor 1963) he acknowledged that semantics are related to 'deep structure' too. But he still detaches grammar too much from semantics: the 'basic element' diverges into a transformational element and a semantic element.
It is apparent, in our opinion, that this divergence does not happen in psycholinguistic behaviour. Is it evident that it should be maintained in a linguistically idealized description of the competence of native speakers of a specific language?
Perhaps here too rules of linguistics may not coincide with laws of psycholinguistics. We think that the 'grammaticalness' of sentences is not simply meaningless, and that the valencies of words and morphemes, i.e. their 'combinabilities' are ruled by both grammatical features and semantic features, that these features must be seen as one whole of 'combinability' (see Howes and Osgood 1954).

'The Gostake Distims the Doshes'

Ogden-Richards (quot. Reichling 1935; Stutterheim 1965) gave this example: 'The gostake distims the doshes.
Is this quite meaningless? Not at all! (Cf. Reichling 1935). If a person says this, we understand that he asserts or pretends to assert something. Further we know that there is meant such a thing as a gostake, that there may be more gostakes, and that the speaker is speaking about a particular one. This gostake is at this moment (or as a general thesis) active, and this in a transitive way. The doshes, − because of their position of a direct object − are in some way undergoing this activity. It is clear that there is more than one dosh, that a particular group is meant. Further at least one distimmer of doshes must be a gostake. And so on. Is this purely meaningless? Quite the contrary. − The same must be said about the example of Chomsky: '*Colorless green ideas sleep furiously*'.
This is pure nonsense (see, however, page 90): *deebs haky the um flutest reciled pav a tofently dison* (Epstein 1962, quot. Hörmann 1967). Chomsky's sentence is grammatically 'combinable' and only contentively 'incombinable' (perhaps!). (I use the term 'content' because the terms lexical and semantical can be misunderstood.) The sentence of Ogden-Richards is grammatically 'combinable', but there is only a virtual or unknown contentive 'combinability'. Epstein's series looks 'incombinable' both contentively and grammatically, but here too something seems to happen: so we may pause a little bit before 'the' and before 'a', and the last 3 'words' seem to be a phrase: 'a tofently dison'.
It is clear, therefore, that it is very difficult to find a series of nonsense-words which is really meaningless. It may be questioned whether nonsense-words actually exist (Wills, quoted by Eggermont 1964). The latter found that deaf children, even when instructed that only nonsense-words would be shown to them, still interpret them as meaningful. Nonsense-words are at least virtually meaningful.

Nuances of Meaning

The inverse: when there is another combination of words, there is another meaning too, at least another *nuance* of meaning. So these two sentences: 'The boy hits the ball' and 'The ball is hit by the boy' can only be identified superficially (Katz and Fodor 1963). In a conversational setting they will be completely unidentical.

The Real 'Depth' of Language: Combinability

Gamelin (1971) is right in saying: 'Syntax and meaningfulness of words work as one whole, supported by STM-function, in sentence processing'. So Katz and

80

Fodor (1963) view the 'grammatical form-classes' (e.g. 'tree' as noun, common noun, 'count'-noun), the semantic 'markers' ('tree' as animate) and the 'distinguishers' ('tree' with a trunk and top) as one hierarchic whole with its selection restrictions (a *big* tree, not a *sandy* tree; *a big tree*, not: tree big a, a tree big etc.), i.e. with its combinabilities. – In my opinion we must see lexical meaning and morphological meaning as one whole of meaningfulness, to be called: '*combinability*'. Here lies the real 'depth' of language.

'Combinability' as the Central Problem in Teaching a Language

'Contentors' and 'Functors'

The 'combinability' of words, – 'contentively' and grammatically – seems to me the central problem in teaching a language to deaf children. The richer these 'combinabilities' are within the rules of the language, the more flexible they are and the better controlled, the better the child will master the language, i.e. the better will be his 'competence of language'.

A 'combinability' of a word is ruled by its content and by its morphology (in a broad sense, see below). There are full semantic words such as *table, love, to shine, blue, further* and so on (let us say nouns, verbs, adjectives, adverbs), called content-words or 'contentors', and so-called function-words or 'functors' (let us call them determiners, auxiliaries, conjunctions, prepositions).

Admittedly (e.g. Fries 1952) the functors 'have no meaning in themselves'. But is this true? To me *the* has a meaning different from *a, that* different from *this* and *the, shall* different from *must, because* different from *although, under* different from *on*, etc. Perhaps we can concede that their meanings are more changeable, more dependent on context, more vague. Therefore their meanings are not as full as those of the contentors. But this does not mean that they are meaningless. Their meaning can best be seen when these words are used in *opposition* to other words of the same class (e.g. *on* the table, *under* the table, almost all words, even the contentors have polar meaning). Thus: these functors too function in our meaningful thinking, and in the building up of our 'world'.

Meaningful Grammaticalness in Children

Brown (1958) found this 'meaningful functioning' to be true already in hearing preschool children. He used for his experiment three sets of 4 pictures, and nonsense-words. E.g. *sib* for one series of 4 pictures. The first picture was as follows: a pair of hands was performing a kneading action with a mass of red material forming it into something resembling a pot. The second picture showed only some of that red material, the third picture only the action of kneading, the fourth only the pot. Brown instructed his young subjects in three different ways:

First way: 'Do you know what it means to sib? In this picture (first picture) you can see sibbing. Show me now another picture of sibbing!' 10 of the 16 children pointed to the picture with only the action of kneading.

Second way (for the first picture): 'Do you know what a sib is?' In using an article as *a*, we indicate immediately that we are speaking about a particular circumscribed object, e.g. a bottle. When we speak about mass-material without bounds as such (Whorf 1956), we do not use an article; we say, e.g. milk or some milk. Here we see now, that 11 of the 16 children pointed to the picture of the particular object: the pot.

Third way: 'Have you ever seen some sib?' 12 of the 16 children pointed to the picture of the red material.

Here we see, clearly, how so-called meaningless morphemes and function-words are already actually working in the manner of thinking of preschool children and in the differentiating process of their growing world.

In the same way Berko's research (1958) has shown how hearing children of 4–7 years of age meaningfully work with plurals, verb-tenses, possessives, derivations and compounds of nonsense-words.

'Action Radius' of Words. – 'Lexical Meaning' of Words

For the reasons mentioned just now I would take 'lexical meaning' in a broader sense (Brinke 1963), i.e. including the content of words but also their grammatical functioning. This has been done more and more in our lexicons too. E.g. I read in Chamber's Etymological English Dictionary (London 1964):

level, *noun*, an instrument for testing horizontality, etc. (6 meanings). – *adjective*, horizontal, etc. (6 meanings). – *verb, transitive*, to make horizontal etc. (5 meanings) (to level to, with, the ground), *present participle* levelling, *past tense* and *past participle* levelled. Etc.

We see: the lexicon gives as much as possible the 'combinability' of this word. If we put this in a diagram, this could be represented by a cog-wheel:

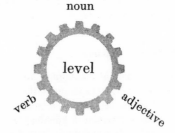

I will explain later why I am using a cogwheel. Of course the cogs of this wheeel are not immediately ready in the mind of a child. The word with its cogs grows by

82

understanding and by producing it, by trying it out by trial and check of combinations with many other words. In an actual utterance only one of the cogs is used. So we must say that the meanings of a word (the cogs) are never simultaneously actual: they are *virtual*. I call the whole set of combinabilities of a word: its *'action-radius'*.

Desemantisized Words?

Only a few words in English are – perhaps! – desemantisized, e.g. *to* with the infinitive. I say: *perhaps*, because by deeper understanding it may be that yet a cryptic meaning is there (Whorf 1956; van Uden 1957 found a meaning of the comparable word 'te' in Dutch). Supposing, however, that a kind of desemantization is really there, we may make a continuum of fullness of content from the desemantisized words up to the most fully semantisized words, e.g. to → the → for → shall → blue → sell → chair → Peter.

Endocentrism and Exocentrism

Before we go over to that continuum, we must discuss briefly another point which is in my opinion very important for our didactics. Bloomfield (1926) distinguishes so-called endocentric and exocentric constructions. In endocentric types the whole construction has the same combinability as at least one of its elements. In exocentric constructions, however, the whole construction has another combinability as do each of the elements. E.g. 'the tall boy'. This is a noun-construction, and boy is a substantive: the whole construction has the same combinability as 'boy'. 'Boy' is in some way the centre of the group, which drags along the other members of the group in the same combinability. The following construction: 'The boy was walking' in the sentence: 'I saw that the boy was walking', is an exocentric construction, because neither 'the', nor 'boy', nor 'was', nor 'walking' in themselves are clauses. The combinability comes from outside ('exo-'): 'I saw that . . .'. Another example: the construction 'on the table' in this sentence: 'Put it on the table', is an adverbial group, although none of the words, 'on' 'the' or 'table' is an adverb. Here too the combinability of the group comes from outside: it is an exocentric construction.

Naming and 'Co-naming'

I would use these terms in a broader sense and apply them to parts of speech, categories of words: endocentric and exocentric words, endocentric and exocentric use of words.
E.g. 'The tall boy'. 'Tall' is a more exocentric word than 'boy', i.e. it points more to

83

another word, is more dependent on context, calls for more words around itself. This is not the case with 'boy', at least much less: this *'substantive'* word labels a special category of beings.

If I say: *'The talking boy,'* at the same time *'talking'* is an adjective, thus not a *'verb'* in its full sense. A verb is only a verb in its full sense when it is exo-centrically used as a verb in a sentence, i.e. morphologically congruent and coherent with the subject and with the events, in its correct serial position. If I say *He came*, the morpheme of the verb *came* is congruent with *He* and with the event: past tense. It takes the second position. In this way a verb does not directly name but only indirectly, i.e. *as* a part of the sentence. It is really 'co-naming'. Consequently I do not agree with this definition of Pei-Gaynor: A verb is 'that part of speech which expresses an action, a process, state or condition or mode of being'. This difinition can be applied to many substantives, adjectives, adverbs, even conjunctions and prepositions! Hartmann and Stork (1972) give this definition, which is not quite right either: 'A part of speech which may function as predicate in a sentence'. This same thing can be said of adjectives.

Adjectives and adverbs are 'co-naming' too. Together they could be called: 'modifiers', defined by Pei-Gaynor as 'a word, expression or entire clause which qualifies or limits the meaning of a word'. The term 'limits' is less useful for children, because *'all* the children', *'many* books', *'always* there' and so on, are not, strictly speaking, 'limiting' phrases according to the comprehension of children. For deaf children it is much more helpful to start with the idea that modifiers make clear the intention, the meaning of the speaker. 'Which children do you mean?' 'I mean all the children'. – 'Which books do you mean?' 'Oh, I mean many books'. – 'Which picture do you mean?' 'That picture that you saw in the tramcar this morning'. Etc.

NB. The expressions 'What do you mean?' ... 'I mean' ... 'Oh, I don't mean that', etc., are very important. Deaf children should understand and use it at least at about 7 years of age.

A *noun*, however, is directly naming: 'That is a table'. Therefore the noun is fully 'naming', independently, in itself, directly: it can be used as a label (see, however, page 129). A noun is a substantive, i.e. something of an 'independent being'. This cannot be said of the other word classes. A substantive is a word by means of which we take something in itself. Each other word, taken in itself, is immediately 'substantivized', i.e. it shifts from its own class to the class of substantives, e.g. that *walking* of yours; *on* is not the same as *in*; I don't like that *blue*; how can you call that *yesterday*? etc. This shifting over opens at the same time other 'combinabilities', namely the 'combinabilities' of a substantive, i.e. it can be a subject, or a direct and indirect object; it can be used with a preposition; it can be used with an article or adjective pointerword, and so on. The 'combinabilities' of its own class are stopped.

84

A Continuum from Desemantisized Words up to the Most Semantisized Words

Now we are prepared to compose the continuum from the desemantisized words up to the most semantisized ones. We can follow the classes, as they are set up by Fries (1952), although I do not agree fully with his theory:

Nouns

↑

Verbs

↑

adjectives
adverbs

↑

auxiliaries

↑

prepositions
conjunctions

↑

deter-
miners

↑

Desemantisized
words.

The nouns could be called 'endocentric'. All other words are more or less exocentric according to their place on the continuum.

Consequences for Our Didactics

The consequences of this for our method are inter alia the following.
In the preschool and the lower grades only the nouns should be placed in paradigmatic lists. The same may be said for the pronouns: I, you, we, and pointerwords such as: that, there, this, here and so on. But it cannot be said of the verbs. This can only be done in higher grades (relevant are the intelligence of the children and their mastering of language). To illustrate, I saw this in a preschool class:

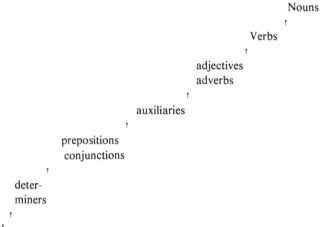

to laugh   to cry

To me this is a mistake. It detaches the verb from its sentence. It must be at least:

85

John is laughing　　　　　　　　John is crying

To do otherwise would be to train the children to use the verb always in its so-called infinitive form, i.e. to use verbs detached from their own nest. In this case: as verbs they will die, or better: they never come to be alive as verbs. E.g. 'Cry you yesterday, laugh all!'

All the more dangerous is it to put prepositions in lists, that is: words still more to the left at the continuum: e.g. in, under, on, of, between, after etc. I saw this in a low class:

under　　　　　on　　　　　behind　　　　in front of　　etc.

At least this must be: under the table, on the table, behind the table, in front of the table, and so on. If we don't do so, we prepare the children to say: 'Cupboard in!' or 'Where is Peter?' Answer: 'Oooh in!'

Dangerous too is the following (in the preschool):

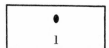　　　　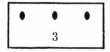　　etc.

This is very abstract for small children. Our numbers, used in daily life, are *adjectives* (modifiers):

'Look for three flowers!'

'All the children receive two sweets'.

'You knocked down only one skittle' . . .

'I told you twice' . . .

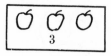　　　　　　　　　　　　　　| • | • | • |
　　　　　　　　　　　　　　　　　　　　　　3

Three apples

(A)　　　　　　　　　　　　　　　　(B)

I like (A) much more than (B). (A = 3 apples, 3 flowers, 3 balls, 3 cars, 3 skittles etc.)
And this is from bad to worse:

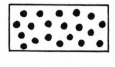

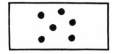

many   few

The same applies to colours. We can use them as nouns, i.e. in themselves: 'I don't like that blue' and so on. But this too is rather abstract for small children. The teacher should use phrases, such as: blue cars, yellow cars, red cars, blue balls, yellow balls, red balls. Etc. Otherwise he prepares: 'Girl ... blue ... red!' (pointing).

In higher grades of course, when the children have already learned very much by natural language, verbs can be classified in themselves, more and more. (Always with prudence, however!) Indeed the word-class which can be listed first after the nouns are the verbs. And so on along the continuum in later years. The danger of this paradigmatic listing, however, is the greater, the more we approach to the left side of the continuum. If we neglect to keep these words in their own settings, i.e. in the phrases, in the sentences and so on, we can be sure that the children will use these words detached from the English system, using them perhaps in their own system: then these words are only loanwords. E.g. if the child says 'cupboard in' then *in* is not functioning as a preposition at all, it is a loanword. Summarizing: we should concern ourselves not so much with paradigmata, but with syntagmata, unless the paradigmata concern accentgroups.

This conforms to the findings of the associative trends of (hearing) children (up to 8 years of age) as opposed to the trends of older children and adults: if we give for instance the stimulus word *boy*, young children will associate *play, school, learning* etc., but older children and adults will associate: *girl, man, woman* and so on (cf., e.g. Brown 1958). Thus the younger children, still in the process of their language-growth, associate syntagmatically, the older ones paradigmatically. Entwistle (1966) found that children make the first paradigmatic associations with the nouns (see above), before those with verbs and adverbs: these are the first 'part of speech' they detect by reflecting unconsciously on language.

Restaino (1969) found that deaf children, trained by *constructive methods* showed a typical behaviour in their word associations: these were artificially paradigmatic (boy → girl, spoon → knife, etc.). Besides they showed a kind of rigid thinking. – Deaf children, trained by more *natural methods*, however, showed more flexibility and more syntagmatic associations (boy → play, spoon → porridge, etc.). The differences of the methods appeared to affect the mind of the children, indeed.

10. RHYTHM AS A LANGUAGE FORM

Rhythm and Phrases

We have already seen that the phrase structure of sentences is in some way also a psycholinguistic entity. I expressed my opinion too that this phrase structure is a result of the dialogic, conversational character of language, by means of which chunks of information can be exchanged between the partners as kinds of 'accessories' or 'components'. Very often we use a phrase as an incomplete sentence; according to G. Miller (1951) 30% of our conversational sentences are incomplete.

Phrases and 'Replacing-words'

These phrases can alway be replaced by pointer-words and question-words, e.g. '*The man with the brown pullover* (who? He!) will come back *tomorrow* (when? Then!) *by car* (how? By what? Like this! By that!). See the reflective exercises page 235, 236. Also this replacing is done continuously and spontaneously, in our conversations and in written language as well. Deaf children don't if not trained in the right way. They will say for instance: 'Daddy and mummy and Francis and I go for a swim ... Daddy and mummy and Francis and I like swimming very much', instead of: 'Daddy and mummy and Francis and I, we all are going for a swim. We like it very much'.

After the children have mastered the question- and the pointer-words, this replacing can be trained as follows:

Find the question-words (c.q. pointer-words) for the underlined phrases:

I am going to visit my grandmother on saturday.

I have a present for her,

Whom? When?
(1) I am going to visit my grandmother on saturday.

What? For whom?
I have a present for her.

her then
(2) I am going to visit my grandmother on saturday.

it, that, this
I have a present for her.

88

Word Order or Word Group?

Can we say more about *what a phrase is*, and how phrases are structured within and between themselves? This may make it the clearer that the acquisition of rhythmic speech cannot be seen apart from the acquisition of grammar (cf. Menyuk 1972).

Historical linguistics (van Uden 1960, Kooy 1973) has shown that the more a language in its diachronic development looses flexions (e.g. Latin to French, Dutch to Suid-Afrikaans), the more the sequential order of the words and their positions in these sequences will play a part, to avoid ambiguities. E.g. the Latin speaker can say: 'Petrus venit' or 'Venit Petrus' with the same meaning, but in French: 'Pierre vient' or 'Vient Pierre' have different meanings. So 'positional categories' of words originate, i.e. some parts of speech call for specific positions within the sentences and phrases (Paardekoper 1971), e.g. the verb takes the second position in a string of words which is assertive, the adjective as a modifier of a noun takes its position immediately before that noun, etc. etc.

Let us first of all emphasize here that word order is not the same as word-group. 'Group' expresses the rhythmic unity of the words. It is not necessary, however, to include more than one word in a phrase. One word can be a phrase, even one word can be a complete sentence ('sentence' defined as an expression of an intention, as 'a grammatically complete *sense* unit' Pei-Gaynor), e.g. *Yes! Indeed! Hallo!*

Consequently, I prefer the term *'accent group'*. This group can be a collection of phonemes only (as in Yes!), a collection of syllables (Tomorrow!) or a collection of words (In the theatre?).

We will see below that the term 'accent group' can, and to me must, be taken in a broader sense, i.e. as a rhythmic unity, so that not only immediate (or continuous) constituents (Bloomfield 1926) can form an accent group, but also 'mediate' (or discontinuous) constituents, i.e. in the so-called 'pincer-construction'. I translate this word from the German linguistics using: 'Zangen-konstruktion' or 'Zangen-bau' or 'Umklammerung' (= gripping, a clamp.) (See van Haeringen 1947). Chomsky (1957) speaks of 'embedding transformations'. E.g. let us compare

$$\text{the boy} \qquad \text{the big boy}$$

We see (or better hear) that *the* and *boy* pinch *big* between them, as a gripping tool (see below). Compare the French: 'le garçon grand', where *grand* is not pinched. That word-order is not the same as word group (accent group), may be illustrated by these examples:

He will come tomorrow. At eleven he will start.
He will come. Tomorrow at eleven he will start.

He will come tomorrow at eleven. He will start.

Peter/said the master/is a rotter.
Peter said:/The master is a rotter. (Reichling 1935.)

Where is/the salt he demanded.
Where is the salt? he demanded.
(Uhlenbeck, in Reichling 1962.)

What disturbed John/was being disregarded by everyone.
What disturbed/John was being disregarded by everyone. (Chomsky 1966.)

Compare this with such ambiguities from mathematics:
$5 + 6 \times 7 = ?$
$(5 + 6) \times 7 = 77$ or $5 + (6 \times 7) = 47$.

NB. In a series of disordered nonsense-words we almost automatically make some chunks of rhythmic units too, for instance the example mentioned earlier from Epstein: deeps haky/the um flutest/reciled pav/a tofently dison. There are some features which call for a pause. These pauses originate accent-groups, which suggest a hidden meaning.

Ambiguity in the Grouping of Words

Chomsky here again (cf. page 74) argues that only a 'deep-structure' is relevant to a specific interpretation of different groupings of words. He asserts that only a single surface-structure may be assigned and that a change-over is only possible by different deep-structures, for instance in the last example above 'What ... was being disregarded' or 'John was being disregarded'. This is seemingly not the case: one person immediately *hears* this, another person immediately *hears* that (cf.

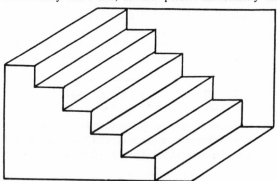

A 'reversible figure'. You see the stairs or the piece of a cornice. There is no deep-structure; there are only two alternative surface structures.

90

the so-called 'reversible figures' in visual perceptual organization, Krech and Crutchfield 1962, see figure page 90). Lackner and Garrett (1973) found that the interpretations are influenced by stimuli or cues received from the environment, quite unconsciously. – Here again the background of *conversation* is relevant to the interpretation. So for example when in a conversation he has been told that everybody felt miserable, the listener will immediately group the words as in the second sentence: *What disturbed/John* . . .. The combinability of a word includes how that word is grouped with other words, which is done by rhythm, not by a deep-structure. We will see below that this rhythmic grouping does not always call for an actual pause, but that a virtual pause exists and suffices. – I think this argument holds for all his examples.

It is a great pity that Chomsky and his followers did not give more attention to the rhythm of language as a real language-form, and to the context of conversation. Perhaps we may say that what Chomsky calls 'deep-structure' coincides on the one side with the homonymy of words (including their multi-dimensional *virtual* combinabilities as we have seen above), and on the other side with virtual pauses and *virtual* groupings. So in my opinion this problem of so-called 'deep-structure' is the problem of the belonging of the *words* to each other, i.e. which combinabilities should be, resp. can be actualized in this phrase, in this sentence.

An important conclusion for our praxis is that we should train deaf children in the rhythmic groupings of the words, throughout, by making them speak rhythmically in phrases, by reading aloud, by finding the virtual and actual pauses themselves (see below reflective exercises page 234).

The Pauses in Language

What is the role of a pause in speech? Does it play a part in language, i.e. in the system, too?

Suci (1967) found that phrases surrounded by pauses are better memorized (see Thorndike, Johnson) than phrases not surrounded by pauses. E.g. 'Let us go by bus/because/it is raining cats and dogs' will be memorized better than 'Letusgobybusbecauseitisrainingcatsanddogs'. Fodor and Garrett (1967) found the same in sentences containing 'pincer-constructions' (= 'self-embedded sentences'), for instance: 'The man/the dog bit/died' was better memorized (STM) and understood than: 'Themanthedogbitdied'. We may consider these findings in connection with those more general ones of memory, clustering and rhythm. These findings mean therefore, in my opinion, that the pauses make the rhythm of phrases more prominent.

I think we must distinguish three kinds of pauses in speech:

(1) Virtual pauses, i.e. which are linguistically possible, according to the phrase-structure, but not actualized, e.g.

91

The sister is not coming tomorrow.
(2) Actual pauses, i.e. which are linguistically possible and are actualized too, e.g.
The sister/is not coming/tomorrow.
(3) Hesitative pauses, which are extralinguistic (Roose 1960), e.g.
The/sister is not coming tomorrow.

I conclude this distinction from several studies. Boomer et al. (1962) found that hesitative pauses were significantly more overlooked by the listeners than actual pauses (called by them: 'juncture-pauses'). Fodor and Bever (1965), Holmes and Forster (1972) offered their subjects tape-recorded sentences, within which a click has been inserted at random places. Their subjects were asked to tell where they had heard the click. They practically never heard it on the exact place, but on a point of a virtual or actual pause. This has to do with the phrase-structure of language. For instance a click was given in the right ear along with '*A*nna', while in the left ear these sentences were successively presented (by means of headphones): (a) 'Your hope of marrying *A*nna was surely impractical', (b) 'In her hope of marrying, *A*nna was surely impractical'. The subjects heard the click in (a) after *A*nna, and in (b) before (Garrett, Bever and Fodor 1966).

Very important is: when reading aloud (it may be the same in silent reading) we usually see 4–5 words ahead. This looking ahead happens significantly according to the coming of virtual or actual pauses, thus according to the rhythmic groupings of the words. For example if we unexpectedly turn off the light, the subject will proceed reading, usually *until* the next pause (Levin and Turner, quoted by Smith 1971). So we see that the graphic and the spoken forms are quite integrated, something we have to achieve in deaf children (van Uden 1975).

Even more important, however, is the following: pauses are related to the *total rhythmic structure* of a sentence, and to its content as well. Goldman et al. (quot. Hörmann 1967, see also Schatz 1954) found that the length of pauses is correlated with the informative content of both preceding and succeeding words, and that this length also functions in the listeners in order to understand the correct content of the sentence.

We mentioned the *hesitative* pauses. Maclay and Osgood (1959) found that hesitative pauses are marked by an extra-linguistic special length, and are preferentially put according to the phrase-structure of the sentences, i.e. on places of the normal virtual or actual pauses.

Consequently pauses are a real lawful tool in expressive and receptive language. They are a living element in the total rhythmic structure of a sentence. In my opinion this is a systematic, i.e. a linguistic tool, which also functions psycholinguistically. It is, however, not an exclusively linguistic tool. Reber et al. (1970) showed about the same for music, i.e. for rhythmically grouped tones (cf. Martin 1972).

'Pincer-constructions'

We have already mentioned what I should like to call 'pincer-constructions'. In my opinion they are related to the phrase structure, i.e. to the rhythmic structure of the sentence. The 'pincer-construction' and the 'compound-construction' are oppositional.

But first I'll give more examples:

He puts his message over.   He takes it over.

in opposition to:

I say, he puts over his message.
He takes over that responsibility.

I draw the links, which may be a symbol of the rhythmic grouping, purposely above the accented syllables of the words between which the pincer works: to me the rhythmic working is exactly between these accented syllables as supports.

He looked the old fence over.

in opposition to:

He looked over / the old fence.

(These two examples are from Francis 1958).

Other examples:

He enthusiastically participated in pursuits,
which for him had acquired value.

in opposition to:

He participated....   which had....

Another example:

Will the boy wash? *I don't think so.*

Is the boy washing? *Turn the light off.*

in opposition to:

The boy will wash,.....is washing.

I think. Turn off....

'*Pincer-constructions*':	'*Compound-constructions*':
Mediate constituents.	Immediate constituents.
Embedding functions.	Clustering functions.
The director's secretary.	The secretary to the director.
How do you plan to manage it?	How will you manage it, do you think?
Mary asked John how to wash the car.	Mary washes the car.
She apparently bought it.	It appears, that she bought it.

Such 'pincer-constructions' are rather often a difficulty in spontaneous, less controlled speech of us hearing, which can be concluded from the many slips in speech, such as:

He participated in pursuits, which had . . . for him had acquired value.

Or we say: *The boy, is he washing?*

I found this example in a study of Maclay and Osgood (1959):

'. . . an interesting problem of doing *a* in a sense *a* structural frequency study of *the alternative* syntactical in a given language, say, like English, *the alternative* possible structures . . .'

There is a tendency to keep words together, to shorten the lengths of 'pincer-constructions':

had acquired,

Is he,

A structural frequency,

The alternative possible structures.

94

Yngve (1962) gives this example of how we organize our sentences: 'He gave the candy to the girl that he met in New York while visiting his parents for 10 days around Christmas and New Year' – in preference to: 'He gave the girl that he met in New York while visiting his parents for 10 days around Christmas and New Year the candy'.

Carol Chomsky (1969) speaks of a 'minimal distance principle'. She found in hearing children of 5–10 years of age that they controlled 'compound-constructions' better and earlier than 'pincer-constructions' (my terminology). – In Dutch there are the studies of van Haeringen (1947) and Uylings (1956) with similar results in adults.

The slips of the tongue mentioned above are found especially in children with 'developmental dysphasia'. I gathered more than 100 analogic slips of the tongue in deaf children, for instance in a 7 year old: 'Mama car, mama by car, mama and I car shopping, many clothes, buy many clothes, clothes for Mary, clothes Johnny, clothes Willy and I ... feast!'

Rhythm and 'Pincer-constructions'

Van Haeringen (1947) thinks that those words, standing at a distance from each other, are felt(?) as logically belonging. I see no logic in these remarkable 'compound' – and 'pincer-groupings'. I feel that it is a rhythmic working, for us hearing an 'intonating' working too. This has been confirmed by the finding of Fodor and Garrett (1967) mentioned above: such 'self-embedding sentences' as 'The man the dog bit died' gave more misinterpretations when read aloud in a flat way (without disturbing the 'logic') than in an expressive way.

Besides I base my opinion on the theory of music (cf. Martin 1972; Farnsworth 1958): a rhythmic whole (the same applies to rhythmic-melodic wholes) stays united even when it is interrupted by other sounds; such an interruption tends to strengthen that feeling of unity; the disrupted parts receive a kind of magnetic attraction to each other, the consequence of which is that the unity of clasping and clasped elements is enormously strengthened; the basis of this magnetic working is always the originally felt unity of the immediate constituent elements, i.e. the opposition between united and disrupted grouping (van Uden 1960).

Let us take this example of a theme in a symphony:

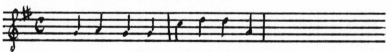

This theme is played by each part of the orchestra in turn, so that the listener will fix it in his mind: indeed it is the fundament of the whole symphony. Some minutes later we hear:

This is an example of a musical 'pincer-construction'. This variety of uniting and disrupting the theme, as Beethoven so often did, enchants the listener.

Let us now apply this to our linguistic functioning. The unit '*the-boy*' is very often used: *the* and *boy* attract each other as it were rhythmic-magnetically. If we say at a certain moment: '*The tall boy*', then that first unit is not crumbled, but strengthened. 'The tall boy' is a phrase the *unity* of which is dependent on 'the boy': this last 'compound-construction' in its turn is strengthened by the alternation with a 'pincer-construction'. Therefore we showed in the examples above how a pincer-construction brings with it a compound-construction as its opposition. Of course all this is ruled by the system of language. So there are a lot of 'compound-constructions' which exclude an oppositional pincer-construction, e.g. 'He is *well up* in the matter' or '*Free of* charge', etc. etc.

If we look now at the 'phrase-structure' of sentences, we must say that the phrases, the accent-groups of the sentences are the oppositions of the pincer-constructions. These last ones are, in their rhythmic working, based on the 'phrase-structure'. So we see again that the phrase structure of sentences is basic in the whole rhythmic structuring of sentences.

Consequences for our Didactics

From experience I can say that this idea is helpful to deaf children, provided that they are orally and rhythmically well trained (signs and finger-spelling or writing do not include sufficient rhythm: see later). It follows from this that we teachers of the deaf must train the children from the beginning in the rhythmic syntagmata such as

- in the cupboard
- nicely written
- late at school
- your blue shoes

and so on, i.e. phrases, spoken in a quick, good tempo.

This work has to start in the preschool or earlier. When the child has learned for instance *ball* and *car*, rhythmic speech training can already start, by speaking from memory: ball-car, ball-ball-car, car-ball-car, car-ball-ball, car-car-ball etc.

etc., each unit 5 or 10 times in a joyful rhythmic way. This exercises at the same time the diaphragmatic and intercostal breathing-muscles (Gutzmann 1905; Hudgins 1937). As soon as possible we go over to phrases such as mentioned above. We train the children to speak whole sentences by heart, rhythmically, 3 times, 5 times, sentences of 6 syllables, of 8 syllables, expanding the STM more and more.

Mistakes against the correct rhythm of the sentences and phrases, tempo included, are as big mistakes as articulatory slips. They are even more dangerous, not only because the intelligibility of speech depends on the rhythm (Hudgins 1942, 1946), but also because of the importance of rhythm to language acquisition (memory for successive data, acceleration of the conversations, control of sentence-structures, thinking in language).

Rhythm and Accentuation

Another aspect of rhythm in language is the accentuation. This accentuation does not solely concern the accentuated words but the flow of the whole sentence, the acceleration of some series of syllables, the lengthening of pauses or retardation of the last syllable before a virtual pause, and the lengthening of some specific syllables. These last lengthenings are integrated with the pitches (usually higher, sometimes lower) and the strengths of voicing (Huggins 1972, quot. Martin 1972). For deaf children see page 102.

There are several rules for the accentuation, by means of which it is a tool in the expressing and receiving of language. This tool is systematic and it is therefore to me linguistic. It is psycholinguistic too. I only point here to:

the opposition between *main accent* and *accidental accent*;
the opposition between *accent of importance* and *accent of contrast*;
the continuous *shifting* of accents in the conversations, also in telling stories, in speeches etc.

'Bound Forms' (cf. Ulrich 1972)

Morphology is defined by Bloomfield (1926): the science of 'the constructions in which bound forms appear among the constituents'. Our problem is: What are bound forms?

First of all (which does not mean, that these are the most important bound forms nor that they are the first in language development, but only that they are the best known) the *flexions*: prefixes, infixes, suffixes, Umlauts, and zero-functions. These are phonemically bound forms.

Some linguists, however, also speak of '*position* categories' (e.g. Paardekoper 1966), or better 'grouping-categories' (Reichling 1947): i.e. that a word has one or more fixed serial positions in sentences and phrases, e.g. the positions of prepositions, of articles, of verbs etc. The 'position-categories' are the 'position-rules'.

'Pivots' and 'Open Class-words'

Hearing children learn these rules by 'becoming familiar with the sounds of units in the temporal positions in which they recur' (Braine 1963). In the beginning children of about 2 years of age use a few words in a fixed position, e.g. *want* sweet, want yellow, never: sweet want, yellow want; Nanny *do* wash, never: do Nanny wash or Nanny wash do etc. Around those positionally fixed words (Braine calls them 'pivots', cf. Ervin, 1963) other words are grouped, as *sweet*, *yellow*, *Nanny*, *wash* etc., called 'open-class-words'. Huttenlocher (1964) found that children easily learn two-five and five-two as well, but not reversals of their 'pivots'. According to Braine (1963) hearing children of about 2 years of age develop a '*pivot-open class-grammar*', of course each child its own, a systematization different from that of the environment. The fixed position of the 'pivot-words' can be the first, or the second (last) position in the series. These words could be designed as: $\boxed{want \ . \, . }$, $\boxed{. \, . \ do \ . \, .}$ etc (see page 68). The fixation of these words may be due to 'rhythmic magnetism', but as a matter of course this is not contrary to semantic features playing a part too (Bloom 1971). Actually these words are 'contentors'. The child of this age does not yet use 'functors'. It is seemingly not correct to consider these 'pivot-words' as precursors of the 'functors' in later language use.

Order of Words Usually Correct

Brown and Bellugi (1964) found that the order of the words used by the children of their investigation (these were a little bit older than those of Braine) was usually kept in that used ('seized') by the mother:

Child:
'Daddy car?'

Mother:
'No, *Daddy* is not coming by *car*.'

This means that that first word-order as such was usually correct.

98

'Telegraphic Speech'

Brown and Fraser (1963) do not speak of 'pivot-open class-sentences' but of 'telegraphic speech', which presupposes that the child would be in some sense aware of something lacking or deleted in his speech, but cannot complete it by some still weak function (e.g. not too good a STM). Perhaps we may say, maybe by the expanding reactions of the mother, that the child becomes more and more aware of something lacking in its speech. The subjects of Brown and Fraser were also a little bit older than those of Braine.

Summary: the Development of Rhythmic Grouping

We see how the rhythmic grouping of words grows in a child, growing to the normal phrase-structures and the pincer-structures of its environment: *pivot-structure → telegraphic speech →correct phrases → pincer construction*.

'Rhythmic Morphemes'

As we have explained we consider these rules as rhythmically based rules. Consequently we may also call these forms 'bound forms': i.e. rhythmically bound forms. Thus we distinguish two kinds of morphemes:

phonemic morphemes, and
rhythmic morphemes (or – if you prefer – 'positional' or 'grouping' morphemes).

Rhythmic morphemes can be described as the special attractive powers in words by which they group into definite serial positions, e.g. expressed in this way: 'prepositions group themselves before nouns'. This does not mean of course, that these rhythmic morphemes always have the same rhythms, but that they are based on the feeling of rhythm. That this feeling of rhythm works in speakers is strikingly illustrated by the verbal memory experiments by Johnson and others. It is a matter of fact that hearing children first learn the rhythmic morphemes, i.e. the correct groupings, helped by the intonations which give them so much pleasure, but that the correct phonemic morphemes still present them with difficulties at 6 or 7 years of age (cf. Pike 1949, Kaper 1959). At 3;0 most children have mastered the normal *rhythmic* structures of sentences (e.g. Menyuk 1964, 1969).

'Pivot-open Class-grammar' in Deaf Children?

If the parents, the house-parents and/or the teacher are not aware of it, deaf children may stick for too long to a kind of 'pivot-open class-grammar', as has been suggested for signing deaf ones by Stokoe (1972). Orally educated deaf children may more or less do the same in their spontaneous utterances, e.g.

'Where water?' (= Could you give me some water?)
'Where home?' (= When will we go home?)
'Where not?' (= Why not?) –
'Finished writing' (= I have finished writing)
'Finished see television?' (= Have you seen the television?). –
'Broken pencil' (= my pencil has been broken)
'Broken skirt' (= my skirt has been torn)
'Broken picture' (= there is something wrong in that picture).

And so on.
We will explain how this development can and should be stimulated to the normal phrase- and pincer-structures of the hearing world.

11. HOW TO DEVELOP RHYTHM OF SPEECH?

Rhythm of Speech

What is the rhythm of speech? Is it sound? If so it will be an almost closed book for deaf children, although not totally. Is it movement of the articulatory organs? Here it is, at least in principle, teachable to deaf children. Examples of rhythm of movement are: marching, dancing, twiddling the thumbs and fingers, and so on. We can say: rhythm of speech is a rhythmic *movement* of the speech organs (breathing-, voice- and mouth-movements), of course integrated with sounds, the latter because the speech-movements 'feed' the hearing, and the hearing (by auditory patterns of *series* of sounds, not by fixed and detached formants) 'feeds back' these movements.

It is not only the auditory function that controls speech, because if that were true a person who becomes deaf postlingually would become mute at the same time. This is, however, not the case: he can carry on speaking even very clearly, although somewhat deteriorated (van Uden 1974; much depends upon his eupraxic functions).

Articulatory 'Distinctive Features'

'Each speech sound is a bundle of features, based on articulatory *and* acoustic characteristics' (Menyuk 1972). MacNeilage (1970) has explained how these motory-sensory processes of speech are programmed both spatially and serially:

100

e.g. when I say 'bah', this pattern is spatial within the mouth, a movement from the lips to the back of the mouth, both supported by the voice, originating from the deeper situated vocal cords. At the same time it is a temporal sequence of movements. The *sound* of speech therefore is only one of the 'distinctive features' (Jacobson et al. 1956). These distinctive features, however, should not be thought of as something static, but dynamic: not so much of detached phonemes, but more of the concatenations of phonemes, i.e. of syllables and words. When we hear a syllable, we scan the *articulatory* Gestalts of the dynamic distinctive features stored in our brain, in order to select the right perceptual reactions. The articulation is the decisive norm of our perceptual interpretations (Stevens and House 1972).

Anarthric subjects can understand speech only to some extent, not perfectly (contrary to Lenneberg 1962).

In the same way Japanese subjects, although speaking English very well, made significantly more mistakes in perceiving the difference between /r/ and /l/, in words such as 'rule' and 'long', than native English subjects: the Japanese language does not have the /r/ in its phonologic system, so the sensory-motory listening of Japanese subjects remained behind in perceiving them, even when they had mastered the English pronunciation (Goto 1971).

So Perozzi and Kunze (1971) found significant correlations in hearing Kindergarten-children between their speech-sound-discrimination and their spoken *expressive* language (and not with their language understanding, which is still very 'global' and general in children of the ages 3 to 5).

Peterson (1952) found that the physical (= acoustical) analysis of the sounds of vowels does not show congruency with the patterns heard. These heard patterns are more congruent with the articulatory movements, i.e. one does not hear a vowel but a speaker articulating a vowel.

Libermann (1957, 1963, 1967) made synthetic plosives and fricatives followed by vowels. He found that acoustically the same sounds are auditorily heard differently according to heard patterns: the acoustically same sound is a /p/ before an /i/ and a /k/ before an /a/, but some acoustically different sounds are all heard as /p/ before /i/. – The phonemes /l/ and /m/ are acoustically not very different, but articulatory the reverse is true. The /m/ is formed with the lips and the /l/ with the tongue – The /k/ in 'key' and 'cool', the /s/ in 'say' and 'soon' are the same phoneme, but acoustically very different; notwithstanding the acoustic differences, the two /k/'s and two /s/'s are more confluent in understanding than /l/ and /m/. And so on. – Here too the heard patterns are more congruent with the articulatory movements than with the acoustic movements of the sounds.

All these findings are very much in favour of a 'motor theory of speech perception'. The criticism of Lane (1965) does not seem to be conclusive, although Libermann and his cooperators neglect the idea of sensory-motory Gestalts and look too much for intermediate coding, or 'translating'-functions, which does not seem to be correct.

101

Indeed: our auditory patterns, Gestalts, are built up by hearing our own speech (circular *motory*-sensory processes).

Consequently we must say that we hear the *movements* of speech: hearing is a motory-sensory process. Mol (1953, 1963) is right in saying that hearing of speech is a lot like lipreading: both are perceptions of articulatory movements. *We hear a speaker articulating.*

Conversation as a 'Duet'

Speech is one of the most *rhythmic* behaviours of man. Hearing speech too. Not only are the articulators involved, but also the breathing mechanisms, even the head, the eyes, the arms, hands and fingers.

The breathing patterns, i.e. the breathing rhythms in speech are 'heard' by the partner. Brown (1962) found breathing movements of listeners significantly related to the breathing movements of the speaker according to rate, depth and variability. We must not forget that rhythmic breathing is the basis of rhythmic speech: if we motorily 'hear' the speech-movements, breathing-movements are included.

It has been found, that a conversation between two persons can be described as a 'dancing together', a duet, that is how strongly the movements of both partners are atuned to each other (cf. Ex 1969, Wiener et al. 1972, Siegman and Pope 1972). For instance the listener puts his cigarette into the ashtray with exactly the same rhythm as he hears the speech of his partner. It is very difficult to execute a tapping movement on an unstressed syllable, for example on *have* in the spoken sentence: '*First* you have to go to New York' (Allen 1967, quot. Martin 1972).

Rhythm and Deaf Children

If the rhythm of speech is not essentially auditory but articulatory too, it may be expected that the basic principle of rhythm in speech and language is accessible to deaf children, notwithstanding the enormous difficulties deaf children have with rhythm, especially with that of speech and breathing (see, e.g. Hudgins 1937, 1957).

I found non-multiply handicapped deaf children of 4–7 years of age, to be 3 years behind normal hearing children in rhythmic development by tapping with a peg and saying baba in a tempo of $\frac{1}{4}$-second, i.e. the syllabic tempo of normal quiet speech (van Uden 1969). – Rileigh and Odom (1972) got other results, but the tempo of their test was too low, so that the children could count the beats. This in a tempo of $\frac{1}{4}$-second, is almost impossible: the child has to get the pattern itself. – At the age of 13 years, after a good rhythmic training according to our 'sound-perceptive method' (van Uden 1952, initiative of Rutten 1941), the difference with hearing children disappeared for patterns such as •• ••• • •• .

Deaf children have a great and basic need for a total rhythmic education from childhood (van Uden 1947, 1952, 1966), the method of which must use sound perception to its fullest extent, so that the child first of all perceives the sounds of its own movements, i.e. of its own speech, of its breathing by means of wind-instruments, or 'blow-organs' (van Uden 1943, 1946, 1955); speech, language and dancing must be integrated.

It may be clear too, that music and dancing continuously train the auditory-vibratory senso-motory functions as such. They train the memory for such sequences and their 'eupraxias'; so indirectly they train the basic functions of speech and language (van Uden 1947, 1952, 1963; Ewing 1954; Nicholas 1967).

An Example of a Lesson for a 'Play-song'

Here is just one example of a lesson in speech, language, music and dancing, given to deaf children of 6–7 years of age (8 children).

On a rainy day.

Teacher comes in. Jeanne feels teacher's coat saying: 'Coat wet!'

Teacher, seizing this: 'My coat is wet!'

Jeanne repeats it: 'Your coat is wet'.

Nelly: 'How?'

Sonja: 'Silly you!'

The teacher quickly puts away her coat in order to seize this beginning conversation and to use if for language . . .

Teacher to Nelly: 'Say: Why is that?'

Teacher to Sonja: 'Say: you are silly!' Both children repeat it.

Anny: 'Why?'

Teacher to Anny:

'Why is the coat wet?'

Anny: 'It is raining . . .'

Now the teacher writes on the blackboard (the names of the children in colour):

Jeanne: '*Your coat is wet*'.

Teacher to Jeanne: 'Say it again, clearly!' Jeanne has to say it rhythmically, showing the rhythm with her arm in a nice, graceful movement while speaking, and in a good tempo:

Your coat / is wet.

Then the teacher writes again on the blackboard:
Nelly: *'Why is that?'*
Nelly has to say it in the same way:

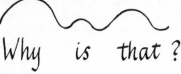

Why is that ?

The teacher writes again:
Sonja: *'You are silly'.*
Sonja has to say that in the same way:

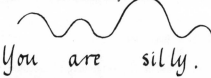

You are silly .

The teacher writes again:
Anny: *'Why is the coat wet?'*
Anny has to say that in the same way:

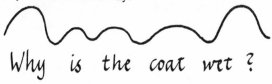

Why is the coat wet ?

Then the teacher writes:
Anny: *'It is raining'.*
Anny repeats this in the same way.

It is raining .

Now all the children have to repeat these sentences in chorus, all moving their hands and arms nice and fluently and speaking rhythmically.
The children are also asked how many syllables each sentence has. They can see it: each movement is a syllable. This is important in order to make the rhythm more conscious and controlled. Next question: 'Which syllable has the accent?' And so on.
Then the teacher makes the children dramatize this. The parts are written on the

104

blackboard: Jeanne, Nelly, Sonja and Anny can see what they have to say. They learn it by heart. After these four children, the other four children have to pretend to be Jeanne, Nelly, Sonja and Anny. In dramatizing, of course, they leave out the movements of the arms, but they speak to each other rhythmically, pretending to converse. They dramatize it all by heart. In the next lesson this episode is used in the music and dance hall. There this conversation is extended as follows.

First the notes have to be found, and this is done in this way.

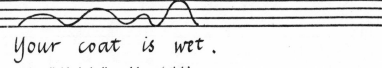

Then each syllable is indicated by a 'stick':

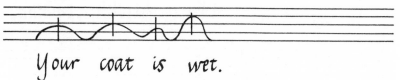

The notes are found at the crosspoints of the waves and the sticks:

All the children have 'blow-organs' with head-phones (for vibration-feeling and/or hearing remnants), on which they can play this melody by blowing.

Each sentence is treated in this way. Of course the children have to learn this. But after some time, it is quickly done.

The lesson results in this 'play-song' which is sung by a man with a nice bass-voice and recorded on magnetic tape:

feeling the coat

Your coat is wet!

Nelly and Anny quickly approach

Why is that?

Sonja quickly approaches

You are silly! silly!

Why is the coat wet?

106 It is raining It is raining It is raining

How this work develops during the years, in the respective grades, up to the time the pupils are 19 and 20 years of age, can be seen in the literature quoted above: more and more the beauty of rhythm of speech is felt and learnt, its phonetic symbolism ('oral mime'), its rhyme, and so on.

Accent of Duration

Deaf children can learn rhythmic speech (provided that the technique of breathing and that of voice-production are well developed) by the accent of duration (de Werd 1942, 1962, van Uden 1952, Speth 1958), i.e. by lengthening the accented syllables. Also in hearing people the accent of duration plays a greater part than has been realized before: see, e.g. the study of *pérmit* and *permít* by Mol and Uhlenbeck (1956, see also Fry 1955). Compare:

To subject, a subject	To object, an object
To digest, a digest	To contract, a contract
Etc.	

Primarily duration and secondarily intensity and/or intonation are the features which make one distinguish the wordclass.
In my opinion the *rule* is this:
when the vowel is a long one, the vowel itself is lengthened;
when the vowel is a short one, the succeeding continuant consonant must be lengthened, e.g. *fast* = faaast, but *fist* = fissst; *hands* = haaands, but *hence* = hennnce,
and the plosives are pronounced more prominently, so peermit in contrast to per-mi*tt*, con*n*tract in contrast to contra*cct*.
As De Werd rightly said, we should present the lengthenings and prominencies to the children a little bit overdone, so that the child, by always spontaneously shortening his reactions, will do it exactly right (van Uden 1952).
This use of the accent of duration has the effect of the children spontaneously giving more intensity to this longer syllable and also raising their voices. This happens in the beginning quite unconsciously, but can be made conscious afterwards by means of the wind-instruments used in our 'sound-perceptive method' (van Uden 1952, 1953). Cf. Gemmil and John (1976).

12. RHYTHM AND MEMORY

Rhythmic Speech and Memory for Language

The rhythmic training of speech is important particularly in relation to the memory for language, and consequently to the thinking of the children (van Uden 1955–1957).

It must be emphasized that words are remembered not so much by their phonemes but first of all by their rhythm. This has been shown by the 'tip of the tongue' experiment of Brown and McNeill (1966). The most important cues for such a retrieval of a forgotten word was its number of syllables and its stress at the beginning or the end of the word.

Krech (1962) summarizes the findings of many researches: 'Any device that aids grouping, no matter how inane, may aid the acquisition process: thus a singsong or melodic reading of items, a rhythmic accenting of every third or fourth item etc.'.

This 'rhythmic memory' is not only auditory as an 'echoic memory' (Murray 1967) but articulatory too. Heim (1973) found in normally hearing subjects that the articulatory pronounceability plays an important part in this memory functioning, a part independent of meaningfulness. He did research with non-syllables (e.g. lpa), syllables (e.g. pla) and words (e.g. pal). There is apparently a kind of 'articulatory memory' for speech, related to the smoothness of its articulatory rhythm. This is open to deaf children too.

Rhythmic Speech and Memory for Non-verbal Items

Speech supports many memory functions which are non-verbal at first sight, for instance memory for colours, figures, pictures etc. We will memorize them, however, by speech encoding processes, as *'green-blue-red'* *'green-blue-red'* etc. Consequently speech may serve thinking by keeping a series of elements of a reasoning process together (Furth 1973). As has been said earlier speech is perhaps the most rhythmic and grouping of activities of men. Thus we may expect that speech is one of the most helpful tools for memory. Bartlett (1932, quot. Kurtz 1953) found that adult subjects who were 'verbalizers' in his memory experiments were at the same time the best 'memorizers'. Kurtz and Hovland (1953) found the same in children.

Thus we must make the most of *this* rhythmic functioning.

Long Term Memory and Short Term Memory

To introduce the problem, imagine a discussion on a topic or the reading of a book. We need a good STM, i.e. a memory for immediate recall, in order to have a good survey on sentences, so that we grasp them as one whole; otherwise we will have difficulties in understanding. But we need LTM too, i.e. a good memory of what was said or read 10 minutes ago, in order to have an overall understanding for the topic, the story of the book, the persons involved, the proceeding of the reasoning etc. – In language-acquisition LTM has a special function in learning the laws of linguistic behaviour, the categorizing of words, their positions in the series, the flexions and so on. There are persons, children or adults, who can immediately repeat a sentence very well, but have a bad LTM. These persons will lag behind more and more in many functions, not the least in language development.

Oral Information and Written Information. Memory Stores?

There seems to be a typical difference between *hearing* and *reading*, and their short term memory and long term memory. When information had been given to *hearing* adults in an oral auditory way, this auditory way had advantages over information gained by reading for the *im*mediate recall. After a week, however, there had been so much forgotten of the auditory information that there appeared to remain no difference between the two ways of giving information (King 1959): perhaps the two ways of information had had the same effect of 'internalizing' which had been stored in the long term 'memory-case'.

It has been concluded that there are 2 memory-cases or -*stores* in our mind (of course not conceived as anatomical data): a LTM-store and a STM-store, or better 'functions'. Mandler (1967, quot. Furth and Milgram 1973) terms them STM = 'primary memory' and LTM = 'organized memory'. This distinction seemingly has to do with the old distinction between perception and apperception. So other useful terms could, in my opinion, be: 'perceptual memory' and 'apperceptual memory'. We prefer the term 'function' instead of 'store'.

Tempo and Memory Processes

Peterson and Johnson (1971) found that the number of units of *speech* to be remembered in STM increases, when the tempo of the input is speeded up. (They suggest a 'buffer-theory' instead of a 'store-theory'.) Additionally Witelson and Rabinowitch (1971) found the tempo of speech increasing the clustering processes for that same STM. – A pilot-research showed us similar effects for the *graphic* form of words (van Uden 1974): tempo increases memory functions.

Conclusion for our Didactics

It can be concluded for our didactics, on the one hand that of course the written form of language is important and helpful to deaf children (as it is to hearing ones) and that we have to train the tempo and the span of STM in this respect, but on the other hand that this should never push aside the rhythmic oral form and its STM, because this last form has its advantages especially for the processes of immediate understanding and reproduction in *conversation*. Both ways of training should be integrated in order to support each other, for an ever better functioning in language.

Memory-span and Rhythm in Hearing People

It has been acknowledged in psychology for a long time (cf. Hofmarksrichter 1931, van Uden 1973) that the perceptual capacity of our senses, including the immediate responses to what has been perceived, i.e. including the STM-function, is limited to 5–6 units, provided the units are *uni*dimensional. Take for instance cards showing dots, numbering 3 through 11, all of the dots being the same size and colour and arranged in random order, and show them one for one tachistoscopically to human subjects. The vast majority of subjects will report correct numbers up to about 5–6 dots; they will make more and more errors in numbers higher than 6 dots, however. George Miller (1956) found in well-trained subjects a limited capacity of 5–9 units ('the magic number 7 ± 2'). – We said: provided that the units are unidimensional. As soon as we arrange the dots in a straight order, e.g. groups of 3 and 3 etc., more and more units can be responded to correctly, because *sub-units* have been formed. These same principles are valid for all modalities, for instance for hearing detached tones in contrast to tones in melodic or rhythmic groupings, for touching dots in relief detached from each other or grouped for the letters of the Braille-alphabet, etc.

There are, however, two differences between the modality of seeing and that of hearing.

(a) It seems to be more difficult to design uni-dimensional *units* in the auditory and motory (articulatory) than in the visual field. At least we group sounds and movements very quickly into rhythmic sub-units. Very many different sound patterns can easily be identified by multi-dimensionality, i.e. comprising differences in length, pitch, intensity etc. of sounds (cf. Pollack and Fick 1954). The same with articulatory patterns. This is the reason that the STM for speech comprises much more than 7 ± 2 words, i.e. by clustering sub-units of rhythmic 'chunks' (George Miller 1956; Neisser 1967 emphasizes this rhythmic *patterning* as being the cue for memory, not so much a new *code* for the sub-units: see Laughery and Spector 1972).

How we hearing memorize can be concluded from a finding by Broadbent (1958, quot. Hörmann 1967). He offered his subjects numbers by means of headphones, through the left headphone, e.g. 7-2-3, exactly simultaneously with this in the right headphone, 9–5–4. The numbers therefore sounded like: 79, 25, 34. The subjects had to tell immediately what they had heard. He never got: 7-9-2-5-3-4, however,

110

but chunks of one side: 7-2-3 and 9-5-4 and 7-2-3. Our immediate memory – it can be concluded – stores rhythmically arranged chunks, not just codes which are closest to each other (provided the successive series is not presented too slowly, Witelson and Rabinovitch 1971).

(b) There is an auditory *'echoic memory'* in normally hearing subjects, lasting about 8 seconds (it does seem to have about the same length in all normal people). If we present series of figures auditorily and disturb the subjects' attention immediately after perception, they can 'hear them back' ('echo') if the disturbing period is no longer than 8 seconds (Murray 1967).

Children of 3 years of age can reproduce sentences of about 6 syllables, at 13 years of age 18 syllables, at 19 years of age 21 syllables (cf. Baker and Leland 1959).

NB.1. There are some normally hearing children with a very low auditory STM for speech, a kind of developmental *dysphasia* (cf. Epstein 1964, Myklebust 1969, Eisenson 1972). These children can utter a sentence like this: 'May I . . . my turn after he he is reading . . . my turn cleaning the blackboard!'. The origin of such a dysgrammaticism is in my opinion simply the fact, that the child at the end of the sentence has forgotten how it has started. The same happens in adults.

NB.2. It should not be forgotten in these considerations that the *content* of the material, its meaningfulness, its logic, some foreknowledge etc. play an important part too, which is especially advantageous to highly intelligent people.

Rhythm and Memory in Deaf Children

Several studies (e.g. Brill 1953, Blair 1957, Hiskey 1966, Conrad 1965, 1970, 1973, Furth 1966, and others) have shown that deaf children are behind normally hearing children in at least some aspects of memory. We will especially discuss here their memory-span in connection with speech and language.

(a) It may be clear that deaf children have no *'echoic* auditory memory'. Ling (1975) found a very short one in severely hard of hearing children (about 3 seconds). What happens in their visual modality is unknown to this day (eidetic memory? cf. Hofmarksrichter 1931).

(b) What about *rhythm*? What about *coding*?

We will confront the problem of *coding* in memorizing functions. Conrad offered his normally hearing subjects detached letters in an only visual way: M, B, C, N, F, G, etc. He found that the mistakes made by his best 'memorizers' (in short term memory) were *confusions* of B with C, not with M or N, or of M with F, not with C of G, e.g. He concluded that his 'memorizers' were during the experiment silently translating the visual letters into auditory patterns, namely Bee Cee Gee eM eN eF and so on, referred to by him as 'acoustic codes' (to me 'auditory' would be a

111

better term, and 'auditory-articulatory' = 'aural-oral' still better; Conrad has been using the term 'articulatory' since 1970). This means: we try to memorize by auditory-articulatory encoding; these codes may be more successful for memory than the visual codes. – Before the age of 5 normally hearing children already show significant auditory-articulatory encoding confusions, and at the ages 9–10 the same quantity of confusions is found as in adults. 'We can now say that at least from about 13 years, hearing subjects predominantly use an acoustic code in short term storage, of verbal material' (Conrad 1964).

As a matter of course Conrad tested his theory on deaf children (1965) because – as he thought – these children cannot encode into auditory patterns, and therefore they will be behind in these memory tasks. He found that his deaf subjects indeed were far behind his hearing subjects.

NB. Locke (1973), applying the same technique as Conrad, found typical fingerspelling confusions in manual deaf children, and Hoeman (1974 b) confusions of signs, for instance of 'lion' and 'sheep' because of the similarity of these signs. Both of them found their deaf subjects behind normally hearing ones.

Also Snijders–Oomen (1958), Hiskey (1966) and Blair (1957) had found that deaf children in such items, where vocalization aids immediate recall, were behind with regard to hearing children, for example in memorizing series of digits, series of pictures, of colours, and so on. I will quote here a finding by Puyenbroek (1966): in his experiments concerning mental calculation of written sums by deaf children, he found that for example in: –

$$A$$
$$57 + 23 + 12 = \ldots?$$

$$B$$
$$572 + 312 = \ldots?$$

A was more difficult than B.

The reason seems to be that the first sum involves more memorizing activities than the second, i.e. three chunks of digits against two.

According to the researches mentioned above deaf children were *not* behind with regard to hearing children in memorizing those materials where a vocalization is very difficult like a series of beads, of paper-foldings, of tapping blocks in a special order (Knox 'Cube Test') and similar functions (cf. also Furth 1966 and his cooperators such as Olsson 1966, Youniss 1971 and others).

But the deaf children tested by Conrad in 1965 were signing children with only a small amount of speech. He repeated his research in 1970 on deaf boys who had better speech (12–17 years of age). He now discovered two groups: boys who used an articulatory coding, similar to that of hearing subjects, and boys who did not. Thomassen (1970) repeated this research in our Institute at St. Michielsgestel. He prepared two different types of series of letters: series according to the

112

model MNF (= eM eN eF) etc. or B C G (= Bee Cee Gee) etc., called homogeneous series, and series according to the model MBNFC (= eM Bee eN eF Cee) etc., called heterogeneous series. I myself had selected the sample of 26 prelingually deaf children, with a normal ability of speech, i.e. without dyspraxic disturbances. *But* these children could not spell according to the letter-names mentioned above: they had never learned to do so. Therefore I took a spelling-experiment, and it appeared that only a few children could spell the letter-names fluently; even these children made many mistakes and could not attain a high tempo. They would call for example F Fee or eF or even Fah, and many letters were pronounced by them without any vowel, for instance B as b (shwah). The result was, as might be expected, that there existed no difference between the memory for homogeneous series and heterogeneous series in these deaf children. Their memory-function, however, did not differ significantly from the memory-function of hearing children for the homogeneous series. These hearing children, who could spell very well, did better in the heterogeneous series than in the homogeneous ones. My interpretation of this phenomenon is: these heterogeneous series were more rhythmic. On the other hand the deaf children showed significantly many typical confusions, which indicated that they had coded orally in this memory-function: they confused D with T, B with P, F with V, S with Z with C. – It may be concluded that deaf children, apart from those with dyspraxic difficulties, *can* perform in this memory investigation as well as hearing children.

NB. Conrad (1970, 1972 b) speaks of '*stuff of thinking*', as if he can conclude from these results whether specific deaf children think orally or not in daily life. This seems to be an inadmissible generalization. Further: it is not sufficient for these investigations that the children *know* the 'names' of the letters, but they should know them *fluently*. He has never checked this out. Further Conrad is not sufficiently aware of the problem of dyspraxia in speech, nor of the consequences of some didactical methods for teaching speech. In 1973 he published a research concerning a connection between reading and that 'stuff of thinking': deaf children who were not 'articulators' were requested to read a paragraph aloud and *immediately* after that to answer some questions. The results were significantly lower than those of the 'articulators'. This does not prove anything, because there are normally hearing and speaking, well reading people with the same difficulties (Edfeldt 1960).

Experience

From *experience* we know (van Uden 1955–1957) that deaf children have difficulty in memorizing verbal material, not only in spoken but in written words and sentences too. Often it seems that they have forgotten at the end of a sentence how

113

this sentence started. I'll give here 6 examples, which every teacher of the deaf can multiply from his own daily experiences.

A deaf child wrote: 'I *am* not hit Mary, but Mary *has* hit me' (adapted from Dutch: Ik ben Marietje niet geslagen, maar Marietje heeft mij geslagen). This child knew very well the active voice. Why did he not correct that first *am*? Why not feedback to that first *am* in order to change it? – How often do deaf children have difficulty in remembering complex expressions! We all know how there are frequent mistakes of contamination, i.e. using two or more complex expressions higgledy-piggledy, e.g. *she took care after the baby* (= a contamination of *take care of* and *look after*), *you are a kill-sport* (contamination of *spoil-sport* and *kill-joy*). – Often they do not follow somewhat longer reasonings, simply because they apparently just forgot the beginning: if you ask how it began, they give wrong answers. – Many teachers adjust themselves to this shortness of memory. For example according to a textbook on First Aid a teacher asked his pupils: 'If one finds a man lying in a dry ditch with his face to the ground, what is the first thing one has to do?' The teacher spontaneously broke up this sentence in more or less the following way: 'You, Peter, are going for a spin. Do you understand? . . . You are cycling along a track. You pass a dry ditch. There, suddenly, you see a man in the ditch. You cannot see his face, because his face is to the ground. Do you understand? . . . What would you do? What should you do first?' This teacher was not only making the abstract task more concrete ('You, Peter!') to show clearly the situation, but also he is, unconsciously perhaps, helping the memory-defect of his pupils, by giving them short clear cut sentences. He is also following an exact chronological order. – I think that difficulties in planning a series of activities which we find so often in deaf children are partly due to shortness of memory. Also the difficulties in reorganizing a story which has not been told in a chronologically correct order (we already mentioned in the example above that the teacher was changing the order of phrases in such a way that the correct chronological order was intact) may be partly due to this defect of memory.

Experiments

From *experiments* we know the following:
Brill (1953) found that hearing children could recall longer *written* sentences than deaf children: the latter's maximum was about 5 words. These deaf children learned fingerspelling and speech, and used signs. – Kates (1972) compared matched groups of purely orally educated, fingerspelling and signing deaf adolescents of 12–16 years of age for the memory of sentences of 7 words, which words have been presented successively in a quick tempo. The children had to write them down. From his findings can be derived an average of 6 words for the purely oral group, and of 5 words for both the fingerspelling and the signing

114

group. Normally hearing children of the same age achieved an average of 7, and those of 8–10 years of age an average of 5 words.

The memory for sentences presented by *fingerspelling*, i.e. successively which is more difficult than simultaneously by reading, is not higher than 3–4 words in prelingually deaf children, educated that way. See page 208.

The memory for series of *signs* seems to be very short too. We did research in this respect with elderly deaf adults, educated in the sign-language of van Beek and using that language (although in its 'low version' cf. Stokoe 1972) all day when conversing among themselves: they lived in an asylum for the deaf. All of them were of normal intelligence. We made a video-recording of a conversation which took place between 5 of them. A first result was that indeed, when these people are conversing among themselves, they leave out almost all flexions, they follow a visual and/or emotional order of signs, i.e. they use only 'low sign-language'. After some time I asked them back, one by one, to my laboratory in order to show them the video-recording, initially the whole tape. Then I showed them the first sentence, stopped the video-recorder and asked them to repeat what they had seen, and so on throughout the sentences of this simple spontaneous conversation. The results were as follows:

Series of signs 1 – 11	Mean percentage of errors	Mean percentage of quite correct reproductions
4 sentences of 1 sign:	4.7%	97.66%
8 sentences of 2 signs:	19.8%	83.16%
12 sentences of 3 signs:	28.2%	73.33%
8 sentences of 4 signs:	41.7%	68.66%
8 sentences of 5 signs:	38.3%	64.33%
3 sentences of 6 signs:	63.1%	55.66%
5 sentences of 7 signs:	76.8%	10.0 %
6 sentences of 8 signs:	70.9%	2.66%
5 sentences of 9 signs:	79.2%	0 %
2 sentences of 10 signs:	71.8%	0 %
1 sentence of 11 signs:	69.9%	0 %

We see that the memory-span for series of signs is about the same as has been found by Brill and Kates for series of written words in manual deaf children. The finding seems to be in agreement with the psychological thesis that our immediate memory holds at about 5–6 unidimensional units. This finding is in agreement with that of Bellugi and Siple (1971) and that of Hoemann (1972) too: very intelligent adult deaf who had been trained in interpreting oral into sign-language and were expert 'signers', could not reproduce strings of more than 5 signs quite correctly. – We would remind you of the research of Tervoort and Verberk (1967,

1974) that deaf children could follow the Key of Fitzgerald, if the series of signs (words) were no longer than 5.

I interpret these findings as showing the consequences of insufficient *rhythm* in series of written words, of fingerspelled words and of signs.

Additionally the *tempo* of signing is limited to about 2 signs per second (Bellugi and Fisher 1972) of fingerspelled letters to about 5 letters per second.

In a pilot experiment (van Uden 1951, 1956) I found that sentences of 5–9 words offered to non-multiply-handicapped deaf children *orally* in a very rhythmic way in a tempo of 3 ± 1 syllables per second, were better memorized both for immediate reproduction and for long term memory than sentences offered to them and copied by them in written form. These were rhythmically well-trained children (music, dancing, use of wind instruments). I mention here the positive correlation found by Heider (1940) between ability to dance and the ability to imitate sentences after lipreading.

We have composed a *test* to determine the *memory for speech* of deaf children: 10 simple sentences of 18 syllables each, composed from words known to deaf 8 year old children of our Institute. Besides the Wechsler Intelligence Scale for Children (WISC) is applied routinely to our children, also the subtest: memory-span for spoken digits. The results are as given on page 117 (van Uden 1969).

According to the Detroit Tests of Learning Aptitude for normally hearing children (Baker and Leland 1958) the average number of syllables correctly imitated at 13 years of age is 18. The average raw score for the Digit Span (WISC) at this age is 10.

We recorded spontaneous conversations between pairs of prelingually deaf children on tape (1966). There was a group of 10–11 year olds and one of 17–19 year olds. What we found according to the *position of the emphasized word* within the sentences, is given below: –

the emphasized word took the first position in 23% of the cases;

the emphasized word took a middle position in 68% of the cases;

the emphasized word took a final position within the sentences in 9% of the cases.

There were no significant differences between the younger and the older groups.

Summarizing: I do not think that it is only a so-called acoustic coding that helps hearing people in verbal memory, but the motor rhythm of speech too, i.e. a way which is also open to the deaf. Whatever is true, I always advised and impressed upon our teachers to make the most of the oral rhythmic training, for a better memorizing, for a fuller mastering of language, for a better thinking in language. To me it is the only possible way. In my opinion an intense training in rhythm of the whole body, of breathing and speech, integrated with sound perception (auditory remnants and vibration feeling), is a must in schools for the deaf.

116

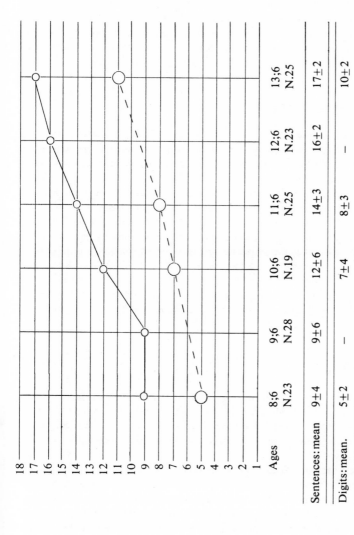

Ages	8;6 N.23	9;6 N.28	10;6 N.19	11;6 N.25	12;6 N.23	13;6 N.25
Sentences: mean	9±4	9±6	12±6	14±3	16±2	17±2
Digits: mean.	5±2	–	7±4	8±3	–	10±2
Stand. score	3±4	–	6±9	7±5	–	10±3

o--o-- = Number of syllables correctly imitated.
O–O-- = Number of digits correctly imitated (sum of the maximum series forward and the maximum series backwards).

This point is wholly connected with the foregoing points, the intentions of sentences, the phrase structure, the combinabilities of words, rhythm as a language form and – the last not being the least – rhythm and memory.

We will meet here the process of memorizing in the Test-Operate-Test-Exit (TOTE)-activity, theorized by Miller, Galanter and Pribam (1960). We look for the mechanism which takes place in the 'black box' of our mind, as far as we can conclude this from findings in verbal behaviour.

Planning and Storage Processes in Speech

We have to explain now how we actively store in producing a sentence. This will clear up something about the linguistic difficulties of deaf children. The conclusion here too will be that they need a thorough rhythmic education in order to attack the enemy on his own field.

We have already seen that we do not produce a sentence according to a Markovian model, but that phrase structures and 'feedbacks' and 'feed-aheads' play important parts. If we group the words in our minds, interrupt groups by making them pinch other words or groups, arrange the whole sentence by intonation and accentuation, or lengthen the pauses according to the information-content of both preceding and succeeding words, then there must be a kind of planning in our mind which is not Markovian, a planning which includes a lot of storage processes. We have explained how these virtual and actualized plans are to be found within the words, as they are stored in our minds according to matrices of stochastic combinabilities.

'Eupraxic Impulses'

Hörmann (1967) gives this example of a failed 'praxia' impulse (failures often show something about faultless behaviour): you are typewriting, you want to type *written* and you type *wriiten*. What happened? You had a rather diffused impulse, a 'praxia', a plan: 'Double!' but by mistake you doubled the wrong letter. (This is a kind of 'dyspraxia').

A more direct example: What do the interpreters of the UNO do? They hear a word in its context, and immediately it is poured out into the mental 'distributor' of the other language, rewired according to its proper contacts and 'combinabilities', and spoken into the microphone: the process flows from a diffuse lexical level to the more precise grammatical level and then to that of the phonetic (cf. Cohen 1965).

So when we produce a sentence, we start with a diffused impulse: we want to say something. Some words give concrete form to that impulse (lexical level) together with their 'action-radius' of 'combinabilities' (rhythmic and phonemic morphemes: grammatical level), from which *one* is selected in order to flow over into the phonetic rhythmic utterance.

From many association-experiments we may conclude that the first word emerging in mind will be a content-word (e.g. Made van Bekkum 1966 found 97% to be content-words). It may, however, also be a function-word which for example has emphasis. But no matter which word it is, it is not at all obliged to be the first word of the sentence to be uttered.

An Example

We will give this example (cf. the 'generative semantics' of McCawley 1968 and of Abraham and Binnick 1969, quoted by Dik and Kooy 1970):
Situation: John and I are walking in an avenue of oaks. Acorns are falling down. I hear this. Then:
I myself:
1. The first word emerging in my mind may be: ACORN-S. It is immediately put in its plural form.
2. FALL(ING) immediately groups with DOWN. The morpheme -ING is retained.
3. The whole phrase ACORNS FALL(ING) DOWN is stored for a moment.
4. HEAR had come up, which immediately groups itself to:
5. I HEAR ...
6. Then ACORNS FALLING DOWN is taken from its store with the morpheme -ING filled in, influenced by the 'feed-ahead' of I HEAR, and the sentence is uttered:

I HEAR ACORNS FALLING DOWN.
Schematized in this way:

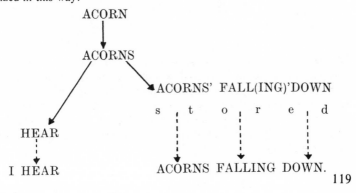

119

Or schematized according to the model of Johnson (1965)

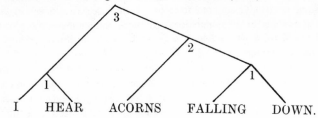

John:
1. YES as his first word . . . Then or together:
2. AUTUMN emerges in his mind.
3. This is immediately grouped as:
    YES. IT IS AUTUMN.
Schematized in this way:

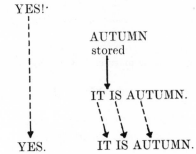

Or schematized according to the Johnson's model:

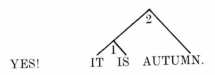

We see that there is continuous structuring, storing, checking, combining, mostly operating unconsciously. This needs a continuous activity of short term memory. If this is defective by lack of rhythmic phrasic training, it will give difficulties in language, in thinking too. If deaf children have not been educated in this way, we can expect a kind of unstructured '*film-thinking*', i.e. the whole story the child is telling, is running off picture after picture, in small units, almost *avoiding any burdening of their STM.*

120

Flexibility and Selective Activity

We can schematize this (ACORNS FALLING DOWN) in another way, in order to illustrate the selective activity in speech, i.e. the need for flexibility. (We warn against an associative concept of the grouping of words.) We symbolize the words with their virtual functions, i.e. with their 'combinabilities', as wheels with cogs. ACORN: noun, singular form, plural form. The selected form is indicated by a flashing light:

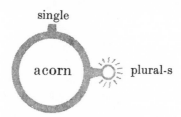

FALL: verb, intransitive, forms: falls, falling, fell, fallen; 13 meanings. – noun, singular form, plural form, 26 meanings. The selected meaning (including form) is indicated by a flashing light.

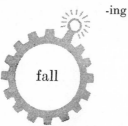

DOWN: adverb, 8 meanings, passing into adjective in predicative use, –preposition, 4 meanings, – verb, transitive, 1 meaning. The selected meaning is indicated by a flashing light:

Influenced by the one intention of an assertion, with a general diffused intuition of

121

the whole, this whole *differentiates* into one rhythm of a phrase in which the words appear: the wheels rush together with their selected cogs:

We see there is a big difference in the richness of combinabilities of words: acorn is rather poor, fall is very rich.

This richness differs of course from person to person: in a child the 'action radius' will be smaller than in an adult, in an illiterate smaller than in a literate, in a professor of physics smaller than in a professor of literature. . . . There must be, however, somewhere a minimum number of combinabilities in a mind, under which minimum the linguistic feeling of a person will be insufficient for his daily life and he will make too many mistakes. This happens in small hearing children, in hearing impaired children, in mentally defective persons etc.

In subjects having normal language, this richness must be very flexible, so that the right combinability is *im*mediately actualized when needed. This immediate readiness of the words with their meanings, called by me the 'transparency' of language, is one of the most striking features of a mother-tongue. When we start to speak a foreign language which we have not mastered sufficiently, there suddenly appears a loss of flexibility: the words are not immediately ready in their right functions, they gear into each other very stiffly; vocabulary, expressions, and structures are limited; most words appear to be screwed down into too few combinabilities. It is clear that this will give many difficulties in receiving and expressing language.

This screwing down of words into too few combinabilities (contentively and functionally) is one of the consequences of programmed and limited presentation of language forms as the constructive method does. We will come back to this point later.

Groht (1958) rightly says: 'The English language is so full of exceptions, that no rule seems to be absolute. . . . No teacher . . . can ever give her pupils all the forms of all the principles they must know.' This happens in all languages. The *only* possible way is to bring the children *to good reading* of normal language on the basis of oral conversation, as we will explain later.

Detecting the System

By 'language' is meant here all that belongs to the system of the language: its semantic structure, its rhythm, i.e. grouping and pincer-functions, its flexions.
The important fact has been found that the normal hearing child finds the system of language mainly by himself (Lewis 1951, 1968; McCarthy 1954; Kaper 1959; Brown and Bellugi 1964; Menyuk 1969; McNeill 1970; Bellugi 1973). Some investigators, such as Chomsky and McNeill, are so astonished by that quick finding of the system of language by a small child of about 3 years of age that they postulate an innate functioning. We think we can best characterize the way children do this with the term: reflecting.

'Reflecting'

Literally speaking 'to reflect' means 'throw back' as the light in a reflector, the image in a mirror. This can be taken biochemically too, e.g. a potato reflects in its taste the ground in which it has grown. – A second meaning is: to look back mentally onto one's own experiences, impressions, images, feelings, thoughts, i.e. becoming conscious of them, organizing and to some extent controlling them. In this way by reflecting we can control our behaviour. – The hearing child reflects on language in both significations, which are ordered chronologically too.

a. A 'Trial-and-Check' Way

a. First, mainly by conversation, the child reflects on language by a trial-and-check way, cybernetically, by storing, comparing, scanning, identifying (TOTE). This process should not be imagined as a conscious reflection, but mainly as an *unconscious* one, even as a bio-physiological process, rather analogic to the reactions of a cybernetic machine finding its way. Think of Wiener's interesting story (1964), where a cybernetically computerized 'chess-player' learns better and better and finally beats its own human builder. ... So what the child actually 'detects' has not so much to do with rules or their applications, nor with 'basic sentence structures' and their 'transformations', but more with laws of behaviour working with the combinabilities of words, before and after them, in a kind of developing 'chemistry'. This language behaviour becomes almost automatic; without thinking on the forms of the codes used, the child is immediately aware of their *content*; language becomes quite transparent. This amount of automation is the measure of the amount of its unconscious reflection on language.

123

b. Finding Rules and their Applications

The child, as a human being, reflects on language in a more directly human way as well, i.e. intellectually by finding rules and their applications. For example a girl of 3;7 years of age asked her father: 'Why do you say birch? It is a tree!' Father: 'Yes, but there are many trees! Birches, and oaks ... That one is an oak ...'. This was a conscious reflection of that child on the meanings of words. – Another example of a girl of 5;4 years of age: 'The railroads'. Father: 'We say railroad, not railroads'. Girl: 'But there are two!' Father: 'Yes, yet they are together only one railroad for one train' ... The language development of a hearing child does not stop at the commencement of the primary school: even learning to read and write enhances this development marvellously. We know from historical linguistics, how the language of analphabets not only changes much more than the language of cultivated people, changes from village to village, from period to period, but also how it in some way remains less structured and primitive (Ellis 1966). The alphabetization of the language in a child makes its language control more and more conscious; it learns a lot of terms; his vocabulary expands immensely; many multiple meanings develop, figurative meanings, metaphors etc.; the analysis of sentences goes deeper and deeper; finally the child comes to the 'belleslettres' stage in its adolescent years.

Difference Between Hearing and Deaf Children

Now we see an almost essential difference between the development of reflection in normal hearing children and that in deaf children. In the latter children, the reflection must be mainly conscious also initially, see also chapter I and chapter V. Yet some unconscious automation comes up, first of all shown by the fact that the orally well-educated deaf child speaks spontaneously, i.e. without any translation from signs or finger-spelling or writing, e.g. a deaf boy of 5 years of age said: 'Mama again milk!', – secondly by the speed and smoothness of their oral conversations (see the examples in the appendices), – thirdly by spontaneous quick rhythmic grouping of words, not yet learned, e.g. an 8 year old boy: 'Perhaps Peter upon the swimming-pool'. Mainly the shortness of the reaction time and the tempo of speech show the automation of language. Besides what has been learned by conscious reflections will become automatized after a time too. This may be compared with the way in which we learn for instance to drive a car: in the beginning very consciously but automatized more and more; a lot of feedback operates cybernetically here. In the same way the automation of language increases more and more by the cybernetical feedback-processes of the *conversations*. ...

Examples of Reflections

a. For the *semantic* structure of language:
'We have eaten milk' said a *hearing* child of 3 years of age, and the mother immediately: 'No, you have *drunk* milk!'
Only relatively seldom, however, does a mother teach her child the meanings of words. The child finds them mainly by himself. This may happen by a process of generalization: I react to this thing here as 'a cupboard', then that one there must be 'a cupboard' too; – or by specialization: the bottle isn't milk but the material in it; – or by individuation: Not every male is 'Daddy' to me, only my father. All this not only applies to names of *objects* but also to relations, processes, feelings, complicated expressions, fine nuances of words and idioms, etc. etc. – It is the conversational situation which stimulates this development.
It also goes for *deaf* children that mainly the conversation should clarify the meanings of words, keeping them as much as possible within their normal settings of phrases and sentences and situations. Very important here is the '*seizing method*': if mother and teacher know the child well, they understand what it is wanting to say, however clumsy its utterances may be. If they give then the child the right expression of its own feelings, we can be sure that it will grasp the meaning, may be in the beginning somewhat roughly, but afterwards specifically too. Pictures are always dangerous in this respect, because it is never quite clear to us what the child is thinking. The process of *reading* (ideo-visual and receptive reading) is indispensably important too. We will explain this further in chapters IV and V.
b. For the *formal* structure:
An example. When a *hearing* child of about 3 years of age says: 'Picture found Peter' or 'Peter found picture', but not 'Picture Peter found' or 'Peter picture found', he shows that he has grasped the positional category of a verb, i.e. that a verb takes the second position in a series of words. Likewise if he says: 'buyed' instead of bought, or 'childs' instead of children (an analogy with kids, boys and girls), he shows that he has grasped something of the morphology of words. He did that himself, because no one has ever said to him 'buyed' or 'childs' or 'picture found Peter'. – We know that the first laws of language found by the child are those of the positions of the 'contentors'; the laws for the 'functors' and for the flexions of the words appear to be more difficult and require one or two years of more 'study' by the child.
Deaf children too detect some formal structures spontaneously. So a 9 year old said: 'Yesterday we laid (meant: laughed) a lot'. This was a moment for the teacher to explain the difference between the 'regular' and 'irregular' verbs. Another child formed: 'yestestday' meaning 'the day before yesterday'. This was an occasion to teach that not all -er syllables are comparative forms. See Russell et al. (1976) and Ivimey (1976).

125

15. WHEN CAN WE SAY THAT WORDS ARE TRULY 'ENGLISH WORDS' IN THE MINDS OF THE CHILDREN?

The response to this is the following: When they use them in the same functioning system as in English, i.e. in the same oppositions of combinabilities. For example when the *hearing* child in Braine's research (1963) says:

- want baby
- want high
- want more etc.

there are some combinations, which could be termed English, and others which are not. So we cannot say that this *want* functions as an English word, yet the word is apparently used by the child in a systematic way. It is a loanword: the child borrows it from the English system of its environment and uses it in its own system. The child itself selects its words from the environment, and slowly it adjusts the primitive combinabilities, which are not English, to the combinabilities of the English system. As soon as the child uses *want* in its English combinabilities, then this *want* has become a true English word.

The same happens in *deaf* children (Tervoort 1953). But here the teacher can use artificial means, e.g. the Fitzgerald Key System. So he can teach the children to use a word such as *want* always in the second position in a sentence. Can we say then that this word functions as a real English word? Not at all! The children learnt a trick, and by means of that trick they use the word, or even only the sign, in the second position, in the sentences. But the word itself does not function in the mind of the child as a real English word, *unless* the child is able to use it mainly with the same rhythmic and phonemic morphemes of English. It is for this reason that I do not understand how a series of even 4 or 5 signs according to the Key could be called 'grammatically correct English' (Tervoort and Verberk 1967, 1974).

16. SOME EXAMPLES ILLUSTRATING TYPICAL EFFECTS OF THE CONSTRUCTIVE WAY OF TEACHING LANGUAGE TO DEAF CHILDREN

Given here are a few examples taken from my collection which I gathered when visiting classes and schools and in my own lessons to deaf children, of what can happen in the verbal behaviour of deaf children as consequences of the constructive methods.

1. A teacher of a boarding school told me how she had been converted from the constructive method. It happened on a free afternoon, when one of her children was visited by its parents. The child came into the parlour and 'unpacked' what it had learnt:

- The table has four legs.
- The chair has four legs.
- The cupboard has no legs.

The parents stood rooted to the ground. What was going on with their child? Was it going to be schizophrenic? ... This teacher went over to a free conversational method.

2. The difference between children, over-trained in verbalizing what they see in the classroom, on pictures etc., and children trained in a conversational free way, is striking. When you show the first children a picture, they are inclined to verbalize what they see, i.e. they dwell on the picture itself. The second ones, however, are more inclined to ask questions: they also think about those things and persons that are not in the picture but connected with it: for them the picture is only one moment in the stream of events (Sr. Theresia van Driel 1964). To me, when a teacher uses pictures, he should ask the children especially e.g.: 'What is mother *saying*?' 'What would the farmer be *thinking*?' etc.

3. Because the 'baked sentences' are baked out very often by using detached elements, in an associating and not in a differentiating way, we can expect the following: a boy, asked to draw on the blackboard this sentence *The boy is going over the soccerfield*, drew this (cf. Jackson 1967):

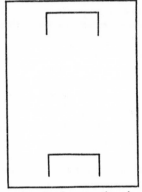

4. Because so much attention is given to the phonemic morphemes, you can expect this:

- *gates* is a verb.
- *garden* is plural.
- *joist* is a superlative, etc. (adapted from Dutch).

5. Trials of baked conjunctive sentences:
The sun is shining because it is nice weather.
We came into the classroom before we went to our places.

Although it is bad weather in the Netherlands, it is nice weather in other countries.

In a composition: first sentence '*Henri who does not like fish went away*' . . . last sentence: '*Henri who does not like fish came back from the errand*'.

This is not free thinking! Language becomes a stiff armour instead of being a light tool. I always think of David, who liked his light duds better than the stiff armour of Saul, and so . . . gained the victory!

17. SUMMARY OF THE FALSE ASSUMPTIONS OF THE CONSTRUCTIONALISTS

We can summarize the false assumptions of the constructive methods as follows (apart from the big danger that these children will converse among themselves in signs more frequently):

1. Logic in the foreground, emotion only in the background.

2. Neglectfulness of the unlimited conversation, e.g. postponing questions after assertions; neglecting the intentionality of language; forgetting this basic principle: Language is first of all a tool of conversation, before it can be a tool of thinking.

3. Making the receptive and the expressive language almost coincide, instead of making the child select his own expressive language (supported by the teacher) from a fund of receptive language.

4. Detaching the words from the sentences in long paradigmatic lists: verb charts, adjective charts, adverb-charts, preposition charts etc. An associating instead of a differentiating procedure. Postponing the global, intuitive grasping of relations in language.

5. Screwing home programmed concepts, words, expressions, sentences, instead of keeping safe, before all, the flexibility of understanding.

6. Neglecting the rhythmic morphemes.

7. Too much writing, not making the most of the oral way.

8. Postponing and for almost all children (except very intelligent ones) omitting the reading of normal books. The following judgment is full of mistakes (M. Miller 1967): '. . . that good reading habit cannot be developed if the pupil be subjected to language above his comprehension'.

III
'The Meaning of Meaning'

(Ogden-Richards 1923)

1. MEANING AS SET IN CONVERSATION

The important point of what meaning is, how it grows in the minds etc. should be studied in the linguistic behaviour in its full form. This full form is: *the conversation in the mother-tongue.* All other forms of language (written forms, audible forms, speeches, conversation in foreign languages, study of foreign languages) are only derivatives of the original behaviour. This must be kept in mind continuously.

2. SIGNIFICANT AND SIGNIFIED

We will introduce the problem with this example. In a certain preschool I found that the teacher had labelled the cupboard in the classroom with a big card:

This was right. But I asked her: 'What is the symbol and what is the meaning?' She said: 'The meaning is that thing of course'. And that was wrong. She had been deceived by the judgment that nouns are names of things or persons. The word 'name' is already misleading because we use it connotatively as a 'personal name' or a name of a very concrete object, such as a city, an inn etc. We cannot refer words directly to the reality itself, however.

It was De Saussure (1916) who distinguished 'signifiant' and 'signifié' (significant and signified). 'Signified' is not the reality itself, but something in our mind. So the 'signified' of 'cupboard' is not that thing there, nor all the cupboards together (as small children and mentally defectives label, Werner 1948), but something abstract which we have formed in our minds by learning the language. The linguistic 'sign' is the unity of the significant and the signified, which as a unity refers to the reality which is not abstract. We must distinguish three aspects in this behaviour:

- something audible or visible which we use as a code (the significant);
- the idea or 'concept' in its broadest sense (the directly signified, wholly integrated with the significant);
- and the reality, the indirectly signified.

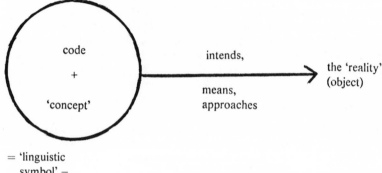

Some linguists reserve the term 'word' for the significant only (e.g. Ullmann 1962). In my opinion it is not consistent. The 'signs' which we use in language are the words. Words have a perceptible (audible, visible) side, and an imperceptible side (cf. Reichling 1935, 1973). These two are integrated. They grow together in a symbiotic way. By conversation, by listening and speaking, by reading and writing, the 'concepts' are formed within the codes used. To me, language is a system of codes and of concepts as well. 'It is trying to decipher the semantics of utterances detached from their behavioural context that students of meaning have gone astray. . . . We might better ask what this individual means (or intends) when he says thus and so' (Krech 1962).

3. TRANSPARENCY

The first point we will discuss is – what I would like to call – the *transparency* of

130

language. This means that we, while conversing in our mother-tongue, do not think of the forms of our language at all, not even of the perceptible side of words, but immediately, through the words, push towards the contents. If we look through our window at a child playing on the lawn in front our house, we don't see the window itself, we see the child. The window is quite transparent. In the same way the words we use in our mother-tongue are transparent. Only when there appear some difficulties in understanding, or in forming a word, we change our attention to the perceptible side of the word itself.

To give another example for this important fact: a driver who is quite accustomed to his car and the roads, is able to think of thousands of things while driving, and at the same time to follow unconsciously the signals along the road. When there is a red light, he will stop immediately. These signals have become transparent for his behaviour.

In the same way we immediately react to the content of what is said to us, and not to the forms themselves. If we are asked unexpectedly and after about 8 seconds (see page 111), to repeat precisely what has been said to us, this will give us much difficulty although we know very well *what* the other has said.

The only way to train *deaf* children up to this transparency is in conversation from the very beginning.

If we want to teach deaf children the *oral* language as their mother-tongue, this conversation must be oral conversation. In this way, oral language will become transparent in their minds.

In the Beginning Too Strong an Identification

It is well known how in the young *hearing* child the words are wholly identified with its 'realities', so that the word is not yet actually an arbitrary 'sign', but an aspect of the meaning or content itself, a 'quality' of the object (Werner 1948); it is still more 'signalistic' than 'symbolic'.

An example from Piaget (1923). He asked a child of 5 years: 'Would it be possible to call this (a picture of a cat) a cow and this (a picture of a cow) a cat?'
Child: 'Yes, of course!'
Piaget: 'Well this is a cat, and that a cow. Has the cow horns?'
Child: 'Yes!'
Piaget: 'But we called this (a cat) cow!'
Child: 'Ooo?' . . . thinking.
Piaget: 'Has the cow horns?'
Child: 'Yes, very small ones!'

In its further development the child will abandon this too strong identification (at least in our Western culture), but the transparency remains. This process develops again by means of conversation, flexible conversation. This flexibility makes the

131

child detect *homonymous* words and forms, and through this their arbitrariness. Notwithstanding this, conversation keeps the language transparent.

The *deaf* child has to be taught this arbitrariness more directly, and as soon as possible. – One of the difficulties against sign-language is that it is too 'signalistic', identifying code and concept too strongly. This hampers flexible thinking.

4. LIVING FULLNESS

The second point in the mother-tongue is its fullness of *connotations*. Osgood (1957) measures this connotative meaning by his 'semantic differential'. Here lie the deep, mostly unconscious roots of language which are the basis of figurative meaning, of poetry and metaphor (Merleau-Ponty, quot. Kwant 1961; Koen 1965; Ricoeur 1973). Language is something like an ice-berg: only the top can be conscious, the main part is unconscious, but therefore not unimportant!

In order to apply this principle in language development, we must make the children fully live the situation through, and give them the language in this full living: i.e. by exchange of ideas and feelings from person to person, i.e. by conversation. The language therefore must be full of normal exclamations, and personal attitudes, not only or mainly of statements. The language of feelings and attitudes has been called 'orectic language' by Lewis (1968), who found deaf children far behind normally hearing children in these types of words in contrast to words with visual contents. – Kates (1965) found deaf children behind in the fullness of conceiving 'social words'.

Further, we need dancing and music together with language. We need plastic arts hand in hand with language.

5. ARBITRARINESS OF MEANING

We spoke about the arbitrariness of the codes in the spoken languages. The third point now is that the *content* of by far the majority of words and morphemes is arbitrary too. Cf. Whorf (1956), Wittgenstein quot. Hubbeling (1965), Ricoeur (1973).

Not only does each culture (including language) *select* its own contents from

132

nature, but the lines drawn between these contents are also usually vague and arbitrary. It is well known that the Eskimos for example have many more words for types of snow than we have (Lenneberg 1953). The Dutch language has many words for types of rain, whereas in some countries of Africa 'rain' means just 'raining cats and dogs'. – Further, the names for colours are not the same in differing cultures, which leads to dissimilar boundaries in the colour-continuum (Lenneberg and Roberts 1956). And so on.

Besides, the contents themselves of many words are just *cultural*. Words as 'cigarette' and 'ashtray' would not have been understood by a mediaeval man, and the meaning of 'feudal' has changed a lot. Here too the boundaries are in the main very arbitrary:

What is the difference between cupboard, case, cabinet, closet etc.?

What is the difference between chair, fauteuil, seat, stool etc.?.

Starting Language Acquisition from 'The Evidence of Things?

All this has to do with our way of thinking, with the world of meanings in our daily life. There is a continuous *interaction* between language and world and vice versa. In general we must say: 'Namable objects will stand out as figures, whereas less namable objects will have background quality' (Krech 1962), and the inverse: objects which stand out as figures will get names sooner than other objects (Sherif 1949). 'Objects' should be taken here in a very broad sense.

The differences of languages and worlds of thinking are felt very strongly in *translation-work*. Each translation presents many difficulties (Weijnen 1947), such as from English into Dutch and vice versa, but even more so from Hebrew or Ishwahili into Western languages and vice versa. How difficult is it to translate deaf children's utterances in 'low version sign language' exactly into spoken language! It is not just 'language' but a world of thinking, which has to be translated. – There are of course so-called 'universals of language' (Greenberg 1963 a.o.) and 'universals of thinking' as well (e.g. Strasser 1962), but these are mixed with so much arbitrariness in all languages that it is impossible indeed to start language-acquisition from the 'evidence of things' (which is often only a socially accepted evidence), from the logic or from the philosophy. We saw this in our criticism on the constructive method.

Concepts?

I heard a preschool teacher of deaf children say: 'My children already have so and so many *concepts*'. The concept of 'concepts' is very difficult here! The contents of language are not only 'concepts', but intentions, images, wants, problems,

133

questions, appeals, needs, feelings, coherences, contrasts, also deixes (Reichling 1935) etc. (cf. Lewis 1963).

Wittgenstein exaggerates of course where he says: 'Don't ask for the meaning, ask for *the use*', but there is some truth in this advice. We learn the meanings mainly just by using them. As St. Augustine said on the concept of time, we must say concerning most of our concepts: 'As long as you don't ask me what it is, I know it!'

Polarity of Meaning

In my opinion we must conclude that there exists a very important phenomenon in semantics: *the polarity of meaning* (cf. Malkiel quot. Ullmann 1967). Here we meet again the basic principle of linguistics and psycholinguistics: opposition (cf. Carroll 1963). We form our meanings mainly by interference and interaction between meanings. We can schematize this in this way, e.g. chair, fauteuil, stool, seat:

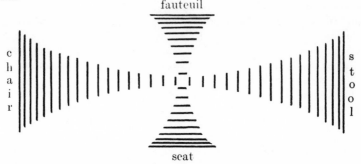

all these 'concepts' have something in common: the lines between them are vague. There are some articles of furniture, which clearly are chairs and not fauteuils, but in some articles the lines fade: John says this and Peter says that.

Our Didactics

A big consequence for our didactics is that of teaching children 'concepts' mainly by polarities. For instance I saw on a blackboard in a classroom of children of about 12 years of age:

a wooden chair
a wooden table
a wooden cupboard etc.

134

It would be much better to do this in the following (of course conversational) way:

That chair there is a wooden one, but this one has steel legs; our windows are steel too; the cupboard is a wooden one, but it is painted, because its wood is not so nice; I don't think that that cross there is a wooden one, it is stone I suppose, but we cannot see it because it is painted, etc.

Therefore if we speak to children about dwarfs, we should also speak of giants; if we talk about pilots, then we also speak of drivers etc. Of course this can only be done in conversation. Our conversations – I think – often work with polarities, especially our discussions.

A dictionary of antonyms would be very helpful in this respect, especially in higher grades, and for difficult concepts such as 'affection', 'humble', 'in cold blood', and so on.

6. SIGNIFICANT AND SIGNIFIED AS ONE INTEGRATED WHOLE, – LANGUAGE AND THINKING

Code and Concept

A consequence of the foregoing is that we cannot detach the significant from the signified. If the boundaries between 'concepts' are formed by using words, and if these boundaries are generally vague and arbitrary, we must say that the significant itself is the boundary of the signified; the code and its way of use is the social watchman of the meaning. The signified and the significant are closely integrated, symbiotized, not merely placed so as to be parallel. The learning of a language is also the learning of a world of thinking: 'Each language is a world-view' (Von Humboldt 1812 quot. Hörmann 1967).

As we have explained above, this holds not only for content-words, but for all phonemic and rhythmic morphemes, for the function-words and for the syntax as well. I think Whorf (1956) is right in supposing that in perceptible language-forms meanings can always be found, if not manifest ones, then cryptic ones.

Another consequence of this is that it will be impossible to explain a language as a system only formally, by means of its forms or codes, as Chomsky (1957) and others were trying to do, and are still trying to do, too much (see p. 79).

Language Coins and Supports Thinking

Language (meaning 'conversation') coins our thinking to a very large extent. Thinking will not *develop* sufficiently if words do not support it. We have already said that 'less nameable objects will (just) have background quality' (Kreach 1962). A second aspect is the short term memory: by rhythmic speech longer strings of words and sentences can be unified: any device that aids grouping, supports memory. So the growth of verbal intelligence and language competence is hampered in children with normal performal intelligence but suffering from too short a memory-span for spoken digits, strings of words and rhythmic patterns (Rispens 1974 for normally hearing children).

This neglect of the connections between language ('*conversation*') and thinking is in my view the big mistake in so many programmes of teaching children with motor disabilities (especially control of the body-scheme), e.g. in the Frostig-programme, the evalution of which is too poor (Myers 1973); in the 'school of thinking' of Furth (1971) and of Wachs and Furth (1974); in the 'Head-start-project' (1964, quot. Mönks-Knoers 1975, i.e. language without conversation); etc.

We will emphasize especially two reasons for the importance of language in our thinking:

a. *Abstraction.* As an instance 'left' is an abstract concept, applicable to the ear, eye, arm, leg of the speaker, but of his opponent too, projected onto the space around them. Compare the many difficulties confronting deaf children in instructions like these: 'Put your watch at the left side of your desk!', 'Which window is left to the door?' etc. (cf. Piaget 1923). As an example: one (signing) deaf adult would explain to another one that he had to go 'to the left around the church' in order to find a special address. The other one imitated this direction wrongly. So he put himself next to the speaker and together they made the same sign 'to the left around the church'. . . . Later it transpired that the other one still took the wrong side, because the tram did not arrive at the front of the church but on its right side. . . .

Examples of concepts which will not be conceived sufficiently without language: duty, shortsightedness, appreciation, freedom, honour, comparison, contrast, difference, and so on. That copper and iron are in some way the same will not be learned without the word 'metal'; beginning and end not without the word 'limit'; pound and meter not without the word 'measure'; 15 and 19 not without the word 'odd'; and so on (cf. the Wechsler-WISC-R 1974).

b. *Figurative meaning.* Only if we can toy with concepts in a non-pictorial way, i.e. by words, can we transfer them to metaphoric thinking (see p. 132 'living fullness'), e.g. 'a left compliment', 'the political left,' 'the whole of nature was laughing', 'an old woman with strawberry goodness', 'a face as old rag' (Dutch poet Aafjes), and so on. – An example: deaf adults were told that heaven is not really above, but that this indication has only a figurative meaning: i.e. of happiness, of sublimity and importance. That 'figurativeness' of 'above' was understood, however, as very very high and far away, as appeared in the discussion afterwards. Compare this with Piaget's example on page 131. See Russo (1975).

So there is a feedback: linguistic codes grow meanings, and meaningfulness evokes, moulds and changes codes (cf. Sherif 1949). Actually significant and signified are integrated into one whole, as we have seen above.

Language and Experience

Many psychologists and pedagogues emphasize deaf children's need for experiences. This should not be emphasized one-sidedly, however. Communication is their very basic need.

It may be clear indeed that especially deaf children need a lot of material to manipulate, to solve problems and so on. According to hearing children: Bühler (1949) found a degree of backwardness in institutionalized children, because they had on the average only 14 objects in their hands a day, in contrast to 71 objects for children in their parents' homes. Deaf children may be institutionalized even within their own homes, *mainly* because they lack the *stimulating power* of language: language, i.e. conversation, stimulates and evokes experiences.

Language *itself*, provided it is learned meaningfully, is an experience as such (cf. Ferreiro 1971). A real conversation is perhaps the highest experience of man! So this enhancement of experience should never be done without language, i.e. without conversation.

'Non-operational' 'Existential' Thinking?

There is still more. We should not forget that Furth (1966, see also his later publications), Piaget (1923, 1963, Ausubel 1968), and his cooperators, limit the term *'thinking'* ('operational thinking') far too much to the quantitative, spatial, physical and logistic field. We will of course not deny the importance of these Piagetian studies, only emphasize a kind of *onesidedness*. Actually children have other thinking problems too, e.g. (cf. Katz and Katz 1936, Church 1961, Helmers 1965, Rieder 1968, Fraiberg 1969, Britton 1970, Gipper 1971): 3;0–4;0 (A child asked its father:) 'What did *your* Daddy do?' – 'Why is Bobby (the dog) never naughty?' – 'Why is the child crying?' – 'Where do these poor children live? Doesn't their father work?' – (Beside a birch:) 'Is it ill, that tree?' – 'Does the lamp feel warm (= its warmth)?' – (laughing:) 'That hot sun is angry' – 'Who are you really afraid of?' – 'What will happen if you fall into deep water and you cannot swim?' – 'Mammy, I dreamt that an elephant had two legs, isn't that funny?' – (When cutting the grass:) 'I am the hay-maker and you are the grass-maker'. 'Didn't try hard enough, did you?' – 'Is delicious nicer than lovely?' – Mary: 'I become police'; Mama: 'That is impossible you are a girl'; Mary: 'I can grow a man!' ... The delight in the nonsense as 'the 24 blackbirds that sang in a pie'. ...

5;0–6;0 'Why do you call that beautiful?' – 'Mammy, how is it, if I do not awaken in the morning, but I am dead?' – 'Mama, it was not a real dog, was it?' – 'May be, the baby was only afraid of a dream!' – (Watching the cutting down of trees:) 'Does it not hurt them, really?' – 'Santa Claus is not honest' – 'That star does not

137

wink at me'. – 'I did not get an ice-cream and yet I have been good' – (To a big engine at the railway station:) 'Swanker!' – 'Mama, does the mouse know that he is a mouse?' – (Theo has fallen:) 'Why is the floor so hard against me?' – 'Do you know how the old man looked in his looking-glass and the looking-glass said nothing'. And so on . . .

Think further of the dependency of the make-believe-play upon language (cf. Britton 1970).

We should like to call this kind of thinking '*existential* thinking'.

Furth and cooperators (1966, 1970, 1973), Oléron and cooperators (1957, 1973) found deaf children far behind in 'operational thinking'. They have been found behind in 'existential thinking' too. See Templin (1954 a–b) and Nass (1964) on deaf children's so-called 'animistic' conception of physical causality (term applied by Piaget); Nass (1965) on deaf children's moral judgment; Lewis (1968) concerning deaf children's difficulties in 'orectic language', Kates (1965) in 'social concepts'.

7. WHAT ABOUT SIGN-LANGUAGE?

What are Signs?

Signs are those conventional movements of arms and hands which replace words. – These signs are mainly esoteric and should be clearly distinguished from the normal gestures. Hirsch (1923) counted 501 gestures of normally hearing children, and 883 of normally hearing adults.

How is it that such an Esoteric Sign Develops?

An example (1957, cf. Hirsch 1961): a deaf child of 2;4 years of age pulled her mother to the cupboard, where a metal box containing cookies had been put away. She dramatized to the mother the whole plan of activities: opening the cupboard, taking out the box, opening the lid (showing her hand in a horizontal position and then turning it upwards by turning her wrist), taking out an illusory cooky, putting it into her mouth with clear eyes and enthusiastically nodding Yes! The mother understood her and gave her a cooky. The consequence of this was that she performed the same drama next day, but a little shorter: she kept standing beside her mother and only dramatized the box and lid and turning the flat of her hand to her mother, meaning 'Give me a cooky', a conventional sign understood by no one except the mother and child.

NB. 1. This development is not a necessary one. There are other mothers who, by good guidance, do not reinforce such signing, but instead mime *orally:* e.g. the

138

child is invited to shape her lips to form /oo/ (in c*oo*ky), preferable with sound, and if the child has done so, it is reinforced. These mothers strive towards the way of oralism. – Other children will do still better: they imitate spontaneously e.g. 'oowy" or 'ohwy' or 'toowy; and so on.

2. It is supposed by many teachers of the deaf that those sign-codes *develop* spontaneously quickly among a group of deaf children: 'generatio spontanea'. This does not seem to be true. Heider (1940) found no more that 8 conventional signs among two groups of normal deaf children of 4–7 years of age living together in a purely oral residential school for the deaf for two years, kept away from any influence of signing deaf. It is a common experience that signs (apart from an introduction by signing deaf) are invented not so much by *low* standard deaf but by those deaf children (think of postlingually deafened and hard of hearing children too) who have more to say *and* have been put into one group with the mentioned low standard deaf: the latter almost compel them to invent more and more dramatizations and signs to make themselves understood.

3. It is supposed too that these signs as a whole are a *language*. But they don't have flexions and their order is not an arbitrarily cultural one; so their syntax can hardly be called linguistic in the strict sense. Stokoe (1971) rightly calls this whole 'a low version of sign language'. They are a collection of '*sign-codes*'.

The Penetrating Influence of these Signs

If we teach deaf children orally in an incorrect way (neglecting 'oral conversation'), these children sooner or later will converse with each other by esoteric signs. They will build up a primitive sign-'language', perhaps a creation of their own. But together with this they build up a primitive own *world-view*, different from ours; their concepts, their images, feelings, denotative and connotative meanings will recede from ours more and more. The teaching of our oral language will be more and more difficult, apart from lack of automation of speech, hearing and lipreading, which does not develop without these functions being continuously challenged.

Signs are Iconic

As far as meaning is concerned, it is the most obvious feature of most 'signs', that they are in some way 'absorbed by meaning', i.e. they are properly speaking not 'names' as arbitrary symbols, but images and/or imitations of their meanings; they are mainly iconic or picturing symbols (cf. Oléron 1952, 1973). This happens in oral language too in the co-called onomatopoeias, such as cuckoo, ping-pong etc., further in the phonetic symbolism as found in poems and 'belles-lettres' (see,

139

e.g. Heider and Heider 1940, Ullman 1975). But what is the exception in oral language, is the rule in sign-language.

Signs are too Signalistic

They will be less symbolistic and more 'signalistic', too 'instrumental', i.e. that the deaf, using signs as their mother-tongue, are not or hardly *aware* of the representational function of these signs (cf. Piaget). The reason is that there are only a few synonyms and almost no homonyms in sign-language. It is eactly by means of these that the child *learns* the arbitrariness of the linguistic *symbols* and so their (representational) function. Thus the way of communication using signs is seemingly more akin to the communicative coding-systems of animals and is less of a human behaviour, less 'distant' from emotions, primary feelings and subjective attitudes. So it is understandable that a chimpanzee can learn to use signs, even to combine them into series of 2 and 3 signs (Gardner 1969, 1974), as a 'signal'-language (cf. Bellugi 1972, see p. 146). – Cf. Glucksberg and Danks (1975).

Signs and Multiple Meanings of Words

It is typical, especially for very frequent words, to have more than one meaning, for instance *table* as a piece of furniture and as a surface on which something is written and as a list of figures, *chest* as a large box and as a part of the body, and so on. I found an average of 5 meanings in the 3,600 words of basic Dutch (see Vannes 1962, cf. for English Williams, 1932), which comprise 95% of our daily conversations and of the content of reading books (Peters and Peters 1973). About 9,000 meanings are very frequent ones. This function of multi-meaning, as we have said above, does not happen so often in signs, even rather seldom, because of their iconicity. This fact hinders deaf children in managing these multi-meanings of words, i.e. to shift quickly from one meaning to another.
Kates (1972) in a sophisticated study found a group of deaf adolescents from combined schools, using speech and signs in their programme of education, behind a matched group (inter alia the same reading level) of purely orally educated deaf in their interpretation of multi-meaning, written words in contexts. This 'combined group' was also behind a similarly matched group of mainly dactylologically (i.e. verbally educated) deaf (Rochester method, see page 205).

Signs and the Figurative Meanings

The absorption in meaning of signs, mentioned above, immediately creates for the signing deaf (i.e. using signs as their mother-tongue, and because of that *in-*

sufficiently verbally developed) difficulties in understanding many abstractions and especially metaphors or figurative meanings such as: 'appreciation', 'short-sightedness', 'contrast', 'honour', 'to hammer at something', 'a victory at any price', 'the attraction of love', 'a pale solitude', 'the tide in the affairs of men', 'then the fat was in the fire', 'be at sea (= astray)', 'chickens come home to roost', etc. etc. (cf. Davidson 1976). So the creativity of linguistic thinking is very limited. For the same reason it is difficult to explain allegories, parables (Russo 1975), the deeper meanings of fairy-tales, poems and so on, to deaf children or adults who think much too visually; it is precisely this overloaded visual thinking which is aggravated by the signs.

Examples of Concrete Difficulties. Ambiguities

Let us give some examples of difficulties, originating from sign-language in prelingually deaf children and adults. Every teacher of the deaf whose children sign very much, can augment them very easily.

'One of the servants of *this* (sign = here) house has died' was understood as: 'died here'.

'The aeroplane *goes* (sign = walking) forward' was not understood; ditto: 'He let himself *go*'.

'How time *flies*' (sign = fluttering) was understood as the movement made by the conductor of an orchestra.

An intelligent child said: 'With *one* (sign of one = only = alone) coat on' meaning: 'Only with a coat on.

'There is an island in the *river* (sign = flowing) 'was understood to be: the island has been overflowed.

One child to another one: 'my father has made a new *roof* (sign = house)', was understood as: 'New house'.

'This street comes to a *dead* (sign = dying) end' was understood as a street with a lot of accidents.

'John's coat was not big enough' was taken to mean: 'John has one small coat, that is enough'. Etc. etc.

A deaf adult would explain to another that he *expected* an accident to happen on a specific corner of the street: 'Car bumping, there, think, perhaps later' ... The deaf partner understood that an accident had already happened, which had the consequence of a very 'lively' conversation full of *misunderstandings*.

8. MEANING OF DEIXES

We mentioned under the subject of language content − : deixes (from Greek

141

deiknumi = I show; Reichling 1935). These are the demonstratives (which I take in a very broad sense) or 'pointer-words' (Hogben and Bodmer quot. Pei-Gaynor 1958): you, yours, I, we, me, mine, that, there, this, here etc. Their 'content' is strictly speaking zero but they point to objects, or to other words, or to groups of words. To me the action of pointing is quite natural and often necessary. If I say: 'The box is there' and I don't point to that place, what I say is nonsense. The actual pointing — mostly with the forefinger, but may also be done with the eyes or a nod — is the only sign in oral language which cannot be excluded. It is interesting to note that we almost always point simultaneously when speaking the pointer-word, and this is difficult for most deaf children of 4–5 years of age: they often either say, e.g. *there* and don't point, or point and do not speak, or speak first and then point or the reverse! They have to learn to point exactly at the same time as they speak. These two have to be closely associated so that pointing (in the situation) calls forth the correct pointer-word, and the correct pointer-word calls forth (at least latently) the pointing sign. To me the deaf child should do this with the pronouns too. There is no danger for a sign-language in this.

Very many deaf small ones as early as 3 and 4 years old cannot point at all! They only grasp or reach as an animal would. And no animal points. The action of pointing is a bodily expression of the mental objectification, i.e. to intend something *as* different and opposite to the pointer (Buytendijk 1957).

9. MEANING OF QUESTIONS

Other difficult meanings for deaf children are those of questions and accentuations.

We have already said above that most teacher's *questions* are not real questions, because there is no need of an answer. The only right way to make deaf children understand questions is to link up with the questions coming spontaneously from the children themselves. Take a boy of 3 or 4 years old, looking for his paintbox; he comes to mother or teacher with some diffuse mouth-movements, arms spread out and a facial mime meaning 'Where?' This is the moment! Mother or teacher says: 'Where is the paintbox?' with a durational-accent on *where?* Perhaps mother knows very well where it is, but she does not yet tell him. She pretends to look for it with the boy, always saying with clear facial mime: 'Where? Where?' asking the boy, if possible, to imitate the question 'Where?' too. The point is here that the word *Where* will enter into the need of the boy. It is a real question for him. A second time mother or teacher will hide the paintbox purposely so as to repeat this 'where-game'. And other things too. The same goes for Who-games, What-games, Yes-no questions etc. When his speech is improving, the boy should be asked to ask the question in its right form, *before* mother or teacher gives the answer, because, as soon as you give the answer the real need for an answer is gone, and the asking for the correct question-form *then* becomes mere formal training. When the child is 5 or 6, questions – i.e. their personally experienced and spontaneously uttered questions – must also be written for him. Of course the form generally has to be corrected, but you always correct the form *before* you give the answer. The question must be kept in a state of tension for the child. You give the child a small note-book, wherein he and you write down his personally experienced questions. By doing this, after a year you will have hundreds of these questions if you like, and the child will be able to ask questions in the right form, and also to understand better and better, questions from other children and from adults.

10. MEANING OF ACCENTUATIONS

What we have said about questions, must be said about the meaning of accents, and here too we link up with the utterances of the children themselves. This, however, can best be done when the child has mastered enough speech and can read reasonably. Peter comes in, for example, and says: 'Saw dog there!' *Dog* will of course have the accent, in his mind at least. Make him say – if possible –: 'I saw a *dog* there', and write:

Make him say this with a nice movement of his hand and arm. The same goes for the accents in questions and calls and wishes etc., spontaneously uttered by the children.

These important language forms too must be noted in each child's individual note-book. The teacher will be especially keen on catching such utterances which contain an accent of contrast, because this is so important for the development of meanings and of understanding, e.g.

![Are we going to swim or do exercises?]

143

Meaning – in my opinion – grows up from four roots, the first two of which are more related to the intersubjectivity of the speaking partners, the latter two more to the objects, i.e. to the system of the codes as such and to the situations represented.

a. Imitation

The hearing child imitates mother in the situation and mother often imitates him, correcting him at the same time, in an enhancing way (Brown 1964). This imitation is a real pleasure for the child, so it reinforces. The child will speak later in that same situation again (Mowrer 1960).

For some difficult children it is necessary to *make* them imitate and to make them experience how pleasing it is to imitate. They need special imitation-exercises as Vatter has already done (Vatter 1891). Note that the Vatter-exercises were at the same time exercises of the body-scheme: teacher spreads out his arms, children spread out their arms; teacher points to his legs, children point to their legs; teacher points to his mouth, children point to their mouths; teacher closes his lips, children close their lips; teacher moves his tongue, children move their tongues etc. It is known that for deaf-blind children this is necessary for a very long time, sometimes also for aphasic children and autistic children (this rule: 'Imitate them and they will imitate you!', cf. Lovaas 1967) who give too little of themselves spontaneously. Don't say that these exercises are too artificial: many lullabies and baby-songs are in fact exercises of the body scheme.

During the whole process of language acquisition, imitation plays an important part. Deaf children must be bent on imitating speech. The following example indicates that there was something wrong in the education:

A boy said to me: 'Long here?' I said: 'Say: How long will you stay here?' But the boy did not follow me. He insisted asking: 'Long here?' and was almost angry that I did not answer him soon enough! This revealed a wrong attitude in the boy. Deaf children indeed must keep an attitude of trial and check, a feeling of wanting to be corrected, and bent on imitating the language of others.

b. Conditioning

By means of conditioning, words are understood as signals (e.g. *milk* said by mother becomes a signal for the child that it will be fed), and words are always used more often and better ('operant conditioning'). The latter reveals the reinforcement of conversation: being understood reinforces the speaker to use such

144

words or forms more and more. (See Pavlov quot. Hörmann 1967; Skinner 1958). Thus the language acquires an instrumental value. Krech (1962) is right in saying: 'To the speaker, speech is like an extension of arms and hands and pointing apparatus; to the listener it is like an extension of eyes and ears or other sensory apparatus'.

According to the laws of conditioning (see e.g. Krech 1962, 1969) the effect is the better if:

aa. the stimulus to be conditioned *precedes* the unconditioned stimulus; bb. the stimulus to be conditioned gives pleasure to the child, moving the child (cf. the 'representational mediating response' of Osgood 1959). For example if the child *likes* to see its mother's face, she will be more successful in training it to lipread; if the first experience of sound-perception is pleasing, sounds will become signals much easier, etc.

Therefore I advised in home-training what I should like to call: the 'anticipatory approach' (van Uden 1963). This approach somewhat contrasts with the 'identifying approach', although both approaches should support each other. According to the 'identifying approach' mother might show a ball to her child and say simultaneously: 'A ball! Do you want the ball?' – According to the 'anticipatory approach' mother will hide the ball, say, just before the moment she expects her child will want it. When the child is looking for it, she will say: 'The ball? Do you want the ball?' – Or another example: before going with the child into the bathroom, mother will prepare before its eyes everything that is needed for bathing it. The child will understand soon what will happen! Then the mother says: 'We will take a bath! Do you like taking a bath?' By doing this the words *ball*, *bath* etc. become signals for the events to come. In my experience the anticipatory method is more effective in teaching lipreading than the identifying method. Of course the identifying method is also worth using: it may be clear that this method leans more on imitating-needs, while the anticipatory method relies more on conditioning.

c. Analogy

It is a matter of fact that the hearing child builds up its *own* language, – which is a spontaneous selection from the language of the environment –, mainly by analogy (Lewis 1951). Analogy, however, presupposes an understanding of a lot of good examples. Although every sentence of an individual is a creation ad hoc that will never be repeated in quite the same way, analogy is the root from which these 'creations' grow. By trial and check the hearing child finds analogies himself, although initially not exactly the analogies of English. Mother helps him, however, to discover the analogies in English. Deaf children must be helped much more. But here too, the best thing will be not to *give* the analogies expressly, but to help the child *to find them himself.* This necessitates a lot of reading material of course, mainly to be found in the diaries of the children and their reading books. We will explain this later.

d. The Sense of Mastery

By means of language we master the world. This can be illustrated by the behaviour of Günther, the son of Stern (1907), 1;6 old. He had understood the word 'Stuhl' (= chair, pronounced 'stool') and suddenly he saw that something else was a 'stool' too. He ran to the chair, pointed to it asking his mother: 'And this?' Mother said: 'Yes, also a chair!' and again to another chair: 'And this?' . . . 'And this?' . . . 'And this?' . . . Their followed quite a period during which he asked for the names of things like a hungry animal: the well-known 'hunger for names'. It must be remarked here that the chimpanzee mentioned earlier, learning sign-language (see p. 140) never did reach this stage (Bronowski and Bellugi 1970). It never came to symbolization. It so happened, however, that when 'reading a picture book' and signing the name of every picture, it stopped at one to which it could not give a name. But this is a purely routine game, not the idea that 'everything has a name'.
Symbolization is neither an association, a conditioned response, nor an imitation, but a 'knowing about associations, a knowing about relations' (Hörmann 1967). Symbolization is in its deepest sense a grasping and a mastering process, it is the outgrowth of the 'ego'. So symbolization is the highest flower in the development of meaning.

12. 'HOMONYMS', 'SYNONYMS', 'ANTONYMS', 'GENERAL WORDS' AND 'METAPHORS'

The 'mastering' described above gives freedom, human freedom. There are, however, two phases in the acquisition of language which enhance this freedom strikingly. (a) The detection of 'homonyms', 'synonyms' and 'general words', and (b) the detection of 'metaphors' (Reichling 1935). We emphasize that the children have to learn these *terms*.

Homonyms and Synonyms

The child detects, say, that a tree has a *trunk*; and an elephant too, – that the nurse puts a *patch* on his wound, but that there is a patch of cabbages too, – that a *swallow* is a fast flying bird, but that he also swallows his food, and so on.

146

We call attention to the many different meanings of *to be*, *to make*, *to have*, *to get* etc. (look in your dictionary). Further the shifting of meanings (the analogy of proportion): 'The body is healthy', 'The situation is healthy', 'You have healthy cheeks'; *or* 'I am a member of that club', 'I go to the club (= house)'; *or* 'The kettle is boiling', 'The whole bus is singing', 'Twelve hands on board', 'All hands on deck' (metonymia), etc.

As soon as we get such a situation with our deaf children, we must make the most of it, saying: 'These two words have quite different meanings; find some more homonyms yourself now!' – in order to make their language more and more flexible. Teach the terms 'homonyms' and 'synonyms' when the children are sufficiently conscious of them. It may be clear, however, that homonyms are more important than synonyms. Some teachers onesidedly emphasize the value of collecting synonyms, not aware of the danger that they are fixing the minds of their children to a kind of rigid thinking within a small field of meanings. Besides many so-called synonyms are not synonyms in their strict sense, because the meanings are nuanced, e.g. 'to watch' and 'to guard'; these nuances are easily overlooked by deaf children.

Mickelson (1969) found a high correlation between meaningfullness of words and the reading ability, in general: verbal learning.

There are homonymous *morphemes* too, e.g. trees (plural) and looks (third person first form of the verb). We should not teach this purposely, however, unless the children make mistakes or detect them themselves. Then we say: 'These are two different flexions, that -s has a double meaning'. Clea, 9 years old, always made many mistakes with the infinitive form of the verb (Dutch –en, e.g. to find = vinden): 'Margriet vinden' instead of 'Margriet vindt . . .' Once she got a postcard from her parents, who wrote that they would come and fetch her 'met de wagen' (= by car). This was a new word for her, for until then the 'wagen' was only the four-wheeled vehicle on the play-ground. So she laughed and said: 'Funny!' But the teacher tried to explain that the 'auto' (Dutch, = car) was also called 'wagen'. She did not follow at first and was astonished that the teacher did not find this funny! She asked then: 'Is it plural?' 'No!' – 'Is it the infinitive?' 'Noooo! . . . It is exactly the same as auto', the teacher said. – From that time Clea was much more conscious of the forms of the verb, as if she had grasped the idea. In language we often just do it, and everyone does it . . . You can't ask 'why?' Later she even exaggerated to the opposite side. She said: 'Toos ironischte . . .' (= Toos – name of a classmate – 'ironiced' . . .).

General Words

Another term which we should teach the children very soon is 'general word', e.g. '*Beautiful*' is a very "general word", can you find examples of something which is

147

beautiful?' And then to words such as *big*, *old*, etc., many substantives like *fluid*, *traffic*, *animal*, *to live*, *to do*, *to happen*, *things*, *clothes*, *furniture*, *material*, *instrument*, *food*, etc. etc.

Antonyms

Still another term is very important: antonyms. For example entrance-exit, beautiful-ugly, up-down etc. These have to do with the meaning of accentuations and the refining of the contents of words. Deaf children have difficulty in thinking about antonymic ideas (Furth 1961, 1966, Restaino 1969).

Metaphors

These phenomena of the vocabulary, i.e. homonyms, synonyms, antonyms and 'general words', have much to do with the flexibility of thinking. This is made clearer with '*figurative meanings*' and 'metaphors'. Here we enter the realm of the highest creativity of man (Padberg 1924, Gullan and Gurrey 1952, Barthès 1967, Smulders 1976), always opening up new pathways, e.g. 'The sun went down like a goldfish' (Timmermans), 'Our life is similar to the work of a type-setter: he puts in type after type and between the series, small blocks of silence; these blocks of silence are the deepest' (van Lierop).

To train them for this you can easily start with so-called 'worn out' expressions, e.g. 'The motor *runs*', 'The *legs* of the table', 'The *arms* of the tree' etc. etc. Then you use a few situations: e.g. you want to switch on the lights but there is something wrong with them, they don't go on; you now say: 'The lights are disobedient!' A child tore his jacket on a nail; you make him say: 'You naughty nail!'. When a child has painted a very colourful picture, you say: 'What a rich painting!' or when it is rather bad: 'What a poor drawing!'. There is a meeting shown on the television and you say: 'A sea of people'. And so on. If the children have learned from many of those examples what a 'figurative meaning' is, it will become easier and easier to teach them the meaning of say 'High winds blow on high hills', 'Not seeing the wood for the trees', 'He knocks his head against a wall', and even: 'You are a *nice* one' (meaning exactly the opposite!) etc. etc. A helpful book may be that of Boatner and Gates (1966).

Make the Children Detect these Phenomena!

But these aspects should first of all be *detected* by the children, more and more. Exactly because we know that these four phenomena are especially difficult for deaf children (cf. Clarke School 1972), who are visualizers all, we must treat them in good time and with purpose. The second grade (7–8 years of age) seems to be an important stage: at the end of this grade these four terms should be known.

13. FOR THE BETTERMENT OF VOCABULARY

Children of about 7 to 12 years of age very often have a hobby in collecting, such as collecting stamps, shells, picture-postcards etc. etc. This tendency should be used for the betterment of vocabulary! The teacher should give his children an alphabetical index, loose-leaf, in which the children can note the new words and expressions they have collected. They then see how their vocabulary grows, and can compare their gains with those of their peers etc., with a growing satisfaction and enjoyment. A parent told me she gave her deaf son something every month for his money-box for every 20 new words, expressions and idioms. . . .

IV

The Importance of Reading in
Language Acquisition

The process of reading and its specific difficulties for deaf children

1. RECEIVING LANGUAGE MORE DIFFICULT THAN EXPRESSING LANGUAGE

Need for More Research in Understanding

Most studies of language acquisition of deaf children deal with their expressive language, usually in its written form only (e.g. Heider and Heider 1940; Tervoort 1953, 1967; Simmonds 1962, Myklebust 1964; Gunderson 1965; Stuckless 1966; Vanden Berg 1971). In my opinion there is a need for more research in the difficulties of deaf children in understanding. Perhaps many problems in expressive language may be cleared up in this way.

The Process of Understanding is More Complicated

I think, in general, receiving language is more difficult than expressing it. Wales and Marshall (1966, quot. Herriot 1970) found that the process of understanding is more complicated than that of producing sentences. This confirms the analysis by Van Ginneken (1922) of both kinds of language use.

One cannot object that a small hearing child learns to receive language at a younger age than he learns to express it: because that expressing is dependent on understanding. What is more difficult to acquire precedes. When the child is able to control almost all simple sentence-structures at the age of 3 years, his learning for understanding is still going on. – This should not be conceived solely as psycholinguistically but directly psychically too: for a very long time that understanding remains egocentric. The child is not yet able to put himself in the place of the other, to get out from his own centre, to put out another centre out there, and to think from that centre out there in an 'ex-sistential' way. So I found it strange that in an excellent book such as 'Natural language for the deaf' by Mildred Groht (1958), learning to read is simply taken for granted. Consequently her book gives more of an 'Expressive natural language' method.

150

2. READING IS MORE IMPORTANT THAN COMPOSITION WORK

To me, reading is more important for deaf children than composition work, not only for practical purposes but most of all, because the enormous arrears of frequency in receiving language can only be made up by reading (Querll 1922, Forchhammer 1930). Reading must give them the source and ground from which expressive language can grow. To me this is the only natural way. I agree fully with the words of Myklebust (1964 p. 328): 'Perhaps (I would say: certainly!) one of the most beneficial and effective ways to improve the level of written language is to raise the level of read language', and all this in the normal forms, with all the oppositions necessary, in the natural situations, at which point it should not be forgotten that the most natural situation for language is the oral conversation.
Of course we will neither exclude nor minimize composition-work. Composition is – after conversation – one of the most important means of converting receptive language into expressive language.

3. SPECIFIC DIFFICULTIES IN LEARNING TO READ

Are there *specific* difficulties for deaf children in learning to read? Yes, there are!

a. General: Putting Oneself in the Place of Another

With respect to the problem of putting himself in the place of another, and thinking from another viewpoint than that of himself, there are here only a few remarks.
This is first of all a problem of general education.

Telling Stories

It is didactically specially trained by conversation and by telling stories. Telling stories is somewhat easier than reading because it is the 'living word of the living present person'. Cf. Gemmil (1976).
Telling stories is very often forgotten by teachers of the deaf. Yet deaf children enjoy it as much as hearing children. Of course there is a small difference between telling to hearing children, because the teacher has to check up again and again whether the children follow well. So telling stories is done in a more dialogic way than with hearing children. Sometimes drawings on the blackboard are necessary, e.g to explain the situation of the story. Sometimes words and sentences have to be written down and so on. But the story itself can be just as thrilling to deaf children.

151

NB. It may be clear that dramatizations with some sentences, and series of pictures or drawings with some sentences are not meant here: this is not *telling* stories!

This work can start at about 7–8 years of age, in the second grade. The content can be a boy's venture, or that of a girl etc., but it is important to weave some stories around animals, such as rabbits, dolphins, dogs etc. etc., involving angels, fairies, ghosts etc., in short, the sphere of fairy-tales. Very soon serial stories are possible, e.g. from Monday through Friday, and – last but not least – the teacher should not forget to compose 'deposits' of the stories for the diaries.

b. A Survey of the Development of Reading in Deaf Children; the Major Difficulty of Growth of the Children's Vocabulary

With respect to reading itself the deaf child is trained in this way:
All the children in the class should have individual diaries.

(a) Ideo-visual Reading

The first step is that they read their own diaries, the stories and the language of which they already know still in a general way. This kind of reading has been called '*ideo-visual reading*' (Décroly 1907, applied to reading-lessons by Sr. Theresia van Driel 1934), *because* the ideas are already in the minds of the children and they read what they know.

These first stories are 'deposits' of the conversations in the classroom (see examples in the appendices p. 258, 270). An example for 5 year old children (cf. the facsimile of Bell):

To the swimming pool.
We were in the swimming pool.
Miss Margaret had to look for John.
He had run away.
'Where is John?'
'Have you seen John?'
'Yes, fortunately I have seen him', said Miss Emmy.
Where?
He stood and watched the small trains full of sand.
'You are a bit naughty!'

The composition of such reading-lessons is not as easy as it looks. They should reflect the conversation and be quite colloquial. So they should not be composed from statements only but should include questions, appeals, calls, exclamations,

152

and a lot of direct quotations. They should not always follow a chronologic order, as in the lesson above: 'He had run away'.

How reading-excercises can be done even in the preschool, will be explained below.

(b) Receptive Reading

The second step is 'receptive reading', i.e. that the children start to read from the diaries of their classmates and friends, the stories and language of which at least part are *unfamiliar*: they now start a kind of 'visuo-ideal reading', i.e. they get *new* ideas from the visual graphic form. The same by reading a letter from home. They start almost spontaneously at about 6 years of age (first grade), led by their curiosity. Actually curiosity is one of the strongest incentives to commence and maintain reading.

The term 'receptive reading' indicates that the child is now receiving ideas more or less unknown to him. – Both 'ideo-visual reading' and 'receptive reading' functions work in every reading-process. For instance if we read a poem which is rather difficult, many ideas are already familiar to us and only a certain proportion of ideas is unknown. The more ideas are unknown, the more the reading will be receptive reading. When a deaf child of 6 begins reading, it is still mainly ideo-visual reading with only a very small proportion being receptive reading. The more its ability to read receptively increases, the larger that proportion of unknown ideas may be.

The Training of Reading

Deaf children need much more *training* in reading than hearing children. How can this be done?

If we give deaf children a reading-lesson and tell them that they should read it, and if their eyes follow the lines of the sentences or even if they read them aloud, we are not at all sure that they are really reading, either ideo-visually or receptively. The same with lipreading-listening exercise: the teacher or a child reads a sentence aloud and the other children have to find that same sentence in its written form. We must *check* whether they *understand* what they are reading. In higher classes of course we discuss the content and find out whether they have taken it in, in the same way as it is done with hearing children. In the preschool and the first and second grades, however, this will usually still be too difficult. Many teachers of the deaf give the following exercises, which are good in themselves although onesided. They ask the children to show them a picture which is pertinent to a special sentence, possibly belonging to several sentences, or a series of pictures which belong to a whole story. They dramatize the events and ask the children to find the sentences belonging to these dramatizations. Inversely, they ask the children themselves to dramatize the contents of sentences, and so on. In addition to this kind of exercise we have proposed others which are not so visual, and less in the line of 'iconic' thinking, so akin to thinking in signs. We distinguish the following five steps.

'Who Says What' – Game

(1) We look for the speakers in the reading-lesson and draw the heads of these speakers with empty 'talk-balloons', e.g. (see lesson page 152.):

The 'say-sentences' (= direct quotations) of the reading-lessons are found, written down on separate pieces of paper, and the children are requested to put the right 'say-sentence' into the appropriate 'talk-balloon'. If they do this correctly, they must have read the sentence to a certain extent. We call this the 'Who says what?' – game.

A 'Scrabble-game'

(2) We cut out the sentences of a reading-lesson, mix them up and ask the children to put them in the right order, a 'scrabble-game'. If they do so, we can be sure that they had read the sentences, at least in an overall intuitive way.

154

Question Work

Development of reading presupposes curiosity, i.e. asking oneself a question and to feel a need for an answer to be found through reading. The children can be educated to this 'problem-solving' reading as follows.

Find the Question-words

(3) We move over to using the question-words. This presupposes that they are known to the children at the end of the second grade (how this should be done, see p. 142). So the teacher already has classified questions on cards, e.g. who-, what-, how-, when-, where-, why-, and what-to-do-questions and so on ('yes-no-questions' too). He can use these question-words now for the reading-lessons, as follows. He underlines special words and/or phrases in the sentences (emphasizing their phrase structure) and asks the children which question-word belongs to which word or phrase, e.g.

Who?   Where?
We were in the swimmingpool

He asks the children: 'Which question-word belongs to *we*?' (Who?). 'Which question-word belongs to *in the swimming-pool*?' (Where?). 'Which question-word belongs to *Miss Margaret*?' (Who?). – And for higher grades: 'Which question-phrase belongs to *had to look for John*?' (What has Miss Margaret to do?). 'Who can make a yes/no-question from *He had run away*?' (Had he run away? Yes). Etc.

Formulate the Whole Question

(4) The children learn to formulate the whole questions, e.g. 'Where have we been?' 'Who were in the swimming-pool?' Etc. – When the children are about 9 or 10 years old, we can again go a little bit further: they are requested to underline some words and/or phrases themselves, and then to formulate questions.

155

'Problem Solving' Reading

(5) The aim of this work is that the children learn to set up questions concerning a whole paragraph in their reading-books, thus to find better and better which problem is explained there, what is the central idea of the paragraph and so on. For instance 'Which reasons for the long journey are explained here?' etc. This work should start when the children are about 12–13 years of age, i.e. in grade 6–7.

An example of a facsimile

From L. Feeney 'Elisabeth Seton. An American woman.', Huntington IN 46750, 1975.
'Shepherdess' is the name of a sailing boat travelling from New York to Leghorn (Italy) and return 1803.

The Shepherdess

A man terribly interested in navigation (or maybe just terribly interested in stunts) once threw five hundred bottles into the Atlantic Ocean at some point on the continent, and he found it was possible for one of them to float to the shores of the United States in a period of seven months.

For what reason were 500 bottles thrown into the ocean?

The little *Shepherdess* was almost four times as fast as that bottle. It crossed from New York to Leghorn in fifty-six days. The *Bremen, Europa, Normandie, Queen Mary, Rex*, stately ships in their day, could probably have crossed ten times during that one little voyage.

How long did the journey take in comparison to modern ships?

Captain O'Brien and his wife were, as may have been suspected by the reader, Irish. The Irish in many situations are difficult people. But I can imagine no more delightful companions on a long sea voyage, especially in the dark nights when

It may be clear that, when the teacher forgets to train his children in *critical* reading, and puts all the emphasis of his teaching on composing and constructing language, the level of reading will remain very low and primitive (cf. Kreye 1972). And because of that, the composition work itself will remain primitive too.

(c) The 'Vocabulary Phase' and the 'Structural Phase' of 'Receptive Reading'

This process of receptive reading embraces two phases also:

(1). The *vocabulary-phase*, i.e. the vast majority of the words used in the paragraph, letter or reading book is known to the child and it can guess intelligently what the content will be. It has been found that hearing children of about 10–12 years of age don't like a book or reading-piece when more than 5% of the words are unknown to them (Peters and Peters 1973); a reading-piece that will be treated in the classroom, however, may permit an amount of 10% of the words to be unfamiliar. This figure can be larger for deaf children. It is up to the teacher to find such reading-pieces, according to the intelligence and language level of his children, of which the children can grasp the general meaning from the whole. From this whole the teacher can proceed to the details.

This vocabulary-phase is *indispensable*, because the structural phase (see below) can flourish only from this basis. Actually this structural phase originates by *reflecting*, does it not (see p. 232)? Such reflecting is impossible or at least very hampered if there is no preceding intuitive understanding of the whole, which is the specific fruit of a well-trained vocabulary-phase. This implies a growth of the vocabulary of at least 10–20 new words and expressions every week in grades 1–3, and 20–30 in the grades 4–8, so that at about 15 years of age the normal reading books for hearing children of 10–11 years can be read, which requires a vocabulary of about 6,000 words with about 11,000 meanings.

By 'normal reading books', I do not mean picture books with texts, but story books written for normal hearing children with only a few pictures.

(2). The *structural phase*, commencing at about 13 years of age, in which additional to the knowledge of the words and the expressions, the structure, the system of the language plays an ever increasing part in understanding, e.g. the parts of speech, the figurative meanings, the humour of language, the analysis of the sentences etc.

A Rating Scale for Reading Level

The whole development of learning to read may appear clearer using the following

157

rating-scale, which we have composed in order to measure the level of intelligent reading in deaf children, 1972.

N.B. 1. Wherever the word '*text*' is used below, we mean solely free normal language which is not limited 'a priori' as regards form or content, in short: 'texts for the hearing'. At least from level 6 on, the texts should not be composed by the teacher himself.
What is meant is a mainly independent understanding, consequently not a text which might be discussed in order to *make* the children understand.
According to scoring: one marks the different norms of understanding which a certain child meets, and the highest norm is the score.

I. *Ideo-visual reading*, meaning that the child only understands texts which express what he already knows and thus the account of his experiences.
1. The child only understands those texts which deal with experiences, which took place no more than 2 months previously.
2. The child can easily understand reading-lessons from his 'diaries', which were dealt with 3 or more months before.
3. The child understands new texts (e.g. letters from home, lessons from the 'diaries' belonging to other children etc.) which are already somewhat outside his own experiences, but which are still strongly connected with them; i.e. they contain analogous experiences.
II. *Receptive reading in the vocabulary-phase*, meaning that the child understands texts which give him new contents, but are mainly understood by more or less guess work on the basis of the vocabulary, familiar to him.
4. The texts still deal with situations which are practically known to the child or can easily be made known by means of limited illustrations, though the experience is new, for instance about a family, a baker, sport, girl- and boy-friends, about going for a walk and travelling in more or less known surroundings.

NB. Here starts a reading level of 9 years old normally hearing children:

5. The texts deal with situations which require fantasy and imagination, for instance fairy-tales, stories from history which took place in different cultures, stories about travels in countries with different cultures, adventures in the same, and such like.
6. The texts have contents as under 4 and 5, but the child can also identify the 'pointers' and 'question-words', mainly independently; he can reorganize texts which are not exactly in the chrono-(logical) order independently if this is not too complicated; and finally he can also understand conversation-texts in which it is not exactly made clear who says what.
III. *Receptive reading in the structure-phase*, meaning the child understands texts

158

which give him new contents, an understanding not only through his own vocabulary, but also through the structure of the language, for instance how words can change in meaning, how they are grouped and belong together, how they are connected by declension and conjugation, what the meaning is of the syntactical structures and such like.

NB. Here starts a reading level.of 11 years old normally hearing children:

7. The texts require understanding of language-humour, of figurative meaning, of allegories etc.; the child can take in longer sentences with several subordinate clauses and the like.
8. The child can give a fair summary of books and other longer reading entities with contents and structures as mentioned under 5, 6 and 7.
9. The child understands texts which come under the belles-lettres, mainly independently.

c. Specific Difficulties

When I say specific difficulties, I mean those which do not occur often enough in conversation, neither in telling stories, nor in composition training.

(a). Difficulties Insufficiently Met in Conversation and Telling Stories

Previously we gave an example of how a teacher broke up a long written sentence into small spoken ones to make it more intelligible for his pupils. He also made the problem more concrete. This – in a moderate way – is a general trend in conversation and telling stories (not so much in speeches) between hearing partners too. Bernstein (1959 quot. Krech 1962) found the following: less long sentences, more elliptic sentences, less conjunctions, less adjectives and adverbs, less abstract expressions, e.g. not so much 'one does not know' but 'you don't know' etc. In reading, however, the children are confronted with longer sentences. The reason is obvious. In reading we can better follow longer sentences as one whole. We can look back for words we had forgotten and so on.
Although written language has some specific characteristics, we should not detach that language from its oral origin. This is why normal hearing children in the ordinary schools are invited by the teacher to read aloud piece by piece in turn, which very often reveals their difficulties in understanding. We should do the same with deaf children, and this can easily be done through the group-hearing-aid: one child reads, the others follow in their own books. Even the deafest children are able to follow this by rhythm (van Uden 1955).

(b). Difficulties in Reading Insufficiently Met in Composition Work

(1) *General warning:*
Don't over-emphasize expressive language. – 'Fixed complexes'.

There is a great danger in over-emphasizing expressive language, – that is the danger of 'screwing home', i.e. fixing in the minds of the children, meanings, language forms etc: leading to a *limited* number of programmed language steps. If we do so, we come to a dangerous loss of flexibility in language; we come to what Nanninga-Boon (1934) has called 'fixed complexes'.

A few examples in order to illustrate what is meant by 'fixed complexes':

A goods-train went to London (adapted from Dutch: een goederentrein ging naar Amsterdam) was, even after explication, understood as a good train. The complex of the limited meaning of good was so fixed in the mind of the child that it could not depart from it, in the same way as Piaget's child, (see above p. 131).

One may say was understood as: only one man.

A teacher said (wanting to tell a story): 'A farmer went to the market to buy *a pig*'. ... Suddenly Peter said: 'Yesterday, pig, on the street, running!' ... The teacher would have done better to have waited a moment and let that flow over him and his children. ... When the complex had been poured out, he could then have continued the story.

A teacher of religion, well prepared to prevent the rearing up of inadequate complexes, told the children: 'You, Peter, you have 3 fishes in an aquarium. But one morning you come to your aquarium, and see that there are 4 fishes! What would you say?' Peter: 'Strange! How is it possible?' Teacher: 'Good! You may also say: Where has that one come from? Repeat after me: ... Well, you, John, you have 10 pence in your pocket. You say to William: Would you like an ice-cream? O Yes! Well, you go to the shop. You look in your pocket, and there you see 20 pence! What would you ask?' John: 'Where has that come from?' Teacher: 'All right! Now we go outside one particular night. It will be a clear night. We will see the stars, so far away, and so many of them. What a universe! You may ask: Where has that come from? Do you have an answer? ...' Peter: 'From God'. Teacher: 'All right, Peter! And now our own earth! It is so small in that universe. We may ask: 'Where has our earth come from?' John: 'Also from God'. Teacher: 'All right, John. And now you yourself! Where have you come from?' John: 'From Sheffield ...'

Every teacher of the deaf is easily able to multiply these examples.

Of course, such complexes will always emerge, with hearing children too. But when you over-emphasize the correct expressive language of deaf children, you have to spend far too much time on this training, because the expressive language costs more of the teacher's time than reading. Consequently, and often alas unconsciously, you limit the language of the children, and then *too* many complexes

160

arise. So I don't agree fully with these words of Groht (1958): 'The wise teacher will do all in her power to keep the deaf child from developing a feeling of insecurity'. I think some feeling of insecurity with a great feeling of trust in the teacher and all other hearing people, (i.e. a feeling of trial and check), is indispensable. It is better than a false feeling of security with too many complexes, when you would never achieve good reading.

Flexibility

Reading first of all asks for *flexibility*. As Miller (1951) found from his experiments in verbal associations, the language we have is shaped according to a profile of probabilities with which words emerge in our mind. This profile works like a 'set'. Thus, if we limit the 'language-fund', the probability of the emergence of this small vocabulary and few language forms becomes too big, dangerously big, so that it masters and imprisons the mind (cf. Solomon and Postma 1952; Johnson, Frincke and Martin 1961). Also, later on when the riches of vocabulary improve, this profile remains too prominent, unless perhaps the children are of the very intelligent type.

(2) Four Specific Difficulties

The Function of Holding Up, Deferring Full Interpretation

The Meanings of Words

The *first difficulty* which is insufficiently approached in composition work is in my opinion (van Uden 1955–1957) the important necessity of deferring full actual determination of meaning. An example may illustrate this.

I once discussed this problem of the deferment function, of revising an interpretation and so on, with a Doctor of Literature. I voiced to him this sentence as an example: 'The waves ... (I purposely waited a moment) were not yet combed'. 'This is absolute nonsense', he said. We called upon another student of literature, a friend of ours, and I again said: 'Do you understand this: The waves were not yet combed'. Together they replied as one: – 'Oh yes, you mean the waves in the hair!' ... –

Other examples. I say: 'Your *table* ... is not complete'. What should you think? If you interpret table as an article of furniture, you may fail, because in the next words it will be clear that I was speaking about the '3 times table' in calculation. If you introspect now in your mind, what is happening there, you may find that you feedback from the words *3 times* to *table* in order to revise your interpretation.

161

You do this by the flexibility the words have in your mind. – Or: 'The *chair* . . . has already been vacant for three years'. – Or: 'That *water* . . . was much too wide'. – Or: 'The *frontier* of France . . ., a car was parked there' (= the border around France? At the boundary-post?). – Or: 'He lived outside the *city*' (= the busy city-centre? The whole community?). Etc. etc.

Don't say that this 'deferment-function' is only needed in very exceptional cases. On the contrary, it is almost continuously working. Let me for instance give the book by Jona and Peter Opei 'The lore and language of school children' (Oxford 1967) as an example of what I mean. Preface first sentence: '*More* than 200 years ago Queen Ann's physician John Arbuthnot, friend of Swift and Pope, *observed* that *nowhere* was tradition preserved *pure* and *uncorrupt* but *amongst* schoolboys, whose Games and Plays are *delivered down* invariably from one generation to another'. The words, (my italics), can only be correctly interpreted one way, by an intuitive understanding of the *whole* sentence, not by an understanding of element by element.

If you take a reading lesson in normal language, you will find that in reading we must very often postpone actual full interpretations, and if we did not do so, our minds should be so *flexible* that they would accept the feedback of the words to come. (Cf. research concerning translating machines, e.g. Reichling 1961, Yngve 1962).

It may be clear that this deferment function is active most of all in words which have a less frequent meaning in the context. So look for the most frequent meaning (at least to deaf children) of: more, observe, nowhere, pure, incorrupt, amongst, delivered . . . in the example above. Precisely because the vocabulary of deaf children is more limited and more primitively profiled, they are so endangered to make misinterpretations by underdeveloped deferment functions, i.e. by rigidity. This is in contrast to hearing children. MacNamara, Cleirigh and Kellaghan (1972) clearly showed how powerfully the context facilitates a special interpretation of words, different from the most frequent one, already present in hearing children of 5 years of age.

Kates (1972) found purely orally educated deaf children of 14 years of age (reading level 4th grade) significantly behind normally hearing children of that same age (although not as far behind as deaf children using signs) in shifting the meaning of known multi-meaning words, not, however, behind 9 year old normally hearing children of the same reading age.

The Groupings of Words

This 'deferment-function' is needed in the grouping of the words too, e.g. 'John said Mary is coming . . . Yes, John will come next week': the latter sentence shows that 'said Mary' was an embedded phrase (= the first sentence was a 'pincer-construction').

We emphasize the *flexibility* of changing the groupings of words.

The Tempo of Reading

Another very important aspect here is: *tempo*. This has to do with Short Term Memory too (cf. Smith 1971, de Leeuw 1970). I said above that I purposely paused for a moment after the words 'The waves' which led my Doctor of Literature astray. A similar difficulty in understanding happens in deaf children (some dyslexic hearing children too) who read in much too slow a tempo. Take this sentence: 'You have cut your finger, what should you do?'. A deaf child read this as follows 'You (2 seconds) have (1.7 seconds) cut (1 second) your (2.4 seconds) finger (4 seconds)', i.e. more than 11 seconds for this short sentence. Then I covered the page with my hand and asked the child: 'What did you read?'. The child did not know it at all! The child pointed at me, saying 'You!', but did not know what had happened in the sentence. Only the rough interpretation of *you/your* (occurring twice in the sentence) had been fixed in its mind.

A conclusion now for our teaching: we must train the memory for language, to speak in a good tempo and to read more and more words in less and less time, and to do this by heart. From all this it is understandable that Olsson (1967) found a significant correlation in deaf adolescents between their speed of visual perception and achievement in language.

What about Composition Work?

This power of deferring is insufficiently trained in composition work. In writing or in speaking we ourselves find the words with their correct determined interpretation and grouping. Not so in reading. The act of reading – as all understanding – presupposes first of all an overall intuitive grasp of the meaning of the whole. Also special words may be interpreted, but always under supervision of the entity, so that feed-backs and feed-aheads can work. We have already seen that reading is not at all a markovian process.

Groupings and Accentuations

A *second difficulty* in reading, insufficiently tackled in composition work, is: the *grouping* of words and the *accentuation*. Thus: the rhythm.

I, too, had some difficulty in understanding these sentences: 'Those subjects with

163

high affiliation need selected more people-pictures than those low in that need'. I halted after 'affiliation' and so I lost the gist. Another example: 'Note that complexity changes occur on specific attributes'. I stopped after 'complexity'. – In composition work, however, these grouping difficulties do not occur.

The same must be said of accentuations. How often must the unwritten accents of the words be understood and read between the lines! Hearing children do so, almost always as a matter of course. Deaf children do not. For instance (the example is taken from an oral conversation):

Teacher: 'How can we film the *growth* of flowers?' (clear accent on *growth*).

Children (16–17 years of age): 'Very easy! You can film the flowers! Nice flowers!'

Teacher: 'I am speaking about the *growth* of flowers, not about . . .'

Some children: ??? Other children: 'Not about houses' and so on.

The children did not see the problem. But they did not understand the accent either. Hearing people immediately understand by the accent: '*growth* of flowers, therefore not their colours, not their forms etc., but their growth'. Deaf children have to learn this purposely. They will be helped in conversation, but in reading there is no help (cf. antonyms).

In teaching to read, it is very often necessary to make children read a text aloud (as we said above), in order to check whether they make acceptably good groupings and accentuations. – And inversely very often our deaf children (even the deafest ones) who did not understand a text ask the teacher to read it aloud to them, with good rhythm, through the microphone of the group hearing aid. After this they often understand the difficult sentence.

The (Chrono)logical Order

A third difficulty is the *(chrono)logical* 'disorder' in many stories. Calon (1950) found – and every teacher of the deaf can confirm this – that deaf children have special difficulties in reorganizing a story the sentences of which do not follow the logical order. An example: –

A	B
1. Mother took her crying baby home.	1. There was a dog barking in the street.
2. There was a dog barking in the street.	2. The baby was afraid and cried.
3. The baby was afraid and cried.	3. Mother took the baby home.
Question: Where was the baby first? Answer: At home.	Question: Where was the baby first? Answer: In the street.

164

Puyenbroek (1966, 1973) found the same with calculations, e.g.

A	B
John had 4 sweets left, because mice had eaten 3 sweets. How many sweets had he first?	John had 7 sweets. Mice had eaten 3 sweets. How many sweets had John left?

A	B
Another example: John buys something for 48 new pence. He had one pound with him. How much change will he get?	John got one pound from his mother. He buys something for 48 new pence. How much change will he get?

A is more difficult than B.

This inner reorganization is also insufficiently trained in composition work.
It must be said that the constructive method – in making itself the reading lessons for the children – generally works according to model B. Neither the deferment functions, nor the inner reorganizations are trained in this way. Of course these children hardly ever reach the stage of reading normal reading books (see Kreye 1972).
Let us compare these 3 drafts of a reading-lesson:

(1) *The butterfly.*

John has got a butterfly.
Mary is very afraid.
Peter is teasing the butterfly.
John lets it fly away.
The butterfly has gone.

(2) *The butterfly.*

'Look! I have got a butterfly!' calls out John.
Mary was very afraid.
'Peter, do not tease him!'
John lets him fly away. Oh! . . .
'Where is he now?' Gone!

(3) *The butterfly.*

John had let his butterfly fly away.

165

Mary was so afraid because Peter teased him!
John was so happy with his butterfly: 'Look! I have
got a butterfly!' he called.
The teacher was a little bit angry with Peter. She
said: 'Peter, do not tease him!'
Away went the butterfly ... Oh!
'Where is he now?' Gone!

The second lesson is much better than the first one. Colloquial English is used, the same as in normal reading-books. The conversation plays a central part. – The third version is more complicated, especially because the temporal order is inversed. The teacher should not neglect this. In conversation too the temporal order is in no way fixed, on the contrary, and this goes for normal reading-books. This inversion of the temporal order makes reading-lessons much more vivid. But it asks more of the children, because they have to organize the correct temporal order themselves. Just this point should be trained. The third version is a good lesson.

The Pointer-words

A *fourth difficulty* is the 'pointer-words'. For reading it is quite necessary for the children to be able to interpret the pointer-words correctly. For example: 'Father has bought a new bicycle, a green one. We like it. I am looking forward to Sunday when we will go out'. Interpret: *one, we, it, I, when.*
In composition work the child should also use many pointer-words, but the interpretation does not present much difficulty, because he knows that interpretation already. This is not so in reading.

The Teacher's Notebook

I omit here the many other difficulties in reading. The teacher should have a note-book, possibly alphabetically ordered, in which he puts the special difficulties he has met in the lessons with his children.

4. WHAT HAS TO BE ACHIEVED?

The Ideal

In my experience of many years in a residential school working with all kinds of deaf children and of teachers, I can assure the reader of this:

All prelingually deaf children in the strict meaning of that term can be educated to read normal, not programmed language. Of course not all to the same level. A realistic ideal for a non-selective residential school for the deaf, taking in all kinds of deaf children in a normal distribution, is the following:

40% of them, when they are about 15–16 years old, can come to read successfully the books of normal hearing children of 11 years and older, through their own age, included books written in the more mature style of adolescents and adulthood (cf. Busemann 1925), = the numbers 7–9 of the Reading Scale page 158 – Many of these children can also learn to read a foreign language (our children learn English, cf. van Uden 1963b). See Appendix.

40% can come to read books written in the style for normal hearing children of about 9–10 years old successfully, when they are about 15–16 years old, = the numbers 5–6 of the Reading Scale.

20% can come to read simply written, normal language about their own environment successfully, = the numbers 3–4 of the Reading Scale.

A Reality

If this is not the case (see e.g. Furth 1966b), there must be something wrong in the education or in the development of the children. For example too many teacher changes; too many inexpert teachers; incorrect methods; lack of home training and/or preschool training (cf. Ewing 1964, Balow and Brill 1975); lack of co-operation by the parents; sign 'language' in free time; and so on. The cause is mainly due to the teachers not composing richly varied diaries with their children in preschool and lower grades, based on conversations. The same must be said for the parents.

We should not over-estimate the normally hearing population, however. Certainly 30–35% of them stick to the reading-levels 3–4–5–6 (Levin and Williams 1970, Sharon 1973–1974, van Uden 1975).

With respect to the three levels of reading mentioned earlier, of prelingually deaf children (in its strict sense), the situation in our Institute school-years 1967–1968 and 1970–1971, with pupils of 16 through 19 years of age (including the multiply-handicapped) was as follows (see further Appendix), see p. 168, top.

The situation is therefore not yet ideal, for a number of reasons. It will be very difficult of course to achieve that ideal, because these 'prelinguals' are so vulnerable. The deep need of these children is often not understood, not even in our high culture.

Even in this last half of the 20th century, e.g. Dutch law (although very loyal to handicapped children) does not yet give these handicapped children all the opportunities they need to achieve their highest potential: e.g. insufficient establishment

Reading-level:	1967–1968 number of children and percentage:	1970–1971 number of children and percentage:
highest level (nos. 7–9):	16 = 24%	19 = 26%
transition phase from 2nd to highest level (no. 6):	15 = 22%	18 = 25%
second level (no. 5):	15 = 22%	26 = 36%
third level (no. 3–4):	22 = 32%	9 = 13%
Total:	68 = 100%	72 = 100%

NB. 20 children of the highest level and the transition-phase were reading simple English books in 1968, 34 in 1971, i.e. 65 and 92% respectively.

of staff, too few facilities for teacher and assistant training, no or very limited possibilities for research and scientific guidance, and so on.

Nevertheless we maintain the ideal to bring these children as far as possible, according to these inciting words of Sr. Theresia van Driel (1934): 'We aspire to the unattainable ideal in order to achieve the highest attainable levels'.

The Cooperation of the Parents. The 'Diaries'

It should be said that the cooperation of the parents is very important, especially in expanding the vocabulary. There are parents who are so cooperative, e.g. in constructing and keeping an index for the growing vocabulary of their child, that their child is easily ahead of its peers in reading intelligently, even notwithstanding a lower intelligence. We discovered several of these children in our research. This cooperation should be stimulated as much as possible. The strongest barrier against a satisfying development of reading is: *lack of vocabulary*, and not so much the difficulties with the structures of sentences. This latter point plays its more important part in the highest levels of reading, nos. 7–9.

I fully agree with these words of Dale (1967, 1968): 'If the family diary is kept carefully and conscientiously for, say, 8 or 10 years, it can be promised (provided the child is not very dull mentally) that *he will read* adequately for his every day needs and it is likely that he will read for pleasure and information throughout the rest of his life'.

There is, however, a phase, in which this ideo-visual reading should be changed more and more to receptive reading (see above). This can start at about 6 to 8 years of age, provided the child has followed the preschool. At about 9 to 10 years

168

of age the writing of diaries should be changed into the composing of albums for specialized objects (unless a child continued his diary for his own pleasure), e.g. from geography, history etc. The diaries should stop being the main reading material, in order not to replace the normal reading books: from that time onwards they have to become 'learning books', in which, e.g. press-cuttings, letters, and also worthwhile compositions of the children, etc. can be collected.

V
Teaching a Mother-tongue to Deaf Children

1. A MOTHER-TONGUE

Children Without a Mother-tongue?

The combination in the title of this chapter looks very paradoxical:
teaching + mother-tongue.

It is said that a mother-tongue is learnt spontaneously and cannot be taught. The linguist Schuy (1955) said that deaf children remain in the exceptional situation of not having a mother-tongue and only using a foreign language (see also Kröhnert 1966). His reasoning seems to be that the oral language they learn in school remains only an artificial language not comparable with a mother-tongue, and the low slang of signs they develop themselves by the communicative actions of the deaf with the deaf cannot be called a language at all, because it has no linguistic system. So he concludes, there is no mother-tongue at all.

I don't think he is right. Take deaf adults — and I have met a lot of them — with whom we can converse orally as easily as with deafened persons. Deaf adults whose spoken and written sentences are mainly correct and who can read the books of the normal hearing according to special levels, do all this directly, spontaneously, i.e. not by translating from another communicative code such as signs, — why should we deny them recognition of their language as being mother-tongue, at least in its third form (see page 22)?

The Spontaneity in Learning a Mother-tongue and Yet Being Taught It

Indeed the *spontaneity* of learning is one of the most striking characteristics of the mother-tongue. A hearing child learns as a child, i.e. by trial and check through these factors: by imitating others, by being conditioned, by finding and following analogies, by feeling master of his own world.

The spontaneity of learning the mother tongue is especially clear in the finding and following of analogies in language, i.e. its structures (Lewis 1951). This aspect becomes effective in hearing children through the enormous frequency in receiving and expressing language. The analogies are rhythmically modelled and seem to present themselves to the child. Also the intonations may be a big help for the correct groupings and flexions. Rhythm and melody are very attractive too.

NB. For example *phrases*: 'Now we are *going to bed*. Do you like *going to bed*?', – *flexions*: 'We wal*ked* in the street and loo*ked* at the shops', – 'You are nice! You did it nice*ly*!'.

This spontaneous process, however, is misunderstood, if it is thought that the mother does not teach. On the contrary, a mother really does teach, though not in the accepted pupil/teacher way by ruling out the child's trial- and check-play. The natural way of teaching the mother follows includes and presupposes trial and check-play. It makes the child search and think. In essence the same way is followed in our reflective method for deaf children. – But let us first trace the path of the hearing child and its mother, before explaining how our reflective method works.

Language Growth as a Differentiating Process

Psychologists say (cf. McCarthy 1954, Barker 1954 quot. Krech 1962; Braine 1963–1964) that during 80% of his wakeful hours a child himself speaks or babbles, or listens to speech of others. This means about three million words a year! The child first forms an enormous fund of receptive language or so-called 'passive language'. Fraser, Bellugi and Brown (1963) investigated this with sentences arranged to pictures. The infants had to indicate which picture belonged to a spoken sentence. They could do so even with such sentences which they could not speak *spontaneously*, i.e. which were not part of their 'active language'. They could even imitate more or less the sentences presented to them, also when they had not understood their content. There was a big difference between their passive and active language. The children now develop their *own* vocabulary by selecting *from* their passive language, and using it in their own system, which is more or less similar to that of the older environment, but not in all aspects.

Their first words are the co-called one-word sentences (Stern 1907): they mean a whole sentence with the intonation of a sentence too (Weir 1962, Menyuk 1969). So it seems to be incorrect to call this stage just a 'lexical phase' (McNeill 1968): the children use the asking, asserting and emphatic intonations, according to the intentions of sentences as parts of their conversations. These intonations are already just the same as those of the older environment.

As Braine (1963) has shown, the child of about 2;0 has 2 word classes: pivots and non-pivots (or open) words. The child starts to combine 2 or 3 words, not as associations or simple strings, but as sentences, because it keeps these strings under the same intonations as the adults. It is in this period that the first combination of question and answer appears, which grows to the subject-predicate structure (Leopold 1953–1954, 1956).

171

Thus from a diffused overall beginning of one word, its expressive language differentiates more and more. By the time it is 2;6 it already has 6 word-classes: verbs, substantives, articles, 'pointer-words', and adjectives. It uses sentences of 3–4 words.

Having reached the age of 3;0 it has the normal language-structure of the adults, of course on a smaller basis of 4- and 5-word sentences, again always comprised under the same intonations, always as parts of the conversations. The following parts of speech will have been added: personal and other pronouns (i.e. special kinds of pointer-words), auxiliary verbs (namely will, can, may, have and similar), adverbs (for instance more, still, very, too and so forth), prepositions (such as in, on, under, to, etc.).

So this process should not be compared with the building of a house, i.e. by the accumulation of bricks, by association, but with the differentiating process from zygote to embryo, to foetus, to baby.

Environment and Child

It may be clear from this summary that the environment plays an important part in the linguistic development of a child: i.e. both the variety of the situations providing opportunity for experiences (compare the city child with that of the country) and the culture of the other persons, of adults as well as of children.

Sometimes it happens that a mother only imitates her child instead of enhancing its progress up to her own level. A kind of *idioglossia* comes into existence. These mothers follow what could be called a diachronic way: they descend to the level of their children hoping to bring them up to a higher level later on. Once my advice was asked in a case of idioglossia between a mother and her two children. These children did not achieve normal speech. My advice was that the mother should immediately stop speaking the jargon of her children and stop responding when her children were using it, but she should always reinforce the use of normal speech and always give the normal example herself. After a year the idioglossia had gone. See also Wood (1964). Instead of following in a diachronic way, this mother had to follow a synchronic way.

Of course the mother has to adjust herself to the capacities of her child, but only in *normal* speech of her own synchronic level, and – it must be said that the mother does this of her own accord – always somewhat more than the child is able to do: the child will at least understand and be 'pulled up' to ever higher stages of language development.

Cases of idioglossia between hearing children and their parents are very exceptional indeed. Not so alas between *deaf* children and their parents. Without good home-training instruction this will even be the rule! There is no need to say how detrimental this is to the deaf child, when it is already so detrimental to a hearing child.

172

It is well known to what extent hearing children can be retarded in an environment of poor language (see e.g. Kellner and Tanner 1958). Vigotsky placed normal hearing infants individually within a group of deaf infants. The quantity of their speech decreased almost immediately (1962).

2. HOW A MOTHER TEACHES

It is not true that a mother does not help her hearing child expressly. Quite the inverse! From our observations (van Uden 1955–1957) and the admirable research of Brown (1964) we know how a mother continuously corrects the language of her baby.

Kinds of Reactions of the Mother

MacNeill (1970) summarizes the kinds of reactions of the mother (and of most adults of the child's environment) to the typical utterances of the small child (as we have seen above: from about 1 until about 6 years of age):
(1) Expansion: the mother repeats the child's utterance by adding the parts she thinks are missing, e.g. child: 'Daddy car', mother: 'Daddy is coming by car'.
(2) Modelling: the mother comments on everything said by the child, e.g. child: 'Daddy car?', mother: 'Daddy is not coming by car, he is taking the tram'.
(3) Prompting: the mother puts a question, asking the child for an answer, e.g. mother: 'Where is your handkerchief?', child: 'I have lost it'. Or inciting, e.g. mother: 'Say: Thank you very much', child: 'Thank you very much'.
(4) Echoing, which aids the child's memory.

The 'Seizing Method' of the Mother and her 'Playing of a Double-part'

Let us give some examples from my longitudinal observations of two mothers, my sister and my sister-in-law:
The mother approaches her baby's cradle. The baby starts to kick and to move its legs and arms, and smiles at the mother. The mother says:
'Would you like some milk?
Come here, my darling!'
What is the mother really doing here? In the first sentence 'Would you like some milk?' the mother interprets the expressive movements of her baby. Every mother knows her baby perfectly and these interpretations will often if not always be right. So the mother 'seizes' what the child *wants* to say and gives him the words which he would use if he could speak. – In the second sentence the mother gives her own contribution to the conversation. This is necessary if a real conversation

173

is to develop. Spontaneous thoughts from *both* sides are needed. This first time the baby will not understand 'Come here, my darling', but the mother takes the child out of his crib, and the second, third or fourth time the child will understand that these words point like a signal to something that is going to happen. We formulate this behaviour by saying that mother *makes herself understood through the situation*. The mother plays *a double-part*: she plays the part of her child, putting the right words into his mouth, and she plays her own part. – And this conversation now develops more and more.

Just 'Expansion' or Conversation?

Cazden (1965) did research on two groups of deprived preschool children (2;6 years of age) of low cultural environment. Group A were the 'expansion children': they received only expansions of their utterances from the teachers and nurses, e.g. child 'Doggy bite', experimenter 'Yes, the doggy bites'. Group B was the experimental group, the 'modelling children': they did not receive expansions but modellings as described above, e.g. child 'Doggy bites', experimenter 'Yes, he is very bad'. Cazden applied pre- and re-tests of language competence on both groups of children and found that group B had achieved better results than group A. – In my opinion, however, it is not so much the 'expansion' and 'modelling' being different between the 2 groups, but more that there was a real conversation only in group B, i.e. an exchange of thoughts.

Tizard and others (1972) did a similar research, giving, however, more attention to the conversation as such. They measured the quality of talk, described in terms of real conversation, i.e. exchange of thoughts, and found a significant correlation with the language-achievement.

How the Mother Converses with her Child

It is one year and one month later. I am sitting in my sister's lounge, and the baby Mariëtta, half crawling and half walking comes up to the long table at which we are sitting. She pulls herself up, looks on the table, sees a dish of biscuits and says: 'Mmmm' ... Her mother says: 'That is nice, isn't it! But you have already had a biscuit'. Here we see the same, as we have described above, again, the mother seizes what Mariëtta wants to say and gives her the right words: 'That is nice, isn't it!' and further-she also gives her own contribution: 'But you have already had a biscuit!' There is a certain progress in the fact that Mariëtta moves her mouth: she uses a vocable as a word: 'Mmmm' ...

Again it is a year later. The following conversation could be noted down. The situation is as follows. Mother, sitting at the table, is preparing an orange for

174

father who is expected home shortly. It is 5 o'clock in the afternoon. The child is kneeling on a chair near the table. Then a conversation starts:

Child (2;2 years old):	*Mother:*
'Mmmm nice!'	'Yes, it is nice, it is for daddy! Daddy likes oranges'.
'Daddy orange'	'Orange' (spoken very melodically).
'Orange' (with the same melody). 'Orange!' 'Orange!' 'Daddy orange!' (a pause).	'Orange! You do talk well!'
'Daddy ... car?	'No, daddy is not coming by car. He is taking the tram!'
'Titia car, eh?'	'No, not today. We will go out by car on Sunday ...
'Daddy orange! Daddy orange!' (skips away). Etc.	See the orange is ready'.

About one month later we could note down the following conversation:

Child:	*Mother:*
'Look mam sheep!'	'Oh what a lovely sheep!'
'Big sheep and small sheep!'	'Yes, that big sheep is the mama of the small sheep'.
'Mama? ... Look mama, big sheep and small sheep running! ...'	'Can't you see that big sheep ...'
'Dog, oh dog, look at dog! Not allowed!'	'The dog is naughty ... That is not allowed! ...'
'Away dog!'	'Yes, the dog must not do that ... His master is calling him already!'
'Master calling ...' Etc.	

We may see clearly how a mother teaches the mother-tongue to a child. We want to emphasize three aspects particularly:

a. At first the child speaks almost only 'contentors'. The mother not only fills in contentors, but also and especially those small 'functors'. Refer to these examples in the text above:

175

Child:	Mother:
Nice!	*That is* nice.
Nice daddy!	*That is* nice. *That is for* daddy.
Car	*By* car
Sheep	*A lovely* sheep.
Big sheep	*The* big sheep
Small sheep.	*The* small sheep
Dog	*The* dog
Not allowed	*That is* not allowed.
Etc.	Etc.

b. At the same time the mother extends the utterances of the child and trains his Short Term Memory almost continuously, specifically the memory-function for *successively* presented data.

c. There are a lot of 'transformations' from child to mother and the reverse. Very often the child uses a question-transformation and the mother a negative assertive one. Or the mother may use an imperative-transformation and the child an assertive one; even passive transformations occur. These transformations appear from the very beginning, especially via the intentions of the sentences. It cannot be said that the positive, active, assertive sentence (so-called 'basic structure') is the first or the most frequent sentence-form a child or a mother uses.

d. Notice that the mother never emphasizes language-forms totally detached from the content and the situation: so 'transparency' is continuously safeguarded.

Now an example given by Brown and Bellugi (1964):

First a small conversation between a mother and her son, 2;3 of age:

Son: See truck, Mommy. See truck!
Mother: Did you see the truck?
Son: No I see truck.
Mother: No, you didn't see it? There goes one.
Son: There go one.
Mother: Yes, there goes one.
Son: See a truck! See Truck, Mommy. See truck! Truck! Put truck, Mommy!
Mother: Put the truck where?
Son: Put truck window!
Mother: I think that one is too large to go in the window ...

Some more examples:

Baby	*Mother*
Baby highchair	Baby is in the highchair.
Eve lunch	Eve is having lunch.
Sat wall	He sat on the wall etc.

176

Notice here again how mother incessantly fills in the function words, which the baby omits! The same function words which cause so many difficulties for deaf children.

Conversation Before Building Up a Vocabulary

Mother seizes what her child says, about 33% of her utterances, – and she plays her own part, about 67% of her utterances: she speaks what she herself wants to say and she seizes the clumsy speech of her child moulding its form. So she starts her work immediately from birth, *before* building up any vocabulary. She finds, led by nature, the crystallization point of language: *conversation*. The mother converses with her child all day. Vocabulary grows by conversation.

3. CONVERSATION AND MOTHER-TONGUE

Characteristics

In conversation, all characteristics of language are concentrated:

a. It is the most natural situation of language (van Ginneken 1909)
b. It guarantees emotionally integrated language
c. True conversation involves spontaneity of all partners, thus its language always arises from the feelings and interests of the child itself: 'following a child-not a method-oriented way' (Myklebust 1964)
d. Expressive and receptive language are balanced
e. It is personal, from person to person with an exchange of thoughts and feelings; not the cold objects are primary, but rather the attitudes towards objects
f. It involves a continuous refinement of meanings by interference and interaction, i.e. by their polarities
g. It involves entering into the attitudes of others, shifting of meanings and attitudes, adjustment and flexibility
h. The accentuations of phrases and sentences are placed in their natural settings and trained in this way, the shifting of accents too
i. It involves a continuous anticipatory behaviour because the partners have to make themselves understood: the encoding processes include the foreseeing of their decoding processes in the other, the correctness of which is immediately checked by the reactions of the partner
j. *Being* understood (= the speaker's utterance was adequate to the situation) and *having* understood (= having given an adequate response to the unity of language

uttered and situation) continuously reinforce the correct choice of words and language-forms, and the correct interpretation of meanings

k. The ability of deferring definite interpretation of parts of utterances and the ability of interpreting them after the whole utterance in the situational setting has been conceived, is continuously trained (see above 'Your table... is not complete')

l. It is the basis of thinking in language and of its 'transparency'

m. It gives the normal everyday idioms.

4. CONVERSATION AND MOULDING THE MIND

The listening attitude of the teacher, his seizing of the children's utterances and giving them back in their right linguistic forms, makes the children themselves more and more listen to the teacher: exchange of thoughts, conversation is born.

The Whole Secret of the Work: the Art of Listening

Experience has taught us that many teachers of the deaf have difficulty in following the 'seizing method' because they cannot listen to their children. They sometimes say: 'My children won't say anything'. This of course is quite untrue; this assertion only shows that the teacher does not give enough attention to what her/his children are wanting to say. He/she cannot sufficiently 'listen'. Scroggs (1975) termed the 'seizing behaviour' of the teacher: 'expansions'. He found in a very suggestive study that some teachers have more difficulty in this listening and seizing function than others, both by lack of stimulating the children to utter themselves, and by presenting their own expressive behaviour too much.

The same happens where the parents are involved, maybe the father or the mother or both of them. We established a clear criterion to find out whether the parents *accept* the deafness of their child whole-heartedly or not. This criterion is: Observe whether they listen to their deaf child! There are some parents who do a lot for their child, except one thing: listen. In some children the consequences may be disastrous: they don't feel accepted and symptoms of a 'desolation-syndrome' appear (van Uden 1973).

It may be clear that the 'seizing-method' is very important to the child-mother relationship. I have known deaf children who unconsciously did not feel accepted by father or mother or both change emotionally like a leaf on a tree, once the parents had learned to follow this 'seizing method'.

Listening is an indispensable aspect of a conversation. How often we see people conversing in such a way that they speak at the same time, interrupt each other continuously, with a lot of misunderstandings because they don't listen to each other. To 'converse' thus means more of addresses *to* each other, because there is no or insufficient *exchange* of thoughts.

In the same way it is impossible to enter into conversation with deaf children unless we continuously listen to what *they* want to say, what they think, what they desire . . . A good teacher of language, or better a good pedagogue of deaf children is always a good listener. If a teacher of the deaf has learned this art of listening, it will be his experience, that he becomes able to explain to the children even the most difficult of expressions, such as: 'he said it with a patronizing and encouraging smile', 'dogskin is being worn a good deal just now', 'it seems so dishonest', 'haven't you got any new gloves?' (observations in the 6th grade 12–17th October 1974), etc. etc.

An Important Pedagogical Consequence: the Deep Influence of a Teacher of the Deaf Upon Character and View of Life of his Children

There is no denying that the teacher of the deaf, following this maternal method in teaching a mother-tongue, has a deep influence upon character and view of life of his children, especially in the first 7 and 8 school-years. This method asks for a '*moving-up system*', i.e. that ideally the teacher keeps his children for at least 4 or 5 school years.

In some sense this influence can be compared with the influence of the parents of hearing children, i.e. those who educate them through and in their mother-tongue, and transfer to them, unconsciously and consciously, their view of life, their religion, their hopes and anxieties, their needs and satisfactions, their ambitions and their memories, their whole way of reacting to persons and events, all incarnated within the mother-tongue. We all know that this influence mostly determines, in some way, one's whole life, right or wrong, equilibrating or disturbing, 'stabilizing' or 'labilizing', 'rigidifying' or 'flexibilizing'. The education, steeped in the mother-tongue, is root and outlook of many conscious and unconscious convictions and aspirations, which hold for many many years and appear almost unchangeable throughout life. – The expert and real teacher of the deaf educates his children much in the same way. I think no teacher has such a high responsibility for his children as does a teacher of the deaf. – The teacher therefore should always keep in mind that he has to educate his children, not for himself but for their parents, although, in these first years, he is mostly able to converse with them much more easily than their parents who offered their child to him can do.

Conversation and Thinking

I said that conversation is the basis of thinking in language and of its 'transparen-

179

cy'. Now we come to this most basic principle of all learning of language, which I would formulate in these two strongly connected theses:

1. A language can be called perfectly mastered when the user thinks in the correct vocabulary and forms of that language (although this can happen in different degrees).
2. Everybody will think in that language in which they converse.

A consequence of this double thesis is that a conversation only then proceeds smoothly when both partners think in the language used in that conversation. The first aim of a teacher of a language is to get conversation going in *that very* language with his pupils, as soon as possible.

With respect to the mother tongue: The child will think in that language in which the environment succeeds in conversing with him; if this is his first language, it will be his mother-tongue.

All this can be supported by every user of a foreign language from his own experience: in the beginning he must translate too much; he keeps on thinking in his own language; but gradually he starts thinking more and more in the foreign one and from that point in time the conversation proceeds better and better. When the user thinks directly in a language, then that language obtains 'transparency'. If he must translate, that language never had or loses 'transparency'.

I met an American who as a Dutch boy of 12 years, the Dutch language being his mother tongue, emigrated to the United States. After some 50 years he came back and appeared to have lost the 'transparency' of his mother-tongue: he told me he had to translate. After about a month of Dutch conversation, thinking in Dutch and its transparency came back.

Thinking in a Language

Psycholinguistics show clearly that there is a continuous circular process, a 'feeding and feeding back', of perceptible speech and inner language. Perhaps De Saussure (1916, conf. Nuytens 1962) separated too much *la langue* from *la parole* ('La langue est essentiellement un dépot psychique'; Chomsky uses the terms 'competence' and 'performance'), seeing that dépot as much too immaterialized and individualistic. Both are quite integrated, however. As Watson (quot. Berlyne 1965) rightly said: 'Thinking is largely a subvocal talking'. Skinner (1957) on the other hand annuls much too much the value of inner language. I don't think he would like it, if I told him: 'Your book 'Verbal Behavior' is only verbal behaviour to me!'

Piaget (1923) perhaps has been influenced by De Saussure in his theory of so-called egocentric speech of children which in his opinion should be a special phase *preparing* the child for socialized speech. So he sees this kind of speech far too

180

much as a soliloquy. Miller (G. 1951) already found that in the phase of that so-called egocentric speech, 90% of the speech of a child is directly social: so it cannot be presumed to be a preparatory phase.

In my opinion it can perhaps be conceived as an imitation of the conversations with the mother (or others). We have already seen that the mother continuously plays a double part, which perhaps makes it easier for the child to imitate conversations. The child often listens to conversations of others too. Vigotsky (1956) may be right in suggesting that these soliloquies are a phase in the language development of children not from in-side to out-side, from egocentricism to social behaviour, but the reverse: from out-side to in-side, preparing more and more the inner language thinking. So we have three phases:

1. conversation with others present;
2. conversation played as a double role without others present as a kind of thinking aloud;
3. inner language subvocal speaking, thinking.

Two Mother-tongues Simultaneously?

Bilingualism

What about bilingualism? Is it possible to master *two mother-tongues* simultaneously?

The experiment is well known where father speaks only German to his child and mother only English, with the effect that the child learns of its own accord to speak German to father and English to mother (cf. Leopold 1949, Haugen in Saporta 1961). This is a kind of bilingualism in its strict sense, so-called 'co-ordinated language'. When the child mixes up the codes from two or more languages, it is called 'compound language' (Ervin and Osgood 1954, Ervin 1961, see Saporta 1961). From the studies in strict bilingualism we may conclude that in principle all oral languages are equally easy for a hearing child and that the manner of coding is determined not by the situation but by the *person* in the situation: for in the same situation the child will speak German to father and English to mother. Ervin and Osgood found that the semantic differential of words in strict bilingualism is not identical in both languages, e.g. the connotative meanings of *wood* will be different from *Holz* (German = wood). This means that the concept-systems of both languages seem to be different and well discerned. This is not the case with 'compound bilingualism': the connotations are more identical. See Carroll (1959), Gekoski (1970).

With respect to the control of language it is clear from many studies (see e.g. Haugen in Saporta 1961, MacNamara 1966, 1967) that compound bilingualism is very bad for the manner of thinking: there is a lot of negative transfer. But also in strict bilingualism the semantic satiety of both languages has been impoverished, e.g. the quantity of associated words by the stimulus-words in such bilinguals is lower than in monolinguals (Jakobovitsch and Lambert quot. Hörmann 1967).

About children speaking at home say, Spanish and in school English, it is evident from several researches that both languages are impoverished (e.g. Holland 1960; MacNamara 1966, 1967). Nuytens (1962) found the same in children speaking a dialect at home and learning General Accepted Language in school. The last writer, however, found also some children who, exactly through the reflecting on the differences of both languages, grew in their ability to master both systems. This is in agreement with the important research of Carrow (1957). She found that bilinguals, speaking Spanish at home and learning English in English-spoken schools, were behind monolinguals in language development, *except* those children who had an I.Q. above 121. These bilinguals were ahead of the monolinguals of the same I.Q. So we see that for only these very intelligent children, they are not only not lagging but ahead, seemingly because they had the ability to reflect spontaneously on their two languages. At the same time this is proof of how important reflection on language can be.

Lambert and Peal (1962) found that the bilingual subjects of their research were more intelligent than monolingual ones, both according to verbal I.Q. and *performance* I.Q. They interpret their better finding as originating from the bilingualism, making these subjects conceptually more flexible. I think the researches of Nuytens and Carrow are more correct in this respect.

So we agree partly with Merleau-Ponty (quot. Kwant 1961) who says that only one mother-tongue in its full and deep sense is possible.

5. CHARACTERISTICS OF TEACHING A MOTHER-TONGUE TO DEAF CHILDREN

Now we can *summarize* our findings in order to apply them to our work with *deaf* children.

Teaching a mother-tongue to deaf children should have – in my opinion – these characteristics:

1. We must enter into conversation with the deaf child as soon as possible.

2. And this in only one language, with all the natural language forms normal in the respective situations.

3. This language should be the oral rhythmical language. So we must come to *oral* conversation with the deaf child as soon as possible, so that he will think in oral ways, the oral language will be transparent, and by doing so can become his mother-tongue.

4. The language which the child should learn must first of all be understood, i.e.

182

receptive language should precede expressive language. This understanding applies not only to the content but also to the grammatical functions.

5. Expressive language should grow from a much larger fund of understood receptive language, which fund must be built up from the conversations, the deposit of which is written down in the children's diaries.

6. The children should be helped more and more to *find* the systematical cues *themselves* by reflecting first of all on their reading material, and on composition work too, in order to make them control, more and more, their own expressive language. These systematic cues should be found not in an associative but in a differentiating way, always starting from the whole, descending to the parts and again ascending back to the whole. These cues, i.e. grammatical rules, should be applied increasingly in conversation, most of all in their composition work. We should use therefore a differentiating grammar. If this is not available, we will have to write our own.

7. Composition work should never be over-emphasized so that reading always remains in the foreground, because only good reading can give deaf children sufficient frequency of language-practice in order to master that language as far as possible.

6. SPECIFIC DIFFICULTIES OF DEAF CHILDREN IN LEARNING AN ORAL MOTHER-TONGUE

The principles mentioned above are quite a programme! In this programme we discounted the many special difficulties of deaf children:

a. A too low frequency of language practice in comparison with hearing children: therefore education in reading should be strongly in the foreground. Therefore help too in finding analogies in the receptive language material. These detected analogies should be crystallized into well-chosen linguistic terms (an attempt at this see p. 234).

b. Difficulties in memory: thus first of all a great deal of oral rhythm practice in language acquisition, (which I would call 'accent-group thinking' or 'phrase structure thinking'), a lot of reading and writing and recording of the learnt language as much as possible in diaries and notebooks.

c. The slow beginning in infant years, in which years the deaf children stay in the one-word phase of expressive language for too long a time, and the lipreading and listening cues are still too limited. Thus an early start with speech lessons is necessary (not later than 3 or 4 years of age, if possible earlier, in methods adequate to childlike behaviour; see a summary below p. 213) and with reading and writing (not later than 4 or 5 years of age) together with an early start of the diaries.

d. The lack of experience in many deaf children, which should be reciprocated by special measures at home, in the boarding school and in class (cf. Furth 1966).

Environment. The Boarding-school

e. The alas often bad *environment* of deaf children in free time (cf. Ewing 1964): i.e. parents and/or brothers and sisters at home constantly using a kind of telegram-style to the child instead of using normal language, or still worse: who use signs ... In the boarding-school: even when the other deaf children are talking, not using signs (which is of course a good situation, necessary for an oral education), this talking is not straight away in normal English. So the most spontaneous conversations of the children do not sufficiently reinforce the use of normal English.

If a normal *hearing* child had such an environment, its language would be impoverished too! This has been shown in such guardian-institutes which follow a horizontal classification of the (hearing) children, i.e. according to the same age. There was a kind of 'linguistic deprivation' (Cazden 1965). Bernstein (1967) rightly calls this 'restricted language' in contrast to 'elaborated language'. One of the first effects of a change to the vertical classification (i.e. to group children of different ages together), was the improvement in the language of the infants (Brodbeck and Irwin 1946, Horn 1948, cf. Tizard et al. 1972).

Experiments in this respect with *deaf* children had the bad effect of enormously increasing a jargon of signs, however, because mainly the grown up children could not yet control themselves in order to talk with the small ones: they created more and more signs (Bern 1950). Research may teach us.

When deaf children live in a residential school, the groups of children should be so small that the children are very much in touch with the hearing adults. This is conclusive especially for the children up to about 12 years of age. – The groups of the residence should be as well selected as the classes of the school.

Hearing playmates, well prepared for this, will be important too. The boarding school should be so organized that these hearing children can be received: e.g. well-equipped sports rooms with stands and so on.

A so-called 'semi-residence', i.e. where the children are at home most weekends, should be preferred to a full-residence (provided the distances are not too far).

A special service for the parents will be very important: there are some parents alas, who have to be 'educated' themselves.

Needless to say, deaf and dumb personnel in school and/or residence, continuously in contact with the children, is a very interfering and often primitivizing and dehumanizing factor. All good faith is pernicious here.

184

Scouten (1967) things that monolingualism in a school for the deaf is only possible by using both finger-spelling and speech. To me this is not monolingualism in its full sense (refer finger-spelling below).

To me it is quite possible and therefore preferable and necessary to use monolingualism in the pure oral way, both in school and in free time. It may be seen from this that in a language teaching school the free time is as important as the school itself.

We explained above that *bilingualism*, both coordinated and compound, is dangerous for by far the most of hearing children. Only one mother-tongue is actually possible.

This is the more conclusive concerning a bilingualism of an oral- and a sign-language, because these are two languages which are not really comparable to each other, seemingly making *reflecting* much more difficult: Charrow and Fletcher (1973) found that intelligent deaf adolescents, children of deaf parents, having started with pure sign-language (American Sign Language or 'Ameslan') from early childhood and learning English afterwards, from 5–6 years of age, using Ameslan outside the classroom and English in the classroom, only *tended* towards a kind of coordinated bilingualism but this unsuccessfully. Even this tendency was not found in deaf children of hearing parents, educated at the same combined school. *Coordinated bilingualism*, i.e. that the 'speakers-signers' are equally conversant in both languages, has not been found in prelingually *deaf* children (see so-called 'total communication' page 195).

What about a *compound bilingualism* of signs and speech?

The origin of this situation is usually that the deaf children are not sufficiently trained in oral conversation and converse among themselves in conventional signs and words. The consequences are deplorable: It is a matter of course that lipreading, auditory training and speech are not developed to full automation and advantage (in prelingually *deaf* children). These functions need a continuous challenge to develop, comparable with such functions as learning to read Braille, to read back finger-spelling and signs, to understand Morse signals, to read the traffic signals quickly enough, to typewrite, to train physically, and so on. Purely oral conversations, as shown in the Appendix of this book, are quite impossible with those 'combined' children. But growth of language-as-such (vocabulary and structure) is heavily hampered too, if not killed.

In my opinion this *jargon* of signs and speech can hardly be acknowledged as 'language' because its system – if any – is too poor: neither the signs have been systemated, nor the words. This slang dominates the children's whole thinking and thwarts any systematized control of language.

Markides (1974, published in 1976) compared 5 classes of a 'combined' school

185

with 5 classes of an oral school, both groups of 30 adolescents matched according to prelingual hearing loss, to intelligence and learning ability, to length of education, and most of all to the *expertise* of their teachers. She found in 10 'demonstration lessons', 5 of them given to 'combined' classes and 5 to oral classes, by their own expert teachers:

(a) that purely oral lessons were not possible in the 'combined' classes. The lipreading of these pupils was much too bad. The number of words used by the teachers in the 'combined' classes was not higher than 38% of that used in the oral classes, and the 'combined' pupils used only 27% of the number of words of the oral pupils. 65% of the communicative means in the 'combined' classes were signs and finger-spelling.
(b) that the communication in the 'combined' classes was very slow and laboured in comparison to the natural pace in the oral classes.
(c) that the written vocabulary of the 'combined' pupils was significantly lagging behind that of the oral pupils.
(d) that the composition work was lagging too. (No data of the reading levels have been published.)
(e) that the intelligibility of spontaneous speech of the 'combined' pupils was significantly much lower than that of the oral ones: 13% of the 'combined' pupils had no speech at all; only 7% of them spoke sufficiently intelligibly in comparison with 60% of the oral pupils; only 3% of the latter spoke unintelligibly.

Kates (1972) compared three matched groups of 30 deaf adolescents, the first one educated monolinguistically orally, the second one in finger-spelling and speech (Rochester-method) and the third one according to the principles of the 'combined' system. The latter pupils were significantly lagging behind the oral ones in almost all aspects of his investigation. This study will be quoted more in detail below.
Rosanova (1970, see Oléron 1972) found a better *memory for* signs than for *words* in signing deaf children. It is a common experience (years ago in our Institute too) that signing deaf children have a bad memory for words, spoken and written, especially for those for which no signs are available (cf. Watson and Scott 1974). They may even sometimes develop a kind of hostility towards words (cf. Blea 1967). (A similar bad memory in hearing students has been found in the learning of those words in a second language for which there is no parallel word in the mother-tongue, Henning 1973.) – Additionally the number of signs is very limited, approximately 4000 at the most (Stokoe 1972). Because for reading the books of hearing children of 11–12 years of age a knowledge of a vocabulary of at least 7000 words is necessary (McCarthy 1954, see 'conversion loss'), there are many words without corresponding signs. These should be added by finger-spelling. We took a random handful of words with no corresponding signs by comparing a normal English dictionary with that of Watson (1964). Within a few minutes we found: abandon, abbreviate, abroad, console, cube, elegant, especial,

flour, furniture, etc. etc. Well then because most deaf persons, using mainly signs, have a weak memory for words (may be finger-spelled, written and/or spoken), the growth of their vocabulary will stick to the 2nd or 3rd Grade level, which alas clearly happens in most schools of the deaf.

For the difficulty of *reflection* in the children using that slang of signs and words, see the study of Tervoort (1953). He made a film of 2 deaf children, 12 years of age, conversing in speech intermixed with signs. It took more than 4 months of his time to find out exactly what these children had said to each other, and to decode their utterances. These children, after all, did not always know exactly themselves what they had said! He had to invoke the help of their peers and even of older children. He found almost the same in his 1967 study (published 1975) on 24 pairs of deaf children, investigated longitudinally for 3 through 6 years. These findings have been confirmed by Rutten (1957) and me (1968), for 'low sign-language'.

The *disappointing* effects in schools for the deaf not following natural methods of teaching language monolingually, may also be seen in the research of Philips (1963) and Craig (1964): all the advantageous effects of home-training and preschool had been lost within 3 years of schooling, i.e. in about the 3rd grade; no significant difference was found between the deaf children who had had home-training and/or preschool training, and the deaf children who had not.

NB. Another reason for this disappointing finding is the 'levelling effect' in all classes, especially those of the deaf: every teacher tries to keep all his children within the work; children who are behind are pulled up, other children receive less opportunities, they are kept back. – That this 'levelling effect' can be prevented has been shown by Balow and Brill (1975): the nursery school classes appeared to be particularly beneficial resulting a higher level of school achievement, even at high school graduation.

These studies *warn* us of three dangerous aspects of our work:

of a lack of proper *selection* of children according to both ability (including multiple handicaps) and achievement when coming into school;

of *formal* constructing methods of language teaching and/or a lack of any method (both of them are very often consequent when there are too many *unqualified* teachers in the school);

and last but not least of any kind of compound bilingualism of speech and signs.

The higher success rate of a *monolinguistic sign-language-method* (with a little bit of speech and lipreading as a foreign language but with much writing and reading, Stokoe 1973), which our Institute used until 1906 (van Beek system 1827), suggests that a school using only or mainly a *systematized* sign-language, in the classroom too (i.e. using one system throughout), succeeds better in teaching its children language than a school with this jargon, calling itself wrongly a 'purely oral school'! (Cf. Tervoort 1967, 1974). I have met teachers of the deaf using sign-language throughout who were very disappointed when visiting such bad oral schools.

But after all a purely or *monolinguistically oral way* is more successful for the education of the vast majority of deaf students than a pure, sign-language method, even when taught as a kind of coordinated bilingualism of sign-language and verbal language, because of the inferiority of signs.

8. DANGEROUS SUGGESTIONS

We will now discuss some suggestions which have been given for the methods of language teaching, and which are not in agreement with the principles mentioned above.

a. Basic Language?

This *advice*, given by Ruffieux (1946), Streng (1958), Jussen (1961), Snijders (1964), Kröhnert (1966), Kreye (1972) and many others, aims at a limitation of vocabulary to the words most frequently used, e.g. so-called 'basic English' = the 3000 most frequently used English words, – further aiming at an enhancement of the didactic frequency of these words, in the language programme, in the reading lessons and so on. Because this has been done, not without success, with hearing subjects in learning foreign languages, it has been thought of as being successful for deaf children too.

Criticism

It is forgotten, however, that these most frequently used words have also on the average the most extended '*action-radius*'.

Howes (1957) did research on free-*associative* reactions to words, i.e. a stimulus-word having given to his subjects, they had to give as many words they could find attached to the stimulus-word. He found a significant correlation between the range of associated words and the frequency of use of the stimulus-word, e.g. 'table' evokes a large range of associated words, but 'ladle' far less.

The frequency of use of words can be found in Thorndike-Lorge's lists (1944, quot. by Hall 1971). But these lists do not render the meanings and the functions of these words. We counted at least 9,000 very frequent meanings of the 3,600 words of basic Dutch (see De La Court 1937, Vannes 1962, Uit den Boogaart 1975). According to content and function they have a lot of combinabilities. Take, for instance, the word 'open'. If we look in the dictionary, we see quite a richness

188

of combinabilities of this simple word. It can be an adjective, a verb or a substantive. A cupboard can be open, but a coat too; a letter can be open by unfolding, so too, may a box; there are a lot of figurative meanings, e.g. keep open house, she has an open hand, I will be open with you, he keeps an open mind, he came into the open, this opened his eyes, etc. etc.

Apparently it is very difficult to compose reading-pieces by using only the basic words. Again and again *less frequent words are necessary*.

An analogic difficulty appears in the simple determination *to find out* which words really occur most frequently. Hipskind and Nerbonne (1970) found in daily adult conversations in Massachusetts 2,268 different words used. The sample embraced about 25,000 words, so that the type-token ratio was 9%. Half of these words, however, had been used only once. About the same has been found by Berger in Ohio (1967). But the largest variance between the two samples was in the types of these 'halves of the words', used only once. So it cannot be concluded that a vocabulary of 2268 words would be sufficient for daily conversation.

Besides the number of *meanings* per word have not been counted in all these studies.

Last but no least: a satisfactory *reading* of reading-books for normal hearing children of 10–11 years of age demands a passive sight-vocabulary of at least 7,000 words, 3,600 of which covering 95% of the text, 3,400 less frequent ones 5%.

It may be clear that a method using basic language cannot be advantageous unless a normal 'action-radius' is developed in the chidlren. For this, these basic words need the help of the less frequently used words in order to make their content intelligible.

Hearing people who already have a *mother-tongue* introduce into this learning of a foreign language the 'action-radii' of the words of their mother-tongue. The more akin this foreign language is to their native language, the better will be the help of the 'basic words' of that foreign language. So a Dutchman will gain much help from such 'basic English' in his first steps in that language, whereas an Indian will have much more difficulty, made the more so, the more his mother-tongue is alienated from English (cf. Weijnen, 1947).

Deaf children, however, have to learn these action-radii from the beginning. Hearing people can fill in the gaps, deaf children cannot. Thus it must be said that the argument mentioned above does not hold.

But if a teacher always uses *natural* language in the situation, in conversation, playing his double role as explained above, he cannot avoid the most frequent usage of precisely the 'basic words'.

Some Help

There may, however, be some help from these lists of basic words. The teacher

189

could use them as a control after the event, e.g. in the 3rd or 4th grade, in order to check whether he perhaps has neglected some very frequently used words. I know of some teachers who did this, but were happy to find that there were no gaps. – It would be very dangerous for the spontaneity and naturalness of his conversation if he limited his vocabulary consciously in an artificial way. He would descend to a kind of constructive method.

b. 'Total Communication'?

(1) Some Preliminary Concepts:

(aa) So-called 'High Sign-language' in Contrast to 'Low Sign-language'

NB. 'Low sign-language', although including facial mime, is not the same as the jargon of signs and speech described earlier. Pure signs are meant here.
Stokoe (1970, 1972) is right in saying that there is a high and a low version of American sign-language ('Ameslan'). – The same can be said of our Dutch sign-language (1827–1906) by Director Rev. M. van Beek (1790–1872, Rutten 1957), composed 150 years ago and still modern in its concept. Van Beek called his system 'Dutch in signs' or '*manual Dutch*'.
(1) Van Beek introduced the flexions of Dutch into his sign system by means of finger-spelling.
(2) Most signs are made by spelling the first letter of the word, e.g. 'day' is made by making a bow with the right arm from left to right, showing the rising and setting sun, the hand showing a *D*; 'week' is made with the same sign, but the hand showing the *W*; 'month' with the hand showing the *M*; and '*n*ight'; and '*y*ear;
There are a lot of similar clusters of signs in his intelligent system. The reason for this invention was to forge a link between the signs and the written words: the first letter of the word has been integrated into the sign. He already experienced difficulty in memory for words in signing deaf children, see p. 186.
(3) The order of the signs is the same as that of the words.
This is the high version of his sign-language. – But as soon as the prelingually deaf (in contrast to postlingually deafened and/or hard of hearing people) are among themselves, they omit these *artificial* introductions, brought in by hearing people (van Uden 1968): so they only use a 'low version' of signs. Nevertheless all the disadvantages, mentioned above (difficulties with figurative meanings, with homonyms, shifting of meanings, groupings and accentuations, with Short Term and Long Term Memory) remain the same in the high version of sign-language too.
The *semantic* difficulties of signs, including those of vocabulary, have already been explained on page 138. We will now explain the *functional* difficulties.

(bb) Why Integrating Signs with Finger-spelling?
Signs, the Written Symbols and Memory

Van Beek saw his 'manual Dutch' as an introduction to *reading*. The deaf should conquer the language mainly by reading. He felt the impossibility of teaching a system of language just by signs. It cannot be said: 'Hearing children learn the *system* of spoken language mainly by hearing and speaking; in the same way deaf children learn the system of (high) sign language by using signs'.
The didactics of Van Beek followed these stages from 5–6 years of age (as soon as a deaf child at that time has been introduced into the Institute):

learning the signs most necessary for daily life;
learning the graphic symbols of these signs (synthetic method);
writing down short sentences according to a language programme;
making the children translate these sentences into 'manual Dutch';
making the children write down sentences signed to them;
introducing reading lessons,
and so on.

I have known several prelingually deaf adults educated this way – some of them well instructed – who read books, wrote rather good letters, could converse in 'high version sign-language' in the main correctly, could speak cautiously, considerately, intelligibly (although lipreading was too bad to converse with them purely orally). They could converse in 'low sign-language' with primitive deaf adults and immediately after that in 'high sign-language' with a teacher of the Institute. (Among themselves they usually made it 'easy' mixing 'low' and 'high'.) There was a *coordinated* bilingualism of sign-language and written Dutch. It must be confessed, however, that their number was very, very small; they were exceptions. – Besides their achievement had been reached, not by signing but by reading and writing. (Of course there were a lot of postlingually deafened and severely hard of hearing people in the Institue in those old times, educated in the same way as the prelingually deaf and reaching on the average higher standards of achievement, but these are not meant in this discussion.)
The background of Van Beek's theory apparently is the difficulty of *memory* for series of signs. In reading the memory of the reader is helped by the *simultaneous* presentation of the symbols. These symbols can be graphic symbols (series of letters) and/or 'hieroglyphic' ones as in the dictionary of signs by Watson (1964), the recent books of fairy tales in signs published by Gallaudet College Press (Kendall department 1972). Van Beek used the graphic symbols and integrated his signs with letters to facilitate the identification.
The shortness of their immediate memory for signs (limited to 5–6 signs) is certainly the reason why deaf people talk in very small units (maybe in long dramatized stories!). So the sentence (Bellugi 1972): 'As he led out his lines, the lapping of the waves against his boat reminded him of his daughter playing in the

waves by their home' was translated into signs, strengthening the iconic thinking: 'Himself thinking about (his) son back in home. Play near water wave. Splash water splash (his) son h-a-n-d (finger-spelled). Splash alike now boat splash boat'. – White and Stevenson (1975) found that the written form of language was more efficient in providing successive factual information, even for deaf fluent 'signers'.

NB. The Short Term Memory function in orally educated deaf children is higher – we found an average memory span of 7–8 spoken words at 13 years of age. Kates (1972) found a group of deaf adolescents from 'combined schools' (see above) significantly behind a matched group of purely orally educated deaf in their memory for *written* sentences and in the average length of their produced written sentences. Markides (1976) too found 'combined' deaf adolescents significantly lagging behind oral ones in the average length of written sentences.

We should not forget that all this has its consequences for the flexibility of thinking and feeling, and for the social adjustment of the deaf (cf. Prick 1956; Prick and Calon 1967).

(cc) Signs and Syntax. Artificiality?

We said that grammar (flexions and orders of signs) is an artificial introduction brought into the sign-language by the hearing, and that the deaf mainly leave it out as soon as they converse among themselves, following other 'rules'. By 'artificiality' is meant here an element or function which is against a proper structure, for instance swimming for a swallow or eating beef for a cow.

First a consequence of the iconic way of signification is that there are strictly *no parts of speech* in sign-language (cf. Stokoe 1972). There is no difference between naming and co-naming functions: each sign is an aspect of its own meaning, with too little relation to other signs or words. For example this sentence in the same order of English, 'The children visited the zoo yesterday' means in signs: 'Children/visiting/zoo/(it was) yesterday'. This order as such means nothing, in contrast to the spoken language where the verb is marked by the second position in the series, the adverb by its position after the direct object and so on. According to sign-language: 'Yesterday/zoo/visiting/children' means the same thing. This does not imply, however, that the minds of the deaf are free in this order or organization, – something comparable to the free order of the words in Latin. On the contrary. Their minds are much more bound to visual and emotional thinking, bound to the situation, lack the objective freedom of a syntax unhampered by the situation as such (see above 'signal'-language).

Secondly Wundt (1908, 1973) already found that signs request a special temporal order which is not congruent to that of words. We say 'cupboard in' because in signing we have first to 'designate' a cupboard before we can sign that we will put something into that cupboard. So the sentence: 'The furious man hit the child' will be expressed in signs: 'Man furious child hitting'. – Another important 'rule' is that a sign which is especially 'accentuated', is put into the front position of the series. For instance if the sign 'hitting' is strongly stressed, the deaf tend to say: 'Hitting child man furious'. This position-effect is the main means of giving 'accent' to a sign, in contrast to the rhythmic accent in spoken language.

All this has been confirmed by Maesse (1935), Oléron (1952, 1973; cf. Herren 1971, Rammel 1974) and Tervoort (1953) with reference to deaf children and adults. Witte (1930) found the same in hearing people, when they were requested to express special sentences using self-made signs. There indeed is a weak influence of education which, however, is so small that it proves rather than contradicts the artificiality of hearing grammar in sign-language. Maesse found in his sample of deaf children that younger deaf children kept these 'natural' rules of signing more purely than older children: the latter children increasingly used the order of the spoken language in which they were educated. But even then the order was hardly ever completely correct: he found a lot of interference between the rules of these two totally different languages. Tervoort and Verberk (1967, 1974) found the same in American deaf children: the visual diagram of sentences, the so-called Fitzgerald Key learned in the classroom, had a real influence on the order of their signs in spontaneous conversations, but here too the original 'rules' of signing were never quite wiped out.

Real 'Linguistic' Syntax in Signing? A 'Sign-language' or a 'Collection of Sign Codes'?

It is questionable whether there is a real *linguistic* (i.e. arbitrary and cultural) syntax in 'natural' 'low version' signing. Consequently it is questionable whether this signing is a real, i.e. cultural, language at all. To me it should be called a 'collection of sign codes' and not a 'sign-language in low version', not a 'language' in its strict sense.

Schlesinger (1970) found that (almost analphabetic) deaf signers had no means of expressing the relations subject-verb-direct object-indirect object, such as for instance 'The cat throws the fish to the pig'. The understanding of these relationships was left to 'nature', i.e. to visually perceptible situations as conceived by the partners. Bode (1974) replicated the experiment done by Schlesinger with alphabetic deaf signing subjects and found that they could express and/or understand these relations, but he did not prove that their means of expression were linguistic, i.e. according to cultural rules. How would they express these relations in: 'John recommends Peter to Willy' or 'John attributes the cause to Peter' or 'The ill man cures the physician'? – Actually Bode found the expressive means of the signs less effective than those of speech, because the deaf made more errors than the hearing control group. The difference was not significant, expectedly so

193

because of the too small a number of subjects. – The assertion by Stokoe (1973) and Tweney (1973) that teaching a sign language to the deaf will facilitate the learning of English since it trains the *basic* functions of language, is not verisimilar. It has been refuted recently by Markides (1976 Ghana West-Africa), who found a group of deaf adolescents educated by sign language significantly lagging behind a matched group of oral ones in learning English as a second language.

The Essential Difference Between the Syntax of Words and of Signs

The essential difference between the order of signs and the order of words is that words are grouped into *rhythmic* units, 'accent-groups', phrases as accentuated arrangements. Series of signs lack grouping according to accentuations, lack the shifting of accents while the order of the elements is kept stable, for example 'Why is your *father* coming tomorrow?' in contrast to 'Why is your father coming *tomorrow*?'

(dd) Signs Most Natural to the Deaf? Sign-language the 'Mother-tongue of the Deaf'?

Some have it that signing is the communicative medium most natural to the deaf (de l'Epée – 18th century – and his followers, and in modern times for example Mindel and Vernon 1971, Stokoe 1972, Furth 1973). What is 'natural' in this respect?
Both hearing and deaf children learn gestures more easily and earlier than words (Meumann 1902). According to Beaver (1932) normally hearing children of 2–3 years of age still use non-verbal means of communication for 32% of the observation time, according to Ling (1974) more than 50% in children below $2\frac{1}{2}$ years of age. So there is a switch-over from mainly gesturing to mainly verbal behaviour at $2\frac{1}{2}$ years of age (in the deaf children of our Institute at $\pm$ 9 years of age). These non-verbal means, including gestures, are replaced by words more and more. – We should not think, however, that these non-verbal means are the same as *conventional* signs. Heider (1940) found that certainly no more than 8 such conventional signs had developed within a group of deaf preschoolers during two years of education. Without help deaf children do not or very slowly develop conventional signs. The sign-*languages* (= cultural systems) known to me were all invented by the hearing. If these signs are introduced, however, within a group of deaf children, they will be picked up very soon. They are rather easy to learn, indeed (at least the sign-*codes*, not their artificial system).
It is correct to call this development 'natural', in two senses: (a) that – without oral help – deaf children will never reach higher communicative codes than gestures

194

and dramatizations and some attempts at lipreading and speaking. (b) Further in the sense that they will pick up conventional signs, if these are presented to them, rather easily. But the statement is *not* true, if one were to assert that deaf children pick up these signs more easily than normally hearing children deprived of words, nor in the sense that deaf children develop a sign 'language' (in a broader sense, i.e. conventional signs sufficient for daily conversations) very easily and soon by themselves. Further, it is *not* true in a deeper *human* sense. Crawling over the floor will be the method of locomotion most 'natural' to handicapped persons with only two short stumps for legs, as can be seen from the beautiful paintings by Brueghel (1525–1569); but now we can fit them with prostheses by means of which they can learn to walk in a more human way, at the same level as their fellow-men; this method of locomotion will be more 'natural' to them as *human* beings. In the same sense, by good education, we can develop the attempts at lipreading and speaking by the deaf, right up to oral conversation, to oral language (which is more than just a prosthesis) by means of which the deaf can live with their hearing fellow-men in a more human way. And this oral language appears to be more 'natural' to them as *human beings*.

(2) What is 'Total Communication'?

(aa) Some Historical Notes

The 'Combined system'

At the conference attended by representatives of all schools for the Deaf of the U.S.A., Washington 1868, Edward Miner Gallaudet (1837–1902) coined the terms 'combined system' and 'combined method', by which he meant a combination of signs, finger-spelling and speech. He regarded speech and lipreading as a higher development, but pointed out that 'the sign language is admitted as a valuable adjunct in all stages of deaf instruction, if it is not acknowledged as the basis of education' (Hodgson 1953). At the International Congress of the Deaf in Milan, Italy, 1880, he defined this system and said that signs were the 'natural language of the deaf' as also the 'mother language of all mankind' (Bender 1970).

The 'Total Communication' – System, or just a Philosophy?

In 1969 Denton described an initiative in the 'Maryland School for the Deaf' (cf. Furth 1966, 1969, 1973; Paget 1953; Gorman and Paget 1969; Wells 1972; Mindel and Vernon 1971; O'Rourke 1972; Schlesinger and Meadow 1972): high sign-language, finger-spelling, reading and writing, lipreading, auditory training

195

and speech, all were to be combined in one whole, used in the classroom, in freetime and at home, from early childhood.

Two characteristics seem to distinguish 'Total Communication' from the 'Combined method':

its systematization, aiming at a coordinated bilingualism of 'High Version sign-language' and 'Oral language, including finger-spelling';

its totality of linguistic codes for, in principle, all the deaf from early childhood, claiming that this integration of so many aspects and modalities of communication does not deteriorate but enhances oral abilities (see below).

I saw a demonstration given by a hearing teacher in order to illustrate the idea. He said, speaking and signing simultaneously, 'I wish I could stay here for several weeks'. The signs kept the order of the words. Some manual cues indicated *could* as subjunctive, *weeks* as plural. – It was exactly the same way of communication as I myself am using every week in my sermons to a small group of very old deaf alumni, educated that way. It is hypothesized by the advocates of 'Total Communication' that the vast majority of the deaf are able to learn this typical kind of coordinated bilingualism: manual English = written English = oral-aural English, so that they become equally conversant in all these modalities according to the situation.

In 'SIGNS for our times' (Gallaudet College, n. 40 April-May-June 1976, American Annals of the Deaf 1976 page 358), however we found that:

After 4 years of debate, an official definition was adopted on the 5th May 1976, by the Conference of Executives of American Schools for the Deaf: 'Total communication is a philosophy requiring the incorporation of appropriate aural, manual, and oral modes of communication in order to ensure effective communication with and among hearing impaired persons'.

This definition is disappointing because the difference with the 'combined method' is rather obscure.

The idea of 'Total Communication' has been propagated in the 'Total-Communication-Movement' in the United States of America, United Kingdom, Sweden and other countries.

Denton (1970 quot. Kent 1971) declared a *right* of all deaf people to 'Total Communication', and Holcomb (1971) spoke of 'Total *Approach*' in so far that not only the schools but also the parents, brothers and sisters and the whole society should adopt 'Total Communication'... These enthusiastic exaggerations presuppose that it has been proven that 'Total Communication' is the best way of education for all deaf people. This is not true at all, rather the opposite.

A Historical Decision at St. Michielsgestel

After the demonstration of 'Total Communication' mentioned above, it became

196

clear to us that this idea was not new. The second successor to van Beek, Rev. F. Slits (1864–1876), combined the sign-language described above with speech and lipreading. Slits' method seemed to be much akin to what is now being introduced in the United States. It was abandoned, however, after about 20 years because speech and lipreading could not be developed sufficiently. The sign-language with only a little speech and lipreading had been maintained until 1906, at which time our Institute went over to the *purely* oral way. What had caused such a radical change to take place? It had become more and more clear that it was impossible to change the 'low' version of sign-language used by the children among themselves into the 'high' version, except in hard of hearing and post-lingually deafened children: the prelingually deaf almost only maintained the 'picturing' and dramatizing effects of the signs. This has been confirmed by my research (van Uden 1968). The director at that time (Rev. A. Hermus 1906–1940) compared the achievement of his children educated in sign-language with those of other schools educated in the purely oral way, and he was convinced that at least reading could be developed by the purely oral way as well as by the 'manual Dutch'. Why then use, he reasoned, such an esoteric and isolating system? ... Within a few years it became evident, however, that, by using the purely oral method, more and better reading could be developed.

Experiences Elsewhere

Crouter's (1911) well-known experiment points in the same direction.
Quigley (1969) found a significantly higher gain in paragraph-reading in those schools which left the signs in favour of speech and finger-spelling (Rochester Method) in a longitudinal study spanning 4 years. Although I do not agree with the Rochester Method, except for a few multiply handicapped deaf children, it is at least a *verbal* method, and its results are constantly better than those of the schools using the 'combined sytem' for almost a century (McClure 1975). – This research confirms the experiences of Hermus and Crouter. Having taught deaf children for more than 30 years, knowing the sign language myself, using it in 'Total Communication'-way, and being able to compare the results of the education of former days and now, I must say that deaf children educated mainly in signs and conversing among themselves mainly in signs will achieve real reading but with much more difficulty and exceptionally. I think the reason is the semantics of the signs, the hampered memory for words and the lack of rhythmic grouping of words.

(bb) Does 'Total Communication' Exist?

We said above that the sign language system of van Beek and the 'Total Communication' system of Slits turned out (for almost all prelingually deaf) to be a

197

slang of 'low' signs, a little bit of speech and almost no useful lipreading. Apparently the children are not able to combine these modalities. One modality, the easiest one, i.e. signing, dominated and ruled out the other ones. There are only a few years of experience with 'Total Communication', and the same tendencies are appearing already. Gates (1971) and White and Stevenson (1975) compared the efficiency of 'Total Communication' (i.e. the combination of signs with lipreading) with that of pure signing for the understanding of messages. They found no difference, in fact more of an interference resulting from lipreading in this situation, because the scores by 'Total Communication' were lower.

The conclusion to all this is that 'Total Communication' for the vast majority of the prelingually deaf just will not exist: it is in essence a system of signs with a veneer of a little bit of verbalization.

The advocates of 'Total Communication' may study the history of the education of the deaf in order to avoid the pitfalls which ensnared so many well-meaning educators in former times: *'l'Histoire se répétera!'*.

(cc) Criticism of the 'Total-Communication'-Philosophy:

Signs, Isolation and Socialization

Towards the Hearing Society

A first bad consequence of using sign-language is that the deaf are educated solely for a deaf community or *ghetto* (Kern 1958). This means a real isolation within the hearing world, a kind of 'apartheid' with all its resentments and other repercussions.

Markides (1976) quite rightly says: 'The ultimate aim of education should be to help the hearing-impaired person to integrate with the hearing society ... Any deviation from this philosophy implies the existence or formation of a 'deaf subculture' with all its undesirable ramifications'. He investigated the attitudes of 'manual' and 'oral' adolescents towards intermixing with the hearing society. The headmasters of the manual and the oral school respectively were asked to consult with their teachers and with two independent assessors and to rate each pupil's social attitudes on a 6-point scale. He found the following, see p. 199, top.

Towards the Other Deaf

It is said that sign-languages keep the deaf further from social isolation when conversing *with each other*. According to my experience, however, there is a lot of misunderstanding among the signing deaf, unless the content of the conversation is kept down to very concrete situations. The more the sign-language (as it is actually used) lacks system, the more it is dependent upon the surroundings and feelings present.

198

Scale:	% of manually educated adolescents:	% of orally educated adolescents:
6. Actively seeks the company of hearing people:	3	23
5. Accepts and enjoys the company of hearing people:	13	37
4. Gets on reasonably well with hearing people:	17	30
3. Tolerates but does not avoid the company of hearing people:	20	10
2. Tends to avoid the company of hearing people:	30	0
1. Actively rejects the company of hearing people:	17	0

Chi-square statistics shows the distribution to be significant.

Spontaneously signed communications by deaf persons have been filmed and translated into a verbal language afterwards (Tervoort 1953, Rutten 1957, van Uden 1968). There were a lot of misunderstandings. As cited earlier: a Dutch deaf signer could not make himself understood by the other signer, in his explanation that he just *expected* (almost the same sign as *waiting*) that there could be an accident on the corner of a street but that such an accident had not yet happened. The partner understood that an accident had happened. The discussion was very lively for an outsider, but essentially it was only about 'no accident' and 'an actual accident?' ... These conversations can hardly be considered as being redeeming from isolation.

Tervoort (1972) published some examples of signed interpretations of orally produced lectures for manual deaf public in the hall. These synchronic translations were filmed. The results are not encouraging, to put it mildly! – Hoemann (1972) confirmed a finding by Gates (1971): he found that almost half of the 10 simple questions translated by qualified interpreters were misunderstood by deaf people. The same Hoemann (1970) had found that normally hearing children among themselves were more successful in transmitting factual information than expertly signing deaf children both by speech *and* by free gesturing without speech. White (1974) found that written messages were better understood than signed ones by deaf adolescents who were skilful signers.

On the effectiveness of *purely oral* communication see the conversations p. 251 through 279, and pp. 135–191 of the 1970-edition of this book; the average amount of misunderstandings was never higher than 5%.

It is to be wished that the 'Total Communicators' will publish similar conversations in their full length.

Recommendations of the UNESCO

We quote here some of the recommendations published by UNESCO (Paris 'Expert Meeting on Education of the Deaf' 30.9–4.10 1974, ED–74/CONF. 645/17, – page 14–15, nrs. 21 through 23):

21. That longitudinal studies be made of the different communication approaches used in programmes for the deaf which will take account of linguistic, social, familial, and psychological factors, and that investigation be made as to how each mode of communication assists or interferes with these factors.

22. That longitudinal research be conducted into real spontaneous conversation of deaf children and adults among themselves, this research to include not only linguistic analysis but study of affective aspects, feelings, misunderstandings, etc.

23. That research be conducted into correlations between work in the classroom in terms of the amount of conversation that occurs there (the 'conversational' as opposed to the 'presenting' approach) and the linguistic growth of children.

Conclusion

I fully agree with these words of the Ewings (1958): 'You place limitations on a deaf child when you make your ultimate goal for him anything less than normal participation in a hearing world'.

(dd) Criticism of Researches Seemingly Supporting 'Total Communication'

General remarks

(1) Nix (1975) is right in pointing out the 'ex post facto' design of these quasi-experiments: they are '*after the fact studies*', which 'simulate experimentation by matching two or more groups of subjects on the basis of preintervention variables *after* the intervention has occurred'. Such a design is very dangerous. He rightly quotes Kerlinger (1964) saying: 'The danger of improper and erroneous interpretations ... stems ... from the plausibility of many explanations'. We will see that this happens in these researches.

(2) Di Carlo (1966) and Owrid (1971) point out that the differences between the groups of children in these researches, although significant, are so small that there is much too much overlap, so that *many overlooked variables* may play a hidden part. We mention: dyspraxia of motor behaviour (not diagnosed in most schools for the deaf, van Dijk and van Uden 1976), disturbance of intermodal integration (not diagnosed in most schools for the deaf), degree and profile of audiogram, profile of intelligence, skill of the teachers and the methods of language acquisition, and so on. Deaf children of deaf parents (the quasi-experimental group in these researches) may be hereditarily deaf, deaf children of hearing parents may be post-natally deafened by illness, which can have more effects than just deafness.

It may be clear that these researches are unsatisfactory and not reliable enough to draw far reaching and generalizing conclusions.

(3) It must be mentioned here that there are, at the moment, just two studies comparing purely oral deaf children and manual-oral deaf children, that of Kates (1972) and of Markides (1976). We saw how the purely oral deaf children were superior to the latter in most and decisive linguistic aspects.

Training Sign-language from Early Childhood?

These researches have been done on deaf children of deaf parents who had had sign-language from early childhood as a real mother-tongue and following that were educated in schools for the deaf using combined methods of signs and speech. These children (mainly adolescents) were compared with deaf children of hearing parents who had had oral home-training and/or preschool (Stuckless and Birch 1964, 1966, Meadow 1967, 1968, Vernon and Koh 1969, 1970, 1971, Schlesinger and Meadow 1972, Brazel 1975; besides two factor-analytic studies of the same purport: Montgomery 1966 and Bolton 1971).

These latter children were at the same schools as the first ones, or lived in a not purely oral environment (although they are *called* in these researches: 'the oral group' or 'the primary oral group', or even 'the intensive oral group'). But their parents tried to converse with them orally, in contrast to the first ones who used the same language in school, in free time and at home.

All these children were prelingually deaf, not multiply handicapped and the vast majority of them had an above average intelligence. Both groups were matched. – Let us call the first group 'deaf-deaf' and the second group 'deaf-hearing'. It was found that speech and lipreading of the deaf-deaf group usually did not lag behind that of the deaf-hearing group. The school achievement, especially in reading, was significantly better in the deaf-deaf group. These children were emotionally better adjusted too. – All these writers concluded that the teaching of a sign-language

201

throughout from early childhood (actually meant as 'Total Communication') is better for deaf children. – These conclusions are not correct.

Particular Criticisms

First. Concerning *communication* and its measurement:
No information at all is given about the results of *auditory training* in these researches on so-called 'Total Communication'. – Too often teacher's *ratings* are used instead of tests without indicating their frame of reference, which makes such ratings very invalid. – Just counting how many phonemes – a very difficult task (how has this been done?) – a deaf child pronounces (Montgomery 1966, 1967) can hardly be called a conversational-*speech*-test! – The scores for *lipreading* gained by these non-multiply handicapped intelligent children were on the average too low. The lipreading-test by Craig (1964) which often was used, is too simple and far too adjusted to the capacities of young deaf children. The results can be expressed more correctly in this way: the achievements of the deaf-deaf group were less bad than those of the deaf-hearing group, instead of saying 'they were better'. – We again emphasize the necessity of recording real *conversations* in the different communicative modes and of analysing them, in order to measure the real communicative skills of deaf children. This 'test' has never been applied in these researches. – (See more examples of oral conversational lessons in the 1968 and 1970 editions of this book. An extensive study of these and more oral lessons is in preparation.)

Secondly: *Conflicting results*:
Lane (1974) compared the scores of paragraph reading of the small sample of deaf-deaf children in the research by Vernon and Koh (1970) with a large sample of orally educated deaf-hearing children: the latter at least did not lag, so that she rightly concluded: 'Early manual communication is not the only variable to account for the differences in reading scores' between deaf-deaf and deaf-hearing children as claimed by Vernon and Koh.
In their 1970-study Vernon and Koh claimed to have shown that the deaf-deaf group was better in the dependent variables mentioned above more so than a deaf-hearing group of children who had followed the courses of the John Tracy Clinic in Los Angeles (oral home-training service). Both groups of children were at the South California School for the Deaf at Riverside, which is not a purely oral school. This claim has been refuted by the fact, that their deaf-hearing sample was biased (Lowell E. L. 1975). The data of the same school, published by Balow and Brill (1975) show that such a deaf-hearing group (not the same sample, but apparently with the same bias) does not have to lag behind a deaf-deaf group so much, notwithstanding the fact, that the first group had had to change from a purely oral preschool education onto a mainly manual one. What would have happened, if that purely oral education had been continued? Smith (1973) found in a purely oral school, that deaf-deaf children were significantly behind deaf-hearing children in the intelligibility of speech.

202

Thirdly: Is 'early manual communication' *the independent variable?*
We have just seen that Balow and Brill leave out 'manual'; they speak of an 'early *system* of linguistic coding and decoding'.

Corson (1973) found the same phenomenon of deaf-deaf children achieving more than deaf-hearing children in a *purely oral* school. These deaf parents were purely oral and taught their deaf children in their home-training according to the oral principles, as did the hearing parents. He thinks the real independent variable is *acceptance* of the deaf child by its parents: 'Deaf parents of deaf children had significantly more positive acceptance towards deafness than did hearing parents of deaf children'. – This has been confirmed by Greenstein (1975) in a research on linguistic development of deaf children of 0;6–3;4 years of age. The deaf parents showed a better acceptance of their deaf child than did hearing parents. This acceptance factor appeared to be correlated positively with language development. 'The children of deaf families tended to do better in ratings and tests of language competence, but the children of hearing parents rated as warmer and more sensitive to their child tended to do as well. The data suggest that the nature of the mother-infant interaction is more crucial than the mother's hearing status'.

Last but not least: the deaf-hearing children were forced to use speech, lipreading and hearing within their parents' homes, *although* they had actually been educated mainly in signs: as children of not purely oral schools the signs were their main means of spontaneous conversation especially among themselves. So these children had been forced towards a kind of *bilingualism.* In contrast to them the deaf-deaf children had been educated quite monolingually.

This state of events explains at the same time why the deaf-hearing group was less well-adjusted. Who can expect anything else of children who are forced to detach themselves from their parents, forced to a kind of maternal deprivation?

Fourthly: *Early manual communication more effective?*
Schlesinger and Meadow (1972) have shown a remarkable growth of esoteric signs in some very young deaf-deaf children, even larger than the amount of words in normally hearing children. They assume that the communication too of the deaf-deaf children would be more efficient than that of orally educated deaf-hearing children by good parent guidance. They forget, however, that very young normally hearing children use a lot of non-verbal means of communication. We saw above that the balance towards mainly verbal communication dips at about 2;6 years of age. Deaf children too will use a lot of non-verbal normal communicative means. Northcott (1975) found, using a questionnaire, that there was no need for an esoteric means of communication in the programmes of parent guidance. Gloyer (1961) and Köble (1964) described the effects of good oral hometraining in longitudinal researches of 3–4 years on individual deaf children, the efficiency of which does not seem to be less than that of esoteric signs. Schlesinger and Meadow have not shown that the esoteric means of communica-

tion mentioned by them was more effective for actual communication than the normal means used by both normally hearing and deaf children in a good programme of home-training. These esoteric means may even hamper the development of normal gestures, because it is impossible to use the hands at the same time for both modes of activity.

Conclusions:

We draw first of all this conclusion: the results of the researches mentioned above only show that the oral way does not exist unless applied *purely*.

A second conclusion is the following: it may be expected alas from the propaganda for 'Total Communication' that more and more deaf children will be detached from their parents, and that it will be increasingly difficult for parents to accept the deafness of their child. They see their child going away from them into another culture which is not theirs. It seems to be unrealistic to suppose that the vast majority of hearing parents will learn sign-language (producing *and* understanding it), and even if such were the case, the cleavage between parents and child is not filled.

NB. *'Iconic' (deaf) children*

There are of course a few deaf children who because of multiple handicaps need a sign-education (see Appendix III).

these are: deaf children with subnormal intelligence;
    deaf children with a pathologically bad memory;
    deaf children with asymbolia for words.

The same happens in a few normally hearing children. These are the overloaded 'image-thinkers', which we would like to call 'iconic children' (and adults).

c. Finger-spelling?

The term 'spelling' has a double meaning, analysing the words in letters, and analysing them in phonemes. Let us call the first: 'alphabetic spelling', and the second one: 'articulatory spelling'. For example, the word 'weigh' and 'way' is alphabetically different in spelling but not so articulatorily. The reverse: 'beau', meaning dandy, is alphabetically the same as *beau*tiful, but articulatorily different.

(1) The Alphabetic Finger-spelling (also called Dactylology)

There are many different systems (Carmel 1975 mentions a lot but even then not all of them):

the two-hand-system by Wallis (1616–1703, see Jeanes e.a. 1972);
the 'stenochirology' of De Haerne (1804–1890, in Belgium, of which system there is nothing known of the speed, but it is said to be very akin to the steno of Taylor 1786);
the 'tipping alphabet' by Dalgarno (1626–1687, the letters are identified using some areas of the inside of the hand, e.g. the *A* on the top of the thumb, *Y* on the top of the 5th finger and so on, which can be shown by using a glove having the letters drawn on it; this system was used by A. G. Bell as a substitute for writing cf. H. Lorm 1881, Schulze 1925, Ritter 1930);
the Swedish one-hand alphabet by Borg (1776–1839);
the one-hand alphabet of Bonet (1579–1633, an elaboration of that of Rossellio 1579, see Abernathy 1959), and several others.

The *manual alphabet of Bonet* is by far the most current one, used – combined with speech – by Pereira (1715–1780) and in our modern times in the so-called Rochester-method. Westervelt (1849–1918, cf. Halpen 1936, Scouten 1942, 1967, Stern 1905, Hester 1963, Jussen 1973, 1975) introduced it into his school in *Rochester* N.Y. 1876, aiming at an oral-manual education. The term 'manual' should be used with caution here, because there is an essential difference between the use of signs, which is an iconic language, and the use of the manual alphabet, which aims at the learning of oral and graphic English. A better term is: '*oral-dactyl*' education.
The same manual alphabet has been introduced in Russia too (Marozova 1965, Morkovin 1960, Moores 1972) in a so-called '*neo-oralism*'. This concerns the problem of integration of speech and manual alphabet. It is possible (our experience confirms this) to train deaf children in such a way that they spontaneously use their hands as they speak and vice versa, even to the extent that they cannot speak a phoneme or word without using their hands; and when they use their hands they spontaneously move their mouths to some degree (Ven 1976). I saw this in children suffering from severe forms of dyspraxia of speech. The Russians claim that deaf children drop the hand-movements after a time when their speech has been achieved. According to our experience this occurs in those deaf children whose speech is spontaneously speeding up, so that its tempo is moving ahead of the tempo of finger-spelling; it does not happen in all of them, however (Ven 1974). – Apart from that, the idea is not at all new, because it was applied a long time ago by Pereira, Westervelt and recently by Hester (1963).

(2) The Articulatory or Auditory (Acoustic) Finger-spelling

The movements of the fingers follow the phonemes, not the letters. This is usually done in such a way that the fingers show how the phoneme and/or the syllable should be pronounced. There are complete systems and incomplete ones.

Complete systems e.g. Lyon (1891), Schulte (1967, 1970, 1972, 1974), Fant (1970), Wolff (1971). As far as I have observed, the tempo of Schulte's system seems to be higher than that of the manual alphabet, it seems to be more rhythmic too. Exact studies of this tempo have not yet been carried out, nor on the Short Term Memory function. Neither have the problems of their integration with speech, nor their independent use been studied yet. Schulte (1974) claims advantages for the teaching of speech and for speech-reading. But the design and the results of the experiments are rather ambiguous and far from conclusive. Effects on auditory training have not been considered. Most of all: no direct oral *conversations* have been investigated.

There are about 20% of deaf children who suffer from a kind of '*integrative dyslexia*', which means that the normal integration of the graphic form and the spoken and/or auditory form is hampered to some extent (van Uden 1974). In a few of these children in which this type of dyslexia is added to a severe dyspraxia of speech, the manual alphabet appeared to be of some therapeutic value: it supports this integration. Nothing is known about the value of the articulatory spelling in this respect. Perhaps some systems, invented for *hearing* dyslexic children, e.g. the 'Fingerlesen' (finger-reading) by Koch (1921, 1967, see a survey by Schultheis 1974) may be of help to these multiply handicapped deaf children.

Other articulatory spelling-systems are *incomplete* and aim at being merely a support for lipreading and/or some difficult phonemes, showing those phonemes which are too hidden (e.g. k, g, h, ng, etc.) or can easily be confused (e.g. m-p-b, n-t-d, etc.), or mispronounced (e.g. S, EE). The movements of the fingers may show the mode of articulation too, and so this spelling is used as a support for speech training: so-called 'sound-signs'. Thus Forchhammer's 'mouth-hand-system' (1861–1934, 1902; Holm 1972), the 'sound-signs-system' of van Driel (1898–1974, 1934), Cornett's 'Cued-speech' (1967, 1970, see also Börrild 1970, Henegar and Cornett 1971, Lykos 1971), French: 'Alphabet des Kinèmes assistés' (Walter 1971).

An abnormal way of speaking to the deaf may be added to these 'supporting systems', e.g. an /L/ pronounced not as a supra-dental, but as a more visible inter-dental, an extended bilabial /W/ or a tongue-point /R/ not usual in normal pronunciation, a too overdone lip rounding for /OH/ or /OO/, too much tension for /EE/, too much facial mime and a kind of grimace, and so on. – Some teachers think it a help towards better lipreading when they speak very slowly, for instance hhoooteelll (= hotel), using a kind of '*spelling-speech*'. This is a grave mistake for several reasons. Besides, lipreading as such is not helped at all by these analytic cues, but much more by nice *rhythm*: hotell.

206

Nothing is known about the *effects* of these incomplete systems upon speech and speech-reading. Our Institute used the 'sound-signs' developed by van Driel for more than 25 years. But experience taught us that first and foremost the advantages of good auditory training made these signs at the least superfluous. In general, they were hampering the development of smooth purely oral *conversation*, and so they have been increasingly left out: they appeared to be harmful to a development of rhythmic speech and to smooth speech-reading-hearing, after auditory equipment had been introduced (1950).

There are no studies as yet concerning the Short Term *Memory* for the different ways of 'supported speech'.

(3) The 'Rochester Method', Finger-spelling Combined with Speech

We will now consider only the manual alphabet as combined with speech of the 'Rochester method', introduced by Westervelt (1849–1918), the founder of the 'Rochester School for the Deaf' U.S.A. 1876.

It is possible to teach deaf children English in this fingerspelled form, i.e. *mainly in its written form.*

There are several problems however.

(a) *Smooth oral conversation is hampered.* So far it is not evident that this extra-oral means of finger-spelling does not deteriorate speech-reading, audition and speech; *experiences* show rather the reverse.

Westervelt himself changed over to the following order of teaching: initially at least some years of purely oral training (alas not as pure as it should have been!), and only then introducing finger-spelling.

Seemingly the Russians had difficulty in stopping the dependency on finger-spelling, in developing enough speech-reading and audition, in at least some of their children, and in changing their 'neo-oralism' into *purely* oral communication (see above cf. Libowsky, quot. Lane, Quigley 1966; Libowsky 1970; cf. Mulholland 1965, D'Audney 1973, 1975, Jürgens and Waesch 1976, Jussen 1976). They organized experimental groups of deaf and severely hard of hearing children, training them in the purely oral-aural way.

NB. After that they will try to find out whether a combination of speech, speechreading, auditory training and early finger-spelling is possible. – They finally have detected that almost all deaf children have residual hearing (see Ewing 1938, Groen 1948, van Uden 1952, Bayne 1968, Nober 1970; they say 'all of them' which is not correct), – and that this hearing, at least for some of the deaf children, will make finger-spelling superfluous. Expectedly they will find that it is harmful to purely oral communication in far the most of deaf children.

207

It would appear from these experiences that it is impossible to expect the majority of the deaf children to use speech, lipreading and hearing, smoothly and freely, i.e. independently of finger-spelling, so that they can *converse* in this way (which is not the same as sometimes using an isolated word or a group of words without finger-spelling).

This is reasonable:

The biological *challenge* to speak and lipread, which is so important for every motivating set of an organism, is lacking (Frisina 1963). In my opinion, the oral way cannot succeed if we don't make the most of it.

If the infants have started with finger-spelling as a conversational tool, this finger language will be their *mother-tongue*. If they converse thus, they will think in that way. It will be very difficult to stop this and to change it into purely oral language to be their main means of conversing and thinking (cf. Novikova 1955, 1961).

We must furthermore not forget the following consideration: while finger-spelling the child sees *his own* finger movements. There is a continuous feedback between this seeing and these movements: an eye-hand coordination. This means that his seeing is 'set' to finger-spelling according to the laws of cybernetics (van Uden 1960). While speaking, however, the child does not see himself. He can feel and hear (with a hearing aid), but must imagine the visual cues of his own speech. This is much more difficult. Thus, the child can do no more than *translate* his easier finger language into the more difficult oral language. Oral communication, if not trained from the beginning in a pure way, cannot but deteriorate.

Quigley (1969), in a longitudinal research spanning 4 years, compared two kindergarten-schools of prelingually deaf children of 4–7 years of age, one using speech with the manual alphabet and the other a so-called purely oral method. The latter children were behind. My criticism of this study is that the environment of these 'oral' children was not purely oral, and that the intelligibility of these orally trained children's speech was not yet reliably measurable at an age of almost 8 years. So we are in doubt as to whether their teachers were expert enough, or whether there were some deaf children in the group suffering from some amount of hidden dyspraxia which very often occurs in deaf children (van Uden 1971, 1974). This study is in no way conclusive. Further White (1972) mentions that it could be shown by a corrected statistical computation that the speech of the oral group was significantly better than that of the finger-spelling group. This may be in agreement with another study carried out by Quigley and Frisina (1961) that the speech of (finger-spelling) children *at a day school* was more intelligible than that of residential children. They say: 'It is this factor of 'oralness of environment' or 'practice effect' which accounts for the differences of speech ability'.

Our main criticism levelled at all those studies is again that no direct oral *conversations* have been investigated.

(b) The *tempo* of expert finger-spellers is no higher than about 5 letters = less than

208

about 2 syllables per second (Fusfeld 1958, Bornstein 1965, Haber and Nathanson 1968, Martsinowskaya 1970, Babbini 1971, Bellugi and Fischer 1972, Zakia 1972), i.e. less than half the tempo of normal speech of even prelingually deaf children (3 syllables per second, van Uden 1971, 1974, cf. Blevins 1972). This too slow a tempo of finger-spelling is a very dangerous obstacle both for the Short Term Memory and for the tempo of accompanying speech. Regarding this last aspect, all teachers of the deaf know very well that, if the tempo of speech in the early years has not been trained sufficiently, resulting in the child acquiring a habit of slow speaking, it is very difficult to speed it up in later years, and if it has been sped up more or less forcibly, many children are going to make a lot of articulatory mistakes. – Last but not least, a habit of too slow a speech gives rise to bad lipreading and poor results in auditory training, for lipreading and hearing are not just sensory but sensory-motory processes.

(c) The *rhythm* of language will not be shown to its full advantage. Pauses will of course be expressed. Accentuated syllables may be expressed by stronger or slower movements. But this is not quite the same as rhythmic grouping of words. So I feel that an important language form is lost, as in written forms too, see (h).

(d) This diminishes again the possibilities of enhancing *immediate memory* for groups of words and sentences, the consequences of which will be shown under (h). Dawson (1976), using nonsense words, found the STM limited to not more than 4 letters.

(e) Only by the purely oral way can we make the most of *auditory training* which is so important for language acquisition, for the control of speech and for the whole behaviour of deaf children.

(f) It has been claimed that finger-spelling has the advantage of a quicker *growth of vocabulary* in infant years (see above especially 'neo-oralism'). This still has to be proved. I am sure that the advantages of finger-spelling, if any, will not compensate for the loss incurred when not making the most of sound-perception.

(g) It has been claimed that the manual alphabet is *quite clear* to deaf children. Fisher and Florence (1973) have pointed out, however, that it is sometimes rather ambiguous: 8 manual letters (V,O,M,E,A,Q,S and U), spelled at conversational rates, gave errors of more than 3% in understanding. – The technique of producing and understanding finger-spelling by expert finger-spellers is that of 'Gestalt'-forming, thus an overall one (Zakia and Haber 1971, Zakia 1972). The producing technique is easily learned, not so the understanding, the reading-back of finger-spelling. It is only seldom learned quite fluently by parents and teachers, because of the lack of challenge (as with lipreading!). As for deaf children themselves, they keep on making many mistakes, especially when less frequent words are used, and/or longer words, word-groups and sentences (Woodford 1973, Markides 1976). This too is a source of more misunderstandings than expected by the advocates of the Rochester Method. No direct *conversations* have been investigated, however.

(h) The 'Rochester deaf children' seemingly have typical *difficulties with the written language* too, although they are on the average significantly ahead of 'combined children' (Quigley 1969, Kates 1972).
Olson (1967) found control of written English in 'Rochester children', measured by the ability to write compositions, independent from the ability in finger-spelling. Apparently their control of English is mainly graphic, i.e. based on the visually simultaneous perception of the written form, not on its successive presentation by finger-spelling as its more difficult form. Kates (1972) found, however, a group of 'Rochester adolescents' significantly behind a matched (i.e. in reading level) group of purely orally educated deaf adolescents in the memory for *written* sentences, the interpretation of multimeaning words, the average length and correctness of produced written sentences. Apparently the words as used by these 'Rochester adolescents' were less context-bound. So it can be questioned whether finger-spelling is of such a help after all to the memory of written text as has been claimed; perhaps the hampered Short Term Memory for finger-spelling is interfering here. On the other hand these 'Rochester adolescents' were significantly ahead of the 'oral adolescents' in finding an associative word to a given word (e.g. house), i.e. they reacted in this respect more similarly to the normally hearing control group of the same age. This can obviously be explained by the fact that younger normally hearing children associate words in a more context-bound way (e.g. house – roof) and normally hearing adolescents in a more context-independent way (e.g. house – dwelling place) (see Restaino in Rosenstein and McGinitie 1969). The 'Rochester adolescents' seemed to be more inclined to this last way of thinking. It is not quite clear whether this is an advantage or not. In normally hearing children this loosening of words from their contexts is an effect of normal linguistic development by the high frequency of varied language; in the 'Rochester children' it may be an artifact of the method.

(i) Last but not least, an education in finger-spelling is an education leading directly to *the deaf 'ghetto'*. This danger should be seen in connection with the difficulty of the hearing in learning to read back finger-spelled language, see (g).

NB. Aphasic deaf children of normal intelligence, or 'dactyl-children'

Myklebust (1960, 1964) speaks of 'lipreading-aphasia', see also Nicholas (1962, 1973). A-phasia, strictly speaking, should be well discerned from dys-phasia, however. Both of them can be congenital (cf. Calon 1950, Prick and Waals

210

1958–1966, Prick and Calon 1950). See Appendix III.

There are a few multiply handicapped deaf children who to me are 'motor-aphasic' ones (van Uden 1955–1957). In my experience so far not more than about 3% of the prelingually deaf constitute such handicapped children, provided that they had had good home-training and good preschool, guided by expert teachers. They cannot be expected to participate in an oral conversation as such, although they can learn a little bit of articulation and make themselves more or less understood in most of the daily situations; but this of course is not the same as an oral conversation. Finger-spelling (or another *verbal* code such as the articulatory alphabets) may be a godsend to them, i.e. among themselves, with the parents and other members of the family, their teachers and house-parents, and with some hearing friends who are willing to learn this.

The main part of language is not learned by fingerspelling, however, but by reading and writing, ideally by 'graphic conversation'. The very weak side of these children is their memory for successively presented visual data (for instance lipreading), in contrast to simultaneously presented ones (van Uden 1971, 1974): usually these children have a strong memory for the graphic form of words and sentences, if taught methodically well, because these are simultaneous visual data. The 'graphic conversation' can be highly facilitated by modern electronic equipment. A 'group graphic aid' is possible, and in fact is in use in one of our departments (van Uden 1975): four severely aphasic deaf children, John, Mary, Christl and Magda follow high school education, Dutch and English included, in a mainly graphic way; each child and the teacher himself has a teleprinter. What John types he sees on his paper, and is printed on the other teleprinters too, all being interconnected. The teacher has a central control panel by means of which he can lock the typekeys of those children who are not 'speaking'. When John is finished and Mary wants to 'say' something, the teacher unlocks Mary's keys and locks the others. At the end of the lesson, the whole text, the whole discussion can be kept by the children in their loose-leaf binders.

There are other ranges of portable electronic typewriters (e.g. Canon Manufacturers 1974), telephone-typewriters (e.g. Bell Laboratories), 'Mediated Interaction Visual Response' using video closed circuits (Wyman 1969), and so on.

It is quite possible to educate the vast majority of these children without signs, in order to prevent image-thinking and to develop satisfactory reading.

There are a few cases, however, in which even finger-spelling, reading and writing alone are insufficient to develop satisfactory communication. Apart from the cases of subnormal intelligence, this can happen with the child having a very *bad memory*. Then we have to go over to signs, not only with the child, but with his parents and the rest of the family too.

Concerning the organization of school and boarding house, see above: monolingualism for deaf children. These children cannot be accomodated with others educated in the purely oral way. (Concerning the term 'asphasia in children' see Ewing 1930, 1967).

d. 'Graphic Conversation'?

This was the method followed by Alex. Graham Bell (1883). The term was really invented by Nanninga-Boon (1934).

This method had the same advantages and disadvantages as finger-spelling. A specific disadvantage was that writing was a very tiring and retarding conversational cue, the effect of which was that it became a stimulus for the children to invent signs for a smoother conversation (see Yale 1931).

I have often met a certain born deaf adult, a hydraulic engineer, who had a perfect control of Dutch, his mother-tongue. He had been educated by his *own mother* by means of 'graphic conversation' up to the age of about 7 years, when he began to learn to speak. His speech, although a little bit too slow, was very intelligible. His lipreading ability was behind, however. During conversation I had to write down many words because he could not lipread them from me. This fine and highly educated man told me that a word for him was first of all a graphic image which he saw before him as if on a screen. The same applied where a sentence was concerned. The graphic form of words was his 'stuff of thinking'. The spoken image was only a side-aspect of linguistic usage to him. He did not know any conventional sign because he had been educated exclusively within a hearing world. Notwithstanding this, his lipreading had not been developed to its highest potential. – In contrast to him, I have in my circle of acquaintances another highly educated deaf born adult, a woman with a perfect control of German, her mother-tongue, and of Dutch too. She can read English. She was educated purely orally from her first year of age, again by her *own mother*, exclusively within a hearing world. She started reading and writing from 6 years of age after a full oral training. There was never a graphic conversation. She can lipread almost perfectly, much better than the engineer. She told me her 'stuff of thinking' is speaking to herself or to a pretended partner. So seemingly much depends upon the *starting-point* of the education.

For the *aphasic* and some of the severely *dysphasic* deaf children, however, this graphic conversation is indispensable.

9. WRITING AND SPEAKING.–
A 'MOUTH TO MOUTH PROCEDURE'. – TEMPO

What then should be the relation between writing and speaking in teaching the deaf?

Lipreading (including listening) and speech should precede reading and writing.

212

Reading and writing are also a help to better lipreading and speaking, however. We may say, in general children will lipread and speak such words better which they can also read and write. So there is an interaction; all 5 forms of language should be well integrated.

At what age should learning to read and write start? In our opinion certainly not later than 4 years of age, first reading (synthetic method) and a few months later, based on drawing, writing. For some children even an earlier start is advisable, especially when a- or dys-phasia is suspected. – These graphic means should be learned mainly and primarily by the 'speech-balloons'. Then there is no danger of hampering lipreading, listening and speaking, even the reverse. – Durkin (1966, 1972, see Pflaum 1974) had found a long term positive effect of this early learning to read in normally hearing children, even through the end of the primary school, especially: 'they could assimilate more information more quickly'. Brzeinsky (1964 quot. Pflaum 1974) had found the same in first through fifth grade children; in older ones only, if they continued an adjusted programme. (Otherwise a levelling effect appeared.) – According to our experience the same must be said of deaf children.

Ideally lipreading, listening and speech should be so far ahead that the children of about 5 years of age can speak all words that they can write, and also some they cannot. Very often, however, this ideal cannot be reached for many reasons, e.g. the school being understaffed. Vatter (1891) would arrest reading and writing until speech had been sufficiently developed, i.e. arrest thinking. He predicted a lot of signs if one went ahead with reading and writing. Perhaps he was right in his prediction. Yet his point of view seems to me too fanatic. I think we must take that risk and not postpone reading and writing. So the first pages of the diaries may contain much reading material which the children understand, also by lipreading (and listening) in an overall way, but which they cannot yet speak. Simultaneously there must be a running-match with speech, so that as soon as possible, speech will be ahead of reading and writing; let us hope it will be so by the time the children are about 6 years old. See Appendix I, how the oral functioning is always kept in the fore-front.

From that time on we must follow more and more – what I would call – a 'mouth to mouth procedure' (van Uden 1955–1957). This means that a new phrase, a new word should first be lipread (listened to) and spoken, before it is written. Many new words and idioms will be understood and expressed immediately. Many others will not. Let us take a difficult one as an example: *persistence*. Let us suppose that a child cannot produce from lipreading more than one syllable. The procedure will be as follows (without using a written form):

– first step: say *siss* (the accented syllable);
– second step: *tence*, then *sisstence*;
– third step: *per*;

– then *persistence*, in a good tempo;
– fifth step: 'Write down now what you have spoken'.

We found (1969) that normal deaf children of 9 years of age and older are able to pronounce every word from 'mouth to mouth', even the longest and the most difficult ones. This ability increasingly enhances the speed of the conversation, therefore too, the speed of thinking, and the growth of the vocabulary.

The *tempo* of speech should not be forgotten. Rhythmic speech includes a quick, good tempo. If the teacher neglects this, the children will speak too slowly. The intelligibility will be unsatisfactory (John and Howarth 1965). They will have more and more difficulty in lipreading because they are not accustomed to the quick tempo of hearing speakers. Short term memory functions will be underfed. Thinking and the processes of inner language will slow down. In emotional situations they will make many slips in speech, stumbling over their own tongues. They adhere to a kind of 'telegraphese'. – The nice tempo of speech for deaf children seems to be that of an orator reading a poem or some piece of the 'belles lettres', i.e. on the average 3 syllables in one second (pauses excluded).

NB. *Dysphasic Deaf Children*

There are some multiply handicapped deaf children (I have found about 25%) who could, in my opinion be termed: dysphasic, in the sense of 'dyspraxic in speech'. These are our 'clumsy speakers'. The disturbance can occur in different degrees, from the border-cases of aphasic-dysphasic to only a slight difficulty. This 'dyspraxia of speech' is just an aspect of a much broader phenomenon, however, affecting the whole personality of the child, i.e. not only his eupraxia as such, including the control of the body scheme and rhythmic comfort, but also his character, including the type of his motivation and sphere of interest, and of his intelligence, his cross-modal functioning (especially the integration of the spoken and the graphic verbal form) and last but not least his memory. A great advantage to most of these children is their strong memory for simultaneously presented data (including the written forms of words), in contrast to successively presented data (e.g. a sequence of paper foldings, and lipreading) (see van Uden 1970, 1974, and van Dijk and van Uden 1976). All this has to be included in both the diagnosis and the therapy.
According to their oral behaviour:
In the first instance they do not come to lipread and speak more than one or two syllables. These are the border-cases close to aphasia.
Some children sometimes have extraordinary difficulties when for example they have to imitate more than three syllables, and yet others struggle with longer sentences only (van Uden 1955–1957; 1964). All these degrees result in *respective* grades of dysgrammaticism.

214

These children need a lot of special help:
First of all, *more individual* speech-training with appropriate methods, at least twice a day for 20 minutes.

In addition to this they need *more written forms* (learning them by heart too) than other deaf children. So when they become about 7 years of age I always advise that they should learn *type-writing*, because this enhances the analytic-synthetic impression of the graphic symbol, of course again: typewriting by heart.

They can and, to me, must be educated to *translate* mentally the written forms as quickly as possible into oral forms, and the reverse. The necessary *integration* of speech and graphic symbol should be trained throughout by a good analysis and synthesis of both speech and writing, writing whilst speaking. An important piece of advice of mine is that the teacher should use transparent strips of paper. The letters are written on it, the child speaks them, holds the strip before his mouth and looks into the mirror: he sees the letter(s) and his moving mouth in one view in one field. This supports integration. The teacher or even better the child himself could also write directly on the mirror with the same effect (van Uden 1971).

Fourth topic of training: I found that lipreading and speech improve significantly when these children have to *lipread from themselves* (van Uden 1970, 1974, van Dijk and van Uden 1976). As soon as they can speak about 10 words correctly (thus as early as in the preschool), this is videotaped and then shown to the children. They have to lipread from themselves. This they like very much! After each word, a portion of the tape is blacked out or a stop inserted: the child after lipreading from himself repeats what he has seen in the monitor. Mistakes are corrected again and again. The tempo of speech is increased continually; they should see themselves speak more and more quickly. Later much longer lists of about 30 or 40 words should be used, increasingly refining the lipreading demands; the same for longer and longer sentences; and eventually whole conversations among the children can be videotaped and shown to them: this enhances their memory for speech tremendously (van Dijk and Ven 1973, Ven 1974, Smits 1975).

Fifthly: for all deaf children, but especially for these ones, auditory training should be given by making them *hear their own voices*, in the same way as explained above according to lipreading from themselves. – The LRS-Method (= Listening-Reading-Speaking-Method) of the Ewings (1964) is of great help. 'Essentially, it depends on the teacher first speaking close to the microphone of the hearing aid while pointing in a book to the words as they are said. Next, the child is asked to repeat the phrase or sentences, while the teacher again points to the words ... Evidence supporting the success is provided by John and Howarth (1965) in a research using this technique with 29 severely and profoundly deaf children. A 56% improvement in speech intelligibility was achieved by getting the children to reproduce the teacher's pattern as nearly as possible. The children concentrated on whatever auditory information they could perceive while watching as the teacher pointed to each syllable (Dale 1967).

These children therefore need a special training *in small groups* for about 3 to 4 years. They should be kept in the oral atmosphere. For some serious cases, however, graphic conversations may be necessary in order not to slow down the tempo of their language-acquisition. During these conversations, what can be spoken is spoken continuously, but *for the moment* not too much time is lost by correcting speech defects or by repeating words or phrases again and again for lipreading. But more and more the oral mouth-to-mouth-procedure will replace the graphic communication.

Finger-spelling?

There is *no need for finger-spelling*.

Instead of finger-spelling I advise — and experience has shown this to be good advice — to teach them the *phonetic alphabet* (as used on the telephone) Andrew, Benjamin, Charlie and so on. This provides an *oral* aid for difficult lipreaders, e.g.: 'I said cap with Charlie not with George', or: 'Say Charlie — Andrew — Peter'.

But first of all they should learn the *phonological cues*, especially for the homophenous phonemes. (This is very useful to the normal deaf children too!) The staff of the school and the boarding house should agree upon clear and simple terms so that each teacher, nurse, guide, etc., the parents too, use roughly the same terms, such terms as: — vowels and consonants; — long vowel, — monophthongs and diphthongs —, and short vowels; — the shwa or 'neutral vowel'; — the tee-aitch; — strong and mild plosives; — fricatives; — nasals, — and so on. This is again of *oral* help to difficult lipreaders. By means of the phonetic alphabet, words or syllables can be spelled, but generally the phonological cues will be sufficient. For example the teacher says 'nor' and the child persistently says ·door'. Then the teacher: 'You are using the plosive; use the nasal: nnor ...'.

Further these children — the normal deaf ones too! — should know precisely *how many syllables* a word, a phrase etc. has, and which syllable has the *accent* (accent of duration).

NB. In some schools, so-called '*speech-signs*' or 'sound-signs', 'articulatory signs' are in use, e.g.

— for a nasal: the teacher touches his nose;
— for the ee: he spreads out his fore- and middle-finger in order to show the stretching of the lips;
— for the ss: he points with his little finger to his lips so as to show the narrow stream of escaping air; etc.

Sometimes these signs have been so multiplied that they become almost a new sort of finger-spelling! I think it is much better to keep the atmosphere orally

216

pure. This can be done in a satisfactory way by means of the phonetic alphabet and the phonological cues. In this way the rewarding feelings of having understood reinforce oralism, not outside signals.

Kinetic Therapy

Needless to say, rhythmical and musical training is very important. Because of their very often clumsy motor-control a kinetic therapy (including rhythmic gymnastics) is indicated. This general training may support the rhythm of speech.

Mouth to Mouth Procedure

More and more it will be possible to teach them *new words*, in the same way as we explained above with the word *persistence*. Some intelligent dysphasic deaf children told me that they saw the letters appearing in front of them when lipreading a difficult word. The written symbol and speech seem to become more and more integrated, with the effect that they become satisfactory and often good lipreaders after several years of training, with a satisfactory language, feeling themselves at home in the hearing world.

Criterion?

Is there any criterion to distinguish between a-phasic and dys-phasic deaf children in the very few 'border cases'? That is: will this child through the very hard work of expert and devoted teachers for 2 or 3 years, having already acquired some speech, acquire in the future *sufficient* speech or not? The distinguishing criterion is whether a true mainly oral conversation will be possible in time or not, especially where the deaf children *among themselves* are concerned. Otherwise they will be compelled to follow a primitive, 'low version' signed communication. – 'In time' means: within a reasonable time of true education, let us say in general before the age of 9 years, pre-supposing the child has been trained throughout from his home training and pre-school years. If this possibility alas must be denied, there will be no true oral education possible, because without conversation there is no true human education. Therefore the humanization of these children will ask for other means of lower standard: finger-spelling and/or (in the worst case) signing. If the children have had home-training, this diagnosis can be drawn up at about 4–5 years of age, in general even earlier (van Uden 1975). We have set up a battery of tests for this diagnosis (in the press).

The previously mentioned hard work in lipreading, auditory training and speech is not fruitless. Indeed, far from it! It should be continued with all possible means. Speech of a few simple words and a little bit of lipreading and 'sound-perception' can already be a welcome help.

Speech is usually developed more easily and sooner than smooth lipreading, at least by expert speech teachers. It can happen that speech is quite fluent and intelligible, even in children who in the beginning needed finger-spelling or 'sound signs' for that, but that lipreading remains behind (see Myklebust's 'lipreading aphasia'). The diagnosis should include both aspects of *conversation*.

Reasons for 'Oral Failures', i.e. Deaf Children Failing to Arrive at Satisfactory Oral Communication

The first reason are alas the unqualified teachers. The teachers' responsibilities are very, very great. The same must be said for the responsibilities of teachers' training. Inexpert teachers will produce a lot of *pseudo a- and dys-phasic deaf* children! Not all teachers are able to teach a deaf child to talk, not even all the qualified ones.

Further: postponement of adequate treatment; – lack of emotional acceptance by the parents, which always hampers communication (cf. Greenstein et al. 1975); – lack of cooperation from the parents in the work of language acquisition; – discontinuity of personnel, i.e. too much falling off of personnel, with too much manpower of insufficient experience; – classes numbering more than 6 children; – an uncontrolled growth of esoteric means of communication of the children among themselves, so that the code of communication within the classroom is different from that outside, with hidden interferences, with as a consequence, the oral behaviour usually being almost destroyed instead of developed from inside.

This list may be a conscience-examination for audiological centres, for parents and for schools for the deaf. So the amount of 'oral failures' can become much bigger than the mentioned 3%. But we should never change the principles of education because of the difficulties in applying them, i.e. we should not advocate 'Total Communication', finger-spelling and so on, as *essentially* required by deaf children in general. Instead, we should be honest and concede that the purely oral way, aiming at the fullest possible integration of the deaf into the hearing world, is alas impossible for certain children just because of the lack of opportunities: 'The children can, but we cannot!'

10. SPECIAL HINTS IN DEVELOPING CONVERSATIONAL DIDACTICS

This cannot be explained here in full (a publication is being prepared in a new book 'A World of language for deaf children', Part III). I will limit myself to giving some hints:

(1) Play a Double Part

Play the double part as a mother continuously does with her hearing child: i.e.

218

seize what the child is wanting and trying to say; give it its normal form; make the child repeat his utterance in that form. For example, your children are doing sums. Peter has finished and says: 'You good or bad?' You grasp this opportunity and make him say: 'Will you correct my work?' . . .

Verbalizing is Insufficient

The so-called 'identification-exercises' of the Belgian Method (Decroly 1907) are somewhat misleading. According to this method the teacher gives little John of the infant school a small card on which is written:

$$\mathcal{I} \ am \ \ entering.$$

John has to go out of the room and to enter showing this card to the other children, or saying: I am entering. This is a wrong way. The teacher should not so much verbalize what the child is experiencing (we normally don't express all our experiences!) but what it is supposed to *want* to say. So when you show pictures, look at what the children are trying to say. This is more important than the verbalizing of what is in a picture. (A typical verbalizing method is that of Kern 1958, 1967).
Seizing what the children are wanting to say! You will experience that language is not only a series of statements or assertions. You will find more of this: calls, exclamations, wants, questions, assertions.

Making Yourself Understood

The other side of the conversation: the teacher should make himself understood, in the preschool – as in hometraining – mainly by the situation. He should arrange the situation in such a way that the children will understand him.
Presupposed is always a good *facial expression* of the teacher and of all those who educate a deaf child, not overdone however, but clear. During home-training and the first year of the preschool the *material* situation should be frequently arranged. For instance: 'Now we are going to play the drum'. No child understands the teacher. So she puts the stick on the table and says again: 'Now we are going to play the drum', and the children will understand her immediately. 'The drum, John. Where is the drum?' etc. – Sometimes a picture must be used. Sometimes the teacher has to look towards a special corner of the room, etc.
The more the children can lipread, the more the *verbal* situation can be arranged. As an example: 'Willy (a child from another class, but known to the other

children) fell into the water!' ... No child comprehends. They look astonished ...
'Now, John! Have you fallen sometimes?' (He had a bad fall some days before).
John: 'Yes! Over!' Teacher (seizing): 'Yes, it is over! But Willy fell into the water!'
... etc.

Conversations in the Diaries

First version: See page 220.

Second version:

A surprise for all of us.

Miss Geoffrey had an envelope.
What would be in it?
'Peter's mother has sent me some pictures', she said.
John was curious: 'Ooh! Where are they?'
Miss Geoffrey showed him the envelope: 'Here they are!'
All the children wanted to look ... Nice pictures of flowers!
'May I give them out?' asked John.
But Mary was a little bit jealous. 'It is my turn', she cried ...
Peter beamed!

In this way a conversation may be visualized for the children.
This visualized conversation may be changed into a completion exercise by cutting out the conversational sentences.
Of course it may very often be necessary for the teacher to make the children say what they have to say in a special situation, as a mother, too, does with her hearing child: 'What do you say now? ...'
It is possible to give preschool children some completion exercises, afterwards, in this way: See page 222, top.

The child has to put the sentence cards in the right places. Ditto: p. 222, bottom.

The teacher should also pay particular attention to what the children are saying *between themselves*. This may often be much more important than what they are saying to him!
As soon as possible, he will make the children dramatize such small conversations from the diaries, in their correct forms. This dramatizing must be allowed to grow out in higher years to small 'sketches' as cabaret artists give, at first all about daily life.

221

222

(2) Conversation on Given Subjects

In higher grades, more and more subject matters should be learned according to a programme (history, geography, arithmetic etc.). This has to be done as much as possible in a conversational way. I will explain what I mean, on the basis of a mistake, a maltreatment of a reading lesson to children of about 9 years old. The reading lesson was this:

Pussy Cat came into the room.
There was a glass of milk on the table.
Pussy Cat sprang on the table.
It puts its nose into the glass . . .
The glass fell down.
It was broken.
And all the milk flowed over the table.
Naughty cat!

> NB. I don't like such a lesson very much. It smells too much like the constructive method explained above. It is much better to start with a reading book full of stories about one central person, e.g. a prince, a baker etc. – This teacher's children had never had diaries, however. So they were not prepared for a higher level of reading.

The teacher made the children dramatize this lesson from line to line. So far, so good. Then she began to analyse the lesson line by line too: Who came . . . etc. etc. Thus there was no conversation at all! In my opinion it would have been much better to have started *conversation*, preferably immediately. How? Well, for example by saying: 'I don't think Pussy Cat was naughty at all!' And so on, and then look for the reactions of the children in order to 'seize' them. Flutter the dovecotes! That is the whole secret.

(3) Optimum Number of Children in a Class

I may point to a study by Hare (1952; with boys) and Slater (1958, with adults) who both found (quot. Krech 1962) that a number of 5 partners is optimum in an effective conversation. This means an average of only ten minutes of speech for each child in a lesson of one hour . . . But this calculation is not correct for several reasons; the real situation is even worse.

Deaf children do not know what another one is saying if they cannot see him. This already becomes difficult in a class of 7 children: one sees the children very often looking to the left, to the right, in order to catch what has been said. If the classes are even larger, e.g. 10 children, it becomes almost impossible and is very tiring too. It seems that the teacher, perhaps unconsciously, understands this difficulty,

223

I forgot my handkerchief!

May I have my comb?

Some more soup please!

You should blow your nose!

because I have observed that he almost continuously repeats for the whole group what one child has said (van Uden 1970). Compare the verbatim reports in the appendices of this book. He plays a 'broadcasting part'.

There is still more: several researches have shown (for hearing children Flanders 1970, for deaf children Craig 1969, and van Uden 1970) that the teacher himself speaks to the class for about 60% of the time. So we must recognize that, when the group is only 5–6 children, there is *only 2 or 3 minutes* per child per hour when he has an occasion to say something! In this way a mother-tongue should be learned . . . And yet it is possible!

11. THE REFLECTIVE WAY TO TEACH THE GRAMMATICAL FORMS

The Motivating Power of Finding Analogies Themselves ('Discovery Learning')

As I explained above we make the children themselves find more and more the system within the language they understand (van Uden 1955–1957). So we do not give them the models, preferably, but we make the children find them themselves as much as possible. In this way the analogies of language receive their surprising, delighting and stirring characteristics, as they have for hearing children. The children are *set* then to these analogies.

I will give two examples from the practice of teaching language to deaf children, the first following a less natural, constructive way, the second following a method of stimulating the child to find the linguistic analogies himself, a method more natural, because it is wholly akin to the spontaneous way of a hearing child.

First example. The teacher wants to introduce a new sentence-form: *I think that* . . . (*it will be nice weather to-morrow*). This is the model and it is written on the blackboard. 'Now find more sentences similar to this model', he says to the children. Children:

John has got a letter from home, saying that his father and mother will come next day. He says: 'I think that my father and mother will come to-morrow'.

Mary: 'I think that the cat will like milk to-morrow'.

Peter: 'I think that we will win the soccer match next Sunday'.

Willy: 'I think that I'll get a letter next week'. Etc.

This way is very dangerous, as may be seen from the first two sentences which are incorrect. The teacher has to correct them. But these corrections obscure the whole procedure to the children and discourage them. – Besides, all the sentences speak about the future, which corresponds to the model, but – at the same time – is screwing down the phrase '*I think that* . . .' into a meaning which is too narrow. This too must be corrected by the teacher, with the same effect of insufficiently motivating the children. Moreover all sentences are 'baked sentences', detached from a normal context of conversation and/or reading and/or composition.

Second example. This will show how a teacher can follow a more natural way by making the children find the models themselves. Here, in our 'reflective way', it is presupposed that the children have at their disposal a lot of reading material which they understand well. The best material in the first years of preschool and first grades are the diaries.

This beginning from reading material is of course a peculiarity to deaf children, in contrast to normal hearing children. Normal hearing children do not need a written, fixed form of language in order to find analogies themselves. They have three advantages: (1) the enormous sea of correct speech in which they swim; (2) the more complete perception of language forms; and (3) the better memory of language forms because of a higher prominence of rhythm, supported by melody. In comparison with this, oral language (finger-spelling too) is too incomplete and too volatile for deaf children. They need *fastened language forms*, on which they can 'land' and which they can explore, categorize and organize, i.e. the written form of language.

The teacher's first aim is that the children *understand* the linguistic forms the use of which he will teach them: expressive language should always be a conversion from passive into active language, from perceiving into producing language. This understanding, however, is only possible by abstraction from many examples of living language. He will do the following. – He knows the content of the children's diaries. Perhaps he knows that an expression such as 'I think that . . .' happened to have been used three or four times in the last ten 'deposits' in the diaries. Then he makes the children find them. This game of finding is very attractive to all children. As soon as a child has found one, he enthusiastically writes it on the blackboard. And then the others. These then are not 'baked sentences' but living ones, taken from living language understood by the children. If they have forgotten, the teacher can repeat the material learnt earlier, and recall to memory the past situations. – Then he makes the children read the sentences and say them aloud by heart, in a very correct rhythm, precisely because this is of such infinite help to memory and makes the analogy so prominent. – He keeps these sentences on the blackboard, for several days, but he does not ask the children to construct any more of these expressions. No. He utilizes every moment in the coming days' conversations, quite naturally, saying himself 'I think that . . .' and making his children express themselves that way as often as the opportunities give rise to do so.

A Typical 'Conversion Loss' in Deaf Children?

Myklebust (1967) uses this appropriate term, meaning the receptive to expressive language ratio. The term includes that language has to be understood (received) first before it can be converted to expression.

Hearing people too have a conversion-loss, i.e. that they understand more language than they use themselves. This may be illustrated by this table concerning the *vocabulary* (cf. Seashore and Eckerson 1940, Smith 1941, McCarthy 1954, Templin 1957, Lorge and Chall 1963, Lorge 1964, Lenneberg 1966):

Age:	*Receptive vocabulary, number of words:*	*Expressive vocabulary, number of words:*	*% of 'conversion-loss':*
3 yrs.	9,300	820	91
5 yrs.	14,000	1,240	91
6 yrs.	23,000	2,327	90
9 yrs.	30,000	4,920	84
10 yrs.	32,000	5,923	83
12 yrs.	45,000	7,470	83
18 yrs.	80,000	11,752	85

The average 'conversion-loss' can be symbolized in this way:

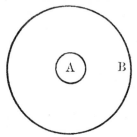

A + B = receptive vocabulary.
A only = expressive vocabulary.

The conversion-loss, quantified in this model, is about 85%. Of course this varies with different people: for a voluminously writing journalist this may be rather small, for a quiet farmer much bigger. The expressive vocabulary of Shakespeare comprised 15,000 words, of Milton 8,000, of Victor Hugo 20,000, of the Italian opera-repertory only 600–800 . . .

NB. It should not be forgotten that only counting the number of words known to a person is an insufficient measure of his vocabulary: the more frequent words have more meanings too, in Dutch on the average 5, ranging from 1 to more than 15. The frequency of the wordmeanings has never been counted to my knowledge. Besides the current multimeaningness should be distinguished

228

from the creative multimeaningness exhibited by poets and other imaginative persons.

There may be a conversion-loss in the *structure* of language too: the amount of structures understood (i.e. receptive language, e.g. 'John's bragging rubbed the other boys up the wrong way') is larger than that we are using ourselves (expressive language). I don't know of any study in this respect, but possibly the amount of conversion-loss is much smaller here than with regard to vocabulary, and may be symbolized in this way (with an estimated conversion-loss of about 30%):

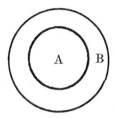

The conversion-loss suffered by many *deaf* people seems to be very different to that of the hearing.

As regards *vocabulary* the conversion-loss is usually much smaller and may be symbolized in this way:

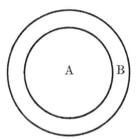

Myklebust (1964) found deaf children of 15 years of age 7–8 years behind normally hearing children in receptive vocabulary. This lag grew from year to year. Silverman-Dresner and Guilfoyle (1972) found in deaf children of 16–17 years of age a *receptive* vocabulary of, on average, 2,500 words. As we have explained above, 3,600 words comprise 95% of the daily conversations of normally hearing adults, with, at a rough estimate, 9,000 very frequent meanings. This study has not counted how many meanings are known to the deaf, but such an amount will be very much behind too. So a receptive knowledge of 2,500 words is very, very insufficient. We can conclude that the *expressive* vocabulary of deaf children must be very close to their receptive vocabulary, suggesting no large 'conversion loss'.

229

This is a very bad situation. – It conditions a reading-level of the 2nd–3rd grade level at the highest. The reasons may be:

(a) An underdevelopment of the *memory* for words. One suspects that deaf children are able to remember only those words which they use routinely, and that they easily forget the many words which they meet only a few times. A perhaps strong dependency on signs again weakens their memory for words.

(b) An unforgivable mistake in the *didactics* of language: the neglect of enhancing the vocabulary of the children from week to week. A growth of 20–30 new meanings every (school)week asks for much concern and hard work, both from the educators (teachers, house-parents and parents) and the children themselves. All this has an escalating effect: because the vocabulary is too small, the children will not come to reading, and because they do not come to reading, the vocabulary does not grow. In our residential school for the deaf at St. Michielsgestel 1975 an average vocabulary of 3,050 words has been found at 14 years of age.

But even when deaf children come to reading with a vocabulary of about 7,000 words, the conversion-loss will be much smaller than in hearing children, because their receptive vocabulary will be much smaller than 45,000 words! So even then many meanings and words in the reading-books will appear unknown. If the children have learned to use a *dictionary*, however, even this barrier can be overcome. *Then* 'the loc has been put on the rails and rides'.

The picture again is different to that of hearing children with respect to the *structure* of language. The conversion-loss here may be symbolized in this way (an estimated loss of 60%):

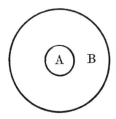

This is what Myklebust (1967) meant principally when he wrote: 'Why is there so great a loss in converting from the inner-receptive to the expressive? Perhaps further reasearch will help us here' ... Indeed, we agree. We would like to give some suggestions which may be helpful to such researches.

In many methods of teaching language, the teaching of *grammar* is far too much *detached* from the language understood, (with respect to the deaf) from reading. 'Baked sentences' are used, and special lessons are constructed in order to illustrate linguistic rules, instead of making the children find these rules themselves as much as possible from their reading material. There is a lack of integration in teaching to read and teaching grammar. This is a mistake. Not only should the expressive vocabulary grow from a fund of receptive language, but the expressive grammar too. Grammatical forms should first be well understood, before they can be converted efficiently into the expressive use. To me this detachment of teaching grammar from the understanding of language is one of the reasons of an eventual abnormal conversion loss in deaf children.

Another reason, I find, is the lack of *conversational* didactics. In conversation, receptive language and expressive language are integrated into one entirity of language behaviour.

We should take note, however, that occurrences may arise, particularly in children educated according to an extreme, *constructive method*, where there is no 'loss' at all. This too is abnormal. When this happens, we can be sure that these children cannot read, notwithstanding given programmed reading lessons, except again the very intelligent ones who are able to guess the meaning of the whole reading-piece from the few words known to them. They intelligently *reconstruct* the whole story. This is of course no real reading.

The Reflective Way Demands a Differentiating Grammar

In teaching grammar, two methods can be followed:
Setting up *an empty diagram* such as that by Fitzgerald or Chomsky and filling it with words. These words are learned beforehand, according to their categories. Or groups of words and/or sentences are constructed and given as models. We call this kind of grammatical 'ruling' an '*associated* grammar'. We have discussed the difficulties against such methods passim in the 2nd chapter of this book.

A normal hearing child, however, detects the rules of the linguistic system, or better the laws of linguistic behaviour, in a '*differentiating* way': starting from the entirety of *sentences*, understood from the expressive melodies, the facial expressions and gestures, according to the situations, – finding *phrases* (= 'accent groups') – detecting *words*, – finding the words and their functional *combinabilities* always within these entirities. See Menyuk (1969), Ferguson and Slobin (1973), Brown (1973). For instance, the example on p. 232, top.

For our Dutch teachers we evolved a *special Dutch grammar* (van Uden and others 1957) using this differentiating way and taking into account the specific difficulties of deaf children, which are not dealt with sufficiently in the grammars for hearing children. In connection with this we wrote a training book for teachers, containing more than 2,000 mistakes made by deaf children, both in receiving and expressing language, in order to make the young teacher interpret them and correct them in the right way, i.e. by making the child *detect* the rule himself (van Uden 1964).

231

1 year of age – first phase

Wouldyoulikesomemilk?

2 years of age – second phase

Wouldyou / like / somemilk?

2½ years of age – third phase

Would / you // like // some / milk?

6 years of age and older – fourth phase

Would you like some milk?

Reflecting upon what?

There are six sources for this work of reflection: the diaries, the notebooks, children's dramas, the receptive reading material, the compositions (by compositions I mean here all kinds of written language, see Groht 1958), and last-but-not-least the conversations. It may be clear that the fixed text in the beginning is almost necessary for this work. It may be very helpful, if the teacher photocopies pages in the diaries or reading books; on these photocopies the children can write and draw all of what they need to do, e.g. the 'schemes of belonging' explained above.

This work can and should start even as early as *in the preschool*. This mainly happens through the changing of words. For example, the 'calendar work' gives the opportunity to children to detect the 'ever changing' verbs.

On Tuesday it is written on the calendar: 'We are *going* to the zoo'. On Wednesday, this sentence should be changed to: 'We *went* to the zoo'. –

Or: 'I am . . .' should be changed to 'We are . . .', 'your block' to 'my block', etc. – Further when the children are *6 to 7 years old* e.g.: 'Find the accent-groups!' 'Find the verbs!' 'Find singular and plural forms!', and so on.

232

Reconstructing, Constructing and Reflecting Exercises

We distinguish three kinds of exercises in language:

(a) *Reconstructing Exercises*

An example from Br. Josefo Dassen (one of our best teachers and headmaster):
The children have learned this reading lesson:

There is no doubt that Mr. Bonar Law gave his life to his country, just as much as if he had fallen in the Great War. The work he did during the war could only have been done by a man of great physical endurance and great intellectual capacity. ... etc.

to be   There — no doubt that Mr. Bonar Law

to give   — his life for the country, just as much as

to have ⎫
         ⎬   if he — — in the Great War. The work
to fall ⎭

to do   he — during the war could only have been —

             by a man of great physical endurance and great

             intellectual capacity . . . etc.

It may be clear that the children have to *re*construct the forms of the verbs, of course by heart.
The same goes for the younger children's exercise, mentioned above page 220: the sentences from a reading lesson are cut out and the child has to correctly reconstruct the lesson in the original order. This same exericise can be done with cut out phrases and even with words.

(b) *Constructing Exercises*

An example: to change an indirect quotation into a direct one and vice versa, or a statement into a question, or a sentence in active voice into one in passive voice, etc. – The same goes for the so-called 'cloze-procedure' (Taylor 1953, Moores 1970, Stuckless and Enders 1972, Meyer 1975), for instance (from Dale 1974):

We are going to — woods tomorrow. We will — early in the morning. — will wear play clothes. — Willis will come with — . Mrs. Daniels will drive — in the car. It — be lovely, but we — be careful. Don't run — in the woods. Don't — lost. Etc.

233

(c) *Reflecting Exercises*

By means of these the child is guided to *detect* the system of language, both semantic and grammatical. We have discussed the semantic side earlier. Now we will give some examples of programmed grammatical reflective exercises. – It may be clear that these are more important than (a) and (b), indispensably important, because the children first of all have to *understand* the language forms before they can be requested to use them. For example, after they have found a lot of accent-groups, by rhythmic speaking, they can learn to understand what is meant by 'accent-groups'; after they have categorized a lot of understood sentences in the passive voice, they can be requested to control this form in their speech and compositions. See the same principle regarding the teaching of questions and accentuations. So *only* on the basis of reflecting exercises, reconstructing and constructing exercises can be introduced afterwards.

> NB. It should never be forgotten that the growth of the vocabulary remains of primary importance, further that the teacher always first of all has to *listen* to his children in order to *seize* their utterances and to react to them. Thus the teacher should not lose too much time, particularly through the reconstructing and constructing exercises! He should prevent all kinds of screwing home his children's thinking.

Examples of Reflective Exercises

Here are some examples of exercises which can be done on the reading material. Of course complete pericopes are always meant when some isolated sentences are given as examples.
Most of these exercises can be given both in the written and oral forms. It may be clear that the oral forms should always be preferred.

We have tried to put the exercises in order of the degree of difficulty.

First Course of Instruction: Children Aged 6–9;11 Years

1. First of all it is necessary to continuously develop a sense of rhythm in language and consequently in speech. 'Look and listen well! What *pauses* have I made in this sentence?', meaning 'What *accent-groups* have I made?' 'Repeat my words exactly, in turn'.

To whom / did Mary / give the ball?

2. John enters and says, with the help of mime: 'Dog outside, bow, wow!' This is

234

'seized' and corrected as follows:

The dog outside barked at me.

The dog outside barked at me .

'Where does the accent lie, John?' It is to be hoped that he can emphasize 'barked' in his speech, which is achieved by lengthening the 'a' (baaaarked).

3. Find the 'question-word' (= a 'substitute-word') which belongs to the underlined words (cf. nrs. 4, 5, 10, 11 and 13):

E.g.: There was the old tree, felled, quite dead.

4. Find the 'pointer-word' which belongs to the underlined words.

E.g.: Mother meanwhile put the potatoes on.

5. Find the accent-group which belong to the interrogative word 'Who?' and underline them. Ditto with 'What', 'What has happened?', 'How?' 'When', 'Around what?' etc.
See nr. 24 and 36. Look for a suitable reading lesson.

6. Find and underline the questions containing a 'question-word'.

E.g.: Have you lost something? Why are you all searching?

7. Underline the questions *without* 'question-words' ('yes- and no-questions'; the term is not quite right, but suitable).

E.g.: 'Will the weather be fine on Sunday?'
   – 'How should I know!'
   'If the weather is fine, where shall we go?'

8. What does *that* belong to? And: What belongs *to that*?

E.g.: a. 'To-morrow at nine o'clock.'
   What does at nine o'clock belong to?
   Mark it with circles and arrows!
   For instance:

'To-morrow at nine o'clock'.

b. 'We went for a walk yesterday.'
What belongs to went for a walk?
As follows:

'We went for a walk yesterday.'

9. What do the underlined words belong to? (Mark this with circles and arrows.)

E.g.: Who left the window open yesterday?
It is <u>not</u> true, what you say.

10. Which of these interrogative sentences belongs to the underlined verbs?

What has happened (to . . .)?
What is happening (to . . .)?
What is (subject . . .) doing?
What did (subject . . .) do? Etc.

E.g.: Mother <u>wanted to put on</u> the potatoes.
But where <u>had</u> the pan <u>gone</u>?

11. What do the underlined question-words (= interrogatives) mean?

E.g.: "<u>Where</u> shall we go to-morrow? May be to the zoo?'
– "<u>When</u> did you say?'

12. Which verb-forms are plural? Which are singular? Which can be both singular and plural? Say why!

E.g.: There <u>are</u> a lot of books on your shelf. But I <u>give</u> you some more. This <u>is</u> a very nice one.

13. What do the underlined 'pointer-words' mean?

E.g.: 'Will you take your hands off <u>them</u>!' mother called from the kitchen to John, <u>who</u> was squeezing the bananas. '<u>They</u> are still far too hard', <u>he</u> called back.

14. Which *underlined* verb is in the finite form?

E.g.: Jack <u>has</u> <u>lost</u> his ball. He <u>says</u>, he <u>has</u> <u>looked</u> for it everywhere. Who <u>would</u> <u>be</u> willing to help him?

15. Which of the *underlined* substantives are plural? Which are singular?

E.g.: The <u>boys</u> were all waiting for <u>Santa Claus</u>. He did not arrive on a <u>horse</u> but by <u>car</u>. The car was also loaded up with <u>Black Peters</u>.

16. What subject belongs to the *underlined* finite form?

E.g.: He came to tell us that nobody would come. But he had hardly said so when uncle and aunt arrived. He always hastens.

17. What finite form belongs to the *underlined* subject?

E.g.: Very slowly a spider came crawling over the table.
'Don't touch it!' cried Mary who was afraid.

18. Find the sentences where the subject is placed *after* the verb.
Find the sentences where the subject is placed *before* the verb.
Find the sentences where the subject is placed *between* the verbs.

E.g.: 'Will you come here please!' shouted mother angrily into the garden. But the boys pretended that they did not hear anything.

NB. At first *underline* the verbs. Later on the children should also *find* the verb.

19. Which accent-group contains a verb?

E.g.: Over there / I see a boy / walking with a dog. Does that dog / belong to him? Can anybody / walk there?

20. Find the sentences without a subject.

E.g.: Go away! – No! – Impossible! – Look at the blackboard!

21. Which *underlined* verbs have a 'pincer-construction'? Indicate this with a link over the top.
Which *underlined* verbs do not have a 'pincer-construction' (we could call this 'compound construction'). Indicate this with a link underneath:

E.g.: 'Can we go swimming to-morrow?'

22. Which *underlined* verb is an infinitive form? A participle form? A progressive form? A finite form?

E.g.: 'Where are you going?' 'There and back again to see how far it is. I never have been there'.

23. Underline the finites in this reading-piece.

John: 'I can jump higher than a house!'
Peter: 'Bet you can't'.
John: 'Bet I can, did you ever see a house jump?'

24. Which *underlined* accent-group is a preposition-group?

E.g.: There is an even bigger stick / behind the cupboard. He who gets it out, is the hero of the day.

25. Which of the *underlined* accent-groups contain a substantive word?

E.g.: He would have come to-morrow, but now he is coming the following day. We have waited for him for a long time.

Second Course of Instruction, Children Aged 10–13;11 Years

26. Underline the 'pointer-words' and add what they mean.

27. Underline the subjects.

28. Underline the verbs and add whether they are finite form, infinitive form, participle form or progressive form.

29. There is already a circle round the substantive word in the subject and around the verb. Now draw circles with arrows round the other words:

E.g.: Upstairs, in the attic, was an old clothes-trunk.

30. Find the subject and the predicate in the underlined sentences. Put a blue line (or ⎯⎯) under the subject, and under the predicate a red line (or ⌄⌄⌄).

E.g.: 'The tree in front of our house was blown down last night'.
'How old was it?' – 'About 30 years I think.'

31. What sort of accent do the *underlined* words have (viz. accent of newness or of contrast)?

E.g.: John and William wanted to go on a journey together. But they did not know yet whereto. To Germany? Or to Belgium? 'I'd rather go to Belgium', said John.

32. Find sentences with verbs in two parts. Underline those two parts.

E.g.: 'Nice that you have won a prize! Who will be presenting the prize?'
'Oh, we have already got that!'
– 'How much was it?'

33. Find the sentences with verbs in two or more parts. Where do we find a 'pincer-construction'? Where is there a 'compound construction'?

E.g.: Nice that you have won a prize! Who will be presenting the prize?'
'Oh, we have already got that!'
'How much was it?'

238

34. Find the finite form of the verb, and the subject belonging to it, and underline these.

35. Then find the 'pincer-construction' and the 'compound construction' of subject and 'finite form' (in pincer-construction, put link over the top, in compound construction, underneath).

E.g.: Do you know, who has been here? I never saw there a friend of mine.

36. Find the preposition groups and underline the preposition.

E.g.: One of these days you will have an accident IN that car.

37. Find the substantive words and underline them. Put two lines beneath those substantive words which form the subject.

38. Which of the *underlined* words is substantive, which is adjectival, which is adverbial?

E.g.: Upstairs, in the attic, was an old clothes-trunk. It was a wooden one, and completely painted brown.

Third Course of Instruction, ⩾ *14 Years of Age*

39. Find the accent-groups with an article, and underline this article.

E.g.: THE youngest child of THE family received A new bike from THE rich uncle.

40. Find the accent-groups with a substantive word without an article.

E.g.: 'Mary, can you go and fetch some buttermilk?' 'How many bottles, Mother?'
–'Well, two bottles will be enough. Go on the bike. On the High Street you will find a dairy'.

NB.: Keep on explaining this difference in using the article! Only in that way one can expect the correct use of the article in the course of time. Remember that the definite article goes back to the pointer-words, and the indefinite article to the numeral one (of many).

41. For the oral lesson: 'Find the accent-groups in (say) the second sentence of this reading-piece. Read that sentence aloud. Listen everybody!' ...

42. For the oral lesson: 'Look and listen well! Where does the *main accent* lie in this sentence? Repeat my words exactly. Listen everybody!' ...

43. For the oral lesson: 'Look and listen well!

239

a. Where do the main- and accidental accents lie in this sentence (resp. main-accent and accidental accent)?

b. Where do the other accents lie? Peter, now you read that aloud and everybody please listen!' . . .

44. Find the accents of newness and of contrast in this reading-piece. Underline the accents of newness with blue and the accents of contrast with red.

45. Find the main and accidental accents in this reading-piece. Underline the main accents with red and the accidental accents with blue.

46. What sorts of '*pincer-constructions*' and '*compound constructions*' can you find in this piece?

> E.g.: That boy hit a hole in here. Do you mean that big boy over there? Yes, he must have hit it hard.

47. Find the 'comparative words' and underline them.

> E.g.: 'He was working on his plane again to-day, just like yesterday. I think it will be better than the last one. If only, it won't be too expensive!' – 'Oh, he is rich enough'.

> NB. Always ask for the exact '*terms of the comparison*'!

48. Find the subordinate clauses with a conjunction and underline the conjunction.

> E.g.: Before we arrived at the castle, we had to cross a rickety little bridge, that spanned a deep ravine. If only we knew that it would hold! We were so wise as to wait, until the guide had safely arrived on the other side! Then we all dared to follow.

49. Give the principal meaning or intention for each sentence of this reading-pieces. Is it an assertion? – Is it a real question? – Is it a call?

> E.g.: 'Have you had a nice trip on your bike?' 'I have indeed! In spite of the rain! Why should that bother us?'

50. Find the 'say sentences' (i.e. direct quotations) and the 'quotations' (indirect quotations).

> E.g.: 'You were asking: why has he given his notice?'
> – 'Yes, do you know why?'
> 'Well, his boss told him that he could do better without him'.

51. Find the passive sentences, and also the active ones, and underline the verbs.

> E.g.: 'Have you posted the letter yet? It is urgent!'
> – 'Yes, it has already been posted'.

240

'If only it will be delivered in time to-morrow! Last week a lot of post was delivered late'.

52. How many parts does the verb (= all verb forms together) in the passive sentences have? – How many parts does the verb in the active sentences have?

53. Who/What is active in these three sentences (= actor), –
Who/What is passive? – Who/What is neither?

> E.g.: 'Have you posted the letter yet?'
> 'It is urgent'.
> 'It has already been posted'.

54. Who/What is active, is passive, is neither?

> E.g.: The children had made a nice snowman. How big he was! But he was ever so proud of himself! In the night, when everything was quiet, he sneaked into the police station. He was not content with the ugly, old cap he had on. There was a beautiful police-hat. 'Will you leave me alone!' the hat said. But no, a bit later the snowman was outside with the nice hat on.

55. An example:

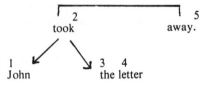

Make the same scheme with the sentences which have an active subject and a passive object (actor → action → goal).

56. Find the transitive and the intransitive verbs.

57. Find the verbs with a preposition of their own.

> E.g.: Do you know what has happened to John? He went to have a look at the new cars with Willy. They had to wait for 2 hours before it was their turn.

Importance of reflecting upon language
Don't say that this reflecting work is not important. For us hearing people it is important too, e.g. in these cases:

(1) when the content of a sentence is difficult;
(2) for very long sentences;
(3) for language of poems;
(4) for emotional a-normal language, using anacoluthons, etc.

241

Stutterheim (1965) gives this example (from Khayyám, translation of Fitzgerald):
'And we that now make merry in the room
They left and summer dresses in new bloom,
Ourselves must we beneath the couch of earth
Descend, ourselves to make a couch – for whom?'

Often 'dresses' is taken as an intransitive verb, which is wrong.

The teacher's notebook

A necessary complement to all this work is the teacher' *notebook*. The children too have theirs. The teacher writes in this notebook the language difficulties of his children. An example:–

A teacher once said to Peter: '*If I were you, I would give it him*'. Peter's answer: 'You can't give!' ...

The teacher noted down this difficulty of understanding in order to grasp the first opportunity to teach it to him and the others. This opportunity came about two weeks later. The teacher told the children of his problem in wanting to move to the country-side but not being able to find a house. (Note the language-forms and the subject-matter of this conversation! Conversation is not at all balderdash!) Peter was astonished, because he lived in the country-side and would have liked much more to live in the city. He said: 'I'd liked much more to live in the city'. The teacher said: 'Now you can say: 'If I were you I would not move'. Say it, Peter!' ...

I'll give here a few more examples of difficult idioms which could be found in the teacher's notebook:

a. It *must* be 12 o'clock, because so many children are coming from school.
b. I left my watch *somewhere. – Somebody* passed our window. (I visited a teacher who was using many of these undetermined words; instead of saying 'Mr Johnson passed our window' he said: Somebody ... The children will ask then: Who was that? These undetermined words are difficult. So *all* is much easier than *some*.)
c. Queen Elisabeth is the *child of* King George.
d. I had *too little* money in my pocket.
e. I was very afraid, but were you *not* afraid too?
f. He laughed on the wrong side of his mouth.
g. Oh my dear! (Mother said this exactly when the child was naughty!)
h. The softer you speak the better will be your voice.
i. I am looking for *the dog who* stole my sausage. Which dog? ...
j. I wish he *would* come.
k. You had better not write that letter!

And so on! Hundreds of notes!

A Reflective Language Lesson (26th February 1976, 4th form, by Mr. Ad van de Boom).

Below we have summarized a lesson to teach the children the difference between 'pincer-construction' and 'compound construction', the former being a difficult sentence-construction which is typical for the Dutch and German language, but which does not occur very often in English. The following lesson may show how the teacher succeeded in making the children discover these constructions.
After the children have well understood this kind of structures by means of a few exercises, they increasingly improve their use of same, in daily conversations, in compositions etc. The teacher also increasingly points to mistakes in these constructions and she can say for example: 'Patricia, you should not use a compound construction here, but a pincer-construction! Try it!' . . .

Subject of this lesson:

Pincer-construction and Compound Construction in Verbs
(first presentation)

The following two sentences (taken from a conversational lesson) form the starting-point:
1. Daddy has, as far as we know, slept until ten o'clock.
2. He can obviously work a lot better when he has slept well

Ad 1.

We speak the sentence.
Who knows what *the subject* is?
What should one ask oneself?
    'Who has slept until ten o'clock? Daddy!'
Now we'll look for the *predicate.*
For this, one should ask oneself:
'What is being said about the subject (Daddy)?'
Use a *demonstrative word*:
    He has, as far as we know, slept until ten o'clock.
(subject and predicate are encircled with the colours brown and green respectively).
What now is the verb in the predicate?
    has   slept
What is *the unchanged (= infinitive) form?*
    have   sleep

243

Now we are going to see *what belongs together*
    slept-until → No!
    until-ten-o'clock → Yes!
We divide the sentence into *accent-groups* in order to see what belongs together:
Daddy has/as far as we know/slept/until ten o'clock.
Who can remember the verbs?
has slept

I make a sentence: Daddy has slept.
Does that belong together? Yes. That is a good sentence.
The verbs are *next to* each other. *However, in the sentence the verbs are not next to each other!*
(the verbs are now written down in red)
Daddy has, as far as we know, slept until ten o'clock.
Which words are placed *between* the verbs?
    as far as we know
This is called '*pincer-construction*'.
We go into the function of a pair of pincers, showing this object.
We pretend to pinch the sentence:

Daddy has   slept

as far as we know

Ad 2.

He can obviously work a lot better when he has slept well. *How many clauses* are included in this sentence? Two.
What is the *subject* of the first clause?
    Who can obviously work a lot better? He (Daddy).
What is the *subject* in the second clause?
    Who has slept well? He (Daddy).
What is the *predicate* in the first clause?
    What is being said about the subject? Can obviously work a lot better.
What is the *predicate* in the second clause?
    What is being said about the subject? Has slept well.

We look for *the verbs:*
He can obviously work a lot better when he has slept well.

244

Is there a pincer-construction here?
 In the first clause → Yes!
 In the second clause → No!
In the second clause we have not a pincer-construction but a compound construction.
The verbs are placed *next to* each other.

Assessment

After the lesson the children received *ten sentences* from the conversational lessons (to be found in the diaries of the children) for homework, with the following exercises:

1. Space the lines when copying down the sentences.
2. Underline all the verbs in red.
3. Look for pincer-construction, using the symbol:
4. Look for compound construction, using the symbol:

Examples of these sentences:
'De moeder van Claudia is in Schiedam gaan wonen. Ze is verhuisd van Rotterdam naar Schiedam.' The *literal* translation into English would be: 'The mother of Claudia has in Schiedam gone to live. She has moved from Rotterdam to Schiedam.' A pincer-construction like this does not occur in English.

Data concerning the children:

Name:	Age:	Home-train-ing:	Kindergarten from the age of 4:	Fletcher-index (ISO) better ear:	Age at which hearing-loss was discovered:	Performance I.Q.:	Remarks:
Claudia	10;0	no	no	82 db. progressive	1;0	average	dysphasia
Margret	9;4	no	no	98 db.	2;0	good	—
Yvonne	10;10	no	no	118 db. progressive	1;4	average	dysphasia
Helen	11;3	no	yes	107 db.	0;10	average	—
Jeanette	10;7	yes	yes	102 db.	1;0	good	—
Monique	11;5	yes	yes	111 db.	0;6	average	integration problems
Patricia	10;3	yes	yes	118 db.	0;4	average	
Inge	9;8	yes	yes	120+ db.	1;0	good	dysphasia
Wilma	11;2	yes	yes	110 db.	0;9	good	—

Results:

Claudia	90% correct
Margret	85% correct
Yvonne	80% correct
Helen	55% correct
Jeannette	75% correct
Monique	60% correct
Patricia	100% correct
Inge	100% correct
Wilma	90% correct

A Growing Grammar: the Children's Notebooks (Sr. Joanni)

The children too should have their notebooks. Some teachers like to hang their classroom full with charts, to be filled with idioms, sentence-models, questions, and so on. Their classroom looks like an always open and growing grammar book where the children can find analogies of language, daily expressions, models etc. Sr. Innocence (1951) told me she preferred not to fill the classroom in this way. She used some blackboards which are filled up during the lessons; and after a week or so she cleans them in order to fill them again. But each child of the class has his own notebook wherein these points noted above are set down. She said: 'The children should have these language forms in their mouths, not on the walls'. This is a question of efficiency of course. There may be a danger that deaf children, when they have the 'grammar always open around them', look for the forms rather than for the contents, lose the setting of these forms in their situations. Another danger is that the short term memory will be 'underfed'. Of course an expert teacher will prevent these dangers.

Application of Found Analogies. – A Code System for Corrections

The more the children get on in the understanding of language forms, i.e. of the grammar, the more this knowledge should be used in *the corrections of their compositions.*
There are 4 kinds of mistakes in the utterances of deaf children:

(a) Omissions, e.g. '(It) fell from (the) table there'. 'It has fall(en)' . . .
(b) Additions, e.g. 'It fell from the table *off* there'. 'It *falling*' . . .
(c) Inversions, e.g. 'It fell the table from there'. 'An up-make' . . .
(d) Substitutions, e.g. 'It *put* from the table there'. 'Many child*s*' . . .

246

The teacher should first ask himself what the child is *meaning* properly, secondly what could be the origin of the mistake.

Myklebust (1965) designed *a code system* for grammar errors, which may be helpful, although his symbols serve diagnostic purposes.

In 1966 I advised a few codes concerning corrections of mistakes in composition-work. In my opinion there should be 3 steps:

– first step: mistakes are just corrected; the reason cannot yet be understood by the child;

– second step: more and more reasons for the corrections can be given. Then more and more simple codes can be introduced.

E.g.

$$At \overset{3}{\ } home \overset{1}{\ } mother \overset{2}{\ } is$$

The numbers are the teacher's corrections for the word-grouping. In later years he may code his corrections in this way:

$$At \overset{o}{\ } home \overset{o}{\ } mother \overset{o}{\ } is$$

The child only knows that the word order is wrong, and has to find the right order himself.

– third step: the teacher does not give codes; he just gives dashes which have to be interpreted by the child himself.

The codes advised by me are the following:

1. $\checkmark$ = omission of a word.

   $\checkmark\checkmark$ = omission of two words.

   $\checkmark\checkmark\checkmark$ = omission of three words. Etc.

2. X = this word should be omitted.

3. $o\,o\,o$ = the word order of these words is wrong.

4. $\diagup$ = wrong word, use another one.

5. $(\diagup\,)$ = wrong part of a word, which should be altered e.g. *mo(o)ning* instead of *morning*.

   $(\mathsf{X}\,)$ = this part should be omitted e.g. *com(e)ing* instead of *coming*.

   $(\cdot\vee\,)$ = omission of a part of a word e.g. *walk(V)* instead of *walks*.

6. ∇ = omission of a punctuation-mark.

247

$\mathcal{T}$ = use another punctuation-mark.

$\mathcal{X}$ = this punctuation-mark should be omitted.

It is of course necessary for all teachers of one school to agree on one code-system.

12. TO SUMMARIZE

Both *reading* and *composition* are based on *conversation*. When we read we converse with the writer or with the persons in the book. This is 'reading between the lines'! Also, composing is a conversation, now with the reader: in composing I am engaged in the reactions of my reader, how, 'he will read between my lines'.

So we come to this scheme of our 'Maternal Reflective Method of language teaching of the deaf':

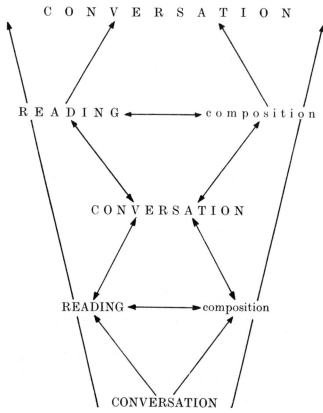

I have expressly put 'composition' in small letters, and conversation and reading in big letters to emphasize the difference in importance.

I fully agree, from my experience, with these words of Groht (1958): 'There are actually many deaf children who have a better command of English than some hearing children'.

Appendices
Appendix I
Verbatim Reports of Lessons in Classes of Children with Difficulties

Verbatim reports will be given of lessons by the teacher and the writer, in two different classes of deaf children, i.e. of different ages, of different abilities, of normal and multi-handicapped deaf children. Particulars of the children will be given at each class.

These verbatim reports had to be translated from Dutch into English. The translation is as faithful as possible.

AFTER ONE YEAR PRESCHOOL

A lesson of one hour 9–10 o'clock 27.9.1967. In the first weeks of 2nd year preschool.

Teacher: Sr. Margret Pouwels

Data of the Children:

Name with particulars:	Age	Had home-train-ing	Had Preschool	Hearing loss of best ear (Fletcher ISO):	Age of Detection of deafness:	Perfor-mance I.Q.
Mt.	5;1	+	1 yr.	90 db.	before 2 yrs.	average
Jt.	5;4	+	has been in a presch. for part. deaf but could not follow	80 db.	,,	good
Pl. dysphasic?	5;5	+	1 yr.	85 db.	3 months	good
Hs. dyslectic? autistiform behaviour	5;1 not in	–	1 yr.	120 db.	±2;0	average
Chl.	5;11	+	2 years un-satisfactory	90 db.	1;2	average

251

Name with particulars:	Age	Had home-train-ing	Had Preschool	Hearing loss of best ear (Fletcher ISO):	Age of Detection of deafness:	Perfor-mance I.Q.
Me. Insuff. react. to sound. Emotional disturb.	4;10	+	1 yr.	85 db.	± 1;0	average
Tr.	6;2	+	2 years un-satisfactory	110 db.	before 2 yrs.	average
(**Nl.** mostly ill, not in the class)	6;5	+	2 years un-satisfactory	105 db.	,,	average

These children had had individual speech lessons during their preschool year(s) about 4 times a week (periods of about 15 minutes). This should be at least 10 times, which could not be given due to lack of personnel. The teacher has had these children during the year 1966–1967.

It is a class with difficulties, referred to in our Institute a B-class, differing from the parallel A-class, i.e. children of the same age but of better intelligence and with fewer difficulties. I thought it better to show the work in a difficult class in order to illustrate more strikingly the manner of teaching in this maternal method.

Layout of the Class

The big classroom has two departments, one for free playing, for teaching lipreading and listening in playing, and for experience, – and the other one – a quieter one – more for strict teaching. The following lesson has been given in this latter department.

In this department are 3 large blackboards, 6 small blackboards, a calendar, a 'lightweek' (van Uden 1960), several charts for idioms etc.

The following texts are already on the blackboards and the charts, as deposits from foregoing lessons:

Blackboard 1:
– Yesterday we were at the fair.
– We got doughnuts.

a bag of doughnuts.
Doughnuts are delicious.

Small blackboards:

1. Look!
Hs. is not looking.
(You are not looking)

2. Don't walk!
You are walking.
You have walked.

3. Take your handkerchief!
Tr. is allowed to take sweets.

4. Me. has fallen.
(I have fallen)
Jt. is falling.
(I am falling).
Don't let it fall!

5. You are playing.
Don't play!
We will play.

6.   —

Chart for pronouns:

We
You
I
altogether
mine
of ... (Tr.)

Charts with question words:

1. *Where?*
There
at Miss Betty's
upstairs
at mother's

2. *What?*
—

3. *Who?*
Rockey
Nelly
Miss Gerry

4. *How much?* (With pictures too.)
one 1
two 2
three 3
four 4
five 5
six 6

5. *When?*
—

The children sit on small chairs in a circle around the teacher. Each child has two hearing-aids, one for each ear, connected with a loop by a listening coil; simultaneously the microphones of these hearing aids are switched on in order to make the children hear their own voices. The teacher has a microphone at her neck, connected with the amplifier and the loop. The hearing aids have been individually adjusted.

The lesson did not go off smoothly this particular morning. Although most lessons go off much better, I preferred to give this example of a difficult lesson in a difficult class, in order to prevent the impression that everything is so easy, and also to show how a good teacher is able to make the most of it.

(S) means: an utterance seized from the children and put in its right form.

The Lesson

Jt. points to Mt. and says: 'fallen'! . . .
Teacher (T): (S) So, have you fallen, Mt.?
Mt. points to upstairs and says: . . . 'sleep . . .'
T. (S) 'upstairs in the bedroom?' To all children: 'Upstairs in the bedroom Mt. has fallen'. To Mt.: 'Not serious is it?'
Mt. shakes her head!
T. (S) 'No!'
Mt. 'No!'

T. wants to put the seats somewhat nearer to the blackboard. She says: 'Get up a moment!' No reactions from the children: nothing from the situation suggests such a command. T. keeps on: 'All of you! Get up! Don't remain seated!' Jt. is the first who understands this. He gets up. All children get up now. 'That's fine! You all have get up! . . . I'll put your seats a little bit forward'. She does so. 'Now you may sit down again. It is finished.' All the children sit down, except Hs. **T.** 'Hs. is a little bit silly!' Hs. sits down too. – Jt. has grasped a changeable card-calendar. He comes to T. with a gesture meaning what should be done now?
T. (S) 'What day is it today? Is it Tuesday today?'
Me. points to the card Tuesday and says: 'Past' . . .
T. to all children (S): 'That has passed'. Me. says: 'That has passed'.
Mt. 'Wednesday!'
T. to all children (S): 'Yes it is Wednesday today. Mt. is clever indeed! And what is Tuesday then?'
Mt. 'Yesterday!'
T. (S) 'Yes that was yesterday! Well Mt. you are clever!' to all children: 'Where can you find it *yesterday* (written)?' There is a small card near the window with the written word: *yesterday.*
T. to Hs. 'Just take that card of yesterday, Hs.! . . . Yesterday! Just take that card!' Hs. takes the card and gives it to the T.
T. 'Thank you, Hs. . . . Can you all see it? Tuesday was yesterday. Mt. has already been clever twice. Fine Mt.!'
Me. is meanwhile quarrelling with Pl., because he is half on her seat (Pl.'s character is not an easy one). She says: 'Mine! . . .' and points to herself.
T. (S) 'That is mine . . . Say it Me.: That's mine!'
Me. 'That's mine' . . .
T. to Pl. 'Stop that! Remain seated quietly again, will you?' Again attention to the calendar.
T. 'That is not yet right!' She points to 26 . . . to Mt. 'What day is it today, did you say?'
Mt. 'Wednesday!' The Wednesday card was already there.
T. 'That is alright!'
Mt. nods Yes . . .
T. (S) 'Say Yes! . . . Say it! Yes!'
Mt. 'Yes!'

254

T. to Me. who is in a temper this morning: 'Me. is a little bit silly today!' To all the children: 'We have a big calendar too! A biiig calendar! This is a small calendar! Jt., you may take the big calendar . . . Jt. is big!' . . . (The calendar is hanging rather high. Jt. is the tallest child of the class.) . . . Hs. stay seated ! Jt. may take the biiig calendar . . . Hs. you are a little bit small today!' Jt. takes the big calendar. On that big calendar *today* has been written against Tuesday, which has to be altered.

T. 'Who has written that?'

Jt. points to himself.

T. (S) 'Say: I'.

Jt. 'I'.

T. (S) 'Right! You have written that. Now Tr. may change it. Tr., you may write!' The big calendar is put on the floor. Tr. writes against Wednesday: *today*.

T. 'What should be taken away?' Tr. crosses the *today* of Tuesday out.

T. 'Very well! Tuesday has passed.'

Me. (who cannot yet write by heart) says: 'Tr. clever!'

T. (S) 'Yes, Tr. is clever'.

Hs. 'Tr. . . . clever!' with a gesture of very clever.

T. (S) 'Yes, Tr. is very very clever! How clever you are, Tr.!'

T. 'Now listen, all of you! I'll think . . . You all should think' . . . Mostly the children themselves come with so many conversational subjects, that the lessons go on smoothly. Sometimes, however, this is not the case. Then T. says: 'We all should think'. The children understand that, and mostly they find very interesting subjects to speak about. But this particular morning the children did not give anything! The T. is always prepared for such perplexities; she has of course enough topics in her mind. So since the children had been at a fair two days ago, (see the text on the black-board of yesterday's conversation), she got acid-drops in the form of sticks, packed in paper wrappings, called 'acid-sticks'. She has not given them immediately to the children, but reserved them for special situations as subjects for lessons. Now they are very useful. The name 'acid-sticks' was unknown to the children. A teacher of course should never waste powder and shot!

T. 'I know something . . . (emphatically:) I have some sweets . . . in the drawer' . . . Immediately the children find a parcel in the drawer. They could not see what was in the parcel.

T. 'Acid-sticks! Ooooh!'

Hs. 'Lollies?'

T. (S) 'You think lollies? No, these are not lollies. What are they? Acid-sticks! Say it! Can't you say it?' . . . Indeed the children could not yet pronounce this word. They tried to babble something.

Hs. (impatiently) 'Openpa . . .!' (= open make = undo it).

T. (S) 'Open the parcel? Should I open the parcel? Will there be many? Many acid-sticks??' . . . T. expected the children to respond to *many*. But they did not. So T. decided to open the parcel. 'Ooooh! These are not lollies, Hs.! These are acid-sticks. These acid-sticks are from the fair! Fair! Who can point to this word *fair?*' (On the blackboard; also fair was a new word and T. wanted to use it again.) Jt. points to *doughnuts*.

T. (S) 'Doughnuts? I said fair! O how stupid! Jt. you are confused. That is wrong.'

Me. 'Wrong!'

T. 'Hs. you are not looking! . . . Who can point to *fair? . . . Fair*, where is it written?'

Me. 'There!'

T. 'Yes, you are clever. What is the fair? Altogether: cakewalk, giant's stride, roundabout, swings . . . All that is the fair!' (The children babble with the T. as best they can.) . . . 'I got these acid-sticks there.'

Mt. 'Cars . . .' with a gesture of bumping.

T. 'Yes, bumper-cars too at the fair'.

Hs. does not understand what Mt. meant by cars. He thinks of the motor-car of Me's mother. On the fair-morning this mother took all the children in her car to the fair. T. and the nurse went there on foot.

Hs. 'Mama' . . . and he points to Me.

255

T. (S) 'Yes, Me's mama was at the fair too!'

Me. 'Altogether car! Mama altogether . . .'

T. (S) 'Yes, you all have been in mama's car . . . Hs., attention please! . . . You all rode in mama's white car.'

Jt. 'Walk you!'

T. (S) 'We walked . . . I was not allowed to go in the car. The car was quite full! Not empty, but full! Quite full! But we walked very quickly! You rode in the car . . . You! Find that word, Me.! Where is it written?'

Me. points to the right word on the chart . . .

T. 'Now I'll write something!' She writes on purpose: *lollies* . . . Immediate reactions of most children: 'Wrong! Wrong! . . .'

T. (S) 'Oh Yes, that is wrong! . . . Acid-sticks! Say it all of you: Acid-sticks!' All the children say something which approximately could be interpreted as 'acid-sticks' . . .

T. 'Hallo! I can't hear it! . . . Say acid-sticks!' . . . While the children babble acid-sticks, she writes it clearly on the blackboard.

Jt. points to each child as if 'co-ordinating' the acid-sticks to the children.

T. (S) 'All the children one each!'

Mt. 'Two?'

T. (S) 'All children two each? No, that is wrong!' She shows the 7 acid-sticks: 'How many are there?'

Pl. (very retarded in speech, see above) shows his 5 fingers.

T. (S) 'Five acid-sticks? No . . . Say it! Five! put away you hand!' Pl. does not say it.

Jt. 'Six!' (Six means for Jt. only: more than five; he does not yet digest higher numbers!)

T. (S) 'Six? Almost! There are seven. Seven acid-sticks: one for Pl., one for Mt., one for Me., one for Tr., one for Chl., one for Hs., one for Jt.'

Chl. points to T. 'One'!

T. (S) 'One for me? No. I have none . . . One acid-stick for every child . . . And for Nl.?'

Jt. 'Ill'.

T. (S) 'Nl. is ill. Nl. has no acid-stick. Nl. is not here'.

Hs. is now fetched by an assistant, who trains him especially in written symbols, because he has some difficulty in this respect. He takes his acid-stick with him! The other children move up to each other on the seats.

T. 'Attention! We are all big, aren't we? (*big* means here: smart, energetic etc.) . . . Where are the small ones? We are not small ones, are we? Where are the small ones? . . .'

Some children: 'There!' pointing to another class i.e. for younger children.

T. 'Yes, at Miss M's class . . . Attention now!'

T. 'How many acid-sticks do we have now?' . . . (Because Hs. has taken his one, there are now 6; this was a point to clear up if possible.) . . . She takes the number-cards 1 to 5. She shuffles them and draws one card, blind: three. She matches this 3 to the 6 acid-sticks and asks: 'Is this right?'

Mt. 'Wrong!'

T. (S) 'Yes, that's wrong! Again a card!' She draws 5, and places this against the acid-sticks . . . 'Is that right?'

Mt. 'Wrong!'

T. (S) 'That's wrong too!'

Me. does not understand T. She thinks T. is looking for number 1 (every child one!). She takes the cards out of T.'s hands and puts them on the floor, in the correct order: 1, 2, 3, 4 and 5.

T. 'It is all right, but I must hear you!'

Me. 'One, two, three, four, . . .

T. 'I don't hear you!'

Me. . . . 'four, five . . .'

T. 'That's right. That's not wrong . . . Give me the cards again!' Me. gives the cards to T.

T. 'Jt., you may draw a card! Come here . . .!' . . . Jt. is coming. 'Don't walk so crazily, Jt.!' (Pl. has

256

some strange behaviour which too often is imitated by the other children. Jt. now is imitating the strange manner of walking of Pl. which could become a bad habit. Therefore the T. could not disregard it.) Jt. draws 3.

T. 'Now show me 3 acid-sticks!' Jt. does it and says: 'Three'.

T. (S) 'Yes, three, that's right. Now Pl.' . . . At this moment the teacher of speech enters in order to fetch Jt. for an individual speech lesson. – Pl. draws: 4.

T. 'Show me as many acid-sticks!' Pl. immediately in one hand silently takes 4 sticks altogether! 'You are clever, Pl., very very clever!' (Pl.'s speech is still very poor, but he is intelligent.)

T. 'Now Tr., come here, will you?' Tr. draws: 2 . . . 'Say it!' . . .

Tr. 'Two!' All the children do the same.

T. 'Pl., your shoes are undone! Both of them!' She ties them (to save time!) . . . 'Pl. is playing! Go and show it to me on the blackboard!' Pl. gets up in order to point to the words (see above). But Me. is quicker, and before him, points to the words with a stick. Then she undoes her shoes too!

T. 'Me. loosens her laces on purpose! That is a little bit silly! Me. does it on purpose!' Me. becomes very shy now and puts her thumb in her mouth . . .

T. 'Me. is sucking her thumb, that is silly too! We are big, Me., all of us!' . . . Pl. now puts all his fingers in his mouth in order to badger Me.!

T. 'All your fingers in the mouth? Your fingers are not sweets! Don't put them in your mouth!' . . . T. tries to divert the attention by singing a baby song which the children can speak fairly well and which they like very much:

– Two hands on the table

– Two hands on the side . . . and so on.

– Show me your mouth . . .

– Show me your nose . . .

– Show me your cheeks . . .

So she catches their attention again . . . at least she thinks so! In a moment Me. is sitting on her lap, thumb in mouth! . . .

T. 'Well, I have a small baby now! . . . Is that thumb of yours an acid-stick? Is it a sweet? Me. has no acid-stick, she has her thumb!' . . . She takes Me. from her lap . . . 'I'll tease you! You have the thumb and I the acid-stick! You have no acid-stick! You have the thumb! . . . Is there still an acid-stick for Me.?' . . .

Me. nods Yes.

T. (S) 'Yes! . . . Say it! Yes!'

Me. 'Yes' . . .

T. 'All right now. Stop thumb sucking!' . . . At this moment Hs. is called for his individual speech lesson . . .

T. 'Jt. is finished. Jt. is coming back.' . . . She then takes one acid-stick, but . . . it is broken!

Chl. points to T.

T. (S) 'Did I break it? No! – – Oooh this one is broken too! . . . What a pity! . . . There are three broken acid-sticks! . . . What a pity! And this one? Broken too! . . .'

Me. points to one and says 'no broken' . . .

T. (S) 'No, this one is not broken . . . Yet! . . . Now four are broken! . . . What a pity! . . . Again another! . . . Five are broken! . . . This one is unbroken . . . For whom is this one?'

All children point to themselves! Chl. points to T.

T. 'For me? . . . Is Hs's acid-stick broken too?' . . . She now writes on the blackboard . . .

Mt. 'Five! Five! Five! Five! Five! . . .'

T. 'You should say that only once! Not so often Five five five' (in order to prevent a wrong concept of five). She writes:

Five acid-sticks are broken. What a pity!

Me. says: 'Wrong! . . . Twice!' And she points to the sentence of yesterday on the blackboard: *Doughnuts are delicious! . . . are, twice.*

T. 'That is allowed! It is not wrong! I may say: Acid-sticks *are* delicious too! . . . How many are not broken? Listen! How many are not broken?' T. takes the opportunity to teach the difference between the plural form *are* and the singular form *is*. The difference *is* – *was* had already been taught on an other occasion, some weeks ago . . . 'One is not broken! Where is it?'

Me. looks for it . . . 'There!' she says.

T. 'O Yes, there it is. Be careful! I'll write it' . . .

One is not broken.

At this moment Hs. comes back from his individual speech lesson. T. to Pl.: 'Pl., it is your turn now' . . .

T. vivaciously to Hs. 'Hs., Look here! . . . Five acid-sticks are broken . . .' She writes in the place of *is* some points:

Five are broken.

One . . . not broken.

'Only one is not broken' . . .

T. was hoping that a child would fill in *are:* One are not broken. Then she could correct the *are* with *is*, because it is only one . . . But then the bell rings and the red lamp flashes (for the children): it is the end of this lessson. T. had to postpone this important point until another lesson, or until the children read it in the diary. There will come enough opportunities to reflect on this change in the verb.

The diary

The setting down of this lesson in the diary (afternoon) was this:

Acid-sticks

> There was a fair in the village.
> We got acid-sticks.
> Hs. said 'These are lollies!'
> The T. said: 'No Hs., these are not lollies!
> These are acid-sticks!'
> Five acid-sticks are broken. What a pity!
> One is not broken.
> Doughnuts are delicious.
> Acid-sticks are delicious too.

One of the exercises will be that the text is phototyped as many times as necessary. The T. will make the children cut out the sentences themselves, so that they see, all the better, that such a sentence is one whole. These loose sentences are disarranged, and the children have to find the correct order themselves. In doing this, they cannot help reading the sentences (van Uden 1955–1957).

Remarks

It may be seen from this verbatim report:

1. how the teacher continuously converses with the children by making herself understood from the situation, and by 'seizing' their attempts to speak: by playing a double part as a mother too does with her hearing baby;

258

2. how badly she is still handicapped by a lack of sufficiently developed speech: she cannot yet make the children say longer sentences, and too many words must be left unspoken; the possibilities would be much nicer if the children instead of 4 speech lessons could have 10 speech lessons weekly; lack of personnel still handicaps the development of the deaf child;

3. how she continuously uses contrasts, i.e. the polarity of meaning (e.g. big and small in different meanings);

4. how she always uses normal language with all its continuous shifting of forms;

5. how deaf children show some consciousness of forms (e.g. is — was, are — is) and how the teacher uses this in a reflective way.

Survey of the diaries of this class

The content of the diaries of these children after 1 year preschool (1966–1967) is the following:

Santa Claus.	Pipo the clown of television.
Two rabbits.	Duck and ducklings.
Birthday.	Naughty dog.
Visit to a farm.	On a journey.
The suitcase.	The Zoo.
Recreation-ground.	The swimming pool.
Grape-Festival.	Butterflies.
Bottles.	Father's pipes.
Blowing bubbles.	Illness.
Presents.	Lost and found.
Balloons.	Sheeps and lambs.
Flowers.	The airplane and the airport.
Thea.	The fair.
	Etc.

The size of the vocabulary in these diaries is 531 words.

Some of these subjects and reading lessons are common to all 8 children, some in particular, with the effect that these books are real loved properties of the children. They are illustrated with many pictures, cut out from magazines, and also with photos of the events, different ones in each book.

Analysis of Communicative Means

Preschool lesson.

Histogram of Communicative means: Teacher and Children together.

Columns ☐   1st purely oral means;
                          2nd speech with gestures and demonstrations;
                          3rd written means.

Columns ▨   non-verbal: 4th drawings;
                                5th gestures, facial expressions and demonstrations
                                without speech;

Column ▦   6th misunderstandings.

80.96%	11.30%	3.87%	0.00%	3.77%	7.28%
1 purely oral	2 speech + gestures	3 written means	4 drawings	5 gestures + demonstrations without speech	6 misunder- standings

GRADE 4 OF THE SCHOOL FOR NORMAL DEAF CHILDREN,
A + B-ABILITIES

Teacher: Mrs. van den Broek

Data of the children

Name with particulars:	Age	Had home-train-ing:	Had pre-sch.:	Hearing loss of best ear (Flectcher, ISO)	Age detec-tion of deaf-ness:	Total Years at school:	Years at this school:	Perf. I.Q.
Alice	9;6	+	2 ys.	100 dB.	1;0	5 ys.	5 ys.	good
Bernie sens. dys-phasia	9;4	−	2 ys.	80 dB.	±2;0	5 ys.	4 ys.	average
Elly	10;0	+	2 ys.	105 dB.	1;0	6 ys.	6 ys.	good
Leentje slight mot. dysph. dyslex.?	10;8	+	2 ys.	90 dB.	0;4	6½ ys.	6½ ys.	good
Trudi slight mot. dysph.	10;9	+	2 ys.	110 dB.	1;6	6 ys.	6 ys.	average
Cora one blind eye	9;4	+	2 ys.	105 dB.	0;6	5 ys.	5 ys.	good
Jeanne slight mot. dysph.	10;3	+	2 ys.	at 500 120 + dB 115 dB.	0;8	6 ys.	6 ys.	good
Lea	8;11	−	2 ys.	110 dB.	1;0	5 ys.	5 ys.	good
Dorien	10;10	−	2 ys.	105 dB.	0;8	6 ys.	6 ys.	average

These children are in the transitive phase from the reading of the diaries, letters, small stories etc., to the reading of books of normal hearing children. The teacher has almost finished the first volume of the Dutch so-called 'Diedeltje-series' for hearing children of 7–8 years of age. Each volume of about 50 pages contains one story. Meanwhile the diaries will still be continued for some years and transformed into learning albums. The children started their notebooks – the teacher has already had one for several years – for expressions and grammar. During the lessons new words, expressions and grammatical items are noted on so-called 'category blackboards' on the wall. From these blackboards the children copy the notes in their notebooks. When the notes have been taken, the blackboards are cleaned in order to be filled again during coming lessons. The 'deposits' of the following lesson, for diary and notebooks, will be given below.

The first part of the lesson is given by the teacher herself, the last part by the writer (U.).

Arrangement of the class-room

1. The children sit around a big table, in which the group-hearing-aid is mounted. The first ones of these group-hearing aids were built in 1951, at our request as follows:

a. They should have such an amplification that as many low tones as possible and every hearing remnant can be used; they have an amplification of 60 – 70 dB.; maximum output at 70 c.p.s. is 105 dB (SPL) and at 1,000 and 2,000 c.p.s. 135 dB (SPL); automatic volume control (data from our audiological department);

b. Each child has – what I have called – a 'mibavo'. It is a box which is so small that it easily can be taken in one hand by a child. In it are assembled a *mi*crophone and a *ba*lanced-*vo*lume-control. 'Balanced volume control' means that the amplification of right and left ear can be differentiated when needed for a different degree of hearing-loss. The differentiation is fixed inside the box by the audiologist. By turning only one knob the child is able to raise or lower the amplification at both ears in this balanced way. The children can be so well trained in sound-perception and lipreading and the combination of these two that the teacher can allow them to use the knob themselves in order to find their most comfortable level of amplification. When a child speaks, it almost automatically takes its mibavo closer to its mouth and switches its microphone on. The other children hear and feel (the low tones are so strong that they can be felt too, and the children have been trained in vibration feeling) what the first child is saying. This is a big help for the conversation among each other (van Uden 1952). The teacher of course has a microphone too, which is on all the time. The earphones for both ears of the mibavo are miniature receivers of different tone characteristics adjusted by the audiologist. – Each child has a wearable hearing aid of his own too, which it used both in free time and at home. But in the classroom, the group hearing aid has been found to be the most efficient equipment for deaf children (cf. Stiller 1976).

c. There is a tape-recorder, used as an 'echo-apparatus' or 'echorder' by means of which the children can hear or feel 'back' what they have said. (There are small mirrors too, which are at hand to make the child see its own speech.)

2. In the corner of the classroom stands a speech amplifier with a mirror, so designed (van Uden 1946), that it has two microphones: one for the teacher and one for the child, in order to make the child both hear and feel as well as see itself while speaking. Our first speech amplifiers were built by Prof. J. Groen (Utrecht died 1975) 1946 with high fidelity headphones, low-pass and high-pass filters and a compression volume control. They have now a maximum output of 140 dB. (SPL). By means of this apparatus the teacher gives his children individual speech lessons 4 or 5 times each week, some children more some children less.

3. The class has a big blackboard, and about 6 charts have been pinned up on the wall with idioms, paradigmatic phrases etc.

Teacher's Lesson (a 'conversational lesson')

NB. It is the last day before the autumn holidays. Some children will be leaving the Institute (a residential school) to-night; they will be fetched by their parents or by other members of the family. The other children will leave to-morrow and will be taken home by the teachers and nurses of the Institute.

The children see that the whole lesson is recorded; this has some influence on their behaviour, making them somewhat too keen to say 'correct' sentences, but in general it does not hurt the lesson. (S) means: an utterance seized from the children and put in its right form.

T. 'We will speak together . . . Listen! I am very very sad! You too, Leentje?'
Children: 'I am not!' Some children: 'Glad!' Some: 'I am glad'.
T. 'Why?'

Lea: 'We are going home today'.

T. (S) 'All right. You can use: because ...'.

Lea: 'Because we go ...'

T. 'Pincer! Use the pincer!' (Dutch construction of the sentences.)

Lea: 'Because we today home go' (correct Dutch pincer-construction, literally translated).

T. 'All right! Elly, you too!'

Elly: 'Yes, today!' Elly repeats the sentence.

Dorien: 'Mogen (= are allowed)'.

T. 'Yes, that is right too ...'

Dorien: 'We go today home 'mogen'' ...

T. (astonished) 'How many verbs do you use? ... You are using two verbs!'

Dorien: 'Elly the same!'

T. 'No, Elly said, ... Now, Elly, say it again!'

Elly: 'Because we today home go' (Correct Dutch construction).

T. 'Dorien says: 'mogen'! Who can use that?'

Cora: 'We 'mogen' today home' (= Wij mogen vandaag naar huis, correct Dutch construction).

T. 'That is nice, you are going home today, but ... I don't believe it! ... Are you going home *today*?'

Cora: 'To-morrow!'

T. 'Cora says: To-morrow! Who is going home *today*? Jeanne, say it!'

Jeanne: 'Dorien and Elly and Leentje and Trudi and I ...'

T. 'Yes' ...

Jeanne: ... 'are going home today'.

T. 'Yes, that is right ... Cora says: 'I am not going home today' ...

Cora: 'Some ...'

T. 'Ssss, say your ss better!'

Cora: 'Some girls, Bernie and Lea and Cora, ... I ..., is ... are allowed to go home to-morrow'. (She corrects herself while speaking.)

T. (S) 'Yes ... are allowed to go home *only* to-morrow'.

Alice: 'Not! Cora, not! Adverb forgot!'

T. 'I don't understand you!'

Alice: 'Not! Adverb!'

T. 'Yes, 'not' is an adverb, but what do you mean?'

Alice: 'Cora, Not! Adverb forgot!'

T. (S) 'You want to say: Cora has forgotten the adverb 'not'?'

Alice: 'Yes, forgot!'

T. (S) 'Say forgott*en*!'

Alice: '*Not*' forgotten'. Cora cannot follow it.

T. to Cora: 'Alice says you have forgotten the adverb not' ...

Cora: 'Why?'

Alice: 'Because some girls, Bernie and Lea and Cora are *not* allowed to go home'.

T. 'I think you are making a mistake! I think Cora is right! What did Cora say? ... Have you forgotten it? ...
Elly, say it!'

Elly: 'Some girl ...'

T. (interrupting) 'Some girls, plural form!' ...

Elly: 'Some girlss, Bernie, Lea and Cora, are allowed to go home to-morrow'.

T. 'That is correct' ... to Alice: 'Cora said *to-morrow*, not *today*! It was correct!'

Alice agrees.

T. 'Thus Cora is *not* going home *today*'.

Alice: 'Why not?'

T. 'Now ask that of Cora herself!'

263

Alice: 'Why is Cora not go . . .'

T. (interrupting) 'Say it to Cora! What did you forget?' . . . to all the children: 'What did she forget?'

Elly: 'Pointer-word!'

T. (S) 'That is right: *a* pointer-word!'

Elly: 'A pointer-word'.

Alice: 'Which pointer-word?'

T. 'Now, to whom are you talking ? to whom?'

Alice: 'To you!' pointing to the teacher.

T. 'Yes, *now* you are talking to *me*, but I asked you to speak to . . .? To whom? . . . To whom *did* you speak?'

Alice: 'To Cora!'

T. 'That is correct! Now say it again!'

Alice to Cora: 'Why . . .?'

T. 'Now a verb!'

Alice: 'Why are you go . . . going today not home?' (Dutch pincer-construction correctly used).

Cora: 'Because the Director won't allow us!'

T. 'La la la! Why are you not going home today? Don't you know? I think I know it! . . . Do you know it, Bernie?'

Bernie: 'No holidays!' All the children laugh.

T. 'No holidays?' . . . to the other children: 'You all laugh, but I think Bernie knows what she means! We are not going on holiday just yet! But this evening! The children are going on holiday this *evening* . . . Will *all* the children at the Institute go on holiday??'

Bernie: 'Some girls . . .' Lea want to say something, she interrupts Bernie.

T. 'Say it, Lea!'

Lea: 'Not allowed by Sister Cornelia' (Sr. Cornelia is the administratrix. Lea uses a Dutch construction correctly).

T. 'Noooo! I don't believe that! I don't believe that! . . . But, yes, you are a little bit right! For Cora is not allowed . . .?'

Lea: 'This evening!'

T. 'Cora is not allowed to go . . .?'

Many children: 'This evening!' . . .

T. 'Cora is not allowed to go alll . . .?

All the children: 'Alone!'

T. '*That* is right! Cora is not allowed to go alone home' (Dutch pincer-construction). 'With whom does Cora go home otherwise?'

Elly: 'With the sister' . . .

T. 'Your ss is not right! sss!'

Elly: 'With the ssissster . . .'

T. 'But that is not true! . . .' to Cora: 'Some times you go home with . . .? With whom?'

Cora: 'With the titter!' . . .

T. 'Ssissster!'

Cora: 'Ssissster . . .' She rectifies herself: 'With Nolly'. (Nolly is her elder brother, 16 years of age, who is old enough to make the journey independently to the Hague, where they live, taking his sister Cora with him).

T. 'Not to-morrow?'

Cora: 'Noo! Because my Nolly must learn! . . .'

T. 'Yes' . . .

Cora: 'Therefore goes later home' (Dutch pincer-construction, correctly used.)

T. 'Exactly! You know what you mean! You are not going home to-day, with Nolly . . . Why not? Say it again!'

Cora: 'Because my Nolly must . . .'

264

T. (interrupting) '... my ...'

Cora: 'My brother ... Because my brother must go to school to learn' (The holidays of the Technical School of the Institute start a day later).

T. 'So Nolly is ...' Bernie wants to say something ...

T. to Bernie: 'What do you want to say?'

Bernie: 'Nolly isn't going on holiday'.

T. (S) 'Nolly isn't going on holiday yet.' All the children are astonished!

Lea: 'Not yet on holiday?'

Cora: '*Not yet* on holiday!!'

Many children want to say something now.

T. 'Wait a moment ... Alice is allowed to talk. To whom?'

Alice: 'To Cora!'

T. 'All right!'

Alice: 'Why must Nolly ... to *learn?*'

T. (S) 'Why must Nolly still learn? ... Say it!'

Alice: 'Why must Nolly the learn?'

T. '*sstill* learn!'

Alice: 'Still learn ... Why must Nolly still learn?'

Cora: 'Because my much too big!'

T. (laughing) (S) 'Because Nolly is big'.

Cora: 'Because Nolly is big.'

T. 'I like to be on holiday ... I am glad with you. I hope ...?'

Some children: 'Nice weather!'

T. to Elly: 'Say it! ...'

Elly: 'I hope during the holidays ...?'

T. '... that ...'

Elly: 'I hope that during the holidays nice weather have' (Dutch pincer-construction, but she forgot *we*).

T. 'Who?'

Lea: 'We!'

T. 'Yes, we! ... Say it again, Elly!'

Elly: 'We hope ...'

T. 'No no, the same sentence! ... I hope ...'

Elly: 'I hope that we during the holidays nice weather have' (Dutch pincer-construction, correctly used).

T. 'I hope so too! I hope that we during the holidays nice weather have' ... to Alice: 'Do you hope so too?'

Alice: 'Yes!'

T. 'Why?'

Alice: 'Because I like ... because I like to mama ... because father and mother at home see!' (She gives an answer to the question, why she likes to go on holiday. She did not understand the question, why she likes to have nice weather.)

T. 'Why do you like nice *weather?*'

Alice: 'Because ... because father and mother, ... father and mother, brother and I go swim!'

T. 'Say it better!'

Alice: 'Because father and mother, brother ...'

T. (interrupting) 'brothersss ...'

Alice: 'Brotherss and I ... go for a swim.'

T. 'That is right! ... But ... for a *swim?*'

Cora: 'I ask Alice!'

T. 'Would you like to ask Alice something? Ask it!'
Cora to Alice: 'Why? Why father and mother and brothers and you go for a swim?'
T. 'Cora, try to use a pointer-word!'
Cora: 'Why . . . you all . . .'
T. 'That is right! Why go you all . . .' (T. introduces the Dutch pincer-construction).
Cora: 'Why go you all for a swim?' (Dutch pincer construction, correctly used).
Alice (astonished): 'Because pleasant!'
T. (S) 'Because it is pleasant!'
Alice: 'Because it is pleasant!' . . . with a gesture of 'of course'.
T. to Alice: 'But you say: You like nice *weather*, because you will go for a swim . . . Why must it be nice weather?'
Alice: 'Because father and mother, brotherss and I go to Helmond, don't like bad weather!' (Helmond is a Dutch town.)
T. 'Use a pointer-word!'
Alice: 'Because we go to Helmond'.
T. 'Where will you go for a swim?'
Alice: 'In the Helmond' with a gesture of 'of course'.
Dorien: 'That is wrong! Not *the*! Not with article!'
T. 'That is very very good, Dorien!' . . . to Alice: 'Don't use the article, so . . .'
Alice: 'In Helmond' . . .
T. 'Now! Alice will go for a swim in Helmond! Alice likes nice weather, otherwise she will get wet in the swimming pool!!?'
Dorien to Alice: 'With what go father and mother, brothers and you . . . to . . .'
T. 'No, I don't mean that! . . . No, Alice is in the swimming pool, and it is raining and she becomes quite wet!'
Elly: 'Which in swimming pool? In indoor bath or outdoor bath?'
T. (S) 'That is nice! Start with: In which . . .'
Elly: 'In which swimming bath . . . verb?'
T. '. . . do you go . . .'
Elly: '. . . do you go . . ., in the indoor bath or outdoor bath, go swimming?'
T. 'You use the verb *go* twice, say it again!'
Elly: 'Do you go in the indoor or outdoor bath for a swim?' (Dutch construction, correctly used).
Alice: 'In the indoor bath' with an 'of course' gesture.
T. 'But why do you want nice weather?'
Alice: . . . ??? . . .
T. 'If you go in the indoor bath, why do you like nice weather? . . . Nice weather for swimming? Still nice weather?'
Alice: 'Because when father and mother, brothers and I go for a swim, out! Then we go home, we go to play!'
T. 'To play, where?'
Alice: 'The garden!'
T. (S) 'In the garden'.
Alice: 'In the garden . . .'
T. 'Yes, that is right . . .' to all the children: 'Alice does not want nice weather to *swim* but . . .?'
Alice: 'to play!'
T. 'That is right . . .' to all the children: 'She wants nice weather not to swim but to play! . . . Say it, Elly!' (Meanwhile Alice's attention wanders.)
Elly: 'You . . . She says that she wants nice weather to . . .'
T. '*not* to . . .'
Elly: '*Not* to play . . . *Not* to swim, but to . . . to play'.
T. 'That is very good, now you, Alice . . . Ooh that is a pity! Alice was not paying attention! I don't

266

think that you know it well enough! ... Do you know what Elly said? ... No, you don't. Alice sat and ... and ...'

Dorien and Lea: 'Dreamed!'

Cora and Leentje: 'Stared ...'

T. 'Yes, Alice sat and stared! ... What a shame! But now ...'

Elly interrupts, wanting to say it again for Alice: 'Alice wants nice weather not to *swim* but to *play*!' The other children speak with Elly. Alice wants to rehabilitate herself: 'I want nice weather, why? because ...'

Elly, helping: 'not to ...'

Alice: 'Not to ...'

•**T.** to Leentje: 'Will you help Alice?'

Leentje: 'Not to play ...' (becomes selfconscious).

T. 'Cora, will you help Alice?

Cora: 'You want not ... You want to swim ... You, you want nice weather not to swim, but to play'.

T. 'Yes, because for swimming you have no nice weather ...?' (Dutch pincer-construction: *have* ... *necessary* = need.) The children say some words such as 'like' and so on; they don't follow it. T. again: 'When you are swimming in the indoor bath, you have no nice weather ...?'

Dorien: 'Not!'

Elly: 'Necessary!'

T. 'That is right, well done! Then you have no nice weather necessary' (Dutch construction).

Alice: 'No nice weather? Why not?'

T. 'Why not? Of course! Not ...? Not ...? Say it!'

Elly: 'Not to swim!'

T. 'Not to swim'.

Alice: 'But when swim finished, then to play'.

T. (S) 'Then we'll play ... Good, first we'll swim, then we'll play! But, listen: Have you nice weather necessary to swim?' (Dutch pincer-construction).

Alice: 'Nooo ... not swim, *buuut* father and mother, brothers and I swimming enough, then home, to play!'

T. 'Thus! You have nice weather necessary to ...?' (Dutch pincer-construction).

Alice: 'To play ...'

T. (relieved) 'That is right! To play ... Now something else!

T. 'I'll speak to Bernie ... You too are going home tomorrow ... Who will be at home tomorrow?'

Bernie: 'Mama. Hubert and Elsje to school'.

T. (S) 'Hubert and Elsje are in school'.

Bernie: 'Hubert and Elsje are in school'.

T. 'So who is at home tomorrow?'

Bernie: ...... ???

T. 'If you are going home, tomorrow, who will be at home?'

Bernie: 'Mama' ...

T. 'Will Daddy be at home too?'

Bernie: 'Is working'.

Elly: 'Which job?'

T. 'Daddy, ... Where? Where will he be working?'

Bernie: 'Working ... miner'.

T. 'But I want to know, Bernie, *where* Daddy works?'

Bernie: 'In Hoensbroek.' (This is a town in the mining district).

T. 'Who else lives in Hoensbroek?'

Lea: 'I!' Several children: 'Lea!'

Trudy to Bernie: 'Your father has ... in the work ...'

T. .... ?? ... to Alice: 'Alice, will you help?'

267

Alice: 'Which your father job?'

T. 'Almost correct ... Who can better it? ... Which ... ?' Several children: 'Which job?'

T. (S) 'Yes, which is your father's job? ... Now say it Trudy!'

Trudy: 'Which is your father's job?'

Bernie: 'Miner! ... O yes, in the mine!'

Cora wants to say something. T. to Cora: 'What do you want to say?'

Cora: 'To Bernie ...'

T. 'All right!'

Cora: 'What time ... What time has your father in the morning and ... evening ... in the evening home come ... Oooh! ... What time has your father in the morning and in the evening home comess?'

T. (S) 'I'll correct it ... What time does ...'

Cora: 'What time does your father leave in the morning and in the evening back home?'

T. 'That is nice ... You only forgot one verb ... What time does your father leave in the morning and ...?'

Cora: 'come back in the evening home' ... (Dutch construction).

T. 'Now say it again!'

Cora: 'What time does your father go away in the morning and come home in the evening?'

T. 'That is excellent.'

Bernie: 'At six o'clock' ...

T. 'Yes, but you should give two answers!'

Bernie: 'Saturday at six o'clock away and at 4 o'clock again back home' ...

T. 'Could you fill in the verb?'

Bernie: 'And papa comes back home at 4 o'clock'.

T. 'Papa leaves at six o'clock and comes back home at 4 o'clock' ...

Elly: 'What time has your father get up?' (Correct Dutch pincer-construction).

T. (laughing) 'Your verb is not correct' ...

Elly: 'How late must your father get up?'

Bernie: 'I don't know.'

T. 'You don't know? ... But you said that your father leaves at six o'clock! What do you think?'

Bernie: 'I think ... about quarter to six!'

T. (laughing) 'If your father is quick enough, perhaps, yes!'

Several children en mass: 'at 7 o'clock' ... 'at half past 7' ...

Dorien to Bernie: 'How your father to mine?'

T. (S) 'You are forgetting the verb! How does your father go to the mine ...'

Dorien: 'How does your father ...'

T. '... go ...'

Dorien: '... go to ...'

T. 'Yes, what? ?'

Elly: 'To the ground!'

T. to Leentje: 'Say it better!'

Leentje: 'To the mine'.

Dorien: 'How does your father the mine. How?'

T. 'I think you want to say two things at once! ... To the mine ...!'

Dorien: 'To the mine'.

Bernie: 'By motor-cycle'.

T. 'That is right ... And how does your father go down *into* the mine? By motor-cycle?'

Several children: 'The lift!' 'By using the lift' ...

T. 'Yes we have seen that. Where did we see that?

Leentje, where did we see the lift, the lift down into the mine? Say it ... Where?'

Leentje: 'Where did we see ...'

T. 'Yes, I'm asking you, where did we see the lift? The lift down into the mine? ... Have you been to

268

Limburg (= the mine-district)? Have you been to Hoensbroek?'
Leentje: 'In a film'.
T. to Jeanne: 'Say it, you too!'
Jeanne: 'By motor-cycle or bicycle or car?'
Dorien: 'No attention!'
T. 'Indeed! Dorien already asked that!' ... to Bernie: 'How does your father go *to* the mine?'
Bernie: 'By using the lift!'
T. ? ? ... '*To* the mine?'
Bernie: '... under the ground'.
T. 'Noo, *to* the mine'.
Bernie: 'By motor-cycle'.
T. 'And how does your father go down *innto* the mine?'
Bernie: 'By using the lift'.

Cora: 'I want to ask Leentje'.
T. 'What do you want to ask?'
Cora: 'Who is going with you on visit to grandma?'
T. (astonished) 'Hey, are you going to grandma?'
Leentje: 'Yes sister!'
T. 'When? this evening already?'
Leentje: 'Not this evening!'
T. (S) 'Not *yet* this evening ... During the holidays?'
Leentje: ... ? ? ? ... Very selfconscious.
T. 'Cora already knows it, for Cora asks ...'
Cora: 'Who else on visit to grandma?'
T. 'That is right, but you forgot a word!'
Cora: 'Who else ... Who go ... Who else go on visit to grandma?'
T. 'Leentje will go to grandma ... Who else will go to visit her?'
Leentje: 'Els and Truusje and I ... All ...'
T. 'The whole family is going to grandma ... Do you like to go to grandma?'
Leentje: 'Perhaps grandma is in Roesselare'. (Roesselare is a town in Belgium.)
T. to all the children: 'Perhaps grandma is in Roesselare'.
Leentje: 'Henk and Truusje, grandma take care ...'
T. 'O, now I understand, ... Grandma take ...?'
Leentje: 'Grandma takes care ...'
T. ... 'of' ...
Leentje: 'Of Henk and Truusje'.
T. 'Grandma takes care of Henk and Truusje' ...
Alice: 'Why? ... Why has grandma ... Father and mother and Els and Truusje go to the grandma!'
T. 'But Leentje is not talking about *that* now!' ... To Leentje: 'Why is grandma taking care of Henk and Truusje? Father and mother can take care of them too! Why is *grandma* taking care of Henk and Truusje?'
Leentje: 'Because my father and mother to den Bosch go' (correct Dutch, pincer-construction; den Bosch is a town in the neighbourhood of the Institute; father and mother are there now for shopping; in the evening they will fetch Leentje.)
T. 'Now I understand ...' to all the children: 'Leentje's father and mother are in den Bosch. Aha!'
Alice and several children: 'Why?'
Dorien: 'In the neighbourhood'.
Elly: 'Where does grandma live?'
T. 'Do you mean which country?'
Elly: 'Belgium! ... Where? Town? Village?'

T. (S) 'Ooh! ... Say: In which place ...'
Elly to Leentje: 'In which place does your grandma live?'
Leentje: 'In Nieuw Kapelle' (Kapel is a Dutch word which also means: Chapel: Nieuw means New).
Elly (astonished over that name): 'Nieuwe? ... Kapel?'
T. 'Nieuw ...'
Elly: 'Nieuw'.
T. 'Kapel*le*'.
Elly: 'Kapelle'.
T. 'In Nieuw Kapelle'.
Elly: 'In Nieuw Kapelle'.
U takes over the lesson.

Deposits for the Diaries

26th October 1967. It was the last day of school. At half past 4 our holidays would begin. But not all the children were going home that evening. Some were going home the day after.
Cora said: 'Bernie and Lea are going home to-morrow'. Alice did not understand 'to-morrow'. She thought that Cora had forgotten the adverb 'not'. That was a misunderstanding.
Some children were not allowed to go home in the evening of 26th October, because they could not yet travel independently. Cora was a little bit sad, because she always went home with Nolly. But his holidays had not yet started. So Cora had to wait until the next morning.
We all hoped it would be nice weather. Alice said that she hoped for nice weather because she wanted to go for a swim. But it was autumn. She would got to the indoor bath. She did not want nice weather to swim but to play outdoors.

Deposits for the children's notebooks

Expressions and vocabulary:

Misunderstanding.
'*To-morrow* we will go on holiday' – Cora had to wait until *the next morning*.
When Bernie goes home, only mama will be *there*.

Grammar:

Pincer:

because we $\overline{\text{today home go}}$

(Dutch construction)

We can $\overline{\text{today home}}$

(Dutch construction)

We have $\overline{\text{no nice weather necessary}}$

(Dutch construction)

In which swimmingpool?

Accent of contrast:
Alice did not want nice weather to go for a *swim*, but to *play outdoors*. What time does your father *leave* in the *morning* and *come back* home in the *evening?*
Father goes *to* the mine by motor-cycle, and down *into* the mine by a lift.

270

Analysis of Communicative Means

Fourth grade lesson I.

Histogram of communicative means: Teacher and Children together.

Columns ☐ 1st purely oral means;
2nd speech with gestures and demonstrations;
3rd written means.

Columns ▨ non-verbal: 4th drawings:
5th gestures, facial expressions and demonstrations without speech;

Column ▧ 6th misunderstandings.

	1 purely oral	2 speech + gestures	3 written means	4 drawings	5 gestures + demonstrations without speech	6 misunder- standings
	94.90%	4.76%	0.00%	0.00%	0.32%	3.02%

Writer's Lesson

'Why do we call a ballpen 'ball-pen'?

U. 'Look!' He takes a pre-shave bottle out of his pocket. Strong reactions from the children! . . . Some children: 'For the beard!' Others don't recognize it.

U. (S) 'Yes, this is for the beard! . . . Is it for your beard, Dorien?'

Dorien: 'No! You!' Several children: 'You!' and 'For you!'

Elly: 'For father!'

U. (S) 'That is for my beard. For father's too! Do you know what this is called? . . . No? . . . This is called: pre-shave'. Dorien repeats it. All the children repeat it now, in turn, from mouth to mouth (see above).

U. writes it now on the blackboard.

U. 'All of you say 'that is for the beard', but why?'

Elly: 'To grow the beard' (child uses the Dutch pincer-construction correctly, literally translated: the beard to grow; Dutch *to grow* cannot be used in a transitive way, – then it has to be changed into: to make grow; this difference will be explained to the children later on, e.g. on the basis of the text in the diaries, see below.)

U. (S) 'Say: To make the beard grow'. (Dutch pincer-construction).

Elly: 'Make the beard grow'.

U. 'To! . . . Again. Look at Elly all of you!'

Elly: 'To make the beard grow' . . .

U. 'All right! . . . You think so, but it is not true!'

Elly makes some plucking gestures on her chin and cheeks saying: 'grow, grow' . . .

U. (S) 'This is stubble' (It was already afternoon, so my chin was rather dark) . . . 'Say it: stubble!'

Elly: 'Stubble'.

U. 'I have stubble. Say it all in turn . . .'

All the children repeat in turn: 'You have stubble', from mouth to mouth.

U. 'But this is not to make the beard grow, but the beard better to . . .?' (Dutch pincer-construction).

Bernie: 'Grow!'

U. 'No, not grow! . . . Better to . . .? The beard better to . . .?'

Lea: 'There off!' (In Dutch this is a good adverbial phrase.)

U. 'Marvellous! . . . Now a verb! . . . In order the beard better there off too . . .?' (Dutch construction literally taken over.)

Cora: 'Pulled' . . .

U. 'What do you say? I don't understand you!'

Lea: 'Pulled' . . .

U. 'O yes . . ., to pull? You mean to pull?'

Lea and several children: 'Pull!'

U. (S) 'To pull . . . That is the infinitive. Not pulled . . . to pull? How would you like it!' (He makes a gesture with his elbow) 'Go on!'

. . . Shall I pull your hair? . . .' All the children laugh.

Alice: 'Does pain you!' (Dutch expression, literally translated).

U. (S) 'Yes that does you pain!' (Dutch pincer-construction.) 'Do you like that, Cora?'

Cora: 'Nooo!'

U. 'All right! Say: Go on!' with an elbow movement.

Cora: 'Go on . . .'

U. 'Say it nicer', he shows how to do it with a gesture of his elbow and facial mine: 'Go on!!' with the correct feeling.

Cora: 'Go on' very well. All the children laugh.

U. 'You will pull my beard? Go on! . . . That means: I don't like it! Stay away!' U. writes the new expressions on the blackboard.

Elly: 'Apparatus'.

U. (S) 'Exactly! Elly speaks of an apparatus! Listen! *An* apparatus . . .' U. draws an electric shaver on the blackboard . . . Most children recognize it. Bernie and Lea apparently do not. 'Is that a hearing aid?'

Elly: 'No no . . . for the beard', she makes the movements of shaving with an electric shaver; many children imitate her. Apparently the children don't know the word *shave*.

U. (S) 'You don't know how to call that? I'll say it: It is an electric shaver' (Dutch 'scheer-apparaat', we don't use the word shaver) . . . 'Say it: an electric shaver! Say it, Leentje!'

Leentje: 'an electric shaver'.

U. 'Nice! Say it all in turn.'

Trudy: 'Electric shaver'.

Lea: 'Electric shin' . . .

U. 'Shinnn? . . . Here, this is the shin!' (showing his shin) All the children laugh. 'Shaver!'

Lea: 'Electric shaver'.

Bernie: 'The electric . . .'

U. (S) 'Not *the*' (pointing) 'There are many shavers; say *an* . . .'

Bernie: 'An electric shaver . . .' All the other children repeat it from mouth to mouth.

U. 'Now listen, Bernie, has your father got an electric shaver too?'

Bernie, with a shrug of her shoulders . . . 'I don't know' . . .

U. to Lea: 'Your father, has he got an electric shaver?'

Lea: 'No'.

U. 'Has your father got a long beard?' Lea laughs.

Lea: 'No', and she makes a gesture of a brush.

U. (S) 'Oo, I see, your father uses a brush!'

Lea (laughing, she is thinking of a shoe brush) 'Noooo! No a brush!'

U. (S) 'No brush? . . . I think your father uses a brush and soap!'

Lea: 'Nooooo!'

U. 'Draw that shaver of your father on the blackboard'.

Lea goes to the blackboard and draws a shaving brush . . .

U. 'Yes, that is a shaving brush!' He writes *brush* next to the drawing. Meanwhile Lea draws a stick of shaving soap . . . 'Yes, that is the soap!' He writes *soap* next to the drawing. Then he imitates what father does when he shaves.

Lea: 'Yes, yes!'

U. 'And then, – listen! – father makes white lather! Say it! white lather!'

Lea: 'White lather' . . . from mouth to mouth.

U. to all the children: 'Say it all in turn: white lather!' All the children repeat it in turn, from mouth to mouth.

Dorien says: 'A white lather' . . .

U. (S) 'No, no article here: white lather'.

Dorien: 'White lather'.

U. 'Look here! I'll draw Lea's father!' He goes to the blackboard and draws a face with lather round the chin and cheeks; he writes *white lather* next to it.

Lea: 'Yes, yes!'

U. 'And then, and then, Lea? And then?'

Lea imitates her father shaving; she shows with her fingers what the Gillette razor looks like.

U. (S) 'Yes, that is a razor! Say it! . . .'

Lea: 'Razor' . . .

U. (S) 'All right . . . article a . . .!'

Lea: 'A razor' . . .

U. to all the children: 'Say it, all of you.' All the children repeat 'a razor' from mouth to mouth.

U. draws this on the blackboard and writes *razor* by it.

273

Lea imitates her father very well.

U. (S) 'Now say that! Father shaves himself like that'.

Lea: 'Father shaves . . .?'

U. '. . . shaves himself like that.'

Lea: 'Father shaves himself like that' (without showing the movement).

U. 'No! You should shave yourself! Like that!' He imitates her pretending to shave, saying at the same time: 'My father shaves himself like thaaaat!'

Lea copies him very well.

U. 'That should be done exactly at the same time', and he repeats it. All the children are doing so now.

U. 'You should say: Like that! . . . Like that! . . . exactly at the same time! . . . all right now!'

U. 'Now . . . attention! . . .' Jeanne wants to say something. 'Jeanne, what do you want to say?'

Jeanne: 'My father has . . .' Jeanne wants to say an electric shaver, but she could not find the word.

U. (S) 'Your father has got an electric shaver!'

Jeanne: 'Yes!' Several children: 'Yes!' or 'My father too!'

U. 'Yes, your father has no brush, has no soap, has no razor, he has an electric shaver!' Many children say en masse: 'My father has an electric shaver!' Elly is showing how father does it.

U. (S) 'My father does it like this!'

Elly: 'My father does it like this!'

U. is imitating her and imitates the sound of the motor into the microphone, pretending to shave himself, rrrr rrrrrrrrr rrrrrrrr (trilling of the tip of the tongue) etc. All the children laugh. 'This is the sound the shaver makes, isn't it?' All the children do the same into their microphones of the mibavo 'Now, listen! That is an electric shaver, an electric shaver . . . Say it: an electric shaver!'

Elly: 'Electric shaver' . . .

U. (S) 'An electric shaver! Say it again! . . .'

Elly: 'An electric shaver'.

U. 'All right we will go on! . . . This preshave is for that electric shaver . . .'

Elly interrupts: 'Pain! When . . . does pain!' (Dutch 'does pain' = hurts).

U. (S) 'That is very good, Elly . . . You are clever! . . . Say: 'Otherwise it will do pain.' (Dutch expression in pincer-construction).

Elly: 'Otherwise it will do pain'. All the children imitate her from mouth to mouth.

U. 'Now look here! Here in the top is a marble, a ball . . .' Some children: 'Yes, a marble' Others: 'A ball!' . . .

U. 'I can turn the ball, look!' . . . Tense silence . . . Dorien inhales . . . 'Nice!' she says . . .

U. (S) 'Yes, that smells nice! Say it! . . .'

Dorien: 'That smells nice' . . . Several children say: 'Nice!'

U. 'You may all try it. Turn the ball!' He gives the bottle to Dorien.

Dorien: 'What?'

U. 'Turn it! Turn the ball . . .' Dorien does it . . . 'The ball is becoming wet . . . Give it to Lea now!' Lea turns it and puts preshave on her lips . . . All the children laugh . . .

U. 'You have no beard!' . . . Lea inhales . . . 'Say: that smells nice!' Lea repeats it. All the children in turn recieve the bottle, turn the ball, many of them saying: 'That smells nice!'

U. 'Now listen, Trudy! . . . Do you have a beard?'

Trudy: 'Noooo!'

U. 'Does the sister have a beard?' All the children: 'Nooooo!' 'Do I have a beard?' All the children: 'Yes!'

Jeanne wants to say something.

U. 'What do you want to say, Jeanne?'

Jeanne: 'Alice's father has moustache' . . .

All the children laugh.

U. (S) 'Yes, he has *a* moustache, that is right . . . I have only a little bit of a moustache! Look here: a little bit of a moustache . . .' All the children imitate, speaking all together.

274

Elly: 'Do you want to have a moustache?' (The child uses the article correctly.)
U. 'No! I don't like to have a moustache . . .'
Elly: 'Why not?'
U. 'I don't think it is nice . . .'
The children don't agree! Several children: 'Nice!'
U. (S) 'Very nice . . . Say that! Very nice!'
All the children together: 'Very nice'.
U. 'All right! I can't help it! I don't like it!' laughs . . . 'Now listen! I'll shave myself with the shaver'. He uses the microphone as an electric shaver . . . The children crow with pleasure! Several children: 'Father too!'
U. 'Now listen!' to Leentje: 'When you get home to-night, you should ask father: Do you use preshave? . . . Listen: Do you use preshave?'
Leentje repeats it.
U. 'All right . . . and ask: Do you have an electric shaver? . . . Say it!'
Leentje and other children repeat: 'Do you have an electric shaver?'
U. writes on the blackboard *electric shaver* next to the drawing there. Meanwhile Elly is showing how father cleans the shaver . . .
U. (S) 'That is right! . . . Father cleans the shaver. Say it, Elly!'
Elly: 'Father clean . . .?'
U. (S) '. . . cleanss . . .'
Elly: 'Father cleans the shaver . . .'
U. shows how he does this. He pretends to open the shaver and blows the hair away . . . Most children recognize that.
Jeanne pretends to clean it with a small brush.
U. 'Yes, father cleans it with a small brush. Say it!'
Jeanne: 'Father clean . . .'
U. (S) '. . . cleanss . . .'
Jeanne: 'cleans the shaver with brush'.
U. (S) 'With *a* brush.'
Jeanne: 'With a brush'.
U. 'That is right . . .'
All the children want to say something now.
Alice: 'Dirty!'
Elly: 'Dust!'
U. 'Yes, dust! Now, what is that dust?'
Some children: 'Hair.'
U. 'Yes, . . . small hair . . . That is small hair'. The children repeat: . . . 'small hair' . . .
U. 'Now listen! . . . This ball here is to become wet' . . . Children: 'Wet'.
Cora: 'It becomes wet'.
U. 'Nice, Cora! . . . Now listen, again: (Dutch pincer-construction) This ball is wet to become . . . Say it, Lea! . . . Ooh, you did not pay attention! You Dorien!'
Dorien: 'That ball is wet to become' . . .
Cora says it too, spontaneously.
U. to Alice: 'Say it, you too, Alice!'
Alice: 'That ball becomes more wet!' . . .
U. 'That is right too! . . . I can do this'. He turns the bottle upside down . . . 'You see, the preshave does not run out of the bottle . . .!' Children: 'Yes!! There!' . . .
U. 'You are right! The bottle leaks a little bit . . . Say it, Alice!'
Alice: 'It lll . . .?'
U. 'It leaks a little bit'.
Alice: 'It leaks a little bit' . . .

275

U. to Bernie: 'Say it, Bernie, you too . . .'
Bernie: 'It leaks a little bit' . . . All the children have to repeat it.
U. writes it on the blackboard. He then takes the lid to put it on the bottle. 'That is the lid . . . Say it! . . . the lid!' The children repeat it. 'Now the lid is on the bottle'. He puts it away in his pocket . . . And then with strong facial mime: 'I have still another ball!' . . . The children look silently . . . He slowly takes a ballpen from his inside pocket . . . The children cry: 'Aaaah!' Some: 'No ball!' with a disappointed face . . .
U. 'Yes, a ball! A very very small ball!'
Cora knows it. She takes her own ballpen and shows the point saying: 'Ball!'
U. (S) 'Yes, that is right, Cora . . . There is a small ball!' Many of the children doubt it . . .
Lea: 'No seee!'
U. (S) 'You don't see it? Say that!'
Lea: 'I don't see it!'
U. 'Really! There is a ball in the point . . . Here, a small ball, look! . . . Explain it to her, Cora!'
Cora to Lea: 'There is! There . . .'
U. (S) 'All right, there is a small ball *in* the point . . .'
Cora: 'There is a . . .'
U. '. . . a small ball . . .'
Cora: '. . . a small ball . . . in the point'.
U. 'That small ball is also wet to become' (Dutch pincer-construction).
Several children: 'Yes!'
U. . . . 'wet to become, not with preshave! . . . With what? ?'
Alice: 'Ink!' Several children too: 'Ink'.
U. 'That is right . . . *with* ink . . . Say that Alice! . . . and all of you!'
All the children repeat: 'With ink'.
U. takes out a red ball-pen. Children: 'Aaaah!' *U.* 'There is a small ball here too!' He takes out a green ballpen! Children: 'Aaaaah!' U. 'Here too is a small ball! They can turn . . .'
Lea interrupts, looking at the inside of U.'s coat, saying: 'one!'
U. (S) 'One more?'
Lea: 'One more'.
U. 'Noo! See here, I have only three! You are seeing double! . . .'
Lea: 'Black? Black ballpen?'
U. (S) 'Do I have a black ballpen too? Say that!'
Lea: 'Do you have black ballpen too?'
U. 'Yes, at home!'
Alice: 'Home? Where?'
U. 'Now, where is my home?' Several children point to the main building . . .
U. (S) 'In the main building? No not there!'
Several children: 'In Nijmegen?'
U. 'No, I moved! That is passed . . . I don't live in Nijmegen any more. I moved . . . Say it Leentje!'
Leentje: 'You moved'.
U. 'That is nice . . . I live there!' He points to another side of the campus . . . The children don't follow.
U. 'I live behind the bakery'.
Cora makes a gesture, tipping with her forefinger against her temple . . . U. imitates her. All the children chuckle!
U. (S) 'Say: I am beginning to see!' . . . TIME . . .

Deposit for the Diaries

Saving:

Mr. U. paid a visit to our class. He showed us a preshave bottle. That is to bring the beard out. Elly thought: 'The preshave is to make the beard grow'. But Mr. U. does not want to make his beard grow. – Men have a beard. Women and children have not. Sometimes men have stubble on the chin and cheeks. Some men have a moustache and a beard. Others don't like to have a beard: they shave it off. Cora thought that men should pull the beard. Imagine! Go on! That would hurt very much. It is very painful.

Lean's father uses a shaving brush and soap. He makes white lather round his chin and cheeks. Then he shaves himself with a razor.

Jeanne's father uses an electric shaver. Elly's father too. They use preshave in order to shave themselves closer. First they put preshave on their beard: then shaving does not hurt. Then they can shave themselves much easier. Otherwise it is somewhat painful. Preshave smells nice. Afterwards the electric shaver must be cleaned with a small brush. The shaver is full of small hair.

The ball in the ballpen

Mr. U.'s preshave bottle had a ball in the top. When father uses the preshave he puts the ball on his chin and cheeks. Then the ball is turned and becomes wetted by preshave. Chin and cheeks become wet too. Mr U's bottle leaked a little bit.

Mr U. also showed a ballpen. In the point of the ballpen is a very very small ball. Therefore it is called a ball-pen. The ball becomes wet with ink to write.

Expressions and vocabulary:
Preshave.
Stubble on chin and cheeks.
To shave.
Imagine! Go on!

Grammar:
The beard grows. –
Preshave is not to *make* the beard grow. (Dutch.)

To pull is infinitive, *pulled* is second form.
Preshave is not in order to pull the hair. Nolly pulled Cora's hair: that was very painful.

A shaving brush

Article:
Lea's father uses *a* shaving brush, and soap and *a* razor.
Father makes white lather.
Elly's father uses preshave and *an* electric shaver.
(Zero functions of the article could be indicated as follows:
°shaving soap
°white lather
°preshave)

shaving soap

White lather

Pincer: (Dutch construction)

In order to make the beard grow ...

An electric shaver

My father shaves himself like this.
My father does it like this.
By using preshave, shaving does not hurt chin and cheeks.
The bottle leaks a little bit.
The lid of the bottle.
Really!
I am beginning to see.

278

Analysis of Communicative Means

Fourth grade Lesson II (Lesson with demonstrations of shaving).

Histogram of communicative means: Teacher and children together.

Columns ☐ 1st purely oral means;
2nd speech with gestures and demonstrations;
3rd written means.

Columns ▨ non-verbal: 4th drawings;
5th gestures, facial expressions and demonstrations
without speech;

Column ▨ 6th misunderstandings.

76.50%	18.47%	0.95%	0.42%	3.66%	0.87%
1 purely oral	2 speech + gestures	3 written means	4 drawings	5 gestures + demonstrations without speech	6 misunder-standings

Appendix II
Achievements

Residential school 'Instituut voor Doven, St. Michielsgestel', The Netherlands.

A. GRADUATES

Survey of *all* strictly prelingually deaf graduates (i.e. with more than 90 dB. hearing loss from early childhood, 'low pass hearing loss' excluded), at 18, 19 and 20 years of age, multiply handicapped included, having been taught from early childhood by preschool-training:

Graduates of the years:	Average Hearing losses in dB., Fletcher-index:	Low stream:	High stream (learning English as a second language):	
			1. Primary level:	2. Secondary level:
1972	103 ± 12	42%	45%	13%
1973	107 ± 15	55%	33%	12%
1974	102 ± 9	43%	26%	31%
1975	111 ± 20	33%	28%	39%
1976	111 ± 18	61%	23%	16%
Average:	105 ± 14	47%	31%	22%

B. LANGUAGE ACHIEVEMENT.

Data concerning strictly prelingually deaf children, *without* severe multiple handicaps, and having had normal instruction at this Institute since 4–5 years of age. Data by the psychological staff of this Institute. Complete publication is in preparation.

1. Growth of Vocabulary Measured by Means of the 'Peabody Picture Vocabulary Test'.

This test was adjusted to normally hearing Dutch children and standardized by Manschot and Bonnema (1974), max. score 100 at 8½ years of age = ± 4,000 words. It was applied at this Institute in 1975. The results are summarized as follows:

280

Ages of deaf children:	Average hearing losses in dB., Fletcher-index:	Raw scores:	Converted into an estimated number of words used by normally hearing children of the same raw scores according to different ages:
6 years	107 ± 13	20 ± 7	460 words (age 2½ years)
8 years	109 ± 18	25 ± 5	1,000 words (age 3 years)
10 years	102 ± 9	49 ± 5	2,000 words (age 5½ years)
12 years	110 ± 17	59 ± 8	2,700 words (age 6½ years)
14 years	102 ± 20	73 ± 15	3,800 words and more (age 8½ and older)

The average gain in vocabulary was 10 words per schoolweek in the age range of 6–12 years, and 15 words in the age range of 12–14 years, rather slow in comparison with the ideal described on page 229, for a number of reasons. – After 14 years of age, the vocabulary of most of the children grows very fast, because they start to read more and more (see reading levels no. 2).

2. Reading Levels:

The 'Metropolitan Paragraph Reading Test' (1958) has been freely translated into Dutch, adjusted to the Dutch environment and standarized on 1,275 normally hearing children of different socio-economic levels in rural-urban primary schools.
In 1974 and 1976 this test was applied on our deaf children. The level of 30 correct answers (max. 44) was found to be the threshold of literacy, i.e. the average reading level of normally hearing non-handicapped children of 10 years of age, having followed regular education from 4 years of age, = level 7–9 of the Reading Scale.

The results for the deaf children of 16 to 19 years of age are summarised as follows:

Raw score (max. 44):	Average reading age of normally hearing children:	Deaf children 16–19 years of age:					
		Performance I.Q.:		Average hearing losses in dB., Fletcher-index:		Percentages:	
		1974	1976	1974	1976	1974	1976
17 or less	7 years or younger	92 ± 13	94 ± 6	105 ± 13	110 ± 18	14	6
18–23	8 years	101 ± 10	104 ± 11	109 ± 13	107 ± 15	20	13
24–29	9 years	105 ± 8	107 ± 13	103 ± 10	111 ± 11	31	53
30–44	10–12 years and older	119 ± 7	116 ± 12	109 ± 14	103 ± 9	35	28

281

More specialized data of the children with Performance I.Q. of 100 and more:

Chronological age:	Average hearing losses in dB., Fletcher-index:		Scores (max. 44) with % of deaf children:							
			17 or less		18–23		24–29		30–44	
	1974	1976	1974	1976	1974	1976	1974	1976	1974	1976
14 years	107 ± 15	103 ± 9	9	0	36	50	36	17	18	33
15 years	111 ± 17	105 ± 14	0	0	31	28	38	28	31	44
16 years	109 ± 15	110 ± 15	0	0	0	18	33	55	67	27
17 years	111 ± 20	102 ± 9	11	0	11	0	33	56	45	44
18 years	109 ± 16	107 ± 14	0	0	22	0	45	66	33	34
Averages of 1974 + 1976 16–18 years:	109 ± 14		2%		8%		48%		42%	

3. Grammatical Control

Composition work by the deaf children has been analysed.

a. In 1969, the compositions by the 16–19 year olds, written for their annual examinations and reports, were collected, for investigation. The children had received 4 or 5 subjects (e.g. 'Our Garden', 'What a shame!' 'Just for pleasure' and so on), from which they had to choose one title for a free composition. The maximum time allowed was 90 minutes. Because the students knew that this task was for their annual report and/or for graduation, they did their utmost. We will call these compositions 'controlled composition-work'.

b. In 1975 the children (9–19 years of age) were given a picture not seen before by them:

They had to write a composition around this picture. This composition was not for their annual report but 'for the psychologist', as the children had been told. The length had to be of at least 25 lines, if possible. The maximum time allowed was 40 minutes. So there was not much time for preparation, neither for control afterwards. We will call these compositions 'uncontrolled composition-work'.

The results of the 16–19 year olds, samples of 100 words, were as follows:
Controlled:

Performance I.Q.	Average hearing losses in dB., Fletcher-index:	% of deaf children:	% of different words:	Average length of sentences:	% of completely correct sentences:
85– 99	103 ± 9	19	72 ± 13	5 ± 3 words	41 ± 11
100–115	107 ± 13	52	64 ± 13	8 ± 4 words	67 ± 9
116 and more	105 ± 11	29	61 ± 6	8 ± 6 words	81 ± 12

282

Uncontrolled:

Perfor- mance I.Q.	Average hearing losses in dB., Fletcher-index:	% of deaf children:	% of diffe- rent words:	Average length of sentences:	% of com- pletely correct sentences:
85– 99	110 ± 16	32	48 ± 9	7 ± 1 words	26 ± 25
100–115	107 ± 15	44	57 ± 5	8 ± 2 words	72 ± 14
116 and more	108 ± 15	24	62 ± 6	11 ± 3 words	77 ± 13

a. *Specimens of Uncontrolled Composition-work Around the Picture*

Very literal translations of these specimens, from Dutch into English, have been made, including as much as possible the particular errors of each child.

Data of the children.

Name with particulars:	Age:	Had home-training:	Had pre-school:	Hearing loss of best ear (Fletcher, ISO):	Age of detection of deafness:	Total years at school:	Years at this school:	Performance I.Q.:
Marti	7;9	+	+	120+ dB.	1;2	4 yrs.	4 yrs.	good
Inge Dysphasia	9;0	−	+	120+ dB.	0;2	5 yrs.	5 yrs.	good
Rick Dysphasia + Dysgraphia	10;9	+	+	107 dB.	0;8	6yrs.	6 yrs.	average
Rob	11;0	+	+	100 dB.	1;0	7 yrs.	7 yrs.	very good
Wim Dyslexia	11;10	+	+	103 dB.	0;5	8 yrs.	8 yrs.	average
Mieke Dysphasia	12;9	+	+	120+ dB.	0;8	9 yrs.	9 yrs.	very good
Gabriel	14;8	+	+	105 dB.	0;3	11 yrs.	11 yrs.	good
Mary Dysphasia	15;3	+	+	118 dB.	0;7	11 yrs.	11 yrs.	good
Lea	16;6	+	+	106 dB.	1;0	12 yrs.	12 yrs.	good
Kees Dysphasia	16;7	+	+	110 dB.	0;11	12 yrs.	12 yrs.	average
Elly	17;2	+	+	105 dB.	0;10	13 yrs.	13 yrs.	good
Jeanne Dysphasia	18;0	+	+	110 dB.	0;6	14 yrs.	14 yrs.	good

Specimens of Compositions

Name: Marti, girl.
Age: 7;9
Mark out of ten given by the teacher: 7

to the wood. tires car sand is broken.
six boys push help
not good street is broken
cannot get right
engine is broken
six boys sand difficult walk

284

Name: Inge, girl.
Age: 9;0
Mark out of ten given by the teacher: 7

About the journey.

Seven people go on a journey.
Where are you going? He go and look, in Germany.
That car could not ride.
Why is it? Because dry sand.
Seven people had to push and help.
The gentlemen do not like it.
It is warm.
There are also plants, grass and trees.

Name: Rick, boy.
Age: 10;9
Mark out of ten given by the teacher: 8

an accident

Mummy said: are we going to african. We said: Yes of course. I have to get a food. Mummy said: That is all right. I must take 15 loaf and 10 lemonade. Mummy said: That is all right. Daddy said: Shall we take a radio. Mummy said: That is all right. I must take sleepbags. grandma has to stay to sister. the car is ready. I'll come in african for about 16 days. Daddy must get petrol in. about 16 litres. Is that ready, Mummy said: Yes, good we leave. Daddy must start very long drive. There is the african. Shall we walk. Daddy said no, else is many animals. There is animals. That is very nice animal. Shall we ride again. I said very careful. Wow what swamp. We must very careful. oh yes I already know that Mummy said. I am afraid of swamp. Daddy said: don't be afraid. we are going to leave. ugh how dirty. the car is in swamp in. 6 persons help to pull no good. oh what shall we do. I 'phone the lorry. That is all right. wait very long time. There is lorry. hip hip hurray, that is nice hello sir. hello sir and madam what is the matter. the car is stuck in the swamp. pull. hurray it is loose. Thank you sir. Good-bye sir and madam we are going to leave. we are going home. hip hip hurray very long drive. There is Home, grandma is Home. I have long ride. I am tired out. I'll go and rest.

Name: Rob, boy.
Age: 11;0
Mark out of ten given by the teacher: 6

Stuck in the mud

The title is about the car which is stuck in the mud.
The family is going to the woods in the car. There are all mud. Don't you know why that is? Because it rained very much yesterday. That is why there are all mud in the woods. These 6 persons want to drive through. Because the car-park is there. That family has bad luck, because they cannot drive through. That is why they have bad luck. 4 persons get out of the car to can get the car back. Yes, they have success. These 4 persons go back into the car. They are going to the other car-park. They stop there. This family all get out of the car. Suddenly there was a rain-shower. The family goes back to the car. They get into the car. This family has bad luck again. They are stuck in the mud again. 4 persons get out of the car again. They pull. Yes, they have success again. They get into the car quickly. After that they went back home. They are never going back to the woods, except in the summer they will.

End or Fin

Name: Wim, boy.
Age: 11;10
Mark out of ten given by the teacher: 6

a little bit terrible story.

A man and lady came to Africa in a car.
And then they came to the big boat to sea, as that has no bridge. Then those 2 people in the car to a village of Africa. That car is on the sand. The tire of the car slips. There came a negroes from the village went walking to the wood.
Oh, those people in the car came from Holland, said negroes.
That man and lady has said that will you push my car. 'brrrrmmm'. Thank you: 'said the man and lady. Now the people sit in the car driven again. Ooooer, The lion came' said the lady. Then the lion sit on the car, as that lion the nails of that beast was scratching on the roof of the car. That man and lady heard 'grrrr'. That man has said, 'that' what is that?' the lady thinks, that beast was the scratching. That animal was out of the car again. Good.

Name: Mieke, girl.
Age: 12;9
Mark out of ten given by the teacher: 8

Mr. Van Andel and their 2 colleagues are going to Africa on airplane. They work at the university. They are going on holiday for 2 weeks. Now they has arrived in Africa (Tanzania). They think a very nice country. The negroes come to fetch them on the airfield. The negroes have to clear away all the cases and put them in the cars. Mr. Van Andel and Mr. Osendorp and Mr. van Made stay in negro's hut with tent. The professor wants that 3 colleagues learn how lives in the jungle. The 3 colleagues hire the negro's car. The next day they are going to the jungle with 5 negroes. They want 1 more car. That is easy, as the other negroes also have to go in the car. They also want guns and pistols. The wild animals live in the jungle (for instance lion, tiger, panther, elephant etc.). The 3 colleagues are little bit afraid, as they have never done it. They see the panther come to them. A negro shoots with the gun. Missed! Again. It is a hit. The panther is severely wounded. Mr. Van Made fetches first-aid box. He puts ointment on the panther's paw, and he puts bandage round it. The panther is unconscious. She has to go to the animal hospital. The negroes carry the panther into the van. All go into the car. They drive to the animal hospital. Suddenly the car stands no longer riding. The car is stuck in the mud. They have bad luck. The negroes and Mr. Osendorp do push the car. Mr. Van Made has to push the car driving. They manage. The negroes are dirty from bare foot.

Name: Gabriel, boy.
Age: 14;8
Mark out of ten given by the teacher: 9

The two students received their degrees in university. Then a professor asked them: 'Would you like to work in Africa as doctors?' 'Yes!' the new doctors said. 'Then I shall recommend you to the tribal chief of a village in Africa.' They went to Africa in a plane and a boat. When they got there, they bought a nice car. Then they drove to a village in Tanzania. Midway they drove through a muddy road. One of the wheels got stuck in the mud. A hunter saw this and ran to his tribe, where he told the news. The tribal chief sent 6 men. Together they succeeded in pushing the car away. 'Thanks' said the doctor behind the wheel. And they drove on, until they arrived in the village in Tanzania. The tribal chief received them cordially and invited them for a dinner. The two doctors did not let this invitation refuse and went with him to his hut. They received some nice food. 'Nice, what titbit is this?' asked a doctor.

286

'Horse-tail with ants and frittered snake!' Then the doctors went red in their faces and ran to a bush where they vomited violently. 'Don't you like it?' asked the tribal chief. 'Yes we do, but we have to get used to it' said the doctor. 'Now it's time to do some work' said the other doctor, whose name is Peter. 'Please come with me' said the tribal chief and he took them to a big hut where he showed them sick negroes. Peter had a look at the sick and declared: 'They have all got smallpox and they have to be vaccinated quickly'. The medicine-man who could not cure the sick people, became jealous and went to the doctors' car to steal the doctor's bag. A doctor, Piet, saw this and wanted to stop him but the medicine-man knocked him unconscious and ran to his own hut. The medicine-man looked at the bottles and syringes and etc. Then the medicine-man found an antidote against smallpox and he hid the bag in the sand. He took the bottle to the tribal chief. He said 'Me can cure the sick'. The chief was dumbfounded and he took the medicine-man to the sick people. The medicine-man opened the bottle and he made a sick man swallow all the medicine. The sick man suddenly stood up, his hair stood on end. Smoke came from his mouth. His tongue was blue. After that he soon died. The tribal chief saw all this. He shouted to the medicine-man: 'You not good medicine-man, you is deceiver'. The tribal chief called all his men and ordered them to put the medicine-man behind bars. A doctor, Piet, woke up and he suddenly remembered everything. He ran to the medicine-man's hut. He suddenly stumbled over a bag. He picked up this bag and ran quickly to the chief. 'Your medicine-man is a useless man and you take me to the sick.' The tribal chief took him. The doctor vaccinated all the sick people, when he saw a dead man. 'Is he dead?' 'The medicine-man had this stuff the sick man swallow' said the chief. 'This stuff is all right but he should not swallow it but be vaccinated.' The medicine-man was taken to the judge who sentenced him, to 5 years.

Name: Mary, girl.
Age: 15;3
Mark out of ten given by the teacher: 8

Holiday to Africa.

Father and mother talked each other about holiday, where go they want to. They thought of Africa. There are the nice country. Mother picked a holiday-book of foreign countries and she saw a nice country in Africa. Then an oldest son came, who came from school. An oldest son is called Peter and he is 22 years old. He had bring report. He has received good marks, and he can go to the form up. An other son came. His name is John and he is 19 years old. He can go to the form up. Father said: 'Listen, I have surprise for you'. John and Peter looked surprise. Father said: 'We are going on holiday, I'll not tell you, where are we going. You can guess 3 times'. John said, 'To France, Spain or England'. Father said: 'Wrong, and you Peter'. Peter said: 'To Switzerland, Germany or Italy'. Father said: 'Wrong, I'll tell you. We are going to Africa by car on the 5th of July. Boys were so glad. John asked mother: 'How long will we be staying in Africa?' Mother answered: 'For 3 weeks'. John said: 'The teacher has tolded us that in Africa is a nice country'. Later on they had to clear up and pack suit cases. On the 5th of July, at 5 o'clock in the morning they had to get up, and they left at 6 o'clock. Father drove the car. They sang in the car. Later parked the car in Belgium. They ate bread and slept in tent. Following day they were in France. After 5 days they were in Africa. John and Peter were so warm, and they wanted to swim. But in Africa there were no swimming-pools. They looked for a nice spot where the tent be put up. They had found it. The let-man said: '. . . . .'. Father did not understand. He could not understand African language. Peter *could* understand African language. He was at university. He told father: 'That negro man said: 'You cannot put up the tent here. It is full. You have to take another road. There you'll see a big tent-spot'. They drove on sandy road. But they did not ride. Father started try. But no success. This sandy road is far too soft and far too dust. 4 Negro men came to help. 1 negro man said to father: '. . . . . .'. Peter said to father: 'He asked: 'We may help with it'. Father said it was all right. Father and mother set in the car, and the car rode little bit. Peter, John and 4 men pushed the car. They found the road. They drove in another road, and looked for another spot. They put up the tent. Following day they walked to the mountain.

They helped with other people. They were so much fun in Africa. After 3 weeks they were back again to Holland.

Name: Lea, girl.
Age: 16;6
Mark out of ten given by the teacher: 6

Car was stuck.

Mr. and Mrs. Janssen had a plan to drive through the wood. They loved nature. Mr. Janssen was a forester and he knew the way of the wood very well. At 9 o'clock in the morning they drove off. Mrs. Janssen said to her husband: 'I hope we'll have a beautiful day to-day'. Her husband said: 'Certainly, you will enjoy the wood'. They lived in Africa. When they were driving in the wood, they saw lots of monkeys, squirrels, etc. Mrs. Janssen thought they were cute and she thought they had cute faces. Sir did not know that 4 or 5 metres ahead there was a mud. He drove on without pay attention. He enjoyed himself and told his wife about his past what he used to do in the wood. Madam wanted to get her bag which was lying on the back seat. Madam at once fell from the front seat and she was now lying on the back seat. Her husband did start and looked his wife how she was. She was all right but she does have bruises on her legs. Sir got out for a moment. He was standing on the mud. Sir looked down and saw a mud. He got back into his car, he told his wife that they were on the mud. Sir said 'Let's try to push the car'. They did so, but it did not work. They went back into the car. Their shoes were dirty. After a few hours they saw African boys. They called for help. They came and looked what had happened. Sir asked them to help. They did so. 2 African boys were pushing at the front of the car and a few boys at the sides of the car. When the man and the lady were pushed on the normal track by the African boys, the man thanked them and gave them 2 dollars for each of them. The boys thanked and went on picking their fruit. The man and lady drove on until it was late. When they came home, they were tired. His wife said: 'What a nice day we have had'. Her husband said yes and asked if his wife was coming to bed. They went to fall asleep straight away. And life goes on.

Name: Kees, boy.
Age: 16;7
Mark out of ten given by the teacher: 6

A car trouble on the way to the zoo.

The family lived on the farm at Oudenbosch. His father was a farmer and his mother was a farmer's wife. They had 6 children. These children all happened to be boys. They wanted to go on a trip to a zoo. It was the 10th of July. Father and mother got up early and they woke up the children. They were ready at half past seven and were leaving. They drove on the motor-way. At nine o'clock they arrived at the border. They did not have to stop but just drove on. Father was nervous because the traffic in Belgium was somewhat different from Dutch traffic. He drove slowly and looks for the sign with 'Antwerp' on it. There wasn't a good road in Belgium. On the road was a lot of thick layers of sand. Father was afraid, as he thought that the car will be stuck. Suddenly the engine was still. They could not go any farther. Father got out of his car and opened the bonnet. He had checked everything. Unfortunately he could not find anything. Two of the children started to cry. Mother said: 'No need to cry, we perhaps go on'. All the children got out of the car. They pushed the car to the petrol station. They had been pushing for nearly half an hour. They had a rest for a while. A little bit later they were at the petrol station. A petrol man asked the driver: 'Will you have petrol?' Father said: 'No, my car is broken down, I don't know what is wrong with that'. That car is repaired. Father said to the children: 'We can no longer go on to Antwerp, but we may go home'. A few minutes later the car was ready. It was late. It was now half past two. 'Now we are going home', father said. After 2 hours they

288

were in Holland. They had a nice meal in a hotel. They all had a plate of chips. Father said: 'We did have a car trouble, by Jove!' When they had finished eating, they just went home. They were home at 6 o'clock.

Name: Elly, girl.
Age: 17;2
Mark out of ten given by the teacher: 4

'A holiday to Africa' was the first prize for the person who filled in crossword puzzle correctly. And I was the lucky one. And I was also allowed to take someone with me. My friend agreed with my suggestion. Thus we left nervously for Spain in our car. There a boat waited which would take us to Africa. The journey had gone very well. We arrived at our destination after a 5 days' voyage. The first night in the hotel we could not sleep at all because of the heat. But when the morning broke we had dressed for the car-trip which we would make to-day with our guide. The guide was part of the prize. Thus we drove on sandy road which led to jungle that morning. Before jungle we stopped and further we walked through jungle which our guide had the way at his fingers' ends. There was a folklore dance held which we would like to see very much. All the negresses had all those beads round their necks and round their arms. They danced and stamped with their feet. I did not understand that they could keep up all day in this such warm weather. I would not keep it up at all. The dance was very beautiful. Suddenly became very dark on this afternoon. The negroes started to dance more quickly and to call and to shout as token of their gratitude that it would start to rain again. And yes, it broke, it was raining cats and dogs. One of the negroes gave us his hut for shelter. When the rain stopped, we had to walk back to our car. The walk back was more difficult than the walk there. When we finally got into our car, we rested for a while before leaving again. The engine started to run. Our car started to move. But a moment later our car would go no farther. The tires were stuck in the mud. I and the guide got out to try if we could push the car out of the mud. A native curiously went to our car.

Name: Jeanne, girl.
Age: 18;0
Mark out of ten given by the teacher: 7

Bad luck in Africa.

Glynn, Rooper and Nelsen are the biologists and come from America. They are going to Africa to film wild animals.
When they arrive in Africa, the negroes take them to the hotel. They are tired and have a rest. The following day Glynn, a big strong man, goes and fetches his car from the airfield. When Glynn comes back, the men already have their film things ready. They go into the jungle. 'Let us first go and film the elephants', Rooper says. They look for the elephants, but they don't see any elephants. Finally they find the tracks of the elephants. They hide the camera in the bush and go away. When the animals go near the camera the camera begins to run. The following day they go back to the place where the camera was. Glynn goes to fetch the camera. 'Oh, my God, that is not possible', Glynn shouts. This shouting startles them and they go to have a look. The camera is completely damaged by the trampling of the elephants. They become angry and drive back with the broken camera. But they are angry and no longer remember the way. They have lost their way and their car is stuck in the mud. Glynn gets out of his car and starts to push the car. But he cannot manage it and Rooper also gets out of his car. He cannot manage it either. 'What are we to do?' Rooper asks. 'Look, there is the village, shall we ask the villagers to push our car out of the mud. 5 Of the villagers come and help. They all push the car out of the mud. The car is free and they thank the negroes and go back to their hotel.
Later on they go to America and tell about their bad luck in Africa. Next year they will go to Africa again to film wild animals.

b. Specimens of Controlled Composition-work

Very literal translations from Dutch into English, including the particular errors of each student.

Data of the students

Name with particulars:	Age:	Had home-training:	Had pre-school:	Hearing-loss of best ear (Fletcher, ISO):	Age of detection of deafness:	Total years at school:	Years at this school:	Per-formance I.Q.:
Gabriel	15;11	+	+	106 dB.	0;3	12 yrs.	12 yrs.	good
Hans	17;10	+	+	107 dB.	0;7	14 yrs.	14 yrs.	very good
Mary Dysphasia	16;6	+	+	119 dB.	0;7	12 yrs.	12 yrs.	good
Leontine Dysphasia	17;10	−	+	110 dB.	0;11	14 yrs.	14 yrs.	average
Mattie Dyslexia	16;2	+	+	97 dB.	0;7	12 yrs.	12 yrs.	average

Specimens of Compositions

Name: Gabriel, boy.
Age: 15;11
Mark out of ten given by the teacher: 9

Fantasy.

In the town of Apeldoorn a boy and an old man occupied with a hobby: building rockets. They had exactly the same rocket-model. But now they wanted to experience a moon-journey themselves.
They cut and sent a form out of 'Sjors-met-zonder-Sjimmie' to Port Kennedy in which they stated that they wanted to pay 50,000 guilders and one cent each for a moon-journey.
Then everything was all right. They took a ship 'Lost with all hands on board', which took them to America. There they met the astronauts Takata Tsjang, John Ford and Boris Poelotja. So they spoke to them in the three languages. On the 1st of January 2000 they left for the moon in their little rocket. The journey lasted 3 days and 1 hour. They had taken food with them for 6 days, however, they wanted to keep some for the return journey and so they starved.
They made a perfect landing. They got in contact with Martians straight away. They were bulb-shaped. They had three eyes and one ear. They had little transmitters on their heads. That was a means of communication for the inhabitants of the moon, the same way as the inhabitants of the earth use their mouths. They ate their food with mouths in the soles of their feet. When they walked, they also ate, if they wanted to. They had 20 legs. They can live for ever, but they did not have sexual organs. The two wings had grown on their backs, so that if they want to they could fly. So the old man of 101 years and the boy had plenty of food, which lies everywhere on the ground. Unfortunately the Martians were war-minded at this moment and they were fighting the Mercurians. The inhabitants of the

290

moon chose for their allies: the Mercurians. Then the war was fought on the moon with the primitive weapons. So the 2 humans fled back to earth in the rocket, landed in the Atlantic, 45.6° latitude east and 30.1° longitude west. No help came and gradually the space-ship started to sink, where the 2 earthlings drowned. They were munched by the sharks.

Name: Hans, boy
Age: 17;10
Mark out of ten given by the teacher: 6

To the cinema.

In the afternoon when school was over at 5 o'clock 5 girls who were called Jolanda, Gertie, Annemie and Ans cycled home. On the way Gertie saw that tonight a nice film is coming in a cinema. Gertie · asked them if tonight they want to go there. Everyone wanted to. And therefore they arranged to come to the cinema at 8 o'clock. Everyone understood it all and then they went home. Jolanda, Gertie and Annemie asked their fathers and mothers. They didn't mind. Then Ans went to ask. Father wasn't at home. Mother was. Mother agreed. Ans became glad and first went to do homework. She did eat of course.
At a quarter to eight Ans's father came in and just Ans had finished her homework. She went downstairs and then saw his father. Ans asked straight away but father wouldn't agree and so she didn't go. She went to bed feeling sad.
5 Minutes later father went upstairs to see if Ans was asleep. The bed had just been filled with pillows to see to it that daddy did not notice that Ans had gone. When Ans heard footsteps she hid in the wardrobe. Father checked and then he was satisfied and locked the door so that she could not escape. Then Ans became a little bit angry and then she had a plan. She went from the window to the gutterpipe and climbed down. The venture is successful.
Ans just ran away at once because it was after eight.
Finally she was at the cinema and then they went inside. They stayed there until the film had finished. Meanwhile Ans's father went to Ans's room to tell her something. Father opened the door and went to Ans. He woke her up but she did not sit up and father got hold of the blankets and complete his surprise he was that she had flown. Father became furious and told his mother. Ans's father decided to stay in Ans's room until Ans had returned.
When the film had finished Ans went home straight away. She climbed up the rainpipe and that is how she entered. Father at once switched on the light so that Ans startled so terribly and could not say anything. Father gave some severe punishment. Ans was sorry and said it to father that she would never do it again. Father heard it and gave her a reward. Father went to the cinema with her.

NB. The following three specimens have been selected because of the interesting topic chosen by the students themselves.

Name: Mary, girl.
Age: 16;6
Mark out of ten given by the teacher: 6

Being deaf, how do I experience it
  how does my environment react.

Then I was about 11 years old. My brother Jan and I were doing the shopping. We cycled in the village. There were 5 boys. They saw I wore a hearing-aid. They gestured to me. They started to talk about deafness. They laughed at me. I didn't feel it nice at all. Jan has heard and seen it all. He went to boys. He started angry with boys. Those boys said: 'That girl is a deaf-mute'. Jan said: 'My sister is

291

not a deaf-mute. She is only deaf. And she can talk'. Those boys began laugh loudly and they didn't believe him. I felt I must angry with boys. I started to talk to boys. The boys were with complete surprise. They could not believe me. They just walked away.

Later I was 14 years old. I went to the village with the neighbour's girl Ineke. We went to the Youth Centre in the village. We were sitting at the table with other girls. We chatted a lot. I did feel happy. Later I saw 5 boys who thought that I was a deaf-mute. These boys saw me too, but they went to sit to another place. One year later I went with Ineke to Youth Centre. I didn't like it so much, because Ineke has a friend. Ineke hardly talked anything to me. When I talked to Ineke, but Ineke half listened to me. Therefore I went to look for other place. I was sitting at the table with 3 girls. I was afraid to start to talk. I did have to persevere. We talked a lot about St. Michielsgestel. 4 boys came to our table. These boys were sitting down. One boy said to me: 'Sorry, that I always used to call you names. I thought I don't like it very much. Let's talk something else'. I felt very happy.

We always went to ' 't putte' at Deurne. I have lots of boy-friends and girl-friends.

Name: Leontine, girl.
Age: 17;10
Mark out of ten given by the teacher: 5

Being deaf, how does my environment react.

Some people feel sorry for deaf people. I think the people a nuisance. Because people are always curious to us. I think people are stupid that people want to stare at us. When we talk to each other they can hear my voice. It happens that people look at us. People gossip about us. Because deaf people make a lot of signs. That is why they think very strange. But I don't need at all, that people need not sorry for us. I don't mind at all being deaf as I can talk and read. Some people find it interesting how deaf people can talk and read. I like it that people want to talk me. But they stare at us. Why do they do it? I think people dare not talk to us or do not want to talk or they make afraid of us. I suggest that people don't know how to speak to deaf people. They don't know exactly either how the deaf is. People want to know much more about deafness. People try want to talk to deaf people. I have to experience a lot about discovering people. I want to talk to the girl, but the girl walks away at once. Because this girl cannot understand me and is afraid of me, for example. We go to a dance. I want to talk to a few friends at the dance. My friends cannot understand me. Because the music is there. When the music has finished then they can understand me. I do find it difficult talk to hearing people. How I feel that I am deaf. That is very bad to think 'I am deaf'. You should not think of how you feel it. But you must simply with other people to chat. The problem always remains hearing the voice.

Name: Mattie, girl.
Age: 16;2
Mark out of ten given by the teacher: 6

Being deaf, how do I experience it, how does my environment react.

When I was small I made many signs when I talked to someone. That is why a lot of people looked at me! There I got a strange feeling in my body. I thought about it a lot later on, that I should make less signs. I have an idea! I always did put my hands under my buttock when I talked to the other girls. I managed it.

But still other people looked at me, when I talked to someone. Those people could hear my voice well, that I am a deaf girl. I didn't mind it so much. I was not upset that everyone looked at me.

Many deaf children often went to the bar for the contact with the other people. I did not agree with that at all because there the music was often too loud. That is why many hearing people had difficulty in understanding from the deaf children.

I have experienced it. In the bar I often had to talk more loudly to my friend. Yet my friend had difficulty in understanding me. I did not often go to the bar with my friend. I did not like it at all. I would much rather to the club than to the bar. In the club I could easy contact with the other girls from the club. I do have a club. It was an Athletics club.

Two boys asked my friend if I could talk well. My friend said to me: 'These boys cannot believe that you can talk well'. I said to two boys: 'Of course I can talk well. My name is Mattie'. They were stupefied. Many deaf children wait till the hearing children talk to them. I thought these deaf children were very stupid. They perhaps thought that we made a lot of signs or we could not talk. I always did talk *first* to the hearing children.

If I did not understand these children well, I had to say to the hearing children: 'You had to articulate well, then I could follow you well'. The hearing children had to know!

End!

Appendix III

Deaf Children Who Cannot Learn to Speak

NB. Literature: Calon (1950), Prick and Waals (1958–1970), Dekaban (1959), Luchsinger and Arnold (1970), Callens (1974), Ansink (1976).

NB. This is an introduction for those who are insufficiently acquainted with neurology, especially the parents of deaf children.

1. HEARING CHILDREN OF NORMAL INTELLIGENCE, WHO CANNOT LEARN TO SPEAK.

a. Eupraxia and the Integration of Senses.

Can everyone able to eat, also learn to speak?
Some years ago I stayed overnight in Mons (Belgium). It was very quiet in the small hotel. I was the only guest that night. There was a young man in the bar, about 20 years old. He looked intelligent but did not speak a word. He did smile kindly when I tried to talk to him. A bit later I asked the hotel-owner who this boy was, as I was curious to know whether he was perhaps a deaf boy. The hotel-owner told me then, not without tears, that the boy was his son. He was not deaf, heard everything. Following an accident with his motor-bike, he had lost all speech. This had happened 18 months previously. In order to avoid a milk-cart he had crashed sideways into a car which was travelling in the opposite direction. He was unconscious when he was taken to hospital and when he regained consciousness he was unable to speak. He was operated on but to no avail. He had had speech-lessons for more than a year, this too without any success.
There was nothing wrong with his jaws, tongue, uvula and throat and he could eat and chew normally. He could also shout 'aah', or 'eh', but could not speak any words, not even 'boo', or bah'. How can this be?
'Learning' means physiologically: 'organizing brain-programmes'.
Our lips, jaws, tongue, uvula and throat are both 'eating-articulators' and 'speech-articulators'. When I chew, my brain, nerves and muscles which are needed for the chewing movement are at work. When I eat a piece of meat I chew differently than when I eat rice pudding. When I suck a sweet I 'articulate' differently than when drinking lemonade. We have learnt these different eating movements. A newly born baby can suck the milk from the mother's breast straight away. When the mother rests the baby's head against her breast the child rounds his lips *of his own accord*, takes the nipple in his mouth and starts to suck. . . . He does not have to be taught; this happens of its own accord, like a reflex, instinctively. Later he *learns* to drink from a cup; this is only partly a natural process. Even later he learns to eat his cereal from a spoon. It is sufficiently known that taking solid food has to be entirely *learned*. There is no child who can do it of his own accord. It sometimes happens that a young deaf child of three or four years of age arrives at our institute and has not yet learned to take solid food. The mother may have been feeding him on cereal only and may not have known how to teach such a deaf child to

294

eat a sandwich, or potatoes, or meat, etc. What happens when a child learns this? His brain is being 'programmed'.

NB. One also says, especially in olden times, 'engrammed', meaning 'inscribed'. The Greek word 'gramma' means: that which is written. 'En' means: in. 'Pro' means: before. Consequently 'programme' means: written down beforehand (also: written down openly). We can illustrate this as follows (the lines are not meant just anatomically):

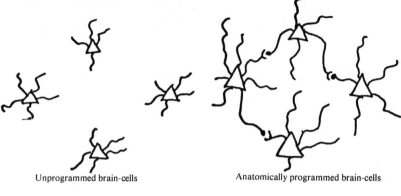

Unprogrammed brain-cells   Anatomically programmed brain-cells

Biochemically programmed brain-cells

One can see that the unprogrammed brain-cells lie together more or less detached. When the brain-cells are programmed, they are interconnected, *integrated*. Together they become a programme, in much the same way as we build a programme into a computer for adding or subtracting, multiplying, dividing, extracting roots, calculating averages, etc. etc.

When a child learns to eat solid food, certain parts of his brain are programmed for a specific behaviour pattern. The better these brain-groups are programmed, the more quickly the child learns to eat.

I have given the brain-cells in the drawing a *pyramid*-shape. These are the movement-cells. Other brain-cells, for example for hearing or seeing or feeling, and for movement-control etc. have different shapes. Naturally these other brain-areas also play a part in the eating-programme. The child *feels* and *tastes* the food in his mouth, *smells* it, *hears* himself chew, *sees* the food beforehand, etc. Consequently

295

learning to eat easily, requires quite a lot of programming of the brain. This programming includes an integration of senses, i.e. intermodal integration. Thus:

Physiologically, 'learning' means: organizing brain-programmes.

When this motor-programming runs smoothly, we call this *'eupraxia'* (dexterity, adroitness). This eupraxia is very strongly connected with eurhythmia, and with the control of the body-scheme (i.e. right, left, under, above, before, behind) and the related positions of the environment. – When this programming is disturbed, we speak of dyspraxia, or even of apraxia, i.e. absence of 'praxia'.
When the 'senses-integration-programming' does not run smoothly, we speak of *intermodal integration* disturbance(s).

b. Eupraxia for Speech and Eupraxia for Eating. Apraxia and Aphasia.

When we speak we use the same articulators as for eating, but this time as speech-articulators. Speaking is not the same as eating. When I eat, I have something in my mouth on which I work. I keep the trachea closed and the gullet open. When I eat, I move the food from the outside to the inside. When I speak, however, I keep the trachea open: I breathe forward and give voice. I have nothing in my mouth on which I work, and articulate forward, to someone who is listening to me. The movements are aimed at producing voice and sounds in many forms.
When, in order to speak, I use my breath, my vocal cords, uvula, tongue, jaws and lips, these speech articulators are guided by programmes in my brain, in *places different* to the ones for the eating-programmes. The programmes for eating are mainly situated under the cerebral cortex, they are sub-cortical (sub = under, cortex = outer grey matter of brain). These sub-cortical brain-areas start to develop before the child is able to speak. So they should, otherwise the child would die. They are more protected, deeper inside the brain, so that they cannot be damaged as easily in an accident. – Let us call the brain-areas for speech, the 'speech-brain-cells', those for eating the 'eating-brain-cells'.
In the case of the youth in the Belgian hotel, the 'speech-brain-cells' were damaged, but not the 'eating-brain-cells'. Therefore he could still eat well, but no longer speak. The 'speech-brain-cells' are more vulnerable than the 'eating-brain-cells', since they lie at the top of the brain, inside the cortex. When someone bumps his head, they are more easily damaged than the 'eating-brain-cells'.
This lacking programming within the 'speech-brain-cells', however, may be *congenital* and/or *prelingual* in some children. It can happen in different degrees from an only slight difficulty through a heavy barrier. When the difficulty is slight, most normally hearing children (and adults) can compensate by their hearing: their *dyspraxia* will not result dysphasia. But if that hearing is impaired, especially when their auditory memory is too short, difficulties in speech may appear: dyspraxia and even apraxia of speech, involving dysgrammaticism. We can term this a special kind of congenital and/or prelingual motor *dysphasia*, or even *aphasia* in heavy cases. – The youth in the Belgian hotel had a *postlingual* apraxia of speech, again a type of motor-aphasia, in the sense of a *loss* of speech by brain damage.

c. Difficulties Both with Eating and Speaking.

It may happen that the muscles of the articulators are *paralysed*, for instance the jaw-muscles. In such a case the brain is in order, but the muscles are not. We say then that there is a peripheral disorder and not a central one. When someone has a paralysed jaw, he has difficulty in learning both to eat and to speak.
It may happen that following an accident both the 'speech' and the 'eating-brain-cells' are damaged.

296

This is of course very serious, even to the extent of the patient only being kept alive by artificial feeding. Some other disorders may occur in the brain. It may happen that the cortical motor-*pyramid*-cells do not co-operate properly, especially with respect to the opposing muscles (the antagonists). These patients show spasmodic, jerky movements. This is called *spasm* ('rigidity'). Even when they hear normally they experience difficulty in speaking. For example they cannot say 'mama', or 'lamb', or 'dance': these become for instance 'p'a'p' ' or 't'a'p' ' of 't'a't' '. Eating is less difficult, but one often sees them spill food, eat slowly, sometimes they may slaver etc.

It may occur that the *controlling cells* do not work properly. These are then the 'extra-pyramidal' cells, i.e. the movement-cells outside the pyramid-cells with the extra-pyramidal nerve-paths. These cells particularly see to it that the movements of our limbs are fluent and even: when the pyramid-cells change over, our limbs go on moving smoothly. One could compare this with the effect a fly-wheel has on a motor. These brain-cells are situated sub-cortically. When they are disturbed, the patients show continuous small jerky (so called 'choreiform') and/or fluent, 'round' movements. They cannot sit still or keep their arms and legs still. The body moves continuously. Only when they are asleep their body is still. This is called *athetosis* (unsteady movements). These patients also have difficulties with speaking and eating.

Spasm and/or athetosis can be so serious that speech is no longer possible. The patient can hear everything and can usually understand well, but he cannot speak himself. They can hardly write either. They can, however, learn to use a typewriter. There are portable electronic typewriters for these patients.

d. Integration Difficulties.

We speak now of difficulties of the integration of senses: so-called difficulties in 'intermodal integration'.

They are seldom so serious that speech becomes insufficient. Typical of these children is that they do speak, but that this has insufficient content. In such cases we speak of *echolalia*, another kind of 'aphasia'. An example:

Doctor: 'What is your name?'
Child: 'What is your name?'
Doctor: 'Don't you know what your name is?'
Child: . . . 'What is your name?'

So the child only repeats, not answering but only acting like a parrot. Such a child does not attain spoken *language*. What is happening here? The words have very little or no meaning. The child finds it difficult to speak spontaneously. He has trouble in finding the correct words, just as he has trouble in interpreting the meanings of the words. These children often are rather silent, not because they cannot speak, but because speech has no meaning enough. This is called *asymbolism* (i.e. the words heard do not become symbols). In less heavy cases we speak of '*dyssymbolism*'. It happens because the heard impressions do not integrate smoothly enough with the rest of the brain, thus with experiences and feelings.

An example: I see a match-box. At the same time I can, *in my imagination*, feel this box, smell it, and also open it and take out a match, etc. All this is integrated, has become one entirety in my notion of the match-box, so in my mind.

In some people this integration is impeded. It does not run smoothly and is too slow. These are the people with many symbolic mistakes, i.e. who have difficulty in finding the right words, and also in interpreting the meanings of the words correctly. Some researches make one suspect that this is to a greater or lesser extent the case in about 20% of normally hearing people. It seldom becomes so serious, however, that an echolalic behaviour with asymbolism (for spoken words) develops.

Another aspect of intermodal integration disability is the lack of integration of the graphic and auditory-articulatory aspects of words. These children (and even adults) make reading mistakes, e.g.

297

reading 'when' for where, 'raining' for ramming or training, and so on, causing a lot of misunderstandings: 'integrative dyslexia', sometimes even 'alexia'. They experience the same difficulty in writing down what they speak. E.g. the child says correctly 'raining', but cannot write it, or even after much treatment still writes earning or rianing and so on: 'integrative dysgraphia'. If this disturbance is not treated in time, it results in the long run into a language disorder, i.e. a lack of memory for words and linguistic structures, lack of linguistic control, poor vocabulary and so on. Then the speech of these children, and even of adults, may stay too primitive.

It may happen in some exceptionally heavy cases, that the eye-hand-coordination is disturbed, i.e. resulting into another type of dyspraxia and dysgraphia.

The combination of dyspraxia and intermodal integration disturbance may result into discalculia: a lack of control of the quantitative structure of experience, thus a lack of seeing the correct numbers of objects and of relating them to each other, a lack of detecting the right mathematical coding and of working up of a quantitative problem. E.g. this problem 'If a cigarette costs 7 cents, how much will cost 3 cigarettes?' is solved as 'Ten cents': the child has added instead of multiplying, not finding the right quantitative working up.

e. Causes?

We quoted one cause: the motorcycle-accident. Other *postnatal* causes are: meningitis, mumps, and so on.

There are many more, first *peri-natal* ones. When a child is born, it must breathe. This it has not done in the mother's womb. This first breathing is a cry (a birth-cry). If this cry holds off, for perhaps a quarter or half an hour, even this can be dangerous, because the brain is starved of enough oxygen. This lack of oxygen is called anoxia, and causes many of the brain cells to die. This may have serious consequences: deafness, blindness, spasm, athetosis, integrative disorders, emotional irregularities etc. The same with immaturity at birth.

Other dangerous causes are *prenatal*, e.g. rubella in the mother during her pregnancy. The rubella virus can penetrate to the child in the mother's womb and nestle itself and grow within the brain of the baby, causing much damage there. Further Rhesus-antagonism (having almost the same effects as anoxia), the mother using drugs, etc.

Heredity is a possible cause too. Then we speak of *congenital* brain-defects.

2. DEAF CHILDREN

We have seen that there are normally hearing people who cannot, or if so only with difficulty, learn to speak because of disorders. When such disorders occur in deaf children, learning to speak is impeded, sometimes to such an extent that they cannot (or insufficiently) learn to speak. This will sooner be the case in deaf children than in hearing children, because hearing people can make up their deficiency more easily with their hearing. Deaf children cannot. The more there is residual hearing, however, the better they can make up. A deaf child with a Fletcher-index of 90–95 dB. can do it more easily than a deaf child with 110 and more dB. loss. Very much depends here upon the ability of the teacher. An expert zealous teacher will grow good oral communication notwithstanding even heavy disorders. An unexperienced and/or lazy teacher will not. There are several other retarding factors: non cooperating parents, lack of early hometraining, a non-oral environment, unqualified educators, too late a diagnosis, emotional disturbances of the child itself, and so on. – Our Institute at St. Michielsgestel, organized in several separate pavilions and departments in order to treat every child according to its individual abilities, takes in all kinds of deaf children, from deaf imbeciles through highly intelligent ones, from children with heavy learning disabilities through highly gifted ones. Only 3% of these cannot learn to communicate orally sufficiently, *if* treated in time.

We shall discuss a few of the difficulties mentioned above.

298

/

a. Eupraxia for Speech. Dysphasia. Aphasia.

Disorder in the speech-controlling part of the brain, the programming of the pyramid cells for speech-movements results dys- or a-phasia. When this programming runs smoothly, we call this eupraxia (see above). The child uses his articulators fluently, he can find and co-ordinate them quickly, and into the bargain, has a nice rhythm. If the children are treated well, by expert speech-therapists, they attain nice, fluent speech, speech-reading and listening.

If this programming runs less smoothly (which in about 30% of the deaf children becomes clearly noticeable), difficulties arise, usually only slight ones. More speech-lessons are required and extra expertise is required from the speech-therapists. In such cases we speak of *dyspraxia of speech* (i.e. 'indexterity' of speech, they are 'indexterous speakers') a form of *motor-dysphasia*. Fortunately these children usually have very good discrimination and memories for simultaneously presented visual data, e.g. series of pictures, geometric figures and so on. So they remember very well what they have seen simultaneously, for example the written word. From a very early age, 2 to 3 years, they can usually learn to distinguish and remember written words quickly. They can be trained to translate these written words into speech. For example they can hardly repeat a word like 'table': it becomes taab, tlaab, laabtel, etc. They mix up the phonemes. They learn to look well at the written word and in this way learn to speak the word correctly. The written word supports the programming of their brain. In this way they can achieve proper speech, to that extent that they *talk* among themselves and do not need sign language or finger-spelling. This applies to 15% of the deaf children. For some children, however, about 10%, difficulties are such that they need very special care: even more expert speech-lessons, small classes and groups etc. in a special department. But they succeed, and they even succeed very well.

About 3–4% of our deaf children experience that much difficulty that particular measures have to be taken. For them our institute has erected another separate department, in 'Eikenheuvel' at Vught, a village very near to St. Michielsgestel. Special care is taken that these children, with normal intelligence, do not arrive at sign-language, as then they would hardly be able to get as far as reading. This would be a pity. At 'Eikenheuvel' they learn to speak through finger-spelling. Finger-spelling is a kind of writing in the air. They especially learn a lot of written language. For this they use not only a 'group hearing aid', but a 'graphic group aid' too by means of Telex-apparatuses. – The vast majority of these children learn to speak quite well in this way, some even very well. Only lipreading and hearing remain stumbling-blocks. Methods have been found to improve these as well, however, among others things by inviting the children to listen to their own speech, to understand it, and also to learn to lipread from themselves. Naturally special equipment is needed. What I have said above, applies particularly to those children who had the correct treatment from an early age, and who had the right home-training. Nearly half of our children at 'Eikenheuvel' come from other institutions, where they often received incorrect treatment, usually because one did not detect or understand their handicap in time. The later a child starts school and the more incorrect the early approach, the more difficult it becomes to put the child right again.

Then there are about 2% of deaf children who will never achieve sufficient speech, even assuming the best of treatment. In such cases we speak of *apraxia of speech*, i.e. a kind of *aphasia*. Even then we need not feel despondent, however, certainly not if the intelligence level is quite good. Cases are known of deaf people who were not able to learn to speak, and yet through reading and writing attained a high degree of development. There are several of these cases at 'Eikenheuvel'.

b. Paralysis, Spasm and Athetosis.

We have discussed these disorders sufficiently above.

c. Integration-dyslexia and Dyssymbolism.

We will find here mainly the same difficulties as with hearing children mentioned above under d.
At least 20% of the deaf children experience difficulty in integrating the written and the spoken image.
It may happen that the deaf child repeats a word correctly especially when there are nice hearing remnants (mouth → mouth, ear → ear), and also copies a word correctly (see → see), but does not read it or write it down correctly (see → mouth and mouth → see). The child repeats e.g. 'ball' nicely, but when you ask him to write it down, he cannot manage it and he writes bll, or aa, or something else. The transfer from mouth-image to written image does not run correctly. This is a kind of dysgraphia as a result of intermodal integration disability.
When 'ball' is written down, they read 'roll', or 'though' instead of 'thorough', or 'calendar, instead of 'colander'.
We call this *integration-dyslexia* (dyslexia means defective reading). One should pay attention to this from an early age, otherwise these children will never get as far as reading. The L(isten) R(ead) S(peak) method of the Ewings will be very fertile, especially for these children.
Usually this integration-disorder will go hand in hand with severe dyspraxia or apraxia (i.e. dysphasia or aphasia), sometimes even with severe spasm or athetosis. Perhaps we should say that especially those dyspraxic deaf children (no. a) who *also* have an integration-disorder, both in a rather heavy degree, need finger-spelling, in order to fill the gap: speech-writing and the other way round. It becomes then: finger-spelling-speech-writing (reading)-finger-spelling-speech.

These same children nearly always have difficulty in attaching the correct meanings to words too, thus in finding words and interpreting them. For example a child may have thoroughly learned the names of colours. Now you ask him: 'William, look for a green colour!'. The child will point to orange or yellow. He may call purple, brown and brown, red, etc. He mixes up the names. The same happens with furniture, figures etc. This is called *dyssymbolism* (defective symbol-awareness or symbolising function). Usually the defect is only slight. If one treats the child in the right way, he will conquer this difficulty and one will not notice it any more in later school-years. But oh dear, if one does not do this! ...
In *rare* cases (perhaps 1% of the deaf children) the disorder is so great that words have no meaning to the child. He does not understand words, and forgets them quite soon etc. etc. He does not use words either when he wants something, not even in finger-spelling, or he finger-spells incorrectly. He will use signs however! He can remember them better, because they more or less *picture* what he means: for example roll, ball etc. Such a child has an *asymbolism for words*. All one can do is to teach the child signs, otherwise he would not be able to converse with other people, which is a necessity. In such a case the parents, brothers and sisters should learn the sign-language as well.

d. A Very Bad Memory.

An example. Some years ago a 20-year old deaf girl and her parents visited our institute. She had formerly been refused admittance to our institute, because she was termed 'mentally retarded' and 'not educable'. The parents hoped that now we would be able to teach the girl, because the methods had been improved considerably. They told us: 'Just see, how nice her embroidery-work is! She cannot possibly be retarded!' I was asked to examine the child. Her insight as such was indeed not too bad, but her memory was extremely bad. She could hardly remember anything. One tried nevertheless to teach her individually, for two years. Without any success though; the girl subsequently attained no language after these two years, and signs were even too difficult for her.
There are cases of deaf children (sometimes hearing ones too) who have such bad memories, that *verbal language* (speech, lipreading, soundperception, writing, reading, finger-spelling) is not possible. The only possibility which remains is the teaching of signs, hoping that at least that will be successful.

e. Too Low an Intelligence.

A few examples:

a. A 3-year old child playing with a doll. She puts a sock on the doll's hand. She has not understood that the sock belongs on a foot. She does not understand the *essence* of the sock, and confuses this with 'putting on', something *incidental*.

b. A 4-year old child has learned to wash his hands after he has been to the toilet. One child first went to wash his hands and then went to the toilet! He obviously had not understood why he has to wash his hands. The *essence* of washing his hands has escaped him.

c. There is a card on the cupboard doorknob. The word 'cupboard' is written on it. A seven-year old child points to a nice knob of another door, which looks very much like the first one, and says: 'Cupboard!', meaning that the knob is called 'cupboard'! He has not understood the *essence* and confuses this with the *incidental*.

d. A 13-year old child puts a used stamp on a letter. He has not understood the purpose of the stamp. The *essence* of the stamp has escaped him. After all the stamp is only *incidental*, the essence is paying for the transport, hence the buying of a new stamp.

'Intelligence' means: observing quickly what is essential and what is incidental.

Some deaf children possess so little intelligence that they hardly understand the meaning of the word 'cupboard'. They confuse it with the knob, or with the room in which the cupboard is standing, or with the door, etc. This defect may be so serious that they cannot really learn a *verbal language*, because their *intelligence* is *sub-normal*. These children may learn to speak a few words, which, however, do not give them the possibility to converse with others. These children have to learn signs.

SUMMARY.

About 3% of the deaf children can learn to speak only insufficiently, namely:

a. Some children with severe apraxia of speech. If intelligence and memory are normal, they can be taught to finger-spell, read and write. The main aim of their education is to get them to read.

b. Some children are only able to learn signs, namely:
– when they suffer from asymbolism for words;
– when they have too bad a memory for words;
– when their intelligence is sub-normal.

A lot depends on the expertise and the dedication of the teaching staff. If they lack the necessary expertise and also the necessary perseverance, the percentage of deaf children who achieve only insufficient speech will become higher. A lot also depends on the age, at which a correct treatment commenced, on the parents' cooperation, and on the child's diligence. If from an early age this cooperation was missing, the percentage will again become higher.

See 'Diagnostic Testing of Deaf Children', in preparation.

SURVEY OF LEARNING DISABILITIES
IN DEAF CHILDREN

1. A weak memory ———————— motor-(primary) dysgraphia

2. Dyspraxia   a kind of
   dysphasia ———————— dyscalculia

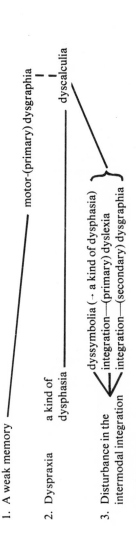

3. Disturbance in the
   intermodal integration

   dyssymbolia (→ a kind of dysphasia)
   integration—(primary) dyslexia
   integration—(secondary) dysgraphia

4. Exceptional:
   a. Disturbance in the visual figure-background perception,
      a kind of visual dysgnosia ———— perception—(primary) dyslexia

   b. Disturbance in the auditory figure-background perception,
      a kind of auditory dysgnosia ———— perception—(primary) dysgraphia

Literature

Abernathy, E. R. An historical sketch of the manual alphabet. American Annals of the Deaf, 1959, pp. 232–240.

Aborn, M., Rubenstein, H. and Sterling, T. D. Sources of contextual constraint upon words in sentences. J. experimental Psychology 1959 (57), pp. 171–180.

Allen, K. E., Henke, L. B., Harris, Fl., Baer, D. M. and Reynolds, N. J. Control of hyperactivity by social reinforcement of attending behaviour. Journal of Educational Psychology, 1967, Vol. 58, (4), pp. 231–237.

Anon. The Older Deaf Child. Rotterdam, 1973.

Ashby, W. R. An Introduction to Cybernetics. London, 1965.

D'Audney, W. W. The Soviet search and research for new methods in deaf education. American Annals of the Deaf, 1975, 120, (1), pp. 42–47.

Ausubel, D. P. The Psychology of Meaningful Verbal Learning. London, 1963.

— Symbolization and symbolic thought: Response to Furth. Child Development, 1968 (39), pp. 997–1001.

Babbini, B. E. I. Manual communication. Finger spelling and the language of signs. A course of study outline for *Instructors,* Institute for Research on Exceptional Children, University of Illinois, Urbana 1971; II Idem for Students, 1971.

Bach, E. An Introduction to Transformational Grammars. New York, 1964.

Baker, H. J. and Leland, B. Detroit Test of Learning Aptitude. University of Detroit, Detroit, 1959.

Bakker, J. Stillees-test 3e–4e lj. L.S. Nijmegen, 1966.

Balow, I. H. and Brill, R. G. An evaluation of reading and academic achievement levels of 16 graduating classes of the California School for the Deaf, Riverside. Volta Review 1975, pp. 255–266.

Barbizet, J. A. Human Memory and Its Pathology. London, 1970.

Barczi, G. Hörerwecken und Hörerziehen. Budapest, 1933.

Barron, F. Creativity and Personal Freedom. Princeton, N.J., 1968.

— Creative Person and Creative Process. New York, 1969.

Barry, K. The Barry System: a System of Objective Language Teaching. Colorado Springs 1893, 1914.

Barthès, R. Elements of Semiology. London, 1967.

Bayne, Sh. Vibro-tactile Thresholds in Pure Tone Audiometry. Unpubl. M. thesis Manchester University. Manchester, 1968.

Beaver, A. P. The Imitation of Social Contacts by Pre-school Children. Child Developm. Monographs no. 7, Teacher's College, Columbia University. New York, 1932.

Becker, K. F. Organismus der Sprache. Frankfurt am Main, 1841.

Bell, Alex. Graham. Upon a method of teaching language to a very young congenitally deaf child. American Annals of the Deaf, 1883 pp. 124–139.

Bellugi, U. Development of language in the normal child, in McLean et al. 1973 pp. 33–51.

303

Bellugi, U. and Fisher, S. A comparison of sign language and spoken language. Cognition, 1972, (1), pp. 173–200.

Bellugi, U. and Klima, E. S. The roots of language in the sign talk of the deaf. Psychology Today 1972 (6), pp. 61–64.

Bellugi, U. and Siple, P. Remembering with and without words, in Problèmes actuelles de psycholinguistique, Colloque C.N.R.S. Paris, 1971.

Bender, R. E. The Conquest of Deafness. Cleveland, 1970.

Benton, A. L. Der Benton-Test. Deutsche Bearbeitung von O. Spreen. 1958, 2d. Basel, 1968.

Berg, D. M. Vanden. The Written Language of Deaf Children. Wellington, 1971.

Berko, J. The child's learning of English morphology, Word 1958 (14), pp. 150–177.

Bergès, J. and Lézine, I. The Imitation of Gestures. A Technique for Studying the Body Schema and Praxis of Children 3 to 6 (and 6 to 10) Years of Age. Paris, 1963, London, 1965.

Berlyne, D. E. Structure and Direction in Thinking. New York, 1965.

Bern personal information, 1950.

Bernstein, B. Social structure, language and learning, in Cecco, 1967, pp. 167–181.

— Class, Codes and Control. London, 1971.

Bieri, E. Die Erscheinungsformen der Sprache und ihre Auswertung im Taubstummen-unterricht. International Congress on the Care of the deafmute, Groningen, 1950, pp. 53–61.

Blackwell, P. M. The application of transformational linguistics to teaching deaf children. Proceedings of the International Congres on the Education of the Deaf, Stockholm 1970, pp. 305–308.

— Language Curriculum. Rhode Island School for the Deaf, 520 Hope Street, Prov., Rhode Island, 02906, 1971.

Bladergroen, W. J. Lichamelijke en geestelijke ontwikkeling van het kind. Amsterdam, 1969.

Blair, F. X. A study of the visual memory of deaf and hearing children. American Annals of the Deaf, 1957, p. 102, pp. 254–263.

Blea, W. A Photographic Study of the Eye Movements of Profoundly Deaf Children during the Process of Reading. University of Kansas, Ed. D., 1967.

Blevins, B. The Myth of 'Total Communication'. Am. Org. for the Ed. of the Hearing impaired, 1972, pp. 2–6.

Bloom, L. Why not pivot-grammar? Journal of Speech and Hearing Disorders, 1971, pp. 40–50.

Bloomfield, L. Language. New York, 1926, 1933.

Boatner, E. B. and Gates, R. The Need of a Realistic Approach to the Education of the Deaf. Calif. Association of teachers of the deaf and hard of hearing and the Calif. Association of the deaf, Nov. 6, 1965.

Bode, L. Communication of agent, object and indirect object in signed and spoken languages. Perception and Motor Skills, 1974, (39), pp. 1151–1158.

Bolton, B. A factor analytic study of communication skills and non-verbal abilities of deaf rehabilitation clients. Multivariate Behaviour Research, 1971, 6, pp. 485–501.

Boomer, D. S. Hesitation and grammatical encoding. Language and Speech, 1965, pp. 148–158.

Boomer, D. S. and Dittman, A. Hesitation pauses and juncture pauses in speech. Language and Speech, 1962, pp. 215–220.

Bornstein, H. Reading the Manual Alphabet: a Research Program for Developing a Filmed Program for Teaching the Manual Alphabet. Washington D.C., Gallaudet College, 1965.

Börrild, K. Problems in connection with the use of technical equipment in a school for the deaf. Proceedings J. Co. Ed. D. Stockholm 1970, I, pp. 60–63.

Braine, M. D. S. The ontogeny of English phrase structure: the first phrase. Language, 1963, pp. 1–13.

— On learning the grammatical order of words. Psychol. Review, 1963, pp. 323–348.

Braine, R. On the basis of phrase structure: a reply to Bever, Fodor and Weksel. Psych. Review, 1965, p. 483–492.

Brannon, J. B. Linguistic word classes in the spoken language of normal, hard-of-hearing and deaf children. Journal of Speech and Hearing Research, 1968, pp. 279–287.

Brannon, J. B. and Murry, Th. The spoken syntax of normal, hard of hearing and deaf children. Journal of Speech and Hearing Research, 1966, pp. 604–610.

Brazel, K. The Influence of Early Language and Communication Environments on the Development of Language in Deaf Children. University of Illinois, Ph.D. Thesis, Dept. of Education, Urbana, 1975.

Brill, R. G. and Orman, J. N. An experiment in the training of deaf children in memory for sentences. American Annals of the Deaf, 1953, pp. 270–279.

Brinke, J. S. ten. Onafhankelijke grootheden in het taalgebruik. Groningen, 1963.

Britton, J. Language and Learning. London, 1970.

Brodbeck, A. J. and Irwin, O. C. The speech behaviour of infants without families. Child Development, 1946 (17), pp. 145–156.

Bronowski, J. S. and Bellugi, U. Language, name and concept. Science 1970, p. 168, 699ff.

Brown, Ch. T. Introductory Study of Breathing as an Index of Listening. Speech Monographs, USA, 1962, p. 79–83.

Brown, R. Words and Things. Glencoe Illinois, 1958.

— 'The first sentences of child and chimpanzee', in Psycholinguistics: selected papers. New York, 1970.

Brown, R. and Bellugi, U. Three processes in the child's acquisition of syntax. Harvard Educ. Review, 1964, pp. 131–151.

Brown, R., Cazden, C. and Bellugi, U. The child's grammar from I to III, in Ferguson and Slobin eds. 1973, pp. 295–332.

Brown, R. and Fraser, C. 'The acquisition of syntax', in Cofer and Musgrave (eds.), 1963, pp. 158–197.

Brown, R. and McNeill, D. The 'tip of the tongue' phenomenon. Journal of Verbal Learning and Verbal Behavior, 1966, pp. 325–337.

Brus, B. Th. Schriftelijke opdrachten, Nijmegen, 1965.

— Eén-Minuut-Test. Nijmegen, 1966, 1975.

Bühler, Ch. Praktische kinderpsychologie. Utrecht, 1949.

Bühler, K. Sprachtheorie. Jena, 1934.

Busemann, A. Die Sprache der Jugend als Ausdruck der Entwicklungsrhythmik. Jena, 1925.

Buytendijk, F. J. J. Algemene theorie der menselijke houding en beweging. Utrecht, 1957.

Calon, P. J. A. Over de persoonlijkheidsontwikkeling bij kinderen met aangeboren of vroeg verworven doofheid. Nijmegen, 1950.

Carmel, S. J. International Hand Alphabet Charts. Studio Printing Inc., Rockville, 1975.

Carmichael, L. Child Psychology 2nd ed. New York, 1954.

Carroll, J. B. Language and Thought. New Jersey, 1964.

Carrow, A. M. Linguistic functioning of bilingual and monolingual children. Journal of Speech and Hearing Disorders, USA, 1957, pp. 371–380.

Carterette, E. C. (ed.) 'Brain Function', Vol. III Speech, Language and Communication. Los Angeles, 1966.

Cazden, C. B. Environmental Assistance to the Child's Acquisition of Grammar. Harvard University, 1965.

Cecco, J. P. de (ed.) The Psychology of Language, Thought and Instruction. New York, 1967.

Charrow, V. R. and Fletcher, J. D. English as the Second Language of Deaf Students. Technical Report nr. 208 July 20 1973, Psychology and Education Series, Institute for mathematical studies in the social sciences, Stanford University, Stanford California, 1973.

Chomsky, A. The Acquisition of Syntax in Children from 5–10. M.I.T. Press, Cambridge, U.S.A. Mass, 1969.

Chomsky, N. Syntactic Structure. The Hague, 1957.

— Aspects of the Theory of Syntax. Cambridge, Mass, 1965.

305

— Topics in the Theory of Generative Grammar. The Hague, 1966.
— Language and Mind. New York, 1968.
— The Logical Structure of Linguistic Theory. New York and London, 1975.
Clarke School. 'Word Study', 'Reading', 'Language'. Northampton, Massachusetts, 1972.
Cobb, S. Borderland of Psychiatry. Cambridge, Harvard University Press, 1948.
Cofer, Ch. N. (ed.) Verbal Learning and Verbal Behavior. New York, 1961.
Cofer, Ch. N. and Musgrave, B. S. (eds.) Verbal Behavior and Learning. New York, 1963.
Cohen, A. Versprekingen als verklappers van het proces van spreken en verstaan. Instituut voor Perceptie-onderzoek, Eindhoven, 1965. Separaat 3593.
Conrad, R. Acoustic confusions in immediate memory. Brit. Journal of Psychology, 1964, pp. 75–84.
— Short-term memory processes in the deaf. British Journal of Psychology 1970 (61). pp. 179–195.
— 'Speech and reading', in: Kavanagh and Mattingley (eds.). 1972.
— Internal speech in profoundly deaf children. The Teacher of the Deaf 1973, pp. 384–389.
Conrad, R. and Rusch, M. L. On the nature of short term memory encoding by the deaf. Journal of Speech and Hearing Disorders, 1965, pp. 336–343.
Cornett, R. O. Cued Speech. American Annals of the deaf, 1967, pp. 3–13.
— Cued Speech Parent Training and Follow-up Program. Bureau Education for handicapped, Washington D.C., 1972.
Corson, H. J. Comparing Deaf Children of Oral Deaf Parents and Parents Using Manual Communication with Deaf Children of Hearing Parents on Academic, Social and Communicative Functioning. University of Cincinnati, Cincinnati, Doctoral Dissertation, Cincinnati Ohio, 1973.
Court, A. De La. De meest voorkomende woorden in het Nederlands, Groningen, 1937.
Craig, H. B. A sociometric investigation of the self-concept of the deaf child. American Annals of the deaf, 1965, pp. 456–478.
Craig, W. N. Effects of preschool training on the development of reading and lipreading skills of deaf children. American Annals of the Deaf 1964, pp. 280–296.
Craig, W. N. and Collins, J. L. Communication Patterns in Classes for Deaf Students. Research Report: U.S. Office of Education, Project no. 7–(0640), Washington D.C., 1969.
Cromer, R. F. Children are nice to understand: surface structure clues for the recovery of a deep structure. British Journal of Psychology 6, (3), 1970, pp. 397–408.
Crouter, A. L. E. The Organisation and Methods of the Pennsylvania Institution for the Deaf and Dumb. Pennsylvania, 1907.
— The Possibilities of Oral Methods in the Instruction of the Deaf: Lecture and Discussion. Nineteenth Meeting of the Convention of American instructors of the deaf, Proceedings, 1911, pp. 138–153.

Dale, D. M. C. Applied Audiology for Children. Springfield, Illinois, USA, 1967.
— The L.R.S.-method. The Teacher of the Deaf, 1966, p. 276–280.
— Deaf Children at Home and at School. London, 1967, 2nd 1968.
— Language Development in Deaf and Partially Hearing Children. Springfield, Illinois, 1974.
Dalgarno, G. Didascalocophus, or the deaf and dumb man's Tutor, Oxford 1680. Reprint in American Annals of the Deaf, 1864, pp. 14–64.
Davis. Hall. Guide for the classification and evaluation of hearing handicap in relation to the international audiometric zero. Trans. Amer. Acad. Ophthalmol. Otolaryngol., 1965, p. 740–751.
Dawson, E. H. An Experiment to Investigate the Optimal use of Finger-spelling in a Teacher/Learning Classroom Situation. The Teacher of the Deaf, 1976, pp. 402–411.
Décroly, O. and Dégany, J. Contribution à la pédagogie de la lecture et de l'écriture. Archives de Psychologie, Brussels, 1907, pp. 308–334.
Derwing, B. L. Transformational Grammar as a Theory of Language Acquisition. Cambridge, U.S.A., 1973.
DiCarlo, L. M. Much ado about the obvious. Volta Review 1966, pp. 269–273.

Dik, J. and Kooy, J. G. Beginselen der algemene taalwetenschap. Nijmegen, 1970.

Dinneen, F. P. An Introduction to General Linguistics. New York, 1967.

Dixon, T. and Horton, D. (eds.) Verbal Behavior Theory and Its Relation to S-R-theory. Englewood Cliffs, N.J., 1968.

Dongen, Br. Ach. v. Tussen Aa en P. Fonetiek en Articulatiecursus. Sint Michielsgestel, 1957, 2nd. 1962.

Driel Sr. Theresia van. De toepassing van de Belgische Methode in onze school. St. Michielsgestel, 1934.

— Handleiding voor de beginnende doofstommenonderwijzer. St. Michielsgestel, 1934.

— personal information, 1964.

Durkin, D. Teaching Young Children to Read. Boston, 1972.

— A six year study of children who learned to read in school at the age of four. Reading Res. Quarterly 1974–1975, pp. 9–61.

Durost, W. N. (ed.) Metropolitan Achievement Test. New York, 1959.

Dijk, J. van and Uden, A. M. J. van. Problems of communication in deaf children. The Teacher of the Deaf, 1976, pp. 70–90.

Dijk, J. van and Ven, Th. van de. Dove dysfatische kinderen. St. Michielsgestel, 1973.

Edfeldt, A. W. Silent Speech and Silent Reading. Chicago Press, 1960.

Eggermont, J. Taalverwerving bij een groep dove kinderen. Groningen, 1964.

Eisenson, J. Aphasia in Children. London, 1972.

Ellis, J. Toward a General Comparative Linguistics. The Hague, 1966.

Entwisle, D. R. Form class and children's word associations. Journal of Verbal Learning and Verbal Behaviour, 1966, (5), pp. 558–565.

— Word associations of Young Children. Baltimore, 1966.

Epstein, A. G. Auditory memory span for language. Folia Phoniatrica, Basel, 1964, (16), pp. 271–289.

Erber, N. P. and Cramer, K. D. Vibrotactile recognition of sentences. Amer. Annals of the Deaf, 1974, pp. 716–720.

Ervin, S. M. Learning and recall in bilinguals. American Journal of Psychology, 1961, pp. 446–451.

— Changes with age in verbal determinants of word association. Am. J. of Psychology, 1961, pp. 361–372.

— Correlates of associative frequency. J. Verbal Learning and Verbal Behavior 1962/1963, pp. 422–431.

— and Osgood, C. E. Psycholinguistics: a survey of theory and research problems. Journal of Abnormal and Social Psychology, 1954, pp. 139–149.

Ervin-Tripp, S. An analysis of the interaction of language, topic and listener. American Anthropologist, 1964, pp. 86–102.

Ewing, A. W. G. Aphasia in Children. London, 1930, New York, 1967.

— (ed.) The Modern Educational Treatment of Deafness. Manchester University Press, Manchester, 1960.

Ewing, A. W. G. and Ewing, E. C. Teaching Deaf Children to Talk. Manchester, 1964.

Ewing, A. W. G. and Ewing, E. C. Hearing aids, Lipreading and Clear Speech. Manchester, 1967.

Ewing, A. W. G. and Ewing, I. R. The Handicap of Deafness. London, 1938.

Ewing, A. W. G. and Stanton, D. A. G. A study of children with defective hearing. The Teacher of the Deaf, 1942, pp. 127–134, 1943, pp. 3–8, 26–30, 56–59.

Ewing, I. R. and Ewing, A. W. G. Deafness in infancy and early childhood. The Journal of Lar. and Ot., London, 1943, pp. 203–226.

Ewing, I. R. and Ewing, A. W. G. Speech and the Deaf Child. Manchester, 1954.

Ewing, I. R. and Ewing, A. W. G. Opportunity and the Deaf Child. London, 1947, New opportunities, London, 1958.

Ex, J. Communicatie van gezicht tot gezicht. Nijmegen, 1969.

307

Fant, L. J. Ameslan: An Introduction to American Sign Language. National Association of the Deaf, Silver Spring, 1970.

Farnsworth, P. The Social Psychology of Music. New York, 1958.

Ferguson, C. A. and Slobin, D. J. (eds.) Studies of Child Language Development. New York, 1973.

Ferreiro, E. Les rélations temporelles dans le langage de l'enfant. Librairie Droz, Genève, 1971.

Fisher, C. G. and Florence, A. H. Finger spelling intelligibility. American Annals of the Deaf, 1973, pp. 508–510.

Fitzgerald, E. Straight Language for the Deaf: a System of Instruction for Deaf Children. The Stick Co., Austin, Texas, 1926, 1937.

Flanders, N. A. Analyzing Teaching Behavior. Addison-Wesley Publishing Co., Reading, Massachusetts, 1970.

Flores d'Arcais G.B. and Levelt, W. J. M. Advances in Psycholinguistics. Amsterdam, 1970.

Fodor, J. A. and Bever, T. The psychological reality of linguistic segments. Journal of Verbal Learning and Verbal Behaviour, 1965, pp. 414–420.

Fodor, J. A. and Garrett, M. F. Some syntactic determinants of sentential complexity. Perception and Psychophysics, 1967, pp. 289–296.

Forchhammer, G. On the Necessity of Sure Means of Communication in the Instruction of the Deaf. Copenhagen, 1903.

Forchhammer, G. Taubstummen-pedagogische Abhandlungen. Leipzig, 1930.

Fraiberg, S. H. The Magic Years. New York, 1964, 1969; De magische wereld van het kind (3d). Bussum, 1970.

Francis, W. N. The structure of American English. New York, 1958.

Fraser, C., Bellugi, U. and Brown, G. Control of grammar in imitation, comprehension and production. Journal of Verbal Learning and Verbal Behaviour, 1963, pp. 121–135.

Freunthaller, G. W. Der gegenwärtige Stand der Taubstummheit auf Wiener Boden. Wien, 1932.

— Over de voorschool, spreekmethode, tijdsduur van het onderwijs. Tijdschrift voor doofstommenonderwijs, 1933.

Fries, C. C. The structure of English. New York, 1952.

Frisina, D. R. Speechreading. Proceedings Intern. Congress on the Education of the Deaf. Washington D.C. 1963, pp. 191–207.

Froeschels, E. Über den Parallelismus zwischen Handigkeit und Zungigkeit. Sprachheilarbeit, 1962, pp. 131–133.

Fry, D. B. Duration and intensity as physical correlates of linguistic stress. Journal of the Acoustic Society of America, 1955, p. 765.

— The development of the phonological system in the normal and the deaf child, in Smith and Miller, G. A. The Genesis of Language. New York, 1966, pp. 187–206.

Furth, H. G. Scholastic ability of deaf children and their performance on non-verbal learning tasks. Journal of clinical psychology, 1961, (17), pp. 370–373.

— Visual paired-associates task with deaf and hearing children. Journal of Speech and Hearing Research, 1961, pp. 172–177.

— Thinking Without Language. New York, 1966a.

— A comparison of reading Test Norms of Deaf and hearing children. American Annals of the Deaf, 1966b, pp. 461–462.

— Piaget for Teachers. Prentice Hall, 1970.

— Linguistic deficiency and thinking: research with deaf subjects 1964–1969. Psychological Bulletin 1971, (76), pp. 58–72.

— Deafness and Learning, a Psychological Approach. Belmont, California, 1973.

Furth, H. G. and Milgram, N. A. Labeling and grouping effects in the recall of pictures by children. Child Development, 1973, (44), pp. 511–518.

Furth, H. G. and Youniss, J. Thinking in deaf adolescents: language and formal operations. J. Comm. Dis. 1969, pp. 195–202.

Fusfeld, I. S. Factors in lipreading as determined by the lipreader. American Annals of the Deaf, 1958, p. 229.
— How the deaf communicate—Manual language. American Annals of the Deaf, 1958, pp. 264–282.

Gamelin, P. J. Sentence processing as a function of syntax, short term memory capacity, the meaningfullness of the stimulus and age. Language and Speech, 1971, (14), pp. 115–134.

Gardner, A. R. and Gardner, B. T. Teaching sign language to a chimpanzee. Science, 1969, pp. 664–672.

Gardner, A. R. and Gardner, B. T. Comparing the Early Utterances of Child and Chimpanzee. Minnesota Symposium on Child Psychology, 1973.

Gardner, A. R. and Gardner, B. T. Teaching Sign Language to the Chimpanzee Washoe. University of Nevada, Nevada, 1973.

Gardner, A. R. and Gardner, B. T. Acquisition of Sign Language in the Chimpanzee. University of Nevada, Nevada, 1974.

Garrett, M., Bever, T. and Fodor, J. The active use of grammar in speech perception. Perception and Psychophysiology, 1966, pp. 30–32.

Gates, R. The Reception of Verbal Information by Deaf Students Through a Television Medium—a Comparison of Speech-reading, Manual Communication and Reading. Proceedings of the Convention of American instructors of the Deaf, Little Rock, Arkansas, 1971, pp. 513–522.

Gekoski, W. L. Effects of language acquisition contexts on semantic processing in bilinguals. Proceedings of the Annual Convention of the American Psychological Association, 1970, pp. 487–488.

Gemmil J. E. Story Telling, Reading and Language Learning. Manuscript Manchester, 1976.

Gemmil, J. E. and John, J. E. J. Time Features in Speech. The Teacher of the Deaf, 1976, pp. 386–402.

Geschwind, N. The apraxias: neural mechanisms of disorders of learned movement. Amer. Scientist, 1975, (63–2), pp. 188–195.

Ginneken, J. van. Het gesprek. Nieuwe Taalgids, 1909, pp. 86–96.
— De roman van een kleuter. 's-Hertogenbosch, 1922.

Gipper, H. Denken ohne Sprache? Düsseldorf, 1971.

Glanzer, M. Grammatical category: a rote learning and word association analysis. Journal of Verbal Learning and Verbal Behavior, 1962–63, pp. 31–41.

Gloyer, J. Vergleich der leib-seelischen Entwicklung des gehörlosen Kleinkindes Jens G. mit der seines normal hörenden Zwillingsbruders unter besonderer Berücksichtigung ihrer sprachlichen Gestaltungskraft. Wissenschaftliche Hausarbeit Universität Hamburg Fachbereich Erziehungswissenschaft. Hamburg, 1961.

Glucksberg, S. and Danks, J. H. Experimental Psycholinguistics. New York, 1975.

Gorman, P. and Paget, Lady G. A Systematic Sign Language. London, 4th ed., 1969.

Goto, H. Auditory perception by normal Japanese adults of the sounds L and R. Neuropsychologica (Eng.), 1971, pp. 317–323.

Goyvaerts, D. L. Modern grammatical theory: a synthesis. ITL Leuven, 1972, pp. 1–21.

Greenberg, J. Universals in Language. Cambridge, Mass., 1963.

Greene, J. Psycholinguistics, Chomsky and Psychology. Penguin Science of Behaviour, Middlesex, 1972, 2nd 1973.

Greenstein, J. M. Methods of Fostering Language in Deaf Infants. Final Report to Health, Education and Welfare Department, Grant OEG-0-72-539. Washington D.C., 1975.

Greulich, M. Aus dem Bildungswesen Gehörgeschädigter in der Sowjet-Union. Neue Blätter f. Taubstummenbildung, 1963, pp. 88–93.
— Der Sprach-Unterricht in den beiden ersten Schuljahren der Sowjetischen Taubstummenschule. Neue Blätter f. Taubstummenbildung, 1965, pp. 37–44.

Groen, J. J. Intern rapport. St. Michielsgestel, 1948.

Groht, M. A. Natural Language for Deaf Children. Washington D.C., 1958.

Gullan, M. and Gurrey, P. Poetry Speaking for Children, I The Beginnings. II Marching Forward. III

Senior Work. London, 1952.

Gunderson, A. N. A linguistic analysis of the written language of the deaf. Volta Review, 1965, pp. 680–688.

Gutzmann, H. Über die Sprache der Taubstummen. Medische Klinik, 1905, pp. 1065–1091.

Haber, R. N. and Nathanson, L. Post-retinal storage? Some further observations on Parks' camel as seen through the eye of a needle. Perception and Psychophysics, 1968, (3), pp. 349–355.

Haeringen, C. B. van. Tangconstructies en reacties daarop. Nieuwe Taalgids, 1947, pp. 322–357.

— Nederlands tussen Duits en Engels. Den Haag, without year.

Hall, J. F. Verbal Learning and Retention. Philadelphia, 1971.

Halpen, R. H. History of Rochester School for the Deaf 1876–1936. Rochester School for the Deaf, Rochester, 1936.

Hamaïde, A. La méthode Décroly. Neuchatel, 1922.

Hammarström, G. Generative phonology. A critical appraisal. Phonetica, 1973, (27), pp. 157–184.

Hare, A. P. A study of interaction and consensus in different sized groups. American Sociological Review, 1952, pp. 261–267.

Hart, B. O. Teaching Reading to Deaf Children. Washington D.C., 1963.

Hartmann, R. and Stork, F. Dictionary of Language and Linguistics. Essex, 1972.

Hartong, C. Danskunst. Rotterdam, 1948.

Heider, F. and Heider, G. M. A comparison of the sentence structure of deaf and hearing children. Psychol. Monographs U.S.A., n. 232, 1940, pp. 42–103.

Heim, J. A comment on R. D. Johnson: reanalysis of meaningfulness and verbal learning. Psychological Review, 1973, (80), pp. 235–236.

Helmers, H. Sprache und Humor des Kindes. Stuttgart, 1965.

Henegar, M. E. and Cornett, R. O. Cued Speech: Handbook for Parents. Cued Speech Program. Washington D.C. Gallaudet College, 1971.

Henning, G. H. Remembering foreign language vocabulary: Acoustic and semantic parameters. Language Learning, 23 (2), 1973, pp. 185–196.

Herren, H. (ed.) L'éducation des enfants et des adolescents handicapés, Tome 1: Les handicapés moteurs, 1969; Tome 3: Volume II: Les aveugles et les sourds-aveugles. Les éditions E.S.F., Paris XVII, 1971.

Herriot, P. An Introduction to the Psychology of Language. London, 1970.

Hester, M., Tully, N. and McCandless, G. Manual Communication. Proceedings International Congress on the Education of the Deaf. Washington D.C., 1963, pp. 211–221.

Hilgard, E. Theories of Learning. New York, 1956.

Hipskind, M. M. and Nerbonne, G. P. The most common words used in conversations: Western Massachusetts Journal of Communication Disorders, 1970, (3), pp. 47–50.

Hirsch, A. P. Die Gebärdensprache der Hörenden und ihre Stellung zur Lautsprache. Im Anhang eine Sammlung von Hörendengebärden. Selbstverlag des Verfassers, Charlottenburg, 1923.

— Zur Genese der Taubstummengebärde. Neue Blätter für Taubstummen Bildung, 1961, pp. 240–252.

Hiskey, M. S. A study of the intelligence of deaf and hearing children. American Annals of the Deaf, 1956, pp. 329–339.

— Hiskey Nebraska Test of Learning Aptitude. Lincoln, Nebraska, 1966.

Hockett, C. F. A Manual of Phonology. Bloomington Indiana, 1955.

— A Course of Modern Linguistics. New York, 1958.

Hodgson, K. W. The Deaf and Their Problems. London, 1953.

Hoemann, H. W. The Development of Communication Skills in Deaf and Hearing Children. The Catholic University of America, Washington, 1970.

— Children's use of fingerspelling versus sign-language in label pictures. Exceptional Children, 1972, (39), pp. 161–162.

Hoemann, H. W., De Ross, D. V. and Andrews, C. E. Categorical encoding in short term memory by four- to eleven-year-old children. Bulletin Psychonomic Sociology, 1974, pp. 63–65.

Hofmarksrichter, K. Visuelle Kompensation und Eidetik bei Taubstummen. Archiv für die Gesammte Psychologie, 1931.

Hofsteater, H. T. An Experiment in Preschool Education. An Autobiographic Study, 1932, Gallaudet College. Bulletin no. 1, Vol. 8. Washington D.C., 1959.

Holcomb, R. Three Years of the Total Approach. Proceedings of the 45th meeting of the Convention of American instructors of the Deaf, U.S. Government Printing Office, Washington D.C., 1971, pp. 522–530.

Holland, W. R. Language barrier as an educational problem of Spanish speaking children. Exceptional children U.S.A., 1960, pp. 42–50.

Holm, A. The Danish mouth-hand system. The Teacher of the Deaf, 1972, pp. 486–490.

Holmes, V. M. and Forster, K. J. Click location and syntactic structure. Perception Psychophysiology, 1972, (12), pp. 9–15.

Hörmann, H. Psychologie der Sprache. Berlin, 1967.

Horn, personal information, 1948.

Howes, D. On the relation between the probability of a word as an association and in general linguistic usage. Journal of Abnormal and Social Psychology, 1957, (54), pp. 75–85.

Howes, D. and Osgood, C. E. On the combination of associative probabilities in linguistic contexts. Am. J. of Psychology, 1954, see Saporta, 1961, pp. 214–227.

Hubbeling, H. G. Inleiding tot het denken van Wittgenstein. Assen, 1965.

Hudgins, Cl. V. Voice production and breath control in the speech of the deaf. American Annals of the Deaf, Washington D.C., 1937, pp. 338–363.

— Speech breathing and speech intelligibility. The Volta Review, 1946, pp. 642–644.

— A comparison of deaf and normal hearing subjects in the production of motor rhythms. American Instructors of the Deaf, Washington D.C., 1957, pp. 200–203.

— The development of communication skills among profoundly deaf children in an auditory training program, in Ewing, A. W. G. (ed.), 1960, nr. 33.

Hudgins, A. V. and Numbers, F. C. An investigation of the intelligibility of the speech of the deaf. Genet. Psychology Monographs, n. 25, 1942, p. 289–392.

Huttenlocher, J. Children's language. Word phrase relationship. Science, 1964, p. 264–265.

Innocence, Rev. Sr., personal information, 1951.

Irvin, J. V. and Marge, M. (eds.) Principles of Children Language Disabilities. New York, 1972.

Irwin, O. C. Infant speech: I. Consonantal sounds according to place of articulation, Journal of Speech and Hearing Disorders, 1947, pp. 397–401. II. Consonantal sounds according to manner of articulation, Journal of Speech and Hearing Disorders, 1947, pp. 402–404. III. Development of vowel sounds, Journal of Speech and Hearing Disorders, 1948, pp. 31–34.

Ivimey, G. P. The Written Syntax of an English Deaf Child: an Exploration in Method. Brit. J. of Disorders of Comm. 1976, pp. 103–120.

Jackson, M. Teaching language. The Teacher of the Deaf, 1967, pp. 79–87.

Jakobson, R. and Halle, M. Fundamentals of Language. Den Haag, 1956.

Jeanes, D. Aid to Communication with the Deaf. Victorian School for deaf children. Melbourne, Australia, 1972.

Jeffres, L. A. (ed.) Cerebral Mechanisms in Behavior. J. Wiley, New York, 1951.

Jett, A. The analogy of learning a language and learning music. Modern Language Journal. 1968, (52), pp. 436–439.

John, J. E. J. and Howarth, J. N. The effect of time distortions of the intelligibility of deaf children's speech. Language and Speech, 1965, pp. 127–134.

Johnson, N. F. The psychological reality of phrase-structure rules. Journal of Verbal Learning and Verbal Behaviour, 1965, (4), pp. 469–475.

311

— Linguistic models and functional units of language behavior, in: Rosenberg St. (ed.), 1965, pp. 29–65.

— The influence of associations between elements of structured verbal responses. Journal of Verbal Learning and Verbal Behaviour, 1966 (5), pp. 369–374.

— On the relationship between sentence structure and the latency in generating the sentence. Journal of Verbal Learning and Verbal Behaviour, 1966, (5), pp. 375–380.

Johnson, R. C., Frincke, G. and Martin, L. Meaningfulness, frequency and affective character of words as related to visual duration threshold. Canadian Journal of Psychology, 1961, (15), pp. 199–204.

Johnson-Laird, P. N. The choice of the passive voice in a communicative task. British Journal of Psychology, 1968, (59), pp. 7–15.

Jürgens, F. W. and Waesch, G. Studienfahrt in die UdSSR. Hörgeschädigten Pädagogik 1976, pp. 268–269. – Ein Bericht über eine Studienreise der Fachgruppe für Blinden- und Gehörlosenschulen vom 4. bis 11. Okt. 1975. Scheuermann, W., Lindenkamp 10, 3201 Diekholzen, 1976.

Jussen, H. Die Erschliessung des verbalen Denkkreises im Taubstummenunterricht. Ratingen, 1961.

— Das Graphem-bestimmte Manualsystem (GMS) als Sprachlernhilfe bei Gehörlosen. Köln, 1973.

— Sprachanthropologische Ueberlegungen zur Anwendung eines graphembestimmten Manualsystems in der Früh-erziehung tauber Kinder. Hörgeschädigten Pädagogik, 1973, pp. 61–78.

— Hörerziehung statt Fingeralphabet?—Kritische Stellungnahme zu einem Bericht. Hörgeschädigten Pädagogik, 1976, pp. 257–259.

Jussen, H. and Kruger, M. Manuelle Kommunikationshilfen bei Gehörlosen. Das Fingeralphabet. Berlin, 1975.

Kaper, W. Einige Erscheinungen der kindlichen Sprach-erwerbung erläutert im Lichte des vom Kinde gezeigten Interesse für Sprachliches. Groningen, 1959.

Kates, S. L. Language Development in Deaf and Hearing Children. The Clarke School for the Deaf, 1972.

Kates, S. L. and Kates, F. F. Social and nonsocial verbal concepts of deaf and hearing children. Journal of Abnormal Psychology, 1965, (3), pp. 214–217.

Katz, D. and Katz, R. Conversations with Children. London, 1936.

Katz, J. J. and Fodor, J. The structure of a semantic theory. Language, 1963, (39), pp. 170–211.

Kellner, P. and Tanner, M. The effect of early deprivation on speech development. Language and Speech, 1958, pp. 269–281.

Kempen, G. De taalgebruiker in de mens. Groningen, 1976.

Kent, M. 'Total communication and the Maryland School for the Deaf', in: Deaf American, 1971, see Watson, D. (ed.), 1973, pp. 53–61.

Kern, E. Theorie und Praxis eines ganzheitlichen Sprach-unterrichts für das gehörgeschädigte Kind. Freiburg im Breisgau, 1958.

— Der freie Sprach-unterricht, Bedeutung, Wesen und Gestalt. Neue Blätter f. Taubstummenbildung, 1967, pp. 177–191.

King, W. H. Immediate and delayed recall of information presented orally and visually. Educational Review, 1959, pp. 125–129.

Klir, J. and Valach, M. Cybernetic Modelling. London, 1967.

Köble, J. Die ersten zweieinhalb Lebensjahre eines hörgeschädigten Knaben. Wissenschaftliche Hausarbeit Universität Heidelberg, Heidelberg, 1964.

Koch, F. J. Fingerlesen Lesen als Gebärdenspiel. Essen, 1st ed. 1921, 12th ed. 1967.

Koen, F. An intraverbal explication of the nature of metaphore. Journal of Verbal Learning and Verbal Behavior, 1965, pp. 129–133.

Kooij, J. G. Is Nederlands een SOV (Subjectum-Objectum Verbum)-taal? Amsterdam, 1973.

Krabbe, J. Beelddenken en woordblindheid. Arnhem, 1951.

Krech, D. and Crutchfield, R. S. Elements of Psychology. New York, 1962, 2nd ed., 1969.

312

Krech, D., Crutchfield, R. S. and Ballachey, E. L. Individual in Society. New York, 1962.

Kreye, H. von Grundstrukturen der Deutschen Sprache und ihr didaktischer Aufbau an Sonderschulen. Marhold, Berlin, 1972.

Kreye, H. von Bildergrammatik. Band I. Münster, 1975.

Krimm-Von, Fischer C. Musikalisch-rhythmische Erziehung. Freiburg i.B., 1975.

Kröhnert, O. Die sprachliche Bildung des Gehörlosen. Weinheim, 1966.

Krijnen, A. Developing the Voices of Very Young Deaf Children. Proceedings of Internat. Cong. on Oral Educ. of the Deaf, Washington D.C., 1967, pp. 664–671.

Kurtz, K. H. and Hovland, C. J. The effect of verbalisation during observation of stimulus objects upon accuracy of recognition and recall. Journal of experimental Psychology, U.S.A., 1953, pp. 157–164.

Kwant, R. C. Fenomenologie van de Taal. Utrecht, 1961.

Lackner, J. R. and Garrett, M. F. Resolving ambiguity: Effects of biasing context in the unattended ear. Cognition, 1972, (1), pp. 359–372.

Lado, R. Language Teaching. A Scientific Approach. New York, 1964.

Lambert, W. E. and Peal, E. The relation of bilingualism to intelligence. Psychological Monograph N., 76, 1962.

Lamendella, J. T. On the irrelevance of transformational grammar to second language pedagogy. Language Learning, 1970, 19, (3–4), pp. 255–270.

Lane, H. L. The motor theory of Speech Perception: a critical review. Psychol. Review, 1965, pp. 275–309.

Lane, H. S. No time for complacency. Volta Review, 1966, pp. 616–622.

Lane, H. S. and Baker, D. Reading Achievement of the deaf: Another look. The Volta Review, 1974, pp. 489–499.

Lashley, K. S. The problem of serial order in behavior, in: Jeffres, L. A. New York, 1951.

Laughery, K. R. and Spector, A. The roles of recording and rhythm in memory organisation. Journal of Experimental Psychology, 1972, (94), pp. 41–48.

Leeuw, M. and E. de. Read Better, Read Faster. Penguin Books, Harmondsworth, 1965, Aula n. 425. Utrecht, 1970.

Lemke, R. Das enthemmte Kind mit choreïformer Symptomatik. Psychiatr. Neurol. Med. Psychol., 1954, pp. 5–10.

Lenneberg, E. H. A laboratory for speech research at the Children's Hospital Medical Center. Journal of Medicine, New England, 1962, pp. 385–392.

— Understanding language without ability to speak; a case report. Journal of Abnormal and Social Psychology, 1962, (65), pp. 419–425.

— Speech development: its anatomical and physiological concomitants, in: Carterette, E.C. (ed.), University Californian Press, Los Angeles, 1966, pp. 37–66.

— The natural history of language, in: Smith, F. and Miller, G., M.I.T. Press, London, 1966, pp. 219–252.

— Prerequisites for Language Acquisition. Proceedings of Intern. Conf. on Oral Education of the Deaf. Washington D.C., 1967, pp. 1302–1361.

— Biological Foundations of Language. New York, 1967.

Lenneberg, E. H., Rebelsky, F. and Nichols, J. The vocalisations of infants born to deaf and hearing parents. Human Development VIII no. 1, 1965, pp. 23–37.

Lenneberg, E. H. and Roberts, J. M. The Language of Experience. Indiana University Publications in Anthropology and Linguistics, Memoir 13. Baltimore, 1956.

Leopold, W. F. Speech Development of a Bilingual Child. Evanston, 1949.

— Patterning in children's language learning. Language Learning 1953–1954, p. 1–14. Das Sprechen Lernen der Kinder, Sprachforum, 1956, pp. 117–125.

Levelt, W. J. M. A scaling approach to the study of syntactic relations, in: Flores d'Arcais and Levelt,

1970, pp. 109–121.

Levin, H. and Williams, J. P. (eds.) Basic studies on reading. New York, 1970.

Lewis, M. M. Infant Speech. London, 1936, 1938, 3rd 1951.

— Language, Thought and Personality in Infancy and Childhood. London, 1963.

— The Education of the Deaf. London, 1968.

— Language and Personality in Deaf Children. London, 1968.

— Language and Mental Development, in: Lunzer, E. A. and Morris, J. F. London, 1968.

— How Children Learn to Speak. Basic Books, Inc. New York, 1970.

Libermann, A. M. Some results of research on speech perception. Journal of the Acoustic Soc. of America, 1957, pp. 117–123.

Libermann, A., Cooper, F. S., Harris, K. S. and McNeilage, P. F. A motor theory of speech perception. Proceedings Speech Communication Seminar, 1962, II. Techn. Institut, Stockholm, 1963.

Libermann, P. Intonation, Perception and Language. Cambridge, Massachusetts, 1967.

Libowski, J. 1970, see Korsunskaja B. D. in Defectologija Moskau 1970 pp. 21–29, Russian text, translated by Lange, W. Methodik des Sprachunterrichtes für gehörlose Vorschulkinder, Sonderschule 1971 pp. 45–64, Fingerzeichensprache im Elternhaus gehörloser Kinder, Sonderschule 1971, pp. 215–222.

Ling, A. H. Memory for verbal and non-verbal auditory sequences in hearing-impaired and normal-hearing children. J. Amer. Audiol. Society, 1975, pp. 37–45.

Ling, D. and Ling, A. H. Communication development in the first three years of life. Journal of Speech and Hearing Research, 1974, pp. 146–159.

Locke, J. L. Children's language coding in short-term-memory. Language and Speech, 1973, (16), pp. 271–278.

Lonergan, B. J. F. Insight. A Study of Human Understanding. Philosophical Library, New York, 1st ed. 1958, 3rd ed. 1970.

Lorge, I. and Chall, J. Estimating the size of vocabularies of children and adults; an analysis of methodological issues. J. of Exp. Education, 32, (Winter, 1963), pp. 147–157.

Lovaas, O. I., Berberich, J. P., Perloff, B. F. and Schaeffer, B. Acquisition of imitation speech by schizophrenic children. Science, 1966, pp. 705–707.

Luce, R., Bush, R. and Galanter, E. (eds.) Handbook of Mathematical Psychology. New York, Vol. 2, 1963.

Lunzer, E. A. and Morris, J. F. Development in Human Learning. Steples Press, London, 1968.

Lykos, C. M. Cued Speech: Handbook for Teachers. Gallaudet College, Cued Speech Program, Washington D.C., 1971.

Lyon, E. The Lyon Phonetic Manual. Rochester Institute for the Deaf, Rochester, 1891.

Lyons, J. Chomsky. Collins Ltd., London, 5th 1972.

Maclay, H. and Osgood, C. E. Hesitation phenomena in spontaneous English Speech. Word, 1959, pp. 19–44.

MacNamara, J. (ed.) Problems of Bilingualism. Ann Arbor, 1967.

MacNamara, J., Cleirigh, A. and Kellaghan, T. The structure of the English lexicon: the simplest hypothesis. Language and Speech, 1972, pp. 141–148.

MacNeilage, P. F. Motor control of serial ordering of speech. Psychological Review, 1970, (77), pp. 182–196.

Made van Bekkum I. G. van der. Commonaliteit en reactietijd bij vrije woord-associaties van kinderen en volwassenen. Ned. Tijdschrift voor Psychologie, 1966, pp. 102–135.

Maesse, H. Das Verhältnis von Laut- und Gebärdensprache in der Entwicklung des taubstummen Kindes. Langensalza, 1935.

Malisch, K. Wesen und Wertung des ersten Sprechunterrichts an Sprachganzen. Heidelberg, 1925.

Markides, A. Comparative linguistic proficiencies of deaf children, taught by two different methods of instruction—manual versus oral. The Teacher of the deaf, 1976, pp. 307–347.

Marks, L. E. and Miller, G. A. The role of semantic and syntactic constraints in the memorisation of English sentences. Journal of Verbal Learning and Verbal Behavior, 1964, pp. 1–5.

Martin, E., Roberts, K. H. and Collins, A. M. Short term memory for sentences. Journal of Verbal Learning and Verbal Behaviour, 1968, (7), pp. 560–566.

Martin, J. G. Rhythmic versus serial structure in speech and other behaviour. Psychological Review, 1972, (79), pp. 487–509.

Marzinovskaya, E. N. Ueber die Daktylsprache. Sonderschule, 1970, pp. 273–278.

— Tempo of oral and dactylic speech. Proceedings of the International Conference, Stockholm, 1970, Vol. III, pp. 493–495.

McCarthy, D. Language development in children, in: L. Carmichael, 1954, pp. 492–631.

McClure, W. J. The Rochester Method and the Florida School. American Annals of the deaf, 1975, pp. 331–340.

McElroy, C. W. Speech and language development of the preschool child. Springfield, 1972.

McGinnis, M. A. Aphasic Children, Identification and Education by the Associative Method. St. Louis, 1963.

McLean, J. E., Yoder, D. E. and Schiefelbusch, R. L. Language Intervention with the Retarded. Developing strategies. London, 3rd, 1973.

McNeill, D. The Capacity for Language Acquisition. Proceedings of a National Research Conference on Behavioral aspects of deafness, New Orleans, 1965.

— Developmental Psycholinguistics, in: Smith, F. and Miller, G. A. (eds.), 1966.

— The capacity for language acquisition. Volta Review, 1966, pp. 17–33.

— On theories of language acquisition, in: Dixon and Horton (eds.), 1968, pp. 406–420.

— The development of language, in: Mussen (ed.), Vol. I, 1970, pp. 1061–1162.

— The Acquisition of Language, the Study of Developmental Psycholinguistics. New York, 1970.

Meadow, K. P. Early Manual Communication in Relation to the Deaf Child's Intellectual, Social and Communicative Functioning. Berkeley University, unpubl. doct. diss., Berkeley, 1967.

— Early manual communication in relation to the deaf child's intellectual, social and communicative functioning. American Annals of the deaf, 1968, pp. 29–41.

Menyuk, P. Syntactic rules used by children from preschool through first grades. Child development, 1964, pp. 533–546.

— Sentences Children Use. Cambridge, U.S.A., 1969.

— The Development of Speech. Indianapolis, New York, 1972.

Meumann, E. Die Entstehung der ersten Wortbedeutungen beim Kinde. Leipzig, 1902.

Meyer, E. Rhythmik mit Gehörlosen, in: Krimm-Von Fischer, C. 1975, pp. 123–139.

Mickelson, N. I. Meaningfulness: a critical variable in children's verbal learning. Reading Teacher, 1969, (23), pp. 11–14.

Miller, G. A. Language and Communication. New York, 1951.

— The magical number seven, plus or minus two: some limits on our capacity for processing information. Psychological review, 1956, (63), pp. 81–97.

— Some psychological studies of grammar. American Psychologist, 1962, (17), pp. 748–762.

Miller, G. A. and Chomsky, N. 'Finitary models of language users', in: Luce, R., Bush, R. and Galanter, E. (eds.). New York, Vol. 2, 1963, pp. 419–431.

Miller, G. A., Galanter, E. and Pribam, K. H. Plans, and the Structure of Behavior. New York, 1960.

Miller, G. A. and Isard, S. Some perceptual consequences of linguistic rules. Journal of Verbal Learning and Verbal Behavior, 1963, pp. 217–228.

Miller, Maj. St.Vincent School for the Deaf, Johannesburg, South Africa, Language scheme for deaf children, approximately 3½ to 12 years of age (adapted from the text 'The Printed Word', by Maj. Miller). The Teacher of the Deaf, 1966, pp. 349–382.

Mindel, E. D. and Vernon, McCay. They Grow in Silence, the Deaf Child and His Family. Nat. Ass. of the Deaf, Silver Spring, Maryland, 1971.

Mol, H. Physical and linguistic principles in the recognition of phonemes. Proceedings of the first Inter-

315

national Congress of Audiology, Leiden, 1953, pp. 140–143.
— Fundamentals of Phonetics. The Hague, 1963.
Mol, H. and Uhlenbeck, E. M. The linguistic relevance of intensity in stress. Lingua, 1956, pp. 205–213.
Mönks, F. J. and Knoers, A. M. P. Ontwikkelingspsychologie; inleiding tot de verschillende deelgebieden. Nijmegen, 1975.
Monsees, E. K. The language curriculum for teachers of language-deficient children. Proceedings of International Congress on oral education of the Deaf. Washington, 1967, pp. 1114–1146.
— Temporal sequence and expressive language disorders. Exceptional Children. 1968, pp. 141–147.
— Structured Language for Children with Special Language Learning Problems. Children's Hearing and Speech Center, Washington D.C., 1972.
Montgomery, G. W. A factorial study of communication and ability in deaf school-leavers. British Journal of Educational Psychology. 1966, (111), pp. 557–565.
— The relationship of oral skills to manual communication in profoundly deaf students. American Annals of the Deaf. 1966, pp. 557–565.
— Vocational Guidance for the Deaf. Edinburgh, 1967.
— Analysis of Pure-Tone Audiometric responses in relation to speech development in the profoundly deaf. Journal of Acoustical Society of America. 1967, pp. 53–59.
Moores, D. Psycholinguistics and deafness. American Annals of the Deaf. 1970, pp. 37–48.
— 'Language disabilities of hearing-impaired children', in: Irvin and Marge, (eds.). 1972, pp. 159–183.
Morkovin, B. Experiment in teaching deaf preschool children in the Soviet Union. Volta Review, 1960, pp. 260–268.
Morozova, N. G. Scientific principles of teaching deaf children in the U.S.S.R. The Teacher of the Deaf. 1965, pp. 139–145.
Mowrer, O. H. Learning Theory and Symbolic Processes. New York, 1960.
Mulholland, A. M. Receptive Language in the U.S.S.R., the Netherlands and the United States. American Annals of the Deaf. 1965, pp. 404–413.
Murray, D. J. The role of speech responses in short term memory. Canad. Journal of Psychology. 1967, (21), pp. 263–276.
Mussen, P. (ed.) Carmichael's Manual of Child Psychology. New York, 1970, I, pp. 1061–1162.
Myers, P. I. and Hammil, D. D. Methods for Learning Disorders. New York, 1969, 1973.
Myklebust, H. R. The Psychology of Deafness. 2nd, New York, 1964.
— Picture Story Language Test. New York, 1965.
— The measurement of language. Proceedings International Congress on oral education of the deaf. Washington D.C., 1967, pp. 1393–1411.
— (ed.) Progress in Learning Disabilities. I, II, III. New York, 1968–1975.

Nanninga-Boon, A. Psychologische ontwikkelingsmethoden van het doofstomme kind. Groningen, 1929.
— Het denken van het doofstomme kind. Groningen, 1934.
Nass, M. L. The deaf child's conception of physical causality. Journal of Abnormal and Social Psychology. 1964, (69), pp. 669–673.
— Development of conscience: a comparison of the moral judgments of deaf and hearing children. Child Development. 1964, pp. 1073–1080.
Neisser, U. Cognitive Psychology. Appleton Century-Crofts, New York, 1967.
Nelson, M. S. The evolutionary process of teaching language to the deaf with a survey of the methods now employed. American Annals of the Deaf. 1949, pp. 230–551.
Nicholas, M. M. o.p. The aphasic child. The Teacher of the Deaf. 1962, pp. 99–108.
— Teaching Speech to Profoundly Deaf Children (unpublished). Manchester, 17, 9, 1965.
Nicholas, M. M. and Maeliosa, M. Sound perception training for the profoundly deaf child. The Teacher of the Deaf. 1967, pp. 161–177.

Nix, G. W. Habilitation of the Deaf Child Through an Auditory-oral Education. Washington, 1974.
— Total communication: a review of the studies offered in its support. Volta Review. 1975, pp. 270–294.
— (ed.) Mainstream Education for Hearing Impaired Children and Youth. New York, 1976.
Nober, E. H. The Development of Audiologic Criteria to Differentiate Between Auditory Thresholds and Cutile Thresholds of Deaf Children. Dept. of Health, Education and Welfare, U.S. Office of Education for the handicapped. Washington D.C., 1970.
— Cutile air and bone conduction thresholds of the deaf. Exceptional Children. 1970, (36), pp. 571–579.
Northcott, W. H. Hearing Impaired Children, Birth to Three Years, and Their Parents, Curriculum Guide. A. G. Bell Association for the deaf, Washington D.C., 1975.
Novikova, L. A. Electrophysiological investigation of speech, in: O'Connor, N. New York, 1961.
Nuytens, E. De tweetalige mens. Assen, 1962.

O'Connor, N. (ed.) Recent Soviet Psychology. New York, 1961.
O'Connor, N. and Hermelin, B. Speech and Thought in Severe Subnormality. New York, 1962.
Odom, P. B. and Blanton, R. L. Phrase-learning in deaf and hearing subjects. Journal of Speech and Hearing Research. 1967, pp. 600–605.
Ogden, C. K. and Richards, I. A. The Meaning of Meaning. New York, 1923, 1930.
Oléron, P. Études sur le langage mimique des sourds-muets. Année Psychologique. 1952, (52), pp. 47–81.
— Conceptual thinking in the deaf. American Annals of the Deaf. 1957, pp. 304–310.
— Appréhension de différences perceptives et présentation simultanée ou successive par des enfants sourds. Revue 'Defectologie'. 1972, (45), pp. 18–23.
— Langage et développement mental. Bruxelles, 1973.
Olson, J. R. A factor analytic study of the relation between the speed of visual perception and the language abilities of deaf adolescents. J. of Speech and Hearing Research, 1967, (19), pp. 354–360.
Olsson, J. E. and Furth, N. G. Visual memory span in the deaf. American Journal of Psychology. 1966, (79), pp. 480–484.
Opei, J. and Opei, P. The lore and language of school children. Oxford 1967.
O'Rourke, T. J. (ed.) Psycholinguistics and Total Communication. Washington D.C., 1972.
Osgood, C. E. Method and Theory in Experimental Psychology. New York, 1953.
— Studies on the generality of affective meaning systems. American Psychologist. 1963, (17), pp. 520–526.
— On understanding and creating sentences. American Psychologist, 1963, pp. 735–741.
— Contextual control in sentence understanding and creating, in: Carterette, E. C. (ed.). Brain function III. Los Angeles, 1966.
Osgood, C. E. and Sebeok, Th. A. Psycholinguistics, Bloomington, 1965.
Owrid, H. L. Studies in manual communication with hearing impaired children. The Teacher of the Deaf. 1971, pp. 151–160.

Paardekoper, P. C. Syntaxis, Spraakkunst en Taalkunde. 's-Hertogenbosch, 1955.
— Inleiding tot de ABN-syntaxis 's-Hertogenbosch, 1966, 4th ed. 1971.
Padberg, H. De mooie taal. 's-Hertogenbosch. 1924.
Paget, R. Education of the totally deaf. Advancement of Science. 1953, (9), pp. 437–441.
Pei, M. A. and Gaynor, Fr. Dictionary of Linguistics. London, 1958.
Perfetti, C. A. Lexical density and phrase structure depth as variables in sentence retention. Journal of Verbal Learning and Verbal Behaviour. 1969, (8), pp. 719–724.
Perozzi, J. A. and Kunze, L. H. Relationship between speech sound discrimination skills and language abilities of Kindergarten-children. Journal of Speech and Hearing Research. 1971, (14), pp. 382–390.

317

Peters, N. and Peters, J. Better reading materials for the content areas. Volta Review. 1973, pp. 375–387.

Peterson, G. E. The information bearing elements of speech. Journal of the Acoustic Soc. of America. 1952, pp. 629–637.

Peterson, G. E. and Barney, H. L. Control methods used in the study of vowels. Journal of the Acoustic Soc. of America. 1952, pp. 175–184.

Peterson, L. R. and Johnson, S. T. Some effects of minimising articulation on short-term retention. J. of Verbal Learning and Verbal Behavior. 1971, (10), pp. 346–354.

Pflaum, S. W. The Development of Language and Reading in the Young Child. Columbus Ohio, 1974.

Phillips, W. D. The Influence of Preschool Training on Achievement in Language Arts, Arithmetic Concepts and Socialization of Young Deaf Children in Residential Schools. Columbia University, New York, 1963.

Piaget, J. Le Langage et la Pensée chez l'Enfant. Neuchatel, 1923, 1930.

— Les praxies chez l'enfant. Revue Neurologie. 1960, (102), pp. 551–565.

— Comments on Vygotzky. Mass. Institute of Technology, U.S.A., 1962.

— The Origins of Intelligence in Children. New York, 1963.

Pike, E. E. Controlled infant intonation. Language Learning. 1949, pp. 21–24.

Pike, K. L. Language in Relation to a Unified Theory of the Structure of Human Behavior. The Hague, 2nd, 1967.

Pollack, J. and Fick, L. Information of elementary multidimensional auditory displays. Journal of the acoustical Society of America. 1954, (26), pp. 155–158.

Postma, C. G. Voorschool en articulatie-onderwijs. Ned. Tijdschr. voor Doofstommenonderwijs, 1936, p. 36–48.

Potter, S. Modern Linguistics. London, 1960.

Prechtl, H. F. R. Het cerebraal gestoorde Kind. Groningen, 1963.

Prechtl, H. F. R. and Stemmer, G. J. Ein choreatiformer Syndrom bei Kindern. Wiener med. Wochenschrift. 1959, pp. 22–29.

Prick, J. J. G. De invloed van afwijkende motoriek of het geheel der persoonlijkheid, mede in verband met de indicatie tot bewegings-therapie. Nederlands Tijdschrift voor Geneeskunde, 1959, pp. 489–495.

Prick, J. J. G. and Calon, P. J. A. Het aphasie probleem na 125 jaar. Nederlands Tijdschrift voor Psychologie. 1950, pp. 369–400.

Prick, J. J. G. and Calon, P. J. A. Een schets van intelligentie en dementie. Amsterdam, 1967.

Prick, J. J. G. and Waals, H. G. van der. Nederlands Handboek der Psychiatrie, I–IV, Arnhem., 1958–1970.

Puyenbroek, J. van. Rekenonderwijs aan dove kinderen. Het Gehoorgestoorde Kind, 1966, pp. 182–191.

— Arithmetic and mathematics: methodical and didactical aspects. In: Anon., Rotterdam, 1973, pp. 25–37.

Querll, W. Die Sprache- und Sprech-entwicklung der Mutterschule. Blätter für Taubstummenbildung. 1922, p. 368, 1925, p. 309 sqq.

Quigley, S. P. See Lane (1966), Volta Review. 1966, pp. 619–620.

— The Influence of Fingerspelling on the Development of Language, Communication and Educational Achievement in Deaf Children. Univ. of Illinois, Urbana, 1969.

Quigley, S. P. and Frisina, D. R. Institutionalisation and Psychoeducational Development of Deaf Children. CEC Monograph Series A. N. 3. Council of Exceptional Children, Washington 6 D.C., 1201 Sixteenth Street, 1961.

Rammel, G. Die Gebärdensprache; Versuch einer Wesensanalyse. Berlin, 1974.

Reber, A. and Anderson, J. The perception of clicks in linguistic and nonlinguistic messages. Perception and Psychophysics. 1970, pp. 81–89.

Reichling, A. 'Over het personale aspect van het taalgebruik', in: De Vooys' Bundel opstellen. Groningen, 1940.
— Annual Report St. Michielsgestel. St. Michielsgestel, 1942.
— De taal, haar wetten en haar wezen. ENSIE II, Amsterdam, 1949.
— A new method of speech training in deaf mutism. Proceedings II Intern. Congress for maladjusted children. Amsterdam, 1949, pp. 325–332.
— Verzamelde studies over hedendaagse problemen der taalwetenschap. Zwolle, 1961, (5th), 1969.
— Grondslagen en methoden der syntaxis: het kryptanalytisch formalisme, in: Verzamelde opstellen, Zwolle, 1961, pp. 73–91.
— Mogelijkheden en grenzen van de machinale vertaling gezien vanuit linguistisch standpunt, in:
. Anon. Automatisering en Taalkunde. Stichting Studiecentrum voor administratieve automatisering, Amsterdam, 1961, pp. 16–23.
— Het woord. Utrecht, 1935, reprint, 1967.
Reichling, A. and others. Taalonderzoek in deze tijd. The Hague, 1962.
Restaino, L. C. R. 'Word associations of deaf and hearing children', in: Rosenstein, J. and McGinitie, W., New York, 1969.
Reuck, A. V. S. de and O'Connor, M. (eds.) Disorders of Language, CIBA, London, 1964.
Ricoeur, P. From existentialism to the philosophy of language. Philosophy Today, 1973, (17), pp. 91–103.
Ricoeur, P. and Marcel, G. Gespräche. Josef Knecht Verlag, Frankfurt/Main, 1970.
Riedrich, H. Tastalphabet für Taubblinde nach Hieronymus Lorm. Dresden, 1947.
Rieder, O. Die Entwicklung des kindlichen Fragens. München, 1968.
Rileigh, K. K. and Odom, P. B. Perception of rhythm by subjects with normal and deficient hearing. Dev. Psychol. 1972, pp. 54–61.
Rispens, J. Auditieve aspekten van leesmoeilijkheden. Nijmegen, 1974.
Ritter, E. Die lautlose Verständigung. Freiburg, 1930.
Robinson, D. N. The Enlightened Machine: An Analytical Introduction to Neuropsychology. Encino, Dickenson, California, 1973.
Robinson, I. The New Grammarian Funeral, a Critique of Naom Chomsky's Linguistics. London, 1975.
Roels, F. Handboek der Psychologie, I–V, Utrecht, 1934–1939.
Roose, H. De pauze als taalteken. De Nieuwe Taalgids. 1960, pp. 220–229.
— Het probleem van de woordsoorten. The Hague, 1964.
Rosenstein, J. and McGinitie, W. (eds.) Verbal Behavior of the Deaf Child: Studies of Word Meanings and Associations. Teachers College Press, New York, 1969.
Ruffieux, F. Der Weg zur selektiven Methode. Neue Blätter für Taubstummenbildung, 1946, pp. 11–25.
Russell, W. K., Quigley, S. P. and Power, D. J. Linguistics and Deaf Children, Transformational Syntax and Its Applications. Washington D.C., 1976.
Russo, A. God of the Deaf Adolescents, N.Y.: Paulist Press, 1975.
Rutten, F. J. Th., personal information, 1941.
— Stervende taal. Film met handboek uitgegeven door Stichting Film en Wetenschap, Utrecht, 1957.
Rutter, M. Maternal Deprivation. London, 1972.

Saporta, S. (ed.) Psycholinguistics, a Book of Readings. New York, 1961.
Saussure, F. de Cours de linguistique générale, Paris, 1916. Course in General Linguistics, New York, 1959.
Savin, H. and Perchonock, E. Grammatical structure and the immediate recall of English sentences. Journal of Verbal Learning and Verbal Behavior. 1965, pp. 348–353.
Schaerlaekens, A. M. The two-word sentence in child language development. The Hague, 1973.
Schank, R. C. and Colby, K. N. (eds.) Computer Models of Thought and Language. San Francisco, 1973.
Schatz, C. D. The role of context in the perception of stops. Language. 1954, pp. 47–56.

319

Schlesinger, H. S. and Meadow, K. P. Sound and Sign; Childhood Deafness and Mental Health. Berkeley, 1972.

Schlesinger, I. M. Transfer of Meaning in Sign Language. Hebrew University of Jerusalem, 1970.

Schmähl, O. Der taubstumme Mensch. Berlin, 1931.

Schmid-Giovannini, S. Sprich mit mir: Eine ganzheitliche Laut-sprach Methode für Kleinkinder von 0–7 Jahren, für Eltern und Erzieher Hörgeschädigter Kleinkinder. Berlin, 1976.

Schmitt, A. Helen Keller und die Sprache. Münster, 1954.

Schulte, K. Ausbau und Systematisierung verwendeter Lautzeichen zu einem 'Phonembestimmten Manualsystem'. Neue Blätter für Taubstummen Bildung. Heidelberg, 1967, pp. 323–328.

— Das Fonator-System und sein Einsatz als Sprechgliederungshilfe bei gehörlosen Kindern. Hörgeschädigte Kinder. 1972, (9), pp. 60–64.

— Phoneme transmitting manual system (P.M.S.) in Fant, G. (ed.) Symposion Stockholm, 1970. Washington D.C., 1972, pp. 255–260.

— Phonembestimmtes Manualsystem (P.M.S.); Forschungsergebnisse und Konsequenzen für die Artikulation hörgeschädigter Kinder. Villingen-Schwenningen, 1974.

Schulte, K. und Roessler, H. Optische Phonemdarstellung als Sprechgliederungshilfe für hörgeschädigte Kinder. Villingen, 1973.

Schultheis, J. R. Lautgebärden als Hilfe für die Primar stufe, ihre integrierende Funktion bei normalen und behinderten Kindern. Sonderpädagogik. 1974, pp. 12–26.

Schulze, I. Das Hand-Tipp-system. Dessau, 1925.

Schumann, P. Geschichte des Taubstummenwesens. Frankfurt a. Main, 1940.

Schuy, Cl. Die sprachliche Situation des Taubstummen. Sprachforum, 1955, p. 146–160.

Scroggs, C. L. The effects of expansions on the communication rate of hearing impaired students. American Annals of the Deaf, 1975, pp. 350–359.

Scouten, E. L. A Revaluation of the Rochester Method. Rochester School for the Deaf, 1942.

— The Rochester Method, an oral multisensory approach for instructing prelingual deaf children. American Annals of the Deaf, 1967, p. 50–55.

Seashore, R. H. and Eckerson, L. D. The measurement of individual differences in general English vocabularies. Journal of Educational Psychology, 1940, (31), pp. 14–38

Sebeok, Th. A. Animal Communication. Techniques of Study and Results of Research. London, 1968, 2nd 1973. — How animals communicate. London, 1973.

Shannon, C. E. and Weaver, W. The Mathematical Theory of Communication. Urbana, 1949. (See also Saporta, 1961).

Sharon. A. T. What do adults read? Reading Research Quarterly, 1973–1974, pp. 148–169, (Vol. IX).

Siegman, A. and Pope, B. (eds.) Dyadic communications in interviews. New York, 1972.

Silverman-Dresner, T. and Guilfoyle, G. R. Vocabulary Norms for Deaf Children, Book VII, Lexington Series. Washington D.C., 1972.

Simmonds, A. A. A comparison of the Type-Token-Ratio of spoken and written language of deaf and hearing children. Volta Review. 1962, pp. 417–421.

Skinner, B. F. Verbal Behavior. London, 1957. (See also Saporta, 1961).

Slater, Ph. E. Contrasting correlates of groups size. Sociometry, A Journal of Research in social Psychology. 1958, pp. 129–139.

Sleigh, P. A study of some symbolic processes in young children. Brit. J. Disorders of Communication 1972, (7), pp. 163–175.

Slobin. D. I. Grammatical transformations and sentence comprehension in childhood and adulthood. J. of Verbal Learning and Verbal Behavior. 1966, pp. 219–227.

— Recall of full and truncated passive sentences in connected discourse. Journal of Verbal Learning and Verbal Behavior. 1968, pp. 876–881.

Smith, C. R. Residual Hearing and Speech Production in Deaf Children. City University of New York, CSL Res. Rep. nr. 4, April 15, 1973.

Smith, F. Understanding Reading; a Psycholinguistic Analysis of Reading and Learning to Read. New

York, 1971.

Smith, F. and Miller, G. A. (eds.) The Genesis of Language. New York, 1966.

Smith, M. K. Measurement of the size of general English vocabulary through the elementary grades and high school. Genetic Psychology Monographs, 1941, (24), pp. 311–345.

Smith, M. K. Measurement of the size of general English vocabulary through the elementary grades and high school. Genetic Psychology Monographs. 1971, (24), pp. 311–345.

Smits, L. F. M. Video en liplezen; beschrijving en evaluatie van een experimentele oefenmethode tot verbetering van de gespreksvaardigheid van oudere dove kinderne. Sint Michielsgestel, 1975.

Smulders, N. and Straates, F. Een onderzoek naar het verstaan van figuurlijke taal door dove kinderen. Sint Michielsgestel, 1976.

Snijders, J. Th. 'Taal en Denken', in: Het doof-zijn beluisterd. St. Michielsgestel, 1964.

Snijders, J. Th. and Snijders-Oomen, A. W. M. Niet-verbaal Intelligentieonderzoek van horenden en doofstommen. Groningen, 1958, 2nd, 1961.

Solomon, R. L. and Postma, L. Frequency of usage as a determinant of recognition threshold for words. J. Exp. Psychology. 1952, (43), pp. 195–201.

Speth, L. Adem en Accent in verband met het spreekonderijs aan dove kinderen. St Michielsgestel, 1958.

Stern, Cl. und Stern, W. L. Die Kindersprache. Leipzig, 1907.

Stern, W. L. Helen Keller. Die Entwicklung und Erziehung einer Taubstummblinden. Berlin, 1905.

Stevens, K. M. and House, A. S. Toward a model for speech perception, in: Tobias, J. V. (ed.) London, 1972, pp. 47–62.

Stoelinga, G. B. A. and Werf ten Bosch, J. J. van der. Normal and abnormal development of brain and behaviour. Leiden, 1971.

Stokoe, W. C. Sign Language Structure: an Outline of the Visual Communication Systems of the American Deaf. Gallaudet College, Washington, D.C., 1960.

— Sign language diglossia. Studies in Linguistics. 1970, (21), pp. 27–41.

— Semiotics and Human Sign Languages. The Hague, 1972.

— Sign language studies. The Hague, 1973.

Strasser, St. Fenomenologie en Empirische Menskunde. Arnhem, 1962.

Streng, A. On improving the teaching of language to the deaf. American Annals of the Deaf. 1958, pp. 553–563.

— Syntax, Speech and Hearing; Applied Linguistics for Teachers of Children with Language and Hearing Disabilities. New York, 1972.

Streng, A., Fitch, W. J., Hedgecock, L. D., Phillips, J. W. and Carell, J. A. Hearing Therapy for Children. New York, 1962.

Stuckless, E. R. and Birch, J. W. The influence of early manual communication on the linguistic development of deaf children. Am. Ann. of the Deaf, 1966, pp. 452–460, 499–504 (Final Report Min. of Education, Health and Welfare, Washington D.C., 1964).

Stuckless, E. R. and Enders, J. L. Three Studies of the Structural Meaning of English for Post Secondary Deaf Students. Min. of Health, Education and Welfare, Washington D.C., 1972.

Stuckless, H. Pittsburgh Test of written language. Volta Review. 1966, pp. 683–695.

Stutterheim, C. F. P. Taalbeschouwing en Taalbeheersing. 2nd print, Amsterdam, 1965.

Suci, G. J. The validity of pause as an index of units of language. Journal of Verbal Learning and Verbal Behavior. 1967, pp. 26–32.

Taylor, W. L. Cloze procedure: a new tool for measuring readability. Journalism Quarterly. 1953, (30), pp. 415–435.

Templin, M. C. A qualitative analysis of explanations of physical causality. American Annals of the Deaf. 1954, I, pp. 252–269, II, 351–364.

— Certain Language Skills in Children. Institute of Child Welfare Monograph nr. 26. Minneapolis, Minnesota, 1957.

Tervoort, B. Th. Structurele analyse van visueel taalgebruik binnen een groep dove kinderen. Amsterdam, 1953.
— Taalstructuur en Taalonderwijs aan doven. St. Michielsgestel, 1955.
— Linguistics in language learning of deaf people, in: Anon. International Research Seminar. 1968, pp. 155–173.
Tervoort, B., Geest, A. J. M. v. d., Hubers, G. A. C., Prins, R. S. en, Snow, C. E. Psycholinguistiek. Utrecht, 1972.
Tervoort, B. and Verberk, A. J. A. Final Report on project number RD-467-64-65 of the vocational rehabilitation administration of the Department of Health, Education and Welfare, Washington, D.C., U.S.A., titled: Analysis of Communicative Structure Patterns in Deaf Children. 1967. The Hague, 1975.
Thomassen, A. J. W. M. On the Representation of Verbal Items in Short Term Memory. Kath. Universiteit, Psych. Lab., Nijmegen, 1970.
Tizard, B., Cooperman, O., Joseph, A. and Tizard, J. Environment effects on language development: a study of children in long-stay residential nurseries. Child Development. 1972, (43), pp. 337–358.
Tobias, J. V. Foundations of Modern Auditory Theory. London, 1972.
Topley, G. H. Seeing Sense. – Hitchen. British National College of Teachers of the Deaf, 1964.
Torrance, E. P. Guiding Creative Talent. Prentice Hall, Englewood Cliffs, 1962.
Tweney, R. D. and Hoemann, H. W. Back translation: a method for analysis of manual languages. Sign Language Studies. 1973, (2), pp. 51–72.

Uden, A. M. J. van. Zichzelf voelen door muziek maken met een clarinet. Ann. Report. St. Michielsgestel, 1943.
— Ontwikkeling van de Geluidsmethode. Ann. Report. St. Michielsgestel, 1946.
— Voelmuziek en Dans voor Doofstommen. St. Michielsgestel, 1947.
— Music and dancing for the deaf. Volta Review. 1949, pp. 386–388.
— De begrippen doofstom, doofstom met gehoorresten, en slechthorend. Ned. Tijdschr. voor Doofstommenonderwijs. 1951, pp. 27–32.
— Een Geluidsmethode voor zwaar en geheel dove kinderen. St. Michielsgestel, 1952.
— An electrical wind-instrument for severly or totally deaf children. The Volta Review. 1953, pp. 241–242.
— Cursus Taaldidactiek voor gehoorgestoorden. Kath. Leergangen, Tilburg, 1955–1957.
— How I teach religion to deaf children. The Teacher of the Deaf. 1956, pp. 42–54.
— Motoriek en verwerving van een klankentaal. Het Gehoorgestoorde Kind. 1960, pp. 179–216.
— Cybernetics and the Instruction of the Deaf. International Congress on Cybernetics, Napels, 1960.
— De ontwikkeling van het tijdsbegrip bij jonge en debiele dove kinderen. Pedagogische nota over zgn. Lichtklokken en Lichtweken. Ann. Report, St. Michielsgestel, 1960, pp. 19–28. (See also: The development of the concept of time with young and with retarded deaf children, in The Australian Teacher of the Deaf. 1963, pp. 5–11).
— Spraak-verstaan, Methode om technische verstaansvaardigheid van dove kinderen te meten. St. Michielsgestel, 1962, pp. 45–53.
— Das gegliederte Ziel der Haus-sprach-erziehung, in Bericht über die Arbeitstagung Früh-erziehung hörgeschädigter, Kinder. Berlin, Aachen, 1963a.
— Dutch deaf children, speaking English to English 'native' listeners. The Teacher of the Deaf. 1963b, pp. 135–141.
— Oefenboek bij de Ned. Spraakkunst i.v.m. de Reflecterende Methode. St. Michielsgestel, 1964.
— Personal Correspondence. 1966.
— The pure oral method in the light of new realisations. Volta Review. 1970, pp. 524–537.
— Waarop reageert de leerkracht in zijn leergesprek met dove kinderen. Unpublished Doctoral Thesis, St. Michielsgestel, 1970.
— Het ritme bij de hoortraining van prelinguaal gehoorgestoorde kinderen; theorie en praktijk,

speciaal bij de hometraining en in de voorschool; een programma voor ritmiek bij de hometraining en in de voorschool. Het Gehoorgestoorde Kind. 1971, pp. 129–143.
— How to teach deaf children to read intelligently. The Teacher of the Deaf. 1971, pp. 373–398.
— 'Congenital deafness and disturbed psychomotor development', in Stoelinga e.a. 1971, pp. 250–258. 250–258.
— The Deep Influence of a Teacher of the Deaf upon the Character and View of Life of His Pupils. International Catholic Conference on religious education of the deaf, Dublin, 1971.
— Teaching an Oral Mothertongue to Deaf Children in Reference to Religious Education. International Catholic Conference on religious education of the deaf, Dublin, 1971.
— They Will Grow . . . by Human Speech. Volta Bureau, Washington D.C., 1972.
— Taalverwerving door taalarme kinderen. Rotterdam, 1973.
— Dove kinderen leren spreken. Rotterdam, 1974.
— Methodische overwegingen over het leren lezen door prelinguaal doven. Het Gehoorgestoorde Kind. 1975, pp. 75–91.
Uden, A. van, Sr. Vincentio and Sr. Joanni. Nederlandse Spraakkunst bij de toepassing van de reflecterende methode. St. Michielsgestel, 1957, 'Addenda en Corrigenda', 1958.
Uit den Boogaart, P. C. Woordfrequenties in geschreven en gesproken Nederlands. Utrecht, 1975.
Ullmann, S. Semantics: an Introduction to the Science of Meaning. New York, 1962, 1967.
— Natural and Conventional Signs. Lisse, 1975.
Ulrich, W. Wörterbuch-linguistische Grundbegriffe. Wien, 1972.
Uylings, E. Praat op heterdaad. Utrecht. 1956.

Vannes, G. Vocabulaire de base du Néérlandais. Antwerpen, 1962.
Vatter, Joh. Die Ausbildung des Taubstummen in der Lautsprache, I, II, III. Frankfurt, 1891–1899.
Ven Th. W. M. van de. Analyse van communicatieve vaardigheden van een groep dove dysfatische kinderen. Scriptie cursus-B Gehoorgestoorden Onderwijs, Katholieke Leergangen Tilburg, 1974.
— Multiply-handicapped Deaf Children. Lecture at the International Congress on the education of the Deaf, Tokyo. St. Michielsgestel, 1976.
Vernon, M. Psychodynamics surrounding the diagnosis of childs deafness. Rehab. Psychol. 1972, (19), pp. 127–134.
Vernon, M. and Koh, S. D. Effects of early manual communication on achievement of deaf children. American Annals of the Deaf. 1970, pp. 527–536.
Vernon, M. and Koh, S. D. Effects of oral preschool compared to early manual communication on education and communication of deaf children. American Annals of the Deaf. 1971, pp. 569–574.
Vigotsky, L. S. Thought and Language. (1956), New York, 1962.
Vivian, R. M. The Tadoma-method: a tactual approach to speech and speechreading. Volta Review. 1966, pp. 733–737.
Vliegenthart, W. E. De uitval van visuele en auditieve waarneming in haar invloed op de vorming van de menselijke persoon. Tijdschrift voor B.O. en Orthopedagogiek. 1961, pp. 105–118.

Wachs, H. and Furth, H. G. A school for thinking. Childhood Education. 1972, pp. 252–255. New York, 1973.
Walter, A. K. A. L'alphabet des kinèmes assistés. Orthopedagogica. 1971, pp. 26–30.
Wason, P. C. The context of plausible devial. Journal of Verbal Learning and Verbal Behavior. 1968, (4), pp. 7–11.
Watson, D. O. Talk with Your Hands. Winneconne, Wisconsin, 1964.
— Readings on Deafness. New York School of Education, New York, 1973.
Watson, P. S. and Scott, E. Disappearing Signs Materials. Center for In-Service Education, P.O. Box 754 Loveland, Colorada 80537, 1974.
Watson, T. J. The use of hearing aids by hearing impaired pupils in ordinary schools. Volta Review. 1964, pp. 741–744.

Wedenberg, E. Auditory Training of Deaf and Hard-of-hearing Children. Stockholm, 1951.

Weir, R. H. Language in the Crib. The Hague, 1962.

Weisgerber, L. Von den Kräften der Deutschen Sprache, I, II. Düsseldorf, 1962.

Wells, J. The Paget systematic sign language. The use of a manual method for accelerating the development of oral language in young deaf children. The Teacher of the Deaf. 1972, pp. 28–39.

Werd, Zr. Rosa de. Iets uit de praktijk van het spreekonderwijs aan dove kinderen. St. Michielsgestel, 1949, 1964.

Werner, H. Comparative Psychology of Mental Development. Chicago, 1948.

— Einführung in die Entwicklungs-psychologie. München, 1959.

Weijnen, A. A. De kunst van vertalen. 2nd, Tilburg, 1947.

White, A. H. The Effects of Total Communication, Manual Communication, Oral Communication and Reading on the Learning of Factual Information in Residential School for the Deaf. Michigan State University, Department of Special Education, Michigan, 1972.

White, A. H. and Stevenson, V. M. The effects of Total Communication, Manual Communication, Oral Communication and Reading on the Learning of Factual Information in Residential School for Deaf Children. Amer. Annals of the Deaf, 1975, p. 48–57.

Whorf, B. L. Language, Thought and Reality. Cambridge, U.S.A., 1956.

Wiener, M., Derve, S., Rubinow, S. and Geller, J. Nonverbal behavior and nonverbal communication. Psychol. Review. 1972, pp. 185–214.

Wiener, N. God and Golem, Inc. Cambridge, Massachusetts, 1964.

Wils, J. A. F. Merleau Ponty's taalbegrip en de moderne linguistiek. Alg. Ned. Tijdschrift voor Wijsbegeerte en psychologie. 1965, pp. 230–257.

Witelson, S. R. and Rabinovitch, S. Children's recall strategies in dichotic listening. Journal of Experimental Child psychology. 1971, (12), pp. 106–113.

Witte, O. Untersuchungen über die Gebärdensprache. Zeitschrift für Psychologie. 1930, (116), pp. 225–308.

Wolff, J. G. Language before speech: a new phonetically-based combined system for the development of language in deaf children. Teacher of the Deaf. 1971, pp. 96–114.

Wood, N. E. Delayed Speech and Language Development. Englewood Cliffs, N.J., 1964.

Woods, W. A. Transition network grammars for natural language analysis. Communications of the ACM. 1970, (13), pp. 591–606.

Woodworth, R. S. and Schlosberg, H. Experimental Psychology. London, 1954.

Wundt, W. Die Sprache, in: Völkerpsychologie, I und II. Leipzig, 1908–1911.

— Language, Its psychology. London, 1973.

Wyman, R. A visual response system for teacher-group interaction in the education of deaf children. Volta Review. 1969, pp. 155–160.

Yale, C. Years of Building. New York, 1931.

Yngve, V. H. Computer Programs for translations. Scientific American. 1962, pp. 668–672.

Youniss, J. and Furth, H. Spatial and Temporal Factors in Learning with Deaf Children: an Experimental Investigation of Thinking. Final Report VRA RD-1305-S, Center for Research in Thinking and Language, The Catholic University of America, Washington D.C., 1971.

Zakia, R. D. Fingerspelling and Speechreading as Visual Sequential Processes. National Technical Institute for the Deaf, Rochester Institute of Technology, Division of Research and Training, Rochester, 1972.

Zakia, R. D. and Haber, R. N. Sequential letter and word recognition in deaf and hearing subjects. Perceptual Psychophysiology. 1971, pp. 110–114.

Zazzo, R., Galifret-Granjon, N., Mathon, T. and Stambak, M. Manuel pour l'examen psychologique de l'enfant. Paris, 1964.

324

Subject and Name index

Aafjes B. 136
Abernathy E.R. 205
Aborn M. 67
Abraham I. 119
abstract 23, 130, 136, 141
accent 54, 93, 104
  of duration, of intensity, of intonation, of
    pitch 107
  '– group' 31, 54, 62, 67, 74, 87, 88–89,
    90, 234
  main –, accidental –, of importance, of
    contrast 97, 143, 164
  rule of – 107
  shifting of – 97
accentuation 97, 116, 143, 148, 163, 177,
    216
  and signs 193
acceptance 178, 203
'accessories' of language 54, 88
achievements 280
'action-radius' 82, 119, 122, 162, 188
active language 28, 128
active voice 78
actual pause 91
adjective 50, 84, 89
adolescent 124, 186, 192
adverb 83, 84
Africa 133
Allen K.E. 102
Allesch S. 59
alphabet
  manual – 25
  phonetic – 216
alphabetic finger-spelling 204
alphabetization 124
ambiguity 74, 90, 141
American Sign Language 185, 190
Ameslan 185, 190
analogy 145

of proportion 147
analysis
  graphic – 77
  phonetic – 77
Anderson J. 92
animals
  communication of – 140
animistic thinking 138
Ansink M. 294
'anticipatory method' 33, 145
antonym 135, 146, 148, 164
apartheid 198
aphasia 210, 213, 296, 299
  congenital – 210
aphasic children 144
'Appell' 57
apperception 109
apraxia 59
  of speech 299
arbitrariness in language 23, 132
Arnaud A. 50
Arnold G.E. 294
article 54
articulation 97
'articulators'
  and 'non-articulators' 113
articulatory
  – code 24
  – finger-spelling 205
  – memory 108
artificial
  – introductions into sign-language 190
  – syntax 192
Ashby W.R. 67
assertion 50, 57, 80, 89, 121
association 69, 119
Astère Sr. 40
asymbolism 297, 300
athetosis 299

325

334

335

336

339

341

'stenochirology' 205
Sterling T.D. 67
Stern C.L. 28, 31, 57, 146, 171
Stern W.L. 28, 31, 57, 146, 171, 205
Stevens K.M. 101
Stevenson V.M. 192, 198
stochastic function 53, 69, 77
Stokoe W.C. 22, 23, 100, 115, 139, 186, 187, 190, 192, 194
storage process 118
Stork F. 21, 84
story-telling 151, 159
Straates F. 148
Strasser St. 133
Streng A. 44, 50, 188
'structural phase' of reading 157, 158
structure 68
    easy and difficult – 56
    of language 20
'stuff' of a cultural language 22
'stuff of thinking' 24
Stuckless E.R. 150, 201, 233
Stutterheim C.F.P. 80, 242
subject-predicate 21, 44, 50, 55, 58, 60, 63, 64, 73
substantive 50, 72
successive memory 176
successive process 22
Suci G.J. 91
suffix 52
Suid-Afrikaans 89
'surface structure' 63, 78, 90
Sweden 196
syllable 104
    lengthening of – 107
symbol 36, 37, 57
    'graphic – and hierographic –' 191
    and integration of senses 300
    linguistic – 140
symbolic function 20, 300
symbolic system 20
symbolization 146
symphony 95
synapse 72
synonym 140, 146, 147
'syntactical eupraxia' 59, 60
syntagma 87
    rhythmic – 96
syntax 135, 194
    artificial – 192
    'conversational –' 60

of sign language 139
signs and linguistic – 193
synthetic speech 101
system 28, 31, 36, 48, 59, 234
    linguistic – 126
    of signals and symbols 20

tactile-kinaesthetic
    form of language 25
tactile-manual language 26
Tadoma-method 25
Tanner M. 173
Taylor I.G. 19
Taylor W.L. 233
teacher 218, 301
    deep influence 179
    unqualified – 187
'telegram-style' 69
'telegraphese' 214
'telegraphic speech' 99
telephone alphabet 216
Telex-apparatus 299
Templin M.C. 138, 228
tempo
    and memory 109
    of reading 163
Tervoort B. 44, 77, 115, 126, 150, 187, 193, 199
test of
    memory for speech 116
Test-Operate-Test-Exit (TOTE) 118, 123
text 158
thinking 23, 56
    abstract – 26
    'accentgroup –', 'phrase-structure –' 183
    animistic – 138
    concrete – 23
    and conversation 179
    deductive – 47
    'existential –' 137, 138
    and figuration 23
    figure-background – 47
    'film –' 120
    flexible – 47
    'graphic –' 212
    'iconic –' 36, 154, 192
    'image –' 36, 204
    inductive – 47
    and language 46, 133, 135, 178
    'non-operational –' 137

343

345

REAP

An International Journal

on

Research Exchange And Practice in Mental Retardation

Editors

Annalise Dupont	Denmark
Herbert C. Gunzburg	United Kingdom
Coen G.A. de Jong	The Netherlands

Coordinating Editor

Sándor Németh   Bishop Bekkers Institute, Utrecht, The Netherlands

As a rule, each issue contains a symposium on a general topic. The topics: prevention, education, treatment and training, and rehabilitation will be recurrent, so that subjects will be dealt with yearly. Next to the symposium, issues carry articles on other subjects of interest. Other features are: 'It functions': short reports on particularly successful projects; letters to the editor, book reviews, a calendar of coming events, and a News column on the activities of international organizations. Each issue contains extensive summaries of all articles in English, French and German.

Themes for symposia to be published in Volume 3 (1977)

'The coordination of services'
'Physical education'
'How to prepare the mentally retarded for leisure time'
'Relationships between family and professionals'

Four issues per year

SWETS PUBLISHING SERVICE – 347 B, Heereweg, – LISSE
A Division of Swets & Zeitlinger B.V.   The Netherlands